T3-BNW-921

NATIONAL INSECURITIES

NATIONAL

INSECURITIES

IMMIGRANTS AND U.S. DEPORTATION POLICY SINCE 1882

DEIRDRE M. MOLONEY

THE UNIVERSITY OF
NORTH CAROLINA PRESS
CHAPEL HILL

Designed by Rich Hendel
Set in Merlo and Franklin Gothic types by
Tseng Information Systems, Inc.
Manufactured in the United States of America

The paper in this book meets the guidelines for permanence and durability of the Committee on Production Guidelines for Book Longevity of the Council on Library Resources.

The University of North Carolina Press has been a member of the Green Press Initiative since 2003.

Library of Congress Cataloging-in-Publication Data
Moloney, Deirdre M.
National insecurities : immigrants and U.S. deportation policy since 1882 / Deirdre M. Moloney. — 1st ed.
p. cm.
Includes bibliographical references and index.
ISBN 978-0-8078-3548-7 (cloth : alk. paper)
1. United States—Emigration and immigration—Government policy—History. 2. Immigrants—United States—Social conditions. 3. Women immigrants—Legal status, laws, etc.—United States. 4. Illegal aliens—Government policy—United States—History. 5. Deportation—United States—History. I. Title.
JV6483.M645 2012
325.73—dc23

2011042855

Portions of this book previously appeared in two publications: "Women, Sexual Morality, and Economic Dependency in Early Deportation Policy," *Journal of Women's History* 18, no. 2 (Summer 2006): 95–122; © 2006 The Johns Hopkins University Press. "Policing Bodies and Borders: Women, Prostitution, and the Differential Regulation of U.S. Immigration Policy," in *Confronting Global Gender Justice: Women's Lives, Human Rights*, edited by Debra Bergoffen, Paula Ruth Gilbert, Tamara Harvey, and Connie L. McNeely (London: Routledge, 2011). Used by permission.

16 15 14 13 12 5 4 3 2 1

In memory of my father,

DAVID R. MOLONEY

1932–1987

Known for his wit, compassion,

and appreciation for a good

narrative

CONTENTS

ILLUSTRATIONS

ACKNOWLEDGMENTS

During the course of the decade spent researching and writing this book, I have benefited greatly from the support and encouragement of many friends, family members, scholars, archivists and librarians, organizations, and students. Early on, the National Endowment for the Humanities (NEH) provided me with a summer stipend that enabled me to visit archival collections in New York City and Minneapolis. A yearlong research fellowship at the Woodrow Wilson International Center for Scholars in Washington, D.C., awarded to me at a critical juncture, provided me with a room of my own to devote to writing, a vibrant scholarly community, and research assistance that was essential to my completing this book. The support I gained there from the entire staff was terrific. I wish to acknowledge the leadership of Lee Hamilton, Michael Van Dusen, and Philippa Strum. Susan Nugent, Lindsay Collins, and many others made my stay there particularly enjoyable.

Two groups of Washington-based scholars, the Immigration History Roundtable and the Red Line group, offered me encouragement and valuable feedback on several chapters. My regular discussions and friendships with my fellow historians Alan Kraut, Tyler Anbinder, Tim Meagher, Tom Guglielmo, Katie Benton-Cohen, and Maddalena Marinari provided me with valuable advice and sharpened my historiographical knowledge. I am grateful to Tyler for reading additional chapters and encouraging me at crucial points, especially in the home stretch. Many meals shared with Philippa Strum, Wendy Williams, Salim Yaqaub, Mary Ellen Curtin, Robyn Muncy, Patricia Sullivan, Marie-Thérèse Connolly, and Matt Dallek sustained me through the revision process and kept me in the Washington political loop. Impeccable research assistance from Mary Klatt, Matthew Dingerdissen, Joseph Humire, Ada Valaitis, and Evan Taparata was vital.

On behalf of the University of North Carolina Press, Desmond King and Erika Lee read the entire manuscript carefully, and each provided insightful and valuable feedback that strengthened the final manuscript.

Elaine Maisner, the editor of my first book, expressed her keen interest in this project and introduced me to her colleague, Chuck Grench, who has also been a great editor and highly supportive through this long process. I sincerely appreciate the dedication of the many others at UNC Press who were involved in the editing and production process.

Donna Gabaccia has been a mentor since we met at my first scholarly conference presentation in Madison, Wisconsin. She, Marlou Schrover, and others working on gender and migration have been wonderful colleagues, as have been scholars whom I interact with regularly at the Social Science History Conference and European Social Science History Conference, including Susie Sinke, Cybelle Fox, Jaime Aguila, Vibha Bhalla, and Enda Delaney. Daniel Kanstroom generously agreed to read my final chapter after we met at an Oxford conference, and Hiroshi Motomura also read the manuscript. Tom Archdeacon, Christopher Kauffman, and Suellen Hoy were also important supporters early on in my career, and I have learned much from each. Landon Storrs, Tyler Priest, Tim Longman, and Regan Rhea have been close friends since graduate school and have supported me in innumerable ways. Landon also shared her expertise on twentieth-century political activism and gave me helpful feedback on chapter 6.

I am deeply appreciative of the archivists and librarians who supported my research at many institutions. Marian Smith, historian at the INS and now USCIS, and Suzanne Harris, of the National Archives, were instrumental in helping me start my archival research and navigate through the sources there. Janet Spikes, Dagne Gizaw, and Michelle Kamalich at the Wilson Center library kept pace with my volume of requests. Daniel Neces, Joel Wurl, now at NEH, and others at the IMHC in Minnesota, Gunnar Berg and the staff of the YIVO archives, and Anthony Touissant and the staff of the Schomberg Center Archives were all extremely helpful. Tim Meagher convinced me to use the archival collection at Catholic University, and I found rich sources materials there.

My Pennsylvania friends, especially Rebecca Kingston, Sara King, and Snezana and Kata Litvinovic, and those at George Mason University supported me as I researched and wrote this book, including Elizabeth Bernard, Cathy McCormick, Maria Eugenia Verdaguer, Dolores Gomez-Moran, Jeannie Brown Leonard, Laurie Fathe, Marcelle Heerschap, Debra Bergoffen, Karen Misencik, Kathy Alligood, and Zofia Burr. Andrew Brenneman and Scott Hensley have remained dear friends since adolescence. My family, Maria Shea Moloney, Brona Moloney and David, Kathleen, Kiera, and Quinn Moloney, Maura Moloney and Eamonn Shea, as well as the entire Shea family, a four-continent Irish diaspora, along with our close family friends, deserve my profound gratitude as well.

NATIONAL INSECURITIES

INTRODUCTION

U.S. immigration laws and policies are hotly debated issues in civic life. Determining who should be allowed into the United States, the equity of immigration quotas, the assignment of refugee status, and the criteria for immigrant deportation are among the issues receiving heightened public attention. Since September 11, 2001, immigration concerns have intensified, leading to renewed debates about the relationship between immigration policy, national origins, civil liberties, and national security. Detention, deportation, and citizenship rights have been the subject of several highly publicized court cases during the past several years; beginning with the *Hamdi v. Rumsfeld* ruling, which determined that aliens or other detainees cannot be held indefinitely and must be accorded due process rights, several Supreme Court and appeals court decisions have determined that the Bush administration's indefinite detention of, and denial of legal rights to, noncitizens in Guantánamo and elsewhere have been unconstitutional.

In one of its first actions, the Obama administration announced that the detention center at Guantánamo Bay would close. But that decision resulted in sharp resistance soon after it was publicized. Immigration reform efforts have also stalled, in large part because of the increasing contentiousness of rhetoric around immigration and religious pluralism (including the proposed Cordoba Cultural Center in New York City, erroneously referred to as the Ground Zero Mosque, and the threatened Koran burning in Florida), fueled by draconian local and state legislation in Arizona and elsewhere and the rise of the Tea Party movement.

In the past few years, tensions between federal agencies such as Immigration and Customs Enforcement (ICE) and local authorities have intensified throughout the United States in regions such as Arizona, where there has long been a substantial immigration population, and in Prince William County, Virginia, where there has not. Competing and often clashing laws and policies have been enacted in many locations to discourage immigrants from living and working in those communities and from availing themselves of local services. Since the 1980s, state and local authorities have become increasingly unwilling to cede immigration control to federal authorities. These new state, county, and local laws have created innumerable problems that were not anticipated by the local and county boards and state legislators voting to support them. They include clashing and overlapping jurisdictions, labor shortages in regions adopting the new policies, a significant escalation in enforcement and court costs, and sharply rising costs incurred by detaining immigrants in local jails and prisons. Such policies expand the potential for racial profiling and other civil liberties–related legal challenges and liabilities and discourage targeted ethnic groups from relocating or establishing businesses in those areas, regardless of their citizenship status.

In 2008 ICE and local officials launched a raid on an Annapolis, Maryland, painting company that employed a large number of Latino workers. They arrested forty-five workers and held several for deportation. Annapolis Chamber of Commerce director Bob Burton objected to the raid. He suggested that racial profiling was a concern and that it would have a "chilling effect" on the city's business climate. That business interests would object to immigration restriction efforts is not new. In the late nineteenth and early twentieth centuries, businesses and corporate interests generally opposed restrictive legislation because inexpensive labor fueled economic growth. Labor unions, including the American Federation of Labor (AFL), were among the major proponents of immigration restriction, beginning with the ban on alien contract labor.[1]

But in recent decades the Republican Party, whose base depends on business owners, has generally supported tough immigration measures. The association between business interests and immigration restriction measures arose from issues related to the Republican Party's increasingly effective use of a "law and order" platform beginning in the early 1980s, rather than from economic interests. The effectiveness of such an emphasis, in turn, depended on racial and urban stereotypes, whether African American or Hispanic. Labor unions, in contrast, now depend on service sector employees to expand its dwindling membership base in the wake of the loss of highly unionized manufacturing jobs. Now that many of those service-sector jobs are held by immigrants, unions no longer lobby for stricter immigration control measures.[2]

Immigrant deportation raids on businesses by ICE affect not only those workers presumed to be in the United States illegally but also their spouses and children, who are sometimes citizens and are often dependent on the immigrant's income. Jakalyn Munoz, a U.S. citizen, born in Washington, D.C., whose spouse was arrested in the 2008 Annapolis raid, stated: "This is supposed to be my country, but it doesn't feel like that. Not when they take your family away and they destroy the lives of your kids." The issue of preventing the separation of families, especially in households with mixed citizenship status, has been a recurring theme in deportation debates since the late nineteenth century, even in the cases of many political radicals.[3]

By 2006 the response of immigrants to this punitive political climate had also changed. They were no longer hesitant to participate in public protests as they once had been, they were better organized, and they held well-attended rallies and demonstrations in Washington, Los Angeles, New York, and several other cities across the country. More than a million immigrants are estimated to have participated in these rallies. In those protests, immigrants employed the rhetoric of the modern American civil rights movement by invoking citizenship and human rights, specifically focusing on harsh immigration legislation that was under consideration by Congress that spring. The protests were one of several factors that prevented the passage of major immigration legislation that year. Another was the political mobilization of Hispanic voters and the fact that, while historically they have tended to support Democrats, in the 2004 presidential election, they voted in substantial numbers for George W. Bush.

Although some Hispanic voters favor stricter immigration enforcement laws and policies, politicians do not wish to alienate this increasingly important voter bloc by supporting immigration laws that are viewed as unduly harsh by many in that community. Moreover, immigrants with permanent residence and third or fourth generation American citizens of Latin descent are concerned that should these laws be enacted they too will face a hostile environment because of their racial identities. That change reflects, to a large extent, the greater political incorporation of Hispanics in the United States, as organizations including the League of United Latin American Citizens (LULAC), established in the early- to mid-twentieth century, successfully mobilized Hispanics.

The Intersection of Race and Gender

Immigrant rights in the United States constitute a major element of a long historical debate over what constitutional and other protections are afforded to noncitizens, especially when the process of deportation or removal is defined as an administrative, not criminal, process, and thus offers insufficient enumerated protections for those facing hearings and possible expulsion. Yet, although governments around the world could and did intervene in cases that pertained to their citizens living in the United States, they were largely unable to monitor closely or extend resources to those outside their own borders in any systematic or sustained way.

This book is a broad historical analysis of United States immigration exclusion and deportation policy. It demonstrates the historical origins of many immigration policy issues in the United States today. I argue that deportation policy has served as a social filter, by defining eligibility for citizenship in the United States and fundamentally shaping the subsequent composition of the American population. I use an intersectional approach to examine how race, gender, religion, and class interacted with one another in the creation and implementation of immigration policy. Racial and gender ideologies and practices converged in ways that compounded the effects of each, although that process was uneven, differed by context, and changed over time. Historically, race and gender have had the most significant impact on the creation of immigration policy and its outcomes; but those factors have always been intertwined with larger social concerns about foreign policy and national security, the economy, scientific and medical issues, morality, and attitudes about class, religion, and citizenship.[4]

Race was used explicitly to define eligibility for admission and citizenship in 1790, when eligibility for naturalization or obtaining U.S. citizenship was denied to nonwhite immigrants. The 1875 Page Law and the 1882 Chinese Exclusion Act further constricted the ability of nonwhite immigrants to settle in the United States. I argue that, even when race was not an explicit basis of enforcement, immigrants were subject to regulation by racially based proxy methods, including the differential regulation of disease, economic status, and religious beliefs by the creation of new categories and definitions and by unstated assumptions. The last-named category, through a constitutionally protected one, was regulated at the borders when immigrants held beliefs outside mainstream Christian traditions. Those immigrants tended to be nonwhite or otherwise associated with non-European religious traditions.

Race was not a stable concept in immigration policy, in part because the definitions of groups and their rights changed according to chronological period, legal definitions that varied by state, federal policies, changes in citizenship eligibility, and local contexts. The eugenics-based ideologies that rose alongside American territorial expansion influenced immigration typologies that subsided in the post–World War II era. But in the past few decades, there has been a resurgence of racially based ideologies, often veiled in racially neutral rhetoric, whether in anti-immigrant invectives against irregular (or undocumented) immigrants, who are predominantly nonwhite, or virulent anti-Muslim sentiment.

Gender ideologies often intersected with race to render nonwhite women particularly vulnerable to exclusion and deportation. The treatment of nonmarital sexual relations at the border was clearly regulated differentially on the basis of race. For much of the twentieth century, inappropriate sexual behavior, or immorality, was defined largely as female—male clients, unmarried fathers, or "procurers" were far less likely to be regulated at the borders than were their female partners. Mexican men proved an exception: they were more likely than white men to be punished by authorities for their involvement in prostitution. The relationship of gender to race was dynamic over time. For example, the "likely to become a public charge" (LPC) provision was a feminized one that affected women of many races and nationalities before the 1930s. After that, federal officials employed it as a strategy to deport Mexican laborers, who were predominately male. In other immigration circumstances, however, such as the separation of young children from their unmarried mothers, race or nationality did not seem to play a decisive factor. In contrast, gender was less critical than race in the differential regulation of illness and in the creation of diagnoses with the purpose of excluding and deporting immigrants on medical grounds. Race and gender ideologies, however, both played major roles in how religion was regulated at the borders.

Labor and economic exigencies often intersected with racial definitions in creating immigration policy. For example, Mexicans were exempt from numerical restrictions based on race and national origins and initially defined as white in the federal census. Mexicans became more vital to the agricultural economy of the West once Chinese and Japanese laborers were excluded in 1882 and 1907 respectively. Even in the early twentieth century, far fewer Mexicans were recorded in immigration statistics than other major immigrant groups.

When the agricultural economy became depressed beginning in the 1920s, however, Mexican immigrants became increasingly vulnerable. In 1930 they were redefined as nonwhite in the federal census. As Kelly Lytle Hernández argues in her recent history of the U.S. Border Patrol, the agency, established in 1924, deepened inequities in the treatment of Mexican immigrants by providing employers with a new mechanism to control their workers. Filipinos also became more vulnerable during this Great Depression. Because of their status as a U.S. colony (or protectorate), Filipinos had been exempt from Asian exclusion laws. But in 1934, the Tydings-McGuffie Act provided for Philippine independence, while simultaneously severely reducing the number of annual immigrants permitted from the country.[5]

Although early federal immigration statistics based on race and nationality are difficult to analyze closely because of continually shifting definitions of race, nationality, and other categories, and although aggregate exclusion or deportation numbers remain small, some trends do emerge that confirm racial bias. From 1895 to 1904, immigrants who were from Asia, the Middle East, Mexico, and Italy had higher rates of exclusion than those from Northern Europe. Japanese had a 3 percent rate; Syrian and Turkish immigrants had just below a 4 percent exclusion rate in this period; Mexicans, 2 percent; and Italians, 1.4 percent, compared to English and Welch at 0.87 percent and Scandinavians at a scant 0.14 percent. Deportation rates remained lower than exclusion, at that point, and occurred only within a year of arrival.[6]

Perhaps most striking in this early-era data is the low number of Mexicans recorded in immigration statistics, relative to their large numerical presence as agricultural workers in the Southwest and elsewhere. In that period, fewer than 3,000 Mexicans were recorded as entering the United States at border stations, as compared to 1.1 million Italians, nearly 78,000 Japanese, and 43,000 Syrians and Turkish immigrants. This suggests that immigration and other federal officials viewed them as migrants rather than immigrants—the way they viewed people arriving by sea—and understood that they were not moving across borders primarily through immigration stations. The reclassification of Mexicans into immigrants would begin to shift only in the years leading to the creation of the U.S. Border Patrol in 1924 and remained contingent on economic needs, since Mexicans were not subject to the numerical quotas imposed by the 1920s national-origins legislation.[7]

Race was less instrumental in those deportations based on political and social ideologies. In the Red Scare following World War I, most of those targeted for deportation were Russian and Eastern and Southern European men who were legally defined as white. That trend reflected the federal authorities' assumptions that those who were neither male nor white were not major political actors. Indeed, given that women had just achieved suffrage and many African Americans and others remained disenfranchised, that attitude reflected reality in the strictest sense of political activity. Women and nonwhites continued to be marginalized in radical and other nontraditional social movements. But as the Emma Goldman, Marcus Garvey, and Claudia Jones cases demonstrate, activists who were nonwhite and/or female who challenged prevailing economic and political ideologies in highly public ways were sometimes targeted for deportation. In those three cases, gender ideologies also played an important role. For example, federal authorities attempted to use the Mann Act against Garvey, Goldman's deportation appeal hinged on her argument that she derived U.S. citizenship through male family members, and Jones's vulnerability arose in part because of her status as a black woman in the white- and male-dominated Communist Party.

My project places several of these issues in transnational perspective by examining immigrant exclusion and deportation policy in the United States from the late nineteenth century until the World War II era, comparing trends among immigrants from Mexico, the Caribbean, Europe, Asia, and the Middle East. It focuses on the consequences of an 1882 immigration law, first revised in 1891, that excluded or deported immigrants deemed "likely to become public charges, persons suffering from a loathsome or contagious disease, persons who have been convicted of a felony or other infamous crime or misdemeanor, involving moral turpitude, polygamists, and also any person whose ticket or passage has been paid for with the money of another."[8]

This study integrates social history with public policy history. It emphasizes the perspectives of immigrants and their advocates as they experienced immigration policy and defended their rights as noncitizens. The richly detailed case files woven into this narrative vividly illustrate the impact that particular decisions had on immigrants' lives. I situate deportation policies in the context of broader Progressive Era and New Deal trends, including economic developments, international relations, gender relations and ideologies, political rights, racial attitudes, and religious life. Early debates over immigrant rights contributed to the modern understanding of universal human rights that emerged following World War II. I illustrate how larger social and political forces were also influential—those include foreign policy concerns, family reunification considerations, the efforts and reaction of immigrant advocacy organizations, and public opinion.[9]

As a social historian of the United States, I emphasize the role of its government agencies, immigrant advocates, and experiences of immigrants themselves. The transnational scope of this topic has led me to draw on a wider disciplinary framework by integrating scholarship of political scientists, anthropologists, sociologists, legal scholars, social activists, and historians of Europe, Canada, and Australia.

Deportation, Exclusion, and Repatriation

Deportation is the state-mandated process by which noncitizen immigrants are expelled from a nation and returned to their countries of origin after residing in the state, on the basis of the administrative determination that they have violated immigration policy or committed a crime. In 1892 just 2,800 people faced deportation from the United States; by 2008 that figure exceeded 358,000. But those statistics mask an array of closely linked administrative processes of expelling immigrants. More common was exclusion, the process by which immigration officials determine that immigrants should not be formally admitted to the United States upon arrival at the border because they are perceived as failing to meet the standards of admission set forth by immigration laws and policies. These immigrants were refused entry upon arrival or shortly thereafter. Until the mechanisms to expel those residing in the United States were in force, exclusion rates exceeded those of deportation.

The distinction between deportation and exclusion is not always clear in law or in implementation. Exclusion, as detailed in chapter 7, has not been a wholly separate process from deportation and makes the fine distinction among those allowed to enter the country and those turned away at the border or port of entry. At times, a clear distinction is made between those deported after being admitted into U.S. territory and those immigrants who were never permitted entry. But the 1953 *Shaughnessy v. United States ex rel. Mezei* case illustrates that the difference was sometimes not clear-cut. Countless other immigrants "voluntarily repatriated" under threat of deportation, because they did not wish to endure detention or were not aware that they could appeal their decision. But the complex question of consent blurs the distinction between voluntary return under such circumstances and mandated deportation.

Early in the federal regulation, "debarment," the term used for exclusion, was employed more often than removal or deportation. In 1906, for example, 12,432 persons were debarred upon landing or attempting to cross a land border, whereas fewer than 700 were deported after residing in the United States for at least a year. Two decades later, the number of debarred aliens, 20,550, still exceeded deportations, 10,904, although by a smaller margin. The mechanisms that allowed for deportation—a much more labor-intensive and administratively complex process than exclusion at borders and ports—had been put into place. Deportation sometimes follows a criminal conviction in the United States but often occurs independently. In such cases, coordination with local and federal agencies is required.[10]

A third closely intertwined process is "voluntary return," in response to apprehension and the threat of deportation or removal. That latter action has since 1954 often exceeded one million immigrants annually and far exceeds the number forcibly deported or removed. In part, this trend occurred because of the lack of administrative capability to hear cases, detain immigrants, and provide for appeals.[11] Some immigrants understand that if formally deported, they are unlikely to ever be admitted to the United States. They also recognize the often inhumane conditions of a lengthy detention in immigration centers, federal prisons, or local and county jails, where there have been instances in which inmates awaiting the outcome of their cases have died because of lack of medical care. Since 1996, expedited removal procedures have allowed U.S. immigration authorities to expel immigrants without any administrative hearing. That process acknowledges that there was in fact a legal and conceptual distinction between exclusion and deportation, even though that distinction had been formally erased.[12]

Over time, the mechanism for exclusion and deportation expanded from an ad hoc, piecemeal process at the state level, rooted in European poor laws, to a national border-focused approach, to a sustained effort to regulate and police the activities of noncitizens sometimes for decades after their arrival. This occurred in several ways: the extension of grounds and length of subjectivity to deportation laws from activities occurring before arrival to activities occurring several years after settlement; an increased level of collaboration among immigration officials with local law enforcement and social service, hospitals, and other publicly funded agencies; and the rise of the FBI and the expansion of its powers to regulate immigration-related matters.

My argument about the significant role of deportation in U.S. society is rights based rather than based on its numerical significance. In fact, relative to those admitted in a given year and the immigrant population as a whole, the aggregate numbers in appendix B suggest that total deportation rates are low. Throughout the twentieth century, deportations averaged just 1 to 3 percent of the total immigrant population admitted to the United States in a given year. Though this seems a relatively small figure, that percentage fluctuated and had a greater impact on some communities in some periods. In a few cases, immigration laws, such as the Chinese exclusion laws, were effective in deterring most of the banned groups from attempting to enter the United States. The cost of intercontinental transportation posed a barrier to those who understood that the likelihood of admission was very low, though some did attempt to cross the borders from Canada and Mexico.

Deportation requires significant resources, especially personnel, to monitor immigrants, review documentation, detain and patrol, and coordinate with federal and local agencies as well as hospitals and charities. These resources were not always available to the immigration agency. The systemization of visa, passport, and communication channels remained rudimentary before the 1920s, a decade when the U.S. Department of State established a visa system in the ports of embarkation and established professional consular officers. Steamship and railroad travel and regulation, along with federal policies pertaining to landholding and property rights, had significant implications for immigration, including the cost and efficiency of immigration routes, and the geographic distribution of potential immigrants and landed immigrants.[13]

By providing a mechanism to exert leverage over noncitizens who resided in the United States, the threat of deportation contributed to the marginalization of immigrants and their stigmatization during periods of national crises. That threat was highly effective in silencing immigrants in the political sphere, in the workplace, and in the community. It further led to retribution efforts by spurned lovers, resentful neighbors, and overzealous public officials. As Reuben Oppenheimer, an attorney and immigrant rights advocate, concluded in the 1930s, immigrants from nations with nondemocratic governments were intimidated by the threat or the process of indefinite detention, deportation, and the impact of their return to their country of origin.

Deportation has been characterized by its unique administrative nature, its retroactivity, and a lack of proportionality between an offense and its outcome. Those features distinguish it from many of the constitutional protections afforded to those facing criminal proceedings, such as the statute of limitations imposed on most crimes adjudicated in the U.S. court system. Immigrants who violated laws between their admission to the United States and obtaining U.S. citizenship had the potential to be deported on many grounds for which there was no statute of limitations. Furthermore, the retroactive nature of many deportation-related policies contributed to a climate where immigrants remained vulnerable until they obtained citizenship. This had a significant effect on early twentieth-century American society, with a foreign-born population of about 10 percent, a ratio that once again characterizes the U.S. population.

Although the deterrent effect of deportations cannot be accurately measured historically, newspaper accounts, personal experiences of returned immigrants, and word of mouth in originating communities certainly played a role in discouraging affected groups of immigrants from seeking to settle in the United States, in much the same way that economic downturns and other events depressed rates of immigration, albeit on a much greater scale.

Deportation has recently been the subject of renewed scholarly interest, alongside other types of "forced migration," particularly modern slavery, human trafficking, impressment into militias and armies, and refugee movements that result from war and major ethnic conflicts, political oppression, denial of human rights, economic depression, and natural disasters. That research correlates with the increasing rates of deportation or expulsion of immigrants in the United States, Canada, Australia, European Union member states, and other countries in recent years.

Refugee policies and immigration regulation are distinct, but those processes have increasingly converged over the past two decades. A liberal refugee policy following World War II served as tacit acknowledgment that democratic nations had not acted generously enough in protecting Jews and others fleeing the Holocaust. Later it reflected an ideological Cold War stance by favoring refugees opposed to communism and socialism. Since the end of the Cold War in 1989, however, many liberal democracies have greatly limited the number of refugees they admit each year, and public attitudes toward refugees have become far less sympathetic. Those denied asylum typically risk politically based or other forms of persecution upon their return to their originating communities. Since the recent global financial crisis, these trends have rapidly accelerated.[14]

Because immigration laws and policies vary by country, my analysis of deportation is specific to the United States and limited to the expulsion of noncitizens. For example, Maria-Teresa Gil-Bazo has recently documented that French citizens have been deported from their own country. In the United States, this is not, in the strictest sense, a legal possibility. Instead, U.S. citizens, whether born or naturalized into that status, must be denaturalized before being removed or expelled from the nation, a process that remains relatively rare. There are some significant exceptions to the notion that U.S. citizens cannot be deported. Minor U.S. citizen children of deported non-U.S. citizens often have no choice but to accompany their parent or parents. U.S. citizens without documentation of their status were detained or deported during immigration raids, such as those of the first Red Scare and the Doak Raids during the Hoover administration.[15]

The definition of deportation that refers to the systematic expulsion of a state's own citizens is a separate process from what I address in this study. For example, the expulsion that was associated with the genocide of Jewish citizens from Germany and its occupied territories during World War II constitutes another meaning of deportation; a state's expulsion of citizen ethnoreligious minority groups within its borders in the later twentieth century is yet another dimension of deportation.

The Emergence of a Federal Deportation Process

Deportation and related forms of immigration control arose as an important function of the modern, industrial state. Control over the composition of a nation's citizenry, its ideologies, and the shape of the industrial workforce increasingly became a transnational project, not simply one that occurred within national borders. Under British rule, American colonies within the broader Atlantic world experienced the close regulation of goods, people, and commerce. With the rapid rise of industrial growth and ease of transportation, and continental expansion, global migration needed to be regulated more systematically than it had since American independence. A comprehensive American immigration policy began to emerge from 1875 to 1882, with the passage of three pieces of legislation—the 1875 Page Law, followed by the Immigration Act and Chinese Exclusion Act in 1882. Between 1882 and the immigration restriction laws of the 1920s that greatly restricted the flow of European immigration to the United States, a series of additional federal laws were passed and policy decisions implemented that restricted the movement of immigrants based largely on concerns over race and ethnicity, poverty, public health, political beliefs, and morality.

Although efforts began in the early national period, sufficient regulatory mechanisms and federal resources did not materialize until the end of the nineteenth century with the emergence of a modern industrial state and an enlarged role for the federal government. Moreover, in large part because of the integral role of immigrants in building a modern infrastructure and an industrial economy in the United States, there were insufficient organized efforts to establish restrictive immigration laws before 1875, with the major exception of Denis Kearney's Workingman's Party and the Know-Nothing Movement.[16]

The Fourteenth and Fifteenth Amendments to the U.S. Constitution, enacted after the Civil War, expanded federal citizenship and voting rights to U.S. citizens regardless of race. But Jim Crow laws at the state level, along with other enforcement mechanisms, prevented many nonwhite citizens from exercising or appealing for their rights. Lynching and other forms of racial violence were widespread in the century following the Civil War. The federal government did not intervene to address the most egregious of those civil rights violations until the modern civil rights movement of the 1950s and 1960s. For nonwhite immigrants, however, ineligibility for citizenship based on race persisted well into the second half of the twentieth century.[17]

The post–Civil War period also led to a major expansion in the power of the federal government and its regulatory power. Congress passed five major immigration laws from 1882 and 1921 that provided grounds for excluding immigrants upon arrival or for their deportation on the basis of poverty, mental and physical health, morality, or political beliefs. Critically, these laws ultimately shifted from assessing those conditions upon entry to expanding deportation criteria to include post-entry conduct. They included the Immigration Act of August 3, 1882 (22 Statutes-at-Large 214), which restricted immigration of "persons likely to become a public charge"; the Immigration Act of March 3, 1891 (22 Statutes-at-Large 1084), which added to the list of inadmissible immigrants those "persons suffering from certain contagious disease, felons, persons convicted of other crimes or misdemeanors, polygamists, aliens assisted by others by payment of passage, and forbade the encouragement of immigration by means of advertisement"; the Immigration Act of March 3, 1903 (32 Statutes-at-Large 1213), which excluded aliens who were anarchists or communists and extended the deportation period to three years after arrival and two to those deported for being likely to become a public charge if those conditions existed before their arrival; the Immigration Act of February 20, 1907 (34 Statutes-at-Large 898), which added to the list of inadmissible classes "imbeciles, feeble-minded persons, persons with physical or mental defects which may affect their ability to earn a living, persons afflicted with tuberculosis, children unaccompanied by their parents, persons who admitted the commission of a crime involving moral turpitude, and women coming to the United States for immoral purposes"; and the Immigration Act of February 5, 1917 (39 Statutes-at-Large 874), which stated that some causes of deportations were to be exempt from statutes of limitation.[18]

This period, especially the early twentieth century, has not received sufficient attention by historians examining immigration policy, largely because the series of immigration laws enacted in this era have been overshadowed by those passed in 1882 and the 1920s. Yet, the period from 1882–1921 was pivotal in the emergence of an increasingly restrictive, national-origins-based U.S. immigration policy. The mechanisms of immigration regulation were established, and debates over which newcomers should be allowed to live in the United States, and which of those were eligible for citizenship, became widespread. The rationale for immigration control was also developed in this era, whether that control was based on racial identity, gender and familial roles and relationships, workforce imperatives, public health, religious views and practices, political and social beliefs, or activism.[19]

In this era the 1911 Dillingham Commission Report was published under the auspices of the U.S. Senate. Its highly biased classifications of various immigrant groups laid the foundation for a federal immigration policy based on legislation enacted in 1921 and 1924 establishing a national quota system that sharply reduced the numbers of Southern and Eastern European and Russian immigrants.[20] The report drew extensively from the increasingly popular eugenics theories of Madison Grant, William Z. Ripley, and other American and European theorists. Immigrant advocates, including the Hebrew Immigrant Aid Society (HIAS), represented immigrants who were in danger of being excluded upon arrival or deported. They also corresponded with the Bureau of Immigration (the precursor to the Immigration and Naturalization Service, now renamed the Bureau of Citizenship and Immigration Services) to address issues of bias.

A helpful way to understand the broad contours of American immigration policy and priorities from the Progressive Era onward is to examine the historical evolution of the name of the agency charged with regulating immigration and naturalization and its continually shifting administrative jurisdiction. While some of those decisions were rooted in logistical and budgetary considerations, those changes also demonstrate the increasingly contested nature of immigration in the United States and the federal government's role in its regulation. Consistent throughout the past century has been the central role of race and ethnicity (or national identity) in shaping immigration and naturalization policy, but other concerns came to the fore in response to shifting social and international contexts. During its first decade, for example, the focus of federal immigration policy was heavily focused on economic issues. The Office of Immigration was first established as an agency within the Treasury Department. One of the agency's major initiatives was to bar alien contract laborers under the 1885 Foran Act. Immigrant workers were widely viewed as undercutting American wages, especially as jobs became increasingly mechanized in this era. A second restriction barred Chinese laborers from entering the United States. Yet many employers voiced their opposition to such restrictive measures in order to maintain cheap labor pools.[21]

This systematic and comprehensive effort also marked the movement of the United States toward a modern state and a developed economy. For the first time, the federal government appropriated resources to determine more systematically who would constitute its population in the future by allocating funds to regulate its borders. Throughout the nineteenth century, a largely immigrant population had laid a complex rail transportation network and increased production in key leading sectors such as textiles and clothing, coal, metals mining, and steel.

Only after much of that industrial infrastructure was built by low-wage workers in highly hazardous conditions were most Chinese immigrants denied entry, and efforts to limit Southern and Eastern European immigrants followed. Outside the South, where African Americans had been historically responsible for most agricultural production, immigrants supplemented output. In fact, Mexican agricultural workers were largely exempt from close immigration control until 1930, because of their critical role in the rapidly developing agricultural and mining sectors of the Southwest and California.[22] Until the Depression, Mexican immigrants were viewed primarily as contingent, nonpermanent agricultural migrants, and their racial identities were still in flux.

In 1885 the agency became known as the Bureau of Immigration, and in 1903 it was transferred to the jurisdiction of the Department of Labor and Commerce. Between 1897 and 1902, former Knights of Labor grand master workman Terence V. Powderly headed the agency. Powderly's appointment symbolized the agency's early concern with immigrants in their role as laborers and their potential to compete with American-born workers and to depress wage scales. By 1906 its role had expanded to encompass the naturalization function, and the agency became known as the Bureau of Immigration and Naturalization. That administrative shift suggested an increasingly closer conceptual and functional link between the determination of who should be admitted into the United States and who should be deemed eligible for citizenship.

By 1913 the functions were split into the Bureau of Immigration and the Bureau of Naturalization, separate agencies within the newly created Department of Labor. In 1933 the agency became known as the Immigration and Naturalization Service, and it moved in 1940 from the Department of Labor to the Department of Justice. Its assignment as an agency within the Department of Justice until 2003 suggests the increasing concern with preventing illegal immigration by the mid-twentieth century that has extended to the recent past. It also reflects the fact that the Bureau of Information (later the FBI) under the influence of J. Edgar Hoover, who eventually headed the agency, claimed a major stake in regulating immigration to deport those whom they deemed subversive political threats, beginning in the World War I era and its immediate aftermath, with the Palmer Raids and first Red Scare.

Finally, the agency has been known since 2003 as the Bureau of Citizenship and Immigration Services and was established under the newly created Department of Homeland Security, in response to the events of 9/11. The agency regulating immigration is now charged with preventing terrorism in the United States, and its enforcement powers have expanded enormously as a result of the passage of the Patriot Act, as well as earlier enforcement efforts designed to strengthen the federal government's power and ability to deport noncitizens.[23] The process formerly known as deportation has been reclassified as "removal." As chapter 7 details, the process remains ambiguous—though not a criminal procedure, many of the features remain nearly identical, such as indefinite detention in jails and other governmental facilities, the issuing of warrants, limited contact with relatives, and appeals. The process of expedited removal allows the federal government to forgo even the limited legal protections afforded to immigrant noncitizens.

An understanding of the historical development of deportation is vital to current immigration reform initiatives, political and community incorporation issues, and citizenship and human rights. This book demonstrates that several current immigration issues originate from much earlier debates over federal immigration policy.

Historiographical Context

This study contributes to the trend of viewing U.S. history from a transnational or global perspective. Daniel T. Rodgers and others have viewed reform movements as products of social, political, and economic influences across national borders. Historians are also interested in analyzing how immigration and other transnational processes influenced the rise of the modern nation-state. Analyzing immigration within the framework of the process of British decolonization and the often simultaneous process of U.S. neo-imperial growth beginning in the post–Civil War era is also helpful. My work contributes both to recent scholarship on U.S. social history, especially immigration and ethnic history, and to a broader discussion of transnational migration and globalization by historians, sociologists, and political scientists.[24]

Two important books on U.S. immigration policy history were published in the 1950s: John Higham's classic *Strangers in the Land* and Robert Divine's *American Immigration Policy, 1924–1952*. Each detailed the major catalysts for immigration laws, highlighted nativism, and focused on eugenicist ideologies in the early twentieth century.[25] That state-focused approach to immigration issues was soon followed by the immense popularity of social history. For several decades immigration and other social historians focused on community studies, the preindustrial and industrial workplace, and social mobility studies, influenced by Herbert Gutmann and other pioneers of the new social history. Historians also embraced anthropological and sociological approaches and quantitative methodologies. Classic examples include Virginia Yans-McLaughlin's *Family and Community: Italian Immigrants in Buffalo, 1880–1930*. Immigration historians also engaged in debates about the nature and process of acculturation, including the uprooted versus transplanted debates that stemmed from Oscar Handlin's 1950 book *The Uprooted*. Rudolph Vecoli's classic article "Contadini in Chicago" initiated this debate, and John Bodnar in *The Transplanted* continued it. Absent in much of that early social history was an analysis of the role of the state in regulating immigration and shaping immigration trends, political incorporation, work patterns, and gender relations.[26]

By the 1990s, however, a subsequent generation returned to the state as a major focus of analysis, a turn that political scientist Theda Skocpol characterizes as "bringing the state back in." But there were significant differences from Higham and Divine in their approaches to immigration policy history. In large part, this was not a break from the preceding decades of historiography but a blending of a state-centered approach with a greater attentiveness to issues of culture, gender, race, and other factors. Perhaps most significantly, the use of archival sources has been far greater than was apparent in studies by Higham or Divine. Recently, Mae Ngai, Aristide Zolberg, Desmond King, and others have published excellent studies on U.S. immigration policy. Each of those studies has addressed the importance of policies and legislation in the interwar period, which had until recently received less scholarly attention than other periods.[27]

A similar trend has occurred among scholars studying immigration in Europe, Australia, and Canada. Since the 1990s many scholars have returned to a more state-inclusive approach to immigration history, including Rita Chin, Marlou Schrover, Philippe Rygiel, and Clifford Rosenberg. Most recently, monographs such as Adam McKeown's *Melancholy Order* and articles by Erika Lee and Kornel Chang have begun to address immigration policies across national boundaries, viewing immigration policies with a multistate, comparative lens, an effort that historians have previously ceded to political scientists.[28]

A related trend in recent immigration and social history, in another return to John Higham's approach in *Strangers in the Land*, has been to examine how racial and ethnic taxonomies that emerged from the Progressive Era writings of Charles Davenport, William Z. Ripley, and others ultimately shaped immigration policy. The popularity of eugenics-based classifications, evident in the 1911 Dillingham Report, commissioned by the U.S. Senate, led to the passage of legislation in 1921 and 1924 that sharply curtailed European immigration. But that classification earlier led to restrictive policies, including those used to reduce Jewish immigration from Russia and Eastern Europe. Alexandra M. Stern is among the historians who have returned to Higham's question of how eugenics ideologies influenced immigration policy.[29]

Immigrant advocates, including those from the Hebrew Immigrant Aid Society, argued that the classification of "poor physique" was unfairly used to exclude or deport Jewish immigrants. INS records reveal that there were significant disagreements among immigration officials in the 1910s about how "poor physique" was defined and diagnosed as well as the influence of eugenics on the creation of immigration policy. Such racial taxonomies contributed to the implementation of immigration policy, including deportation policies, during the Progressive Era.[30]

Despite a renewed focus on the history of U.S. immigration policy over the past decade, especially on the impact of the Chinese Exclusion Act, there has been relatively little focus specifically on the history of U.S. deportation policy since Jane Clark Perry's study was published in 1931. Daniel Kanstroom's recent book is an exception. His impressive study is primarily a legal history of deportation. In contrast, my social history approach incorporates significant case files from the National Archives, emphasizes the role of immigrant advocate groups, and roots deportation issues firmly in the historical context of larger social trends, such as Progressive Era reform movements, eugenics ideology, the Red Scare, and the New Deal. Mae Ngai's book on how the concept of illegal immigration emerged as a significant category in the United States incorporates a discussion of deportation policy, but she does not analyze gender to a significant degree.[31]

Kanstroom and Ngai provide excellent macrolevel analyses of federal immigration policy, but such an approach tends to minimize agency among immigrants and their advocates. My study also emphasizes the lived experiences of immigrants who were affected by exclusion and deportation—whether that was through separation from their infant children, indefinite detention, or, in particularly extreme cases, death. By highlighting the interplay between immigrants, immigration officials on the ground and in Washington, the Department of State, international consulates in the United States, immigrant communities, immigrant advocates, the press, members of the public, politicians, and other stakeholders, my study places deportation within a larger transnational framework of debates over the role of immigrants and citizenship and emphasizes that immigrants and their advocates contributed significantly to those debates.

Martha Gardner and Eithne Luibhéad have each addressed the impact of U.S. immigration policy on females and have effectively embedded race into their analysis. Martha Gardner's analysis of the impact of gendered assumptions in the enforcement of immigration law shares similarities with my first chapters—both of us draw from case records to focus on definitions of marriage, prostitution, and poverty and economics, though her work does not center on deportation specifically. Luibhéad discusses deportation in a larger framework of immigration policy, but much of her research focuses on the post–World War II period. She makes a particularly vital contribution to gender and immigration policy through her analysis of how sexual orientation and heteronormative assumptions have influenced federal policy and its enforcement. That perspective is shared by Margot Canaday, who analyzes the heteronormative assumptions underlying immigration laws and policies in *The Straight State: Sexuality and Citizenship in Twentieth-Century America*.[32]

In contrast to the work of Ngai, Kanstroom, Gardner, and Luibhéad, my study emphasizes the impact of immigrant advocates, and situates both race and gender within the context of larger transnational historical developments, including mobilization against white slavery, international investigations, and foreign policy issues. I also incorporate a state-building approach to deportation. In contrast to previous scholarship I discuss how immigration policy is shaped at multiple and often conflicting levels of government: local, state, federal, and international, as well as the competing interests and agendas of government agencies and federal branches. By focusing on deportation and exclusion policies in particular, my study reveals much about debates about who was fit for citizenship at the borders and following settlement and how those decisions were made at several levels—on the ground; among policy makers, the media, and immigrant groups and organization; and in a wider international context. As a historian interested in the relationship between immigration, religion, and ethnicity, I emphasize the role of religion and religious organizations in immigration policy and deportation in ways that have not yet been systematically addressed.[33]

Immigrant advocacy organizations, precursors to contemporary non-governmental organizations (NGOs), influenced the creation and implementation of U.S. immigration policy in ways that have not been fully recognized. Groups such as the Hebrew Immigrant Aid Society (HIAS), the National Catholic Welfare Council (NCWC), and members of local ethnic and immigrant communities helped to shape the contours of immigration policy, or the outcomes of individual deportation cases. Though a challenge to find sources depicting the deportation process from the perspective of immigrants themselves, they do exist, even when filtered through the lens of the U.S. government or immigrant assistance organizations. But that strategy worked best when advocates and immigrants hewed to a narrative of vulnerability, such as mothers separated from children or spouses, or orphaned refugee children. Radicals, non-European immigrants, and others were less likely to evoke sympathy.

HIAS was particularly successful in appealing its clients' deportation and exclusion decisions, because it had a group of dedicated attorneys working on their behalf, had strong relationships with congressional representatives, especially in New York, and ensured that immigration issues were well publicized in the Jewish community through local and national organizations and publications. The Catholic Church in the United States had several motivations to intervene on behalf of immigrants. Immigrants from Eastern and Southern Europe, and increasingly from Mexico, were a major source of church membership in the United States and the basis of its future growth and success. Social welfare efforts, such as those established by NCWC, demonstrated the institutional maturity of the church, its ability to care for its own, and an alternative to Progressive Era Protestant and humanist charitable and reform efforts. Both HIAS and the NCWC were motivated to demonstrate publicly that they had achieved middle-class respectability by establishing such initiatives for their needy immigrant coreligionists. Both stressed the ethos of family unity as a rights principle, such as the NCWC's use of the term "fireside relatives."

Historians of medicine have also published interesting research on immigration policy based on public health issues and racialized assumptions underlying those restrictive efforts. For example, Amy Fairchild's research addresses medical examinations and public health issues at Ellis Island and at other ports, but she does not situate those issues within a broader social history framework. She argues that relatively few immigrants were excluded or deported for medical illness and states that the LPC provision was the commonly used category. The LPC provision is a critical but underanalyzed provision of immigration policy. It accounted for the majority of deportations in this era and had a major impact during the Great Depression and during policy debates in the 1990s. A 1987 dissertation analyzed the clause, but that research focused extensively on the administration of the policy and was never published. Fairchild relies on aggregate immigration statistics, which can be misleading without a close examination of the case files of those deported for LPC. In reading those records, it is evident that the LPC provision was often used in cases when immigrants were suspected of prostitution, criminality, or were otherwise undesirable, because it was easier to prove.

This study uses a comparative framework that demonstrates that pluralistic nations began moving to increasingly restrictive policies in this era. Rather than focusing on a particular ethnic group or two, I have consciously chosen to incorporate a broad selection of groups from Europe, Mexico, the Caribbean, the Middle East, and Asia. Such a comparative approach allows immigrant historians to understand how different groups experienced immigration regulation, and the differential impact of policies by gender, region, religion, and national/ethnic origins. But such a comprehensive approach gives less attention to specific immigrant groups' unique histories and motivations for immigration, as well as to community and institution-building approaches following arrival.

Chinese immigration, however, is foundational to my analysis for several reasons. First, Chinese immigrants were the first to be regulated at the federal level, through the 1875 Page Law and the Chinese Exclusion Act of 1882. These laws influenced the development of subsequent policies that restricted, excluded, and deported immigrants from other regions of the world, such as those policing female sexuality. The mechanisms of immigration control, including the use of photographic identification, were first developed to police Chinese immigrants and later became widely implemented. Moreover, several Chinese exclusion-based cases became landmark Supreme Court decisions with lasting implications for immigrant rights. These included *U.S. v. Wong Kim Ark*, *Chae Chan Ping v. U.S.*, and *Yick Wo v. Hopkins* in the late nineteenth century.[34] The ban on Chinese laborers also increased the importance of Mexican immigrants in the Southwest. Unlike Chinese laborers, Mexican immigrants were first viewed by many as temporary migrants. Following the Exclusion Act, Chinese immigrants faced exclusion on medical grounds, especially for trachoma and hookworm, which were diagnosed at much higher frequencies than for other groups.[35]

Whiteness Scholarship

My understanding of the racialization of immigration policy has been informed by scholars of immigration history writing in the past two decades, and also by whiteness studies, an area of research that has intersected with immigration history in that period. David Roediger's study on the social construction of race and economic competition between Irish and African American workers launched a wider debate about permeable and contextual racial definitions of Italian, Jewish, and Eastern European immigrant workers by historians, including James Barrett and Matthew Frye Jacobson. Thomas Guglielmo takes issue with some of those earlier works, suggesting that Italian immigrants' access to citizenship, their settlement outside of the segregated South, and legal rights insured that they were "white," despite their often darker complexions, their Catholicism, and low skill levels relative to native-born white Protestants. Eric Arnesen and others have also questioned whether whiteness studies is a particularly new approach and have debated the theoretical framework of the field.

Several issues arising from the debates about whiteness are helpful to my analysis. I agree that context was important in framing racial identities, a point that scholars of whiteness often emphasize. Historians have discussed how class, education, language, and region of settlement all influenced the treatment of nonwhites in any given era, as did how they were classified in state and federal censuses, immigration statistics, and other official documents. Mexican Americans sometimes consciously chose to describe themselves as Spanish, thus "whitening" themselves by identifying as Europeans.[36]

Glaringly absent from most of these works, however, is a systematic analysis of how racial construction or identity was shaped by gender, especially economic roles of men and women. Like the field of labor history that influenced these writers, many of these studies are situated in male-dominated or exclusively male workplaces or organizations. Indeed, Eric Arnesen's robust critique of whiteness as a category of historical analysis does not cite the lack of attention to gender as a major weakness in the approach. Karen Brodkin, an anthropologist, offers one exception. In her book on Jewish immigrants she explains how decisions about married women's labor force participation contributed to the whitening of American Jews. April Schultz has addressed how immigrant domestic servants can be viewed in the context of whiteness, and Gunther Peck has discussed gender and whiteness in the context of prostitution. With some exceptions, then, most of the gender analysis within whiteness studies has emerged from literary theorists.[37]

Another issue that I find problematic about the historical literature on whiteness is the assumption that Europeans and others learned about racism, and its use as a strategy for economic mobility and social acceptance, only within a U.S. context. It is certainly true, as David Roediger and other historians emphasize, that during the nineteenth century, there were strong alliances between antislavery activists, such as Frederick Douglass, and Irish leaders such as Daniel O'Connell, in the quest for Irish independence. But Roediger seems to conclude that racism was unknown to Irish and other European immigrants before their arrival in the United States. Certainly, direct exposure to those of African origins was uncommon, as compared to in the United States, or London, where Africans had lived for generations. Yet, as scholars from Winthrop Jordan on have described, Europeans had developed a racial perspective, and an associated vocabulary, before settling its American colonies.[38]

Irish, German, Italian, English, French, Spanish, and Dutch citizens also held eugenicist ideologies during the late nineteenth and early twentieth centuries, whether or not they participated directly in the slave trade or the process of colonization. In fact, many of those countries have more recently restricted citizenship rights of those born outside their borders and within them. Italians, including Cesare Lombroso and Giuseppe

Sergi, promoted eugenicist ideologies that arose first in discussions about northern and southern Italians. Peter D'Agostino takes issue with those who view the eugenics movement of the early twentieth century as an Anglo-American system later exported to Europe rather than a system that emerged as a global phenomenon.[39]

Certainly the legacies of slavery and colonization had a major impact on the development of racism and its embrace by immigrants seeking incorporation into the mainstream of American society. But even those countries whose citizens were relatively unlikely to live alongside those of a different race developed racial ideologies of their own. In the late twentieth and early twenty-first centuries, many Europeans who remained in their countries of origin developed racial biases and nativism outside of a purely American context, partly resulting from their widespread exposure to American entertainment. Therefore, whiteness scholars assume that immigrants brought with them little in the way of racial consciousness and developed it only in an American context.

U.S. Deportation Policy in a Global Context

My approach to immigration policy incorporates a transnational perspective. U.S. immigration officials traveled to Europe and to the Mexican side of the border to investigate conditions among immigrants bound for the United States. I further demonstrate how immigrant cultural traditions and practices often clashed with immigration policy implementation. Foreign policy and international economic issues also affected the implementation of deportation policy, as well as the disposition of individual cases. The project fits squarely within the trend of immigration and other social historians examining how policy and legal issues shaped social concerns, rather than viewing political and social history in isolation. It also traces the history of immigration policy from a relatively unregulated matter before the Civil War, to its early and uneven regulation at the state level, and finally to its more uniform treatment as a federal matter.[40]

Placing U.S. social and policy trends in a broader context also challenges narratives of American exceptionalism. The United States implemented immigration control measures in a larger global context. In fact, in the late nineteenth and early twentieth century immigration control measures were simultaneously being implemented in Canada and Australia, two Commonwealth nations that, like the United States, had been British colonies. As settler nations, early immigration policies in those three societies shared many features. Their leaders initially sought permanent economic migrants to build their infrastructures and to fuel industrial and agricultural growth. It was only by the late nineteenth century that political developments enabled these three societies to regulate immigration—for Australia and Canada that change was the creation of a Commonwealth government that preserved formal political ties to Great Britain. In the case of the United States, it emanated from an exponential growth in the size of the federal government, a process that began with the Civil War. Each nation also needed to appropriate resources, personnel, and a system of effective documentation at its major points of entry and, later, its immigrants' points of departure. Finally, each had a significant indigenous population that had been legally and socially subjected to the white settler population. These settler nations' early racial and legal dynamics—indigenous peoples interacting with a predominantly European settler population (and, in the case of the United States, a multiracial dynamic, with a significant population of enslaved African Americans, especially in the South, and Spanish and Latin American peoples in California, Texas, Florida, and the Southwest)—influenced the contours of their subsequent national immigration policies. That context was a vital one in understanding what occurred when large numbers of Eastern and Southern European, Asian, and other nonwhite immigrants began migrating. Although many economic migrants to these countries intended to stay temporarily or seasonally, eventually a significant portion of those circular migrant groups settled permanently.

As settler nations, the United States, Canada, and Australia formalized their immigration policies earlier than most European countries. In contrast, early Western European immigration patterns were, as Leslie Page Moch terms it, largely "local, circular, chain, and career." Many Europeans who migrated in the preindustrial era were labor migrants, but others were paupers and religious refugees.[41] High population growth in nineteenth-century Europe, alongside mechanization and landholding consolidation, reduced demands for immigrant laborers relative to Canada, Australia, and the United States. These three countries drew increasing numbers of Europeans who might have previously migrated locally or regionally within the continent.

"Populate or perish" described Australian efforts to encourage European migrants. Known colloquially as the White Australia policy, it remained in place until 1973. The first act passed by the new Commonwealth parliament in Australia in 1901 was the Commonwealth Immigration Restriction Act (IRA). Potential immigrants who could not write out a passage of fifty words in a European language were excluded. This law was specifically designed to prohibit Asians and other non-Northern Europeans from settling in Australia.

In addition to establishing racial categories, the Australian government excluded migrants according to characteristics that bore striking similarities to those inscribed in the 1891 U.S. law. The proscribed groups were "persons likely to become a public charge upon the public or charitable institutions, idiots and insane persons, persons suffering from an infectious or contagious disease of a loathsome or dangerous character, persons convicted of crimes 'not being a mere political offence' and sentenced to imprisonment for one year or longer, and prostitutes or persons living on the prostitution of others."[42] One substantial difference between the U.S. and Australian acts was an exception that provided for politically based dissent. That feature acknowledged Australia's role as place of exile for those opposing British rule.[43]

Following its acquisition of Commonwealth status, Canada's immigration regulation function was placed under the newly established Department of Agriculture in 1868 (until it moved to the Department of Interior in 1892). The first comprehensive immigration law in 1869 excluded any "Lunatic, Idiotic, Deaf, Dumb, Blind or Infirm" person immigrating apart from a family, as well as those who were paupers.[44] That law did not provide any mechanism for removal until 1887. By the mid-1880s, provisions to bar Chinese immigrants were enacted and, as in the United States, such laws were later broadened to include many Asian groups. There existed a few important differences between early U.S. and Canadian regulations—Canadian law envisioned immigrants as promoting agriculture, given Canada's more rural economy; there was a family unity provision for those immigrants who were seen as medically unfit; and the undesirability category was initially stated as a principle rather than a policy or mandate.[45]

Canada enacted anti-Asian immigration legislation similar to that in the United States. First, Canada increased the head taxes for Chinese immigrants beginning in 1885 and then passed a Chinese Exclusion Act in 1923 (repealed in 1947), and signed the anti-Japanese Gentleman's Agreement at the same time as the United States. In 1914, a group of Indian Sikhs on the *Komagata Maru* were refused landing upon arrival in the port of Vancouver, although, because of their British citizenship, they arrived not as immigrants but as intercolonial migrants. After returning to Calcutta, passengers were fired upon by British officers and several passengers died. Canada also interned 22,000 Canadian citizens of Japanese heritage and Japanese aliens during World War II. In 1967 Canada liberalized its immigration policies.[46]

Deportation and other immigrant regulation policies are by definition state-specific—they are highly influenced by a nation's system of government, including the role of the judiciary, race relations, the role of activists, media representation, and public attitudes and ideologies. Policies are also influenced by the history of settlement and the labor systems that emerged. Immigration, however, occurs in a wider global context that includes economic development and displacement, labor demands, shifting national boundaries, international relations priorities, and more recently, terrorism. Since World War II, the development of a code of universal human rights and international bodies to regulate and standardize the treatment of migrants has also affected deportation procedures. This book addresses both the state-specific and broader considerations of U.S. deportation policy.

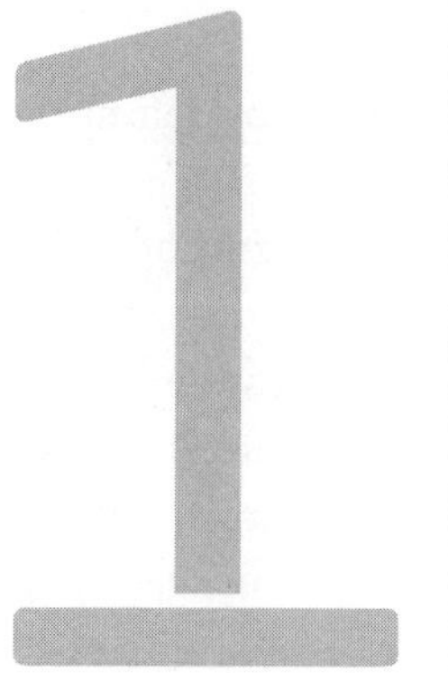

WOMEN, SEXUALITY, AND ECONOMIC DEPENDENCY IN EARLY U.S. DEPORTATION POLICY

In 1909 Caterina Bressi was deported to Naples, Italy, with her young, American-born child, having been charged with prostitution. She spent some months sleeping on the streets of Naples, until a group of wealthy women there provided her with funds to return to the United States, where she supported herself by obtaining a low-wage job at an Illinois candy factory. Bressi claimed she was raped by a co-worker at gunpoint and became pregnant. In 1910 the twenty-three-year-old woman was ordered deported by Chicago immigration authorities on grounds that she was likely to become a public charge. Her deportation order was overturned by Illinois Federal District Court judge Kenesaw Mountain Landis on a writ of habeas corpus. Judge Landis concluded that there was insufficient evidence to suggest that because Bressi had once practiced prostitution and would soon become the sole support of two children that she would necessarily become a public charge. Immigration officials defended their decision to deport her a second time. "There can be no doubt that a woman of loose morals who, while attempting to maintain an appearance of respectability, consents to occasional acts of illicit sexual intercourse is by that defect of character rendered likely to become a public charge." The official added that Bressi was unlikely to earn enough to support her family on such a low wage, especially since she was soon to enter a period of confinement.[1]

Bressi's case neatly captures the relationship between sexual morality issues and women's economic roles that emerged in the context of the United States' rapidly industrializing society. By the early twentieth century, growing public concerns over nonmarital pregnancy and prostitution (commonly referred to as "white slavery") helped to shape immigration policies concerning the exclusion and deportation of female immigrants

Caterina Bressi, with her child. (51777/231, RG 85, Entry 9, National Archives)

arriving in the United States. That scrutiny of female immigrants occurred in an era in which American citizenship itself was being contested on several levels. Native-born women had renewed their mobilization for federal voting rights and had begun to challenge many assumptions about their social roles. Women's rates of employment and educational attainment increased in this period, leading to concerns of "women adrift" in urban settings and the rise of organizations such as the YWCA. In this era African Americans formed the NAACP and other organizations to fight Jim Crow segregation policies, and the United States expanded its political territory to include the Philippines, Panama, and Puerto Rico. Questions about what legal status these countries' inhabitants had in relation to the United States was widely debated. A major impetus for federal regulation of immigration arose from labor leaders, who sought to limit the number of alien laborers arriving in the country, on the grounds that they depressed American wages. Other early proponents of restriction included those opposed to Asian immigrants on the West Coast and eugenicists who feared the effects of large-scale immigration, as well as officials in states such as New York, who sought to reduce the cost associated with the growing number of immigrants requiring public institutional care and charity.

Thus, concerns about immigrant women reflected larger social debates about who was fit for American citizenship and how the large influx of immigrants would shape American society and its institutions. Moreover, settlement house workers and other Progressive reformers widely perceived immigrant women, in their roles as mothers or potential mothers, to be the primary transmitters of critical cultural and moral values to the next generation. Their maternalist perspective, which emphasized the special place of mothers and children in society, was evident in settlement programs and in reforms such as the Sheppard-Towner Act, which provided medical care to mothers and infants.[2]

Regulating nonmarital sexuality at the borders, including nonmarital births and common-law marriage, ensured that the immigrant women who were admitted would become both moral citizens themselves and the mothers of moral citizens. Citizenship and political rights for immigrant women was not an issue that began only upon their arrival. Their countries of origin also shaped their relationship to the polity and influenced their economic status, as in the case of women in newly independent Ireland. As discussed in the next chapter, widespread public fears about an international white slavery epidemic led to three Bureau of Immigration investigations: in Europe, New York City, and along the Mexican border. Those inquiries also reveal much about attitudes about the relationship between sexuality, race, religion, nationality, and morality.

The 1875 Page Law first addressed concerns about immigrant women's morality by placing major constraints on the immigration of unmarried women from China, casting them as likely to engage in prostitution. The Chinese Exclusion Act and the Immigration Act of 1882 constituted the first major federal laws regulating immigration to the United States. That 1882 law, revised in 1891, allowed for the exclusion or deportation of immigrants who were determined to be likely to become public charges, suffering from a loathsome or contagious disease, or convicted of a felony or other infamous crime or misdemeanor, involving moral turpitude. Before the 1882 Immigration Act, there were some efforts by the states to regulate immigration at incoming ports, using boards or commissions, but there was no systematic effort to limit immigration and no federal government agency authorized or granted a budget to regulate the flow of immigrants. Over the next few decades, additional laws were passed to regulate immigration and to strengthen and broaden the scope of deportation policies and deepen the mechanism for enforcement of those laws and policies to the major ports of immigration, along the Canadian and Mexican border, and in many cities across the United States that became destinations for immigrants.

Between 1900 and 1909, more than 8.2 million immigrants arrived in the United States, primarily from Europe. In fact, the percentage of immigrants arriving in the United States totaled just less than 11 percent of the U.S. population, a ratio that was its second highest in history until the 1990s. The influx of immigrants from Europe began to slow by World War I. By the 1920s a series of immigration restriction acts greatly reduced the flow. The national quota system did not place numerical restrictions on immigrants from Canada or Mexico, though they were subject to other forms of regulation, based on public health restrictions, for example. By the Great Depression of the 1930s, large numbers of immigrants, especially Mexicans, were deported or pressured to repatriate to their countries of origin.[3]

Some of the state-level policies carried over to federal policy, including precedents about "paupers" and pregnant women. The "likely to become a public charge" (LPC) provision was a modern incarnation of traditional Anglo-American poor laws, which reinforced prevalent views about women's economic vulnerability and dependency on male wage earners. Therefore, female immigrants became vulnerable especially to the LPC provision but also to increasing social concerns about women's morality.[4] These two issues were intertwined, because women who immigrated outside family structures were viewed as far more economically vulnerable than men. If they were unable to earn a living in industry or domestic service, they might turn to prostitution, as had women such as Caterina Bressi. Indeed, for many women in industrializing capital economies, prostitution served as one of the few profitable alternatives to domestic service or low-paid factory jobs. As with domestic service or factory jobs, there was a clear demand for such work in the United States.

Because it was easier to prove, women who were suspected of prostitution or who lived with their partners or children outside of a formal marriage were often excluded on the basis of the LPC provision rather than on grounds of prostitution or moral turpitude. Indeed, LPC and other provisions related to economic dependency were the most common reason for exclusion, in large part because it was an easier charge to substantiate. In 1916, for example, 10,263 people were excluded at the ports of entry and returned to their countries of origin on the basis of the LPC provision. That number equaled 55 percent of those excluded that year. Additionally, 1,431 immigrants were deported after having resided in the United States because they were or were deemed likely to become dependent on public funds or to become inmates of public institutions.[5]

In the first two decades of the twentieth century, women of all nationalities constituted about a third of all immigrants arriving in the United States, but they were proportionately more likely than men to face LPC charges, especially if they were unmarried and traveling outside a family structure. In contrast, the numbers of immigrant women excluded from the United States on the basis of prostitution ranged from 80 in 1892 to 510 in 1917, and in six years no immigrants were excluded for prostitution. The mean number of immigrant women excluded annually for prostitution in the years from 1892 to 1920 was 131. The number of immigrant women deported on grounds of prostitution (after having resided in the United States) remained low, generally fewer than 200 per year before 1920. Thus, immigrant women who were excluded or deported from the United States in these years generally found that immigration officials used provisions of the LPC clause more than those of prostitution.[6]

By 1910, female immigrants traveling alone from Europe, Mexico, the Caribbean, Asia, and the Middle East were routinely scrutinized to determine their moral, familial, and economic status. Female sexual behavior had previously surfaced in state-level immigration policies. In Pennsylvania, for example, state officials developed a policy of deporting single, pregnant immigrant women in the 1880s. In 1884 Pennsylvania noted in "The Second Immigration Report of the Board of Commissioners of Public Charities for the Year Ending June 30, 1884" that seventeen persons were returned to Europe that year. The report writer noted with typical Victorian delicacy, "Twelve (12) of those were incapacitated for labor on account of illness, or inability, and five (5) were *enciente* [*sic*]." A similar situation was reported by Frederick Busch, keeper of the Erie County Almshouse, who noted that his agency had assisted a twenty-four-year-old German woman who had been sent alone to the United States by the father of her child and was later returned to Germany by the State Board of Charities. When immigration was regulated by the states, there were relatively few legal mechanisms and virtually no resources expended to address immigration law. Therefore, there was little enforcement regulating immigrants from Europe until the close of the nineteenth century.[7]

Some early principles determining the grounds for deportation influenced the development of federal policy. For example, the policy of excluding or deporting women who were pregnant on the grounds of their likelihood to become public charges carried over to federal policy following the passage of the Immigration Act of 1882, which transferred the enforcement of immigration policy to the federal government. Even when written as gender neutral, immigration laws and policies concerning sexual morality, economic independence, and public health had significantly divergent effects on men and women. Ultimately, the policies that sought to prevent women who had sexual relations outside of marriage, defined by evidence of prostitution, nonmarital pregnancy, or adultery, restricted all women's ability to immigrate to the United States unaccompanied by husbands or fathers. By the early twentieth century, the Bureau of Immigration used its gate-keeping authority to promote marriage between partners who were not legally married, a policy that shares similarities with federal initiatives designed to encourage heterosexual marriage initiated during the Bush administration. The richly detailed case files and administrative records of the Bureau of Immigration, housed in the National Archives, offer crucial insights into attitudes toward those female immigrants who immigrated independently from their families and how those who faced exclusion or deportation proceedings were treated.[8]

The close regulation of single female immigrants marked a significant change from earlier in the nineteenth century, when Irish and Scandinavian women regularly immigrated to the United States alone to serve as domestic servants, just as in the colonial era many young women arrived as servants or indentured servants. Though some of those women ultimately became dependent on charity and engaged in prostitution, concerns about immigrant women's morality were not as widespread as they were by the 1890s.[9] Moreover, in prior eras of significant immigration, women's immigration remained largely regulated by communities and institutions in the countries of origin. Once in the United States, immigrant women's moral regulation continued in the ethnic communities in which they settled, rather than by the state. But during the Progressive Era, the United States began to industrialize rapidly, and urban centers grew as a result of regional migration from rural areas and immigration. As women entered the industrial workforce in unprecedented numbers, social concerns about sexual morality intensified.

On the West Coast, anti-Asian sentiment led to new measures designed to severely restrict Chinese immigrants and others from immigrating to and settling in the United States. During the nineteenth century, Chinese immigration to the United States was overwhelmingly male, a situation that, coupled with antimiscegenation laws and the men's ineligibility for citizenship status, made Chinese immigrants' permanent settlement difficult. By 1875 the Page Law made it even more difficult for Chinese women to immigrate to the United States because of their suspected involvement in prostitution. By the 1880s the number of immigrants from Europe was surging, and these "new" immigrants from Eastern Europe, Italy, and elsewhere rapidly changed the composition of urban areas in many regions of the country. Many immigrant women sought work in factories and in other industrial settings at the same time that rural American-born women moved into urban areas looking for employment. But as the numbers of young single women employed in wage labor increased, so too did concerns about their sexual morality.

The proportion of female immigrant workers in various ethnic communities varied significantly. Italian women, for example, were less likely than other groups (including Irish, Scandinavian, or Jewish women) to immigrate to the United States or to work in urban factories or in domestic service. Many chose instead to immigrate within Europe or to oversee family farms while their male relatives sought the higher-paid work available to men in the United States. Indeed, the proportion of Italians and Syrians immigrating to the United States in this era was heavily skewed toward men.[10]

Regulating Relationships, Promoting Marriage

In addition to investigating the white slave trade, immigration officials interrogated women about the intimate details of their sexual lives during board of special inquiry hearings and interceded when they received care in hospitals and other institutions. In some cases, officials provided women with reprieves if they promised to reform their behavior and allowed them to remain in the country if they agreed to marry their partners. That opportunity for redemption was not available to all women, however. Implementation of the policy was often racialized—relationships between men and women could be categorized differently depending on those immigrants' nationalities and the perception of those women's fitness for American citizenship. In some cases, immigrant women faced deportation as a result of being unmarried mothers, living in common-law marriages, or engaging in prostitution. Officials could intervene dramatically in the lives and bodies of immigrant women, beyond simply physically inspecting them at the border or port of debarkation.

In the nineteenth century, deportation policies and procedures often assumed that women were economically dependent on men, even when those female immigrants had work experience. Women traveling alone or with children were often vulnerable to the LPC charge in ways that women immigrating as wives and daughters accompanied by their male relatives were not. Affidavits of support submitted on behalf of female immigrants facing deportation proceedings were generally written by their male relatives in the United States. Immigrant women facing deportation on LPC grounds often brought with them skills suitable for an industrializing society. But their skills were not often recognized by immigration officials to the same extent as men's. Therefore, immigration laws and policies concerning morality were frequently based on erroneous assumptions about women's moral vulnerability and economic dependency in this era. Yet immigrant women were increasingly participating in the workforce as they constituted a growing segment of the industrial and service sectors in their countries of origin and in the United States.[11]

During their deportation hearings, where they were often without legal representation, women were questioned in detail about their sexual practices and histories. Three Danish sisters, Anna, Caroline, and Elvine Wang, living in the United States apart from male partners, were deported with three children, because those children were born outside of marriage. The third and youngest sister, Elvine, aged twenty-two, was childless and employed as a cook. As the immigration official on the case noted, "Standing alone she would doubtless be regarded as admissible, but having arrived with her sisters, her case should, in my opinion, stand or fall with theirs." The youngest sister had admitted having sexual relations once. The official concluded that "These three sisters seem to represent an undesirable lot." Although the issue of whether fornication constituted moral turpitude was contested within the Bureau of Immigration, he recommended that their appeal be dismissed on the grounds that they were members of an undesirable class and as LPC.[12]

That same day, in another case, an immigrant couple, Paul Overlie and Anne Moen of Norway, were successful in appealing their exclusion order. They were engaged, but not yet married and were excluded at the border on charges of fornication, a crime of moral turpitude. But, according to their case file, the couple "claim[ed] to be engaged, that their intentions are honorable and that they will marry just as soon as they can get started in this country. They admit having intercourse, but only after betrothal." Though Commissioner Clark recommended exclusion, Commissioner-General Daniel J. Keefe overruled this decision, noting, "Their marriage would render them admissible. As they are in every other respect desirable immigrants, I recommend that their appeal be sustained on condition that they are married before being landed."[13]

A second case shared several similarities. Two Swedish immigrants, Johan Jansson and Helga Johanson, appealed their exclusion on grounds of moral turpitude. They were engaged for "a number of years" but had been living together before marriage, stating that economic circumstances and military service had delayed their marriage. Each wore a betrothal ring engraved with the date December 24, 1908, and stated their willingness "to marry at once." Daniel Keefe stated, "Under the circumstances, however, I do not think these aliens could be properly excluded on the grounds taken by the board. Their intentions appear to have been sincere and honorable toward one another and they have regarded themselves virtually married. They are desirable immigrants in every respect." Indeed, their case file notes that they were married at the Quebec Immigration Station before being admitted to the United States on August 10.[14]

Immigration officials imposed harsher penalties on some immigrants whose partnerships were widely accepted in their countries of origin. For example, in parts of the Caribbean common-law marriages remained routine and culturally sanctioned, and in Japan relationships that did not conform to conventional Western ideals of marriage were commonly accepted. Yet such relationships subjected women, and much less frequently, their partners, to deportation once they arrived in the United States.

Caroline Stewart, a Jamaican-born domestic servant and the mother of a thirteen-year-old daughter with James Butler, was deported in 1912 after arriving in Jacksonville, Florida. Stewart and Butler had a long-term relationship, he readily acknowledged paternity of their child, and the couple had known each other since childhood. Yet his assurances that he would make her "his bona fide" wife were insufficiently convincing to authorities, in part because he was the father of other children outside of marriage and thus was "morally irresponsible." That both Stewart and Butler were parents, but neither had ever been legally married, posed a problem for immigration authorities. Stewart's attorney appealed the deportation decision on the grounds that she "would not be an undesirable citizen, and that she comes to this country to marry a man who is a sober, law abiding person of good character," and that her testimony "does not show that she is guilty of a crime involving moral turpitude." Moreover, Stewart was unlikely to become a public charge—in fact, she had more than $200 in her possession when entering with less than $50 signaled poverty. Yet, despite these mitigating factors, her appeal was denied. Though he had been in the United States for just ten months, it does not appear that James Butler, also a Jamaican, faced any charges arising from the case. The fact that both were Jamaican might well have led immigration authorities to scrutinize their relationship carefully. As Caribbean immigrants, and as people of color, they would have been perceived as less desirable future citizens than European immigrants and so would be less likely to be allowed to immigrate after agreeing to marry legally.[15]

In 1912 Ysabel Hernandez, a twenty-year-old dressmaker from Cuba, failed in her appeal. She had previously been deported from the United States on LPC charges. The bureau officials did not believe her explanation that the man who met her at the port in Tampa was her brother Preciliano and that she was joining "her lover" Rudolfo Gonzalez so they could be married, a statement that was verified by a notary public who accompanied her brother to the immigration office. Despite the subsequent intervention of an attorney, who submitted an affidavit on her behalf, she was deemed to be coming over for immoral purposes, in part because of inconsistencies in details about her brothers, but also because "there is no family resemblance between the two aliens and that the appearance of the appellant is very unfavorable."[16]

In appealing their deportation or exclusion orders, some Northern European immigrants enjoyed advantages that nonwhite immigrants did not. Legal representation was not enough to secure successful appeals for either Stewart or Hernandez, whereas in the Moen and Johansen cases no attorney was necessary in their achieving entry to the United States. Further, the two women who were deported each had defined occupations, whereas the two women whose appeals were successful did not have occupations listed in the records. Moreover, the immigrant male partners of Stewart and Hernandez seem to have suffered no negative consequences arising from their relationships. The fact that Moen and Johansen arrived alongside their partners rather than alone might have served as an additional mitigating factor in their cases.

In 1903 Theodore Roosevelt famously expressed his concern that, by limiting family size, elite native-born white women were committing "race suicide," while immigrants, African Americans, and others continued to bear large numbers of children. Such anxieties were commonly expressed among elites in the Progressive Era. Therefore, promoting marriage and families among "old" stock, Northern European Protestant immigrants, while discouraging it among others, might have profound effects on the future composition of the American population. As middle-class and elite women became better educated, independent, politically active, and self-sufficient, many traditional ideals of domesticity, marriage, and gender roles came into question. Immigration regulation served as a means to reinforce traditional marital and domestic norms among potential citizens and deny access to those who did not conform to them.[17]

Common-law marriages did not always present an insurmountable obstacle for immigrants wishing to remain in the United States. Harold Wood, an immigrant minor from Wales, saw his case resolved favorably. He and his mother, who had earlier been widowed from Harold's father, had immigrated to Missouri with her common-law husband, Edward Bewen. Wood's mother had understood that she was eligible for citizenship when Bewen was naturalized, because Missouri had recognized common-law marriages at the time of Bewen's naturalization. Before the 1922 Cable Act, women in the United States automatically took on their husband's citizenship, while their minor children derived their citizenship status from their mothers. Because Wood was a minor child at that time, the Bureau of Immigration determined that he, too, was eligible for American citizenship. Therefore, enforcement of that federal law remained contingent on whether a particular state recognized the legality of common-law marriage. By 1910 there was a decline in the number of states that recognized common-law marriages and its privileges. Though allowing for some variations in state laws in its enforcement of immigration policy, the federal government increasingly sought to normalize a narrower definition of marriage that would preclude common-law relationships, premarital sex, or other domestic relationships among immigrants.[18]

Natsu Takaya, a Japanese woman who had once worked as a hospital nurse, was deported for prostitution in 1908. In Japan, she was a mistress (or concubine) of Kogero Sumida, who paid for her passage to join him in Portland, Oregon. Yet, after some months of living together, in an affidavit, Sumida accused Takaya of having "deserted" him and further accused her of prostitution. In her testimony, she denied having sexual relationships with anyone else in the United States but testified that Sumida tried to force her into prostitution to pay down his debts and that he had assaulted her when she refused. The rift between them caused a street fight among members of Portland's Japanese immigrant community, and this altercation was what likely led to the Bureau of Immigration investigation. Sumida, having testified to paying her passage with the intent of continuing his relationship with her, was sentenced to a year in prison for importing a "female alien for immoral purposes," but immigration officials declined to initiate deportation proceedings against him. Takaya, unlike most women, asked that her deportation hearing be suspended until her brother could be present in order to ensure that her statements were being interpreted correctly. The case occurred during the same year that the Gentlemen's Agreement between the United States and Japan was being negotiated. That agreement severely curtailed Japanese immigration to the United States. That policy decision undoubtedly had a significant influence on immigration authorities' perceptions of Japanese immigrants' right to remain in the United States.[19]

Some relatives of immigrants from the Middle East requested that U.S. authorities intervene when their relatives engaged in sexual conduct that violated the cultural norms of their communities of origin. Middle Eastern immigrants often expressed their concerns that the immigration process, which disengaged women from moral regulation by male family members and increased their relatives' exposure to American values, broke down the traditional moral codes governing their society. In direct contrast to the view of U.S. immigration authorities, who articulated the moral threat

Natsu Takaya. (51777/52, RG 85, Entry 9, National Archives)

to society as arising from immigrant value systems, and in some cases their religious beliefs, many Middle Eastern families believed that American values were the source of their erosion.

A Syrian woman, Mary Lias, came under investigation in 1908. Her Bureau of Immigration case file noted that she was "maintaining immoral relations with another Syrian named George, whose brother is anxious to have the woman deported." She was reported to have been married in Syria and to have returned there after having lived in the United States without her husband, to give birth to a child conceived outside of marriage.[20]

Harold Cook, the lawyer representing her alleged lover's brother, noted that "on her promise of future good behavior she was assisted to return to this country, but that in a short time her actions were even worse than before." Cook maintained that his client was interested in Lias's case for two reasons: that he "wishes to get his brother, who has always born[e] a good reputation, away from this woman, and the other is that the Assyrian people who come to this country seem to have very little respect for our laws relating to marriage and co-habitation, and that he and some others desire some action to teach them proper respect for laws of civilized society." It is unclear how Lias's case was ultimately resolved.[21]

In 1914 Malake Sultan was deported from Ellis Island after being charged with making false and misleading statements. Though she represented herself as a widow, a status entered on the ship's manifest, she was accused of leaving her husband and child abroad and having been a "concubine" to one man and having sexual relations with others.[22] Zahia Antony, a native of Syria, was deported because as a married woman she posed as the wife of another married man to gain entry to the United States from Canada. Though she sustained herself economically as a peddler, immigration officials recommended that she be deported on LPC grounds.[23]

It is highly improbable that those Middle Eastern immigrant women would have faced deportation proceedings had their relatives or members of the immigrant community not notified American immigration authorities about their situations. Their families and community members requested the Bureau of Immigration to intervene as allies in their efforts to ensure that women did not deviate from community cultural norms once in the United States. More generally, however, any immigrant woman who came into contact with public or private institutions while in the United States (e.g., in the course of receiving medical services or charity), risked the chance that administrators would alert immigration officials to her case.

Several other deportation cases arose after husbands, former husbands, or spurned lovers contacted the police or immigration officials to bring charges of adultery or prostitution against their former partners. Such actions served to magnify immigrant women's vulnerability as noncitizens and as women. In 1910, for example, Hilma Olson, a Norwegian immigrant living in Minnesota, faced deportation proceedings when her husband, Matthias, accused her of committing adultery with several men, including during a period in which the couple was separated. On the day that she was arrested, her husband, Matthias, initiated divorce proceedings against her. Her children, ages eight, five, and four, were sent first to a Children's Home in St. Paul and then into foster care with different families, though their father had the financial means to support them. Her lawyer asserted that "this woman is a victim of conspiracy, that her husband is insanely jealous, and that the ends of justice will be attained by allowing her to remain here." He further concluded that her husband subjected her to "cruel and inhuman treatment." Perhaps the most effective argument in her successful appeal, though, was the uncertain fate of her three young children after she was deported.[24]

A spurned lover seeking revenge brought Sarah Kevin's case to the attention of immigration authorities, and her case ultimately resulted in questions about whether she was a "fit" mother. Indeed the former lover's deep obsession with her case suggests that today he might be found guilty of harassment. Kevin, a widow of a British officer with four children, had come to Pennsylvania to join her sister. In his correspondence with immigration officials, her former lover, Edward Aves, an English architect, claimed that he and Kevin had married in Pennsylvania. He also stated that he had obtained custody of her children, who remained in England, but that she "had gotten past his control" by deserting him. He further charged that charity workers had forced Kevin into a marriage with a Mr. Nordberg, an American citizen, in order to keep Aves away from her. He also called into question her mental stability.[25]

In response to Aves's complaint, bureau authorities investigated Kevin's situation. They traced Kevin, who "denied her marriage with Mr. Aves, and did not know why he was troubling her so, that she wanted nothing to do with him." Earlier, while employed as a maid, Kevin was "besieged with letters and phone calls from Mr. Aves." Later, following her marriage to Nordberg, Kevin stated that she was "contented in her present circumstances, she also claims that she wants to be rid of Aves." Felix Ansart, the lawyer who Aves claimed had handled legal matters regarding his custody claim, stated that Aves's claims were false. Indeed, Aves could not legally remarry because, in a twist recalling *Jane Eyre*'s Mr. Rochester, it was discovered that his wife was institutionalized in England. He was also dismissed as "peripatetic" and unable to pay board or earn a living, a situation that led to Kevin's leaving him. Though Aves first appeared to be respectable and truthful, characteristics that had first led immigration officials to investigate his charges against Kevin, his claims were later determined to be fraudulent and unreliable.[26]

Although Kevin had admitted engaging in prostitution after leaving Aves, and was assisted by workers in the Charity Organization Society and another charity agency involved in assisting "fallen women," it was her spurned lover, not the charity workers, who sought to have her deported, as a retaliatory measure. Kevin did remain in the United States, because the charges brought by Aves were deemed false. In dismissing the case, the immigration official noted, "I am glad to report that she is now legally married to a worthy seafaring man named Nordberg, and residing in a respectable section of Baltimore City, and she is particularly desirous that Edward L. Aves not be informed of her whereabouts."[27]

Unlike most women facing the possibility of deportation because of their prostitution activities, Kevin gained support through the testimonies of several influential members of her community—the upper-class reformers who helped to rehabilitate her, an attorney in Pennsylvania, and the state's attorney in Maryland. The fact that she had remarried to a stable breadwinner, though he clearly belonged to a lower class than her first husband, undoubtedly assisted her case. Although most immigrant women were not subjected to deportation proceedings through the retaliatory actions of relatives or male partners, as we have seen they were made more vulnerable because any sexual activity outside a legally recognized marriage contract had the potential to lead to deportation and possibly even a permanent separation from their children. Today, many immigrant women in the United States, particularly undocumented workers, remain subject to the threat of deportation by their partners, other family members, or their employers. Because many women's immigrant status is tied to that of their partners, family members, or employers, they remain vulnerable to physical, emotional, or financial exploitation or abuse as a result of their insecure immigration status.[28]

Immigrant women traveling alone were vulnerable to deportation on

LPC grounds, whether or not they had employable skills. Women who were pregnant outside of marriage or were suspected of prostitution were most likely to face deportation charges. Yet such women were usually charged not with prostitution or moral turpitude but with LPC or an excludable illness. That situation might have occurred to avoid stigmatizing them, but also because those other charges were easier for officials to sustain. Therefore, Bureau of Immigration deportation statistics and categories often obscure the larger debates and discussions over issues of women's morality that arose in such proceedings, and aggregate data about the reasons for deportation are often misleading. For example, whereas the numbers of women "rejected" on grounds of prostitution in 1907 numbered just 18, the number of male and female immigrants rejected on LPC or pauperism grounds was 7,898.[29]

Occasionally, immigrant women facing exclusion or deportation were provided with the possibility of redemption. In deportation hearings, women usually declined legal representation, and as a result their sexual histories were often recounted in detail. Women's physical appearance, demeanor, and dress became important determinants of whether they would be granted clemency by immigration officials. In granting a reprieve to women who had violated sexual mores, officials often noted their well-groomed and respectable appearance. In 1908, for example, Louisa Maud Bruce, an Englishwoman who had separated from her husband and entered the United States under the pretense of being married to another man, was allowed to remain in the United States. An immigration official noted, "Her appearance is not that of a dissolute person . . . she appears respectable." Therefore, if a young woman appeared contrite and had the demeanor of a respectable member of the middle class, she was more likely to be perceived as a potential citizen and given the opportunity to remain in the United States. Conversely, as the Bressi and Hernandez cases illustrate, the lack of physically respectable appearance often contributed to the bureau's decision to deport or exclude women.[30]

The practice of scrutinizing single women constitutes an important aspect of my larger argument that even when written as gender neutral, immigration laws and policies concerning morality, economic independence, and public health had divergent effects on men and women. Publicity surrounding these cases also reveals the widespread sentiment among immigrant advocates, such as the Hebrew Immigrant Aid Society (HIAS), and those sympathetic to them in the press. Several women's deportation cases stirred controversy in the immigrant and alternative press. Women were often described sympathetically and portrayed as victims of male aggressors, rather than as moral transgressors. One such well-publicized deportation case occurred in 1913. Annie Hof was an unmarried German domestic servant in her early twenties and mother of an eight-month-old baby born in the United States. Hof was ordered deported, and she left her child in the United States, in the words of one journalist, to "become motherless, homeless, and a charge on the community." The Bureau of Immigration officials defended the agency against claims that they had been unduly harsh toward the woman, noting that both her children were illegitimate, that she was employed in a disorderly house, and had been a public charge.[31]

Immigrant Mothers Facing Deportation

Three deportation cases of Irish immigrant women in the 1910s and 1920s illustrate the impact that immigration law, community standards, and qualifications for citizenship had on women's lives and, in some cases, their ability to remain with their young children. Irishwomen were far from the only immigrant women who were scrutinized on the basis of sexual morality or economic dependence. But unlike women from many other countries, Irish women had a long tradition of migrating alone and by the late nineteenth century had formed the majority of all Irish immigrants to the United States. They had remitted a great deal of income to their remaining family members in Ireland and demonstrated their ability to earn an independent living. They gave generously to church-building initiatives in the United States and supported the Land League and other nationalist and charitable causes. Generally speaking, they enjoyed a superior reputation to Irish men and, though exaggerated, a reputation for chastity.

In the two decades before 1922 independence, Irish immigrant women's sexuality came under greater scrutiny at the U.S. borders as well as in institutional settings, such as hospitals and charitable institutions. That represented a significant shift from the relative ease with which they immigrated to the United States and earned their living as unmarried women.[32]

Before formal Irish political independence from Britain in 1922, Irish women leaving for the United States symbolized the lack of economic alternatives under British colonization. Limited land availability made marriage difficult in rural areas and the lack of industrialization restricted the number of nonagricultural jobs. After political independence was achieved, the Irish government and society began to use emigration as a safety valve itself, allowing emigration to address chronically high levels of unemployment and to serve as a method of banishment for those who did not conform to the gender and other social norms that were prerequisites to national citizenship, a concept that was narrowly defined for women. Irish independence, then, did not always yield the promise of greater freedom for women. Thus, in both the United States and Ireland, decisions about whether to exclude or deport women at the borders were often discussed in terms of whether they deserved or had earned citizenship.[33]

In the United States, immigration laws similarly filtered out those who did not conform to prescribed gender expectations by making it increasingly difficult for unmarried women to immigrate outside of a nuclear family unit. Therefore, immigrant women were sometimes caught in transit as expectations for sexual behavior as well as gender roles narrowed and formalized in the political and legal codes in both their originating nation and the receiving societies. Indeed, some women and their children lost the right to be considered citizens of one of these countries.

The idea of Irish women's chastity, a central tenet of Irish nationalist rhetoric, became integral to the Catholic identity of Ireland after independence. In large measure, it was their reputation for chastity that in the nineteenth century provided Irishwomen with a larger degree of social freedom to migrate alone than many other immigrant women. But their sexual behavior became closely regulated in the twentieth century. In Ireland, this occurred during the William T. Cosgrave administration and intensified in the De Valera years. The new Irish state imposed censorship on materials deemed indecent by the Catholic hierarchy, including the work of authors such as James Joyce.[34]

Eamon De Valera, the politician who dominated Irish politics for much of the twentieth century, though not elected prime minister until 1932, was the man most closely associated with promoting a strong adherence to the strictures of the Catholic Church that so strongly stigmatized nonmarital pregnancy and birth. Following Irish political independence, and especially under De Valera's presidency, Ireland became a quasi-theocratic state as Irish law and policies became intertwined with Catholic theology and the church's hierarchy. The Irish Constitution inscribed the ideal that married women remain outside the workplace to care for their children. The document prohibited divorce until a referendum lifting that ban on it passed by a slim margin in 1995. The imposition of a strict Catholic standard of sexual morality had significant and often severe consequences for women in both the United States and the newly independent counties that formed the Irish Free State, later Éire, or the Republic of Ireland.

Crossing national borders led to greater scrutiny of one's physical condition, including pregnancy, and of one's morality, both of which were central to definitions of citizenship in the Progressive Era United States and, ultimately, in the new Irish state. Therefore, Irishwomen and other female immigrants arriving at the U.S. borders continued to be presumed to be economically dependent on men, despite strong evidence to the contrary, particularly among Irish immigrants in the late nineteenth century and early twentieth centuries.

It was in this shifting political climate that Maria O'Malley, a married Irish woman with a child, faced deportation on LPC grounds (the most common reason for exclusion and deportation of immigrants), despite the fact that she was destined for the household of her sister in Chicago. In 1913 the Bureau of Immigration letter denying her appeal noted that "she has been separated from her husband only a month. It may be they could effect a reconciliation if she were returned to Ireland." In this case, U.S. immigration officials sought a resolution that would promote marriage, with little regard for its long-term impact on the woman or her children or its practicality. Indeed many immigrant women were admitted to the United States on the condition that they marry their common-law partners.[35] But as O'Malley's sister, Patricia O'Brien, wrote to the secretary of labor, "She did not desert her husband, but he deserted her and baby, and left them to starve. They have no one that can take care of them in Ireland, and if they are sent back, it means their being thrown into the street, as they have no place to go." O'Brien promised to take care of them, noting that she and her husband are "good citizens." O'Malley's nine-month-old son died while hospitalized. Congressman James McDermott of Illinois agreed to provide reimbursement for the child's burial and hospital expenses and seems to have intervened to stay the deportation order, but it is unclear how O'Malley's case was ultimately resolved.[36]

In 1912 Mary Terrell was the subject of a highly publicized case that illustrated for many immigrants the harshness with which William A. Williams, the commissioner for immigration at Ellis Island, was enforcing immigration policies. Terrell, an unmarried woman in her early twenties and mother of a three-year-old child, described in *Fair Play* as "a comely and well-behaved Irish seamstress from Queenstown," had arrived on the *Lusitania*. An anonymous tip led her to a Board of Special Inquiry hearing upon her arrival. She told the board that she had been raped in her family's house and had been banished from her town by the parish priest. Once in the United States, she was excluded from admission to the United States and placed on a ship to Liverpool. The journalist reporting this case concluded his article by calling for Williams's resignation. A notation indicates that the editor of *Fair Play* was Marcus Braun, who just a few years earlier had undertaken a major European study of prostitution for the Bureau of Immigration. The case led to a revision in how immigration officials handled Board of Special Inquiry procedures after they acknowledged that she had not been apprised of her right to appeal the board's decision to deny her entry.[37]

Several years later, Mary Murphy, an Irish woman from County Donegal, also faced deportation on grounds that she was "likely to become a public charge," with an additional notation that she was "mentally defective" at the time of her entry to the United States in 1925. But the fact that she gave birth as a single mother was what ultimately led to her deportation, because officials at the State Infirmary in Tewksbury, Massachusetts, had contacted the Bureau of Immigration the day after she gave birth to a daughter. The infirmary noted that she had tested at below normal intelligence and concluded that, because of her "inability to care for herself from the sex standpoint, she is not desirable material for citizenship." Yet, after her arrival in the United States, she had worked as a chambermaid at several Boston hotels, and she had an aunt in Roxbury, who might have assisted her financially.

Two years earlier, Murphy had given birth to a son, who was placed for adoption, and she returned to work. Like Mary Terrell, she was deported without her child. Though the Department of Labor had requested that the State Department issue her a passport that would enable her to leave the United States with her child, the Irish consul agreed to issue a passport to the mother but refused her permission to bring the child. Had the infirmary's authorities not intervened, it is likely that she could have continued earning a living as a chambermaid and possibly retained custody of her child.[38] Here, Murphy's nonmarital pregnancy was deemed unacceptable by at least three governmental bodies: the state of Massachusetts, which removed her first child from her custody, probably without her consent; the federal Bureau of Immigration, which found two official (and one unofficial) grounds for her deportation; and the Irish Free State, which refused permission for her to return to Ireland with her child. Although the Irish woman was declared fit for Irish citizenship, her American-born children were not, even though minors at this time were generally viewed as having the right to share their mother's citizenship, as they still do today. Without the ability to share their mother's citizenship, and without her ability to remain in the United States, such children became, in essence, involuntary U.S. citizens and orphaned wards of the state.[39]

Concerns about the sexual morality of female immigrants intersected with concerns over their economic roles in the new industrial economy, as well as with prevailing middle-class views of immigrant women and their children as dependent on male breadwinners to whom they were married. When immigrant women did not conform to such American social norms, they became highly vulnerable to exclusion or deportation proceedings. Moreover, immigrant women whose partnerships were acceptable in their countries of origin as well as those whose behavior in the United States deviated from the accepted sexual norms of their countries of origin also faced harsh consequences when encountering immigration authorities. Indeed, American norms about marriage were themselves undergoing change in this era, as common-law marriages became less frequently recognized and a standardized, narrower legal definition of marriage prevailed.

Yet, all immigrant women were subject to intense scrutiny about their personal lives if they immigrated as single women or were unaccompanied by a father or husband. These new immigration policies, while resulting in the actual deportation of a small number of women, had larger consequences for immigrant women in general. As we have seen, patrolling women's sexuality and economic status at the borders reduced migration opportunities for women in general, subjected them to intense scrutiny by the state, constricted the contours of their personal relationships, and in some cases permanently separated them from their infant children.

We have also seen that the enforcement of immigration policies concerning women's sexuality differed according to their race and ethnicity. Even when their personal relationships and economic means were similar, white, Northern European women were sometimes treated more leniently by immigration officials than immigrant women from the Caribbean and other regions. Today, women, who now often constitute the majority of immigrants from their societies, can remain vulnerable to the threat of deportation by U.S. immigration officials through the retaliatory actions of their employers or their family members, to whom they must rely for their immigration status or their economic livelihoods, especially if they are undocumented workers.

Promoting marriage as a means to avoid deportation has significant parallels to recent federal policies designed to encourage marriage among lower-income women in a context in which the very definition of marriage itself is subject to debate. Like the federal policy on deporting pregnant women who entered the United States, this current federal marriage initiative had its origins in state policy. In the early 1990s Governor Tommy Thompson of Wisconsin initiated a program designed to provide incentives for low-wage women to marry, in order to decrease their dependence on state assistance. That policy, known informally as "wedfare," served as a model for a similar federal program in the George W. Bush administration, after Thompson was appointed as the secretary for health and human services. That effort later became part of a larger Bush administration effort to promote heterosexual marriage, alongside its support for the Defense of Marriage Act and funding for the "healthy marriages" initiative designed to reduce divorce rates through religiously based counseling.[40]

Though marriage policies have not been emphasized during the Obama administration, same sex marriage has become a more pressing concern. Contemporary issues surrounding same sex marriage have close parallels to heterosexual marriage and immigration issues in the early twentieth century. Specifically, those include reconciling state and federal definitions of marriage and questions about the derivative citizenship rights and immigration status accorded to spouses. Given that many nations now recognize same sex marriage, U.S. officials now need to address such issues as an immigration and a foreign policy matter and not simply as a domestic issue.

DIFFERENTIAL REGULATION

INTERROGATING SEXUALITY IN EUROPE, IN URBAN AMERICA, AND ALONG THE MEXICAN BORDER

In contrast to men, women immigrating to the United States in the late nineteenth century usually came accompanied by family members—their husbands, parents, or occasionally siblings, or to join relatives who had arrived earlier. The small number of female immigrants who arrived by themselves had fewer and lower-wage employment options, often domestic work or factory work. The same scrutiny faced by immigrant women involved in nonmarital partnerships and those who gave birth to children while single was eventually extended to those suspected of prostitution. Beginning in 1909, U.S. immigration officials focused much of their regulatory efforts on the transnational "white slave" trade, the practice of importing women from continental Europe (including Russia) to serve as prostitutes. Bureau officials initially viewed these prostitution rings as highly organized operations run much like other international cartels, as did many transnational organizations developed to curtail them. That view, however, was largely dispelled after immigration officials conducted several lengthy investigations, often in conjunction with the local police, to uncover prostitution rings among immigrant women and their usually male "procurers," or pimps. Marcus Braun launched a multicity investigation of prostitution in Europe. His colleague, Helen Bullis, undertook an extensive study of prostitution among immigrants in New York City. As a result, transnational prostitution was increasingly attributed to two causes: a lack of strict moral standards among many Europeans and economic issues.[1]

A third investigation centered on cities and towns along the border with Mexico, particularly those in Texas and Arizona. That investigation and its outcomes differed in significant ways from the European and New

York investigations. First, fewer resources were expended on investigations along the Mexican border. Second, male procurers were more likely to be arrested and deported than those in New York. Lastly, evidence of the use of violence and coercion toward young women brought into brothels did not greatly concern federal immigration officials or result in further investigation or arrests.

These investigations reveal the assumptions U.S. government officials made about European and Mexican society and the threat that immigrant prostitution rings posed for U.S. citizens. By focusing their efforts on external threats imported from abroad, such investigations rarely explored the demand side of the equation—the extent to which native-born American male clients, rather than immigrant men, employed these services. Prostitution in locations such as San Francisco and along the Mexican border served to maintain a stable labor force, while addressing the shortage of women in regions where economic growth was rapid. Whereas Asian men found that bringing their family members to the United States was a virtual legal impossibility, European and Mexican men often discovered that bringing their wives and families to border areas was a financial impracticality. The widespread presence of prostitutes allowed for continued economic growth through the labor of men (whether immigrant or not) who were unmarried or living apart from their families for extended periods. Although women suspected of or engaged in prostitution were never deported on moral turpitude grounds in large numbers, concerns about immigrant prostitution were nevertheless pervasive. The Mann Act, passed in 1913, prohibited the transportation of women across state lines for immoral purposes and is still in effect today. Although originally enacted as part of a moral panic, it soon became used more broadly against those in relationships outside of marriage.

The moral turpitude clause sometimes affected immigrant men who served as "procurers," those accused of adultery or bigamy, and rarely those engaging in prostitution themselves, but efforts to exclude or deport immigrants over concerns about sexual morality had more profound effects on women. Unsurprisingly, immigrant men who frequented prostitutes were rarely, if ever, subject to deportation on grounds of moral turpitude. As Jane Clark Perry, an early historian of U.S. deportation policy has noted, the court system debated the definition of moral turpitude (and the actions that subjected the immigrant to deportation) and often applied it inconsistently, because criminal classifications at the state level were different. Crimes constituting moral turpitude included those related to sexuality but extended to gambling, narcotics use, larceny, assault, and murder.[2]

Technical questions arising in the application of morality codes in deportation cases included whether the activity or behavior in question was habitual or ongoing, whether the objectionable incidence happened before arrival in the United States, and how long an immigrant had been in the country. Immigration officials, for example, had difficulty deporting women on prostitution charges if they had been in the United States for more than three years, unless they had strong evidence that a woman had engaged in prostitution or other immoral acts before her arrival. In 1910 immigration laws were expanded so that immigrant women suspected of having engaged in prostitution could be deported from the United States without regard to the length of time they had been in the country.[3]

The regulation of morality through immigration laws, and specifically exclusion and deportation policy, was intertwined with prevailing attitudes about women's economic dependence on men. The threat of immorality was defined as an external one, which immigrants brought with them from their own societies, rather than as a response to changes within American society, culture, and its economy. In some cases, immigration officials recognized a legal distinction between prostitution and a woman's lack of chastity, but having more than one encounter with a man or accepting gifts from him sometimes exhibited a level of moral turpitude sufficient for deportation. Historian Kathy Peiss has written about the practice of "treating," whereby young working-class women frequenting places such as dance halls or amusement parks informally exchanged sexual favors for gifts and money to supplement their low factory wages. Indeed for many working women in urban America, the line between prostitution and socializing with men was a blurry one. Yet solutions designed to reduce the demand for prostitution, on the part of immigrant or native-born men, and the ensuing spread of communicable diseases were not widely debated in discussions about white slavery.[4]

An International White Slavery Investigation

The Bureau of Immigration became involved in investigating prostitution and limiting it in response to a widespread alarm over the "white slave traffic" that emerged in the late nineteenth century. This investigation was a classic Progressive Era enterprise. Experts were confident that they could address a social problem by first carefully studying it, gathering appropriate facts, and developing a solution that was either volunteer based or government based, and sometimes both. Women and religious reformers were particularly interested in this issue, and they established various programs to address it. Port assistance programs, including the St. Raphael Society, L'Association des Oeuvres de Protection de la Jeune Fille, the Young Women's Christian Association, the National Council of Catholic Women, and the National Council of Jewish Women, emerged in Europe, South America, the United States, and elsewhere.

Historians have debated whether women were being drawn into prostitution rings under false pretenses or whether the idea gained social currency when changes accompanying industrialization and women's increasing levels of employment raised concerns. The evidence suggests to Ruth Rosen, for example, that women were sometimes forced into prostitution against their will.[5]

Many scholars argue that the fear of white slavery was an example of moral panic, a collective fear that arises from rapid social changes. These panics, according to Stanley Cohen, who coined the term, and other sociologists, have tended to focus on the corruption of youth. In the case of white slavery, that panic occurred in reaction to rapid changes in urban areas—including an increase in immigration, technological and economic transformations, and the evolving composition of neighborhoods.[6]

Middle-class reformers, especially women, demonstrated their concern for young women by organizing efforts to prevent the spread of white slavery, either by forming groups specifically designed to address it or by expanding their existing activities to include such work. Their efforts complemented other Progressive Era social purity campaigns and laid the groundwork for further public engagement that would ultimately result in women's suffrage. By engaging in such reform efforts, women in Jewish and Catholic organizations in the United States and England advanced some additional goals. They could both reinforce their new middle-class status and work toward limiting an activity that could harm the reputations of their minority religious communities at a time when large numbers of their coreligionists were arriving from Europe and elsewhere. In that way, Catholics and Jews sought to strengthen the position of their religious communities in the majority culture.

Unpacking White Slavery

The label "white slavery" is another relevant dimension to the differentiation in resource allocation. The choice of the term "slavery" intended to connote the brutal and inhumane treatment of African Americans and African slaves, who were forcibly brought to Europe, its colonies, and later, the United States. It also consciously linked the transnational religiously based movement to that of the abolitionist movement earlier in the nineteenth century, which had now been broadened beyond Quakers and other liberal Protestant denominations to encompass Catholics throughout Europe and in the United States.

But the term also emphasized that the victims of coercion were white. As several scholars have noted, the term "white slavery" had been used before the late nineteenth century to describe the condition of Massachusetts women workers employed in the Lowell textile mills and the Lynn shoe factories. In Europe and in the United States, it was used widely as a metaphor for labor exploitation more generally. As Eric Foner and David Roediger have each detailed, it was used in much the same way as the term "wage slavery." Before the Civil War, southerners, seeking to defend slavery, used the term to argue that northern abolitionist factory owners were hypocritical in their opposition to slavery because they continued to exploit workers in their mills.[7]

Gradually the term came to be used specifically to refer to prostitution, by emphasizing the exploitation and coercion of its young, unsuspecting victims. Historians such as Judith Walkowitz have written about prostitution in Victorian London and the agitation against it. Three decades after the panic took hold in England, Jane Addams and other American reformers began focusing on white slavery in the United States. Addams published *A New Conscience and an Ancient Evil* in 1912, incorporating research from the Juvenile Protective Association of Chicago.[8]

Addams's first chapter establishes a strong parallel between prostitution and racially based slavery: "Thus the generation before us, our own fathers, uprooted the enormous upas [toxic tree] of slavery" and deemed modern-day prostitution "a twin of slavery." The first example she discusses is of Marie, an adolescent "convent-bred" Breton girl whose father's age and economic misfortunes led her to leave school to seek work in Paris. The adolescent then immigrated to Chicago under the guise of performing in an acting troupe.[9] Addams also attributes prostitution among immigrants as an outcome of either undue influence by a male lover, a stranger, or an acquaintance offering what appears to be genuine help or strained family relationships. Young women who arrived in Chicago from rural areas were particularly vulnerable to prostitution, whether they migrated from neighboring states or from Europe or Russia. She also noted how jealous partners sometimes used deportation to exact revenge on women.[10]

Addams discusses at length the structural economic inequalities that led women to engage in prostitution, including the narrow range of viable opportunities for young immigrant women in the urban United States. Although she does not discuss it in significant detail, she notes that domestic service rendered women particularly likely to become prostitutes. She also emphasizes how women employed for low wages in department stores and cafés came into contact with male procurers.[11]

Though her book is clearly focused on white women, Addams briefly addresses African American women's specific vulnerability. She argues that decreased occupational opportunities and housing discrimination led to African American women's high concentration in domestic service, especially in neighborhoods where prostitution was widespread. She notes the irony of the U.S. abolishing slavery as an institution only later to render African American women vulnerable to this particular form of sexual slavery. She further notes that their court testimony against white men was less likely to be believed because of their race.[12]

Scholars Janet Beer and Katherine Joslin discuss the idea of white slavery as concerned with "poor women adrift in the city [who] became unwitting victims of sexual slavery, a depiction that avoided a more powerful image of urban working women forging neighborhood communities and organizing labour unions, claiming their place in the city and even reshaping the manners and mores of the middle class." It is somewhat ironic, then, that Jane Addams and her friend, Charlotte Perkins Gilman, a writer and an early women's rights advocate, who through both their words and their actions challenged traditional expectations about women's roles, and the image of women as victims, joined in this campaign.[13] Yet, despite her middle-class bias, her traditional views of sexual behavior, and her maternalist perspective, Addams offered a trenchant critique of social inequality that would resonate with activists working on global human trafficking issues today.

White slavery narratives reflected middle-class anxieties about immigration, "race suicide," women's power, and rapid urbanization. They portrayed young women and girls as powerless and gullible. Neither Mexican women, who were defined as nonwhite, nor older European (often French or Jewish) women who worked as prostitutes in mining towns or small cities along the southern border, fit seamlessly into this narrative of exploitation. As a result, their personal safety was largely ignored by both local police and federal immigration officials.

Braun's European Investigation

Within the Bureau of Immigration, a growing concern over nonmarital pregnancy and prostitution also spanned the Atlantic. On March 31, 1909, Marcus Braun, a Bureau of Immigration official, sailed from New York on the *Lusitania* to undertake a major, five-month investigation in Europe on the impact of the international white slave trade on immigration to the United States. In some ways, his trip resembled a European grand tour, taking him to the capital cities of London, Paris, and Berlin and to several smaller cities, including Warsaw and Odessa. Throughout his travels, he frequented cafés and kept a regular record of his activities, much as if he were writing entries in a travel diary, noting carefully the particular cultural practices of the locals. In other ways, however, his voyage shared characteristics with other Progressive Era fact-finding tours in which American reformers sought to determine how Europeans had addressed certain social issues. Indeed, his European investigation in the service of U.S. immigration policy was very much like the one eugenicist Harry H. Laughlin conducted in the early 1920s as a representative of the Carnegie Institute and a "dollar a year" man for the Department of Labor. Laughlin would testify before Congress during the debate over the national-origins legislation, as discussed in chapter 4.[14]

Braun's reports reveal a great deal about American fears of prostitution and the perspective that the United States population had stronger moral values than did that of Old Europe. His reports highlight his view that the United States was superior to the countries that he visited. Through the prism of his investigation, Braun interpreted the United States as a more enlightened and forward-looking society because it did not permit prostitution, in contrast to the older cities of Europe, which, in its permissiveness, allowed immorality, the exploitation of women, and corruption to flourish. Yet, perhaps ironically, Braun acknowledged that in many European countries, including France and Germany, prostitution was closely regulated on public health grounds. Several cities required prostitutes to undergo regular physical examinations, and those found to have sexually transmitted diseases were sanctioned. In fact, these early European efforts to regulate prostitution were at the vanguard of public health initiatives designed to contain the spread of disease.

Braun arrived at two major conclusions: that there was very little coordination among those involved in prostitution, and that most women engaged in the prostitution voluntarily, rather than having been ensnared under false pretenses. He therefore countered the notion, often asserted by reformers, that there was a prostitution industry that organized "traffic" or cartels, in much the same way that the international narcotics industry is organized today. He maintained that those engaged in prostitution were united by an informal "esprit de corps." Yet, Braun agreed with reformers that women were exploited economically by their employers by having their wages garnished or being charged exorbitant rates for clothing.[15]

Braun further asserted that on the West Coast, Jews formed a significant percentage of pimps and in Seattle particularly, "70% of all the prostitutes in this city are Jewesses." In Russia, he concluded, "the whole 'business' of prostitution is almost exclusively in the hands of Jews."

That assertion reflected commonly held stereotypes about Jews in this era. As Mara Keire has argued, Progressive Era journalists such as George Kibbe Turner, influenced by anti-Semitism, advanced the trope of prostitution as a worldwide Jewish conspiracy.[16]

The trope of significant Jewish involvement in transnational prostitution was widespread. Donna Guy, a historian writing about prostitution in Argentina in the late nineteenth and early twentieth centuries, has noted that as Jewish immigration from Russia and Eastern Europe increased, Jewish religious organizations worked to prevent prostitution among Jewish women. While Guy argues that many Jewish women were involved in the Buenos Aires trade, she concludes that anti-Semitism fueled concerns that were disproportionate to the actual extent of Jewish participation in prostitution. In fact, most prostitutes in the country were nonimmigrant Catholics, a fact that did not lead to controversy.[17]

Immigration officials' conclusions about prostitution were also shaped by eugenicist ideologies of the era. The notion that some women were hypersexualized and engaged in prostitution to satisfy their sexual appetites, rather than for economic reasons, was a well-known cultural stereotype in the era. Cesare Lombroso, an Italian criminal anthropologist, who published research on female criminals in the late nineteenth century, argued that women who became prostitutes were biologically predisposed and had physical features that differed from "normal" women. For example, prostitutes were more likely to experience the early onset of menstruation, to become sexually active as children or early adolescents, and to "clearly manifest exaggerated and unceasing lustfulness." Lombroso argued that prostitutes were more like men than like "normal" women, whom he characterized as frigid. These stereotypes also arose from the perception among many Americans that Europeans (and the French especially) were more morally corrupt than Americans, a perception that was clearly evident in the Braun report.[18]

Paris was Braun's major destination, largely because of its longtime reputation as a center of prostitution and vice. He also concluded that Paris was an important point of origin for immigrant prostitutes in the United States. He estimated that "75% of all French and Belgian women and girls and 90% of the Japanese females arriving in this country are prostitutes, and that Paris furnishes more prostitutes to the United States than all other countries combined."[19]

In stemming the threat of prostitution, however, the United States would have to act unilaterally, without the full cooperation of its European allies. Braun expressed his frustration at the indifference to prostitution expressed by many officials that he interviewed. "European sentiment is wholly out of sympathy with Section 3 of the immigration laws, and no cooperation can be expected in the enforcement thereof. Abroad, prostitutes and prostitution are regarded as 'necessary evils,' and our attempts to discourage or to obliterate same are regarded as 'farcical' and 'hypocritical.'" In Belgium, Braun reported, "and for that matter in all Europe, . . . a woman who is of age can do with her body whatever she pleases and if she does not violate any of the existing regulations, which are mostly made by the Local, Municipal or Police Authorities, no one will or can interfere with her or her movements." Revealing more than a hint of contempt for the perceived moral permissiveness of Europeans, Braun concluded that most European women participate in prostitution "of their own volition, a fact which speaks well for the moral condition of the countries investigated."[20]

Braun's European investigation created diplomatic tensions. He reported that M. Hennequin, the French undersecretary of the interior, objected to Braun's investigation, stating his position that such actions were "the province, jurisdiction, and duty of the French police authorities." Braun found other French officials, including the future prime minister Georges Clemenceau, more helpful, perhaps because France had been a signatory in a major international agreement to address white slave traffic. But in their subsequent meetings, Hennequin continued to question Braun's right to investigate a matter that was legal in France. He further stated that he was not sympathetic to U.S. immigration laws and that, as an internal U.S. affair, the French government was not obligated to assist in the matter. Braun's increasingly strained interactions with Hennequin led the latter to register a complaint with Henry White, the American ambassador to France.[21]

Braun's report heightened the Bureau of Immigration's efforts to closely scrutinize women arriving in the United States for evidence that they might be engaging in prostitution. Braun's investigation confirmed the view that Europeans had fewer strictures against prostitution and would not serve as strong allies in containing it within their borders. They concluded that the United States needed to be ever more vigilant under such circumstances.

Special Inspectoress Helen Bullis embarked on an investigation of houses of assignation in the Tenderloin District of New York City. Her study assessed how the business was organized in the city and the role of immigrants in the business. She compiled a list of known houses of prostitution, their proprietors, and the names and nationalities of the "inmates." More cursory investigations of prostitution in Chicago and among French Canadians in New England were initiated as part of this effort to combat white slavery.[22]

These "white slavery" investigations occurred just before the release of the 1911 Dillingham Commission's report that influenced the later immigration restriction laws that greatly reduced immigration from Europe. The Dillingham Commission drew extensively upon eugenicist typologies based on perceived national characteristics, including physical health, intelligence, and moral behavior, as rationales for limiting immigration. The national characteristics addressed in the white slavery investigations were similarly used to place limitations on women's immigration. By policing women's bodies and moral fitness both at the borders and in the cities of origin, U.S. officials rendered immigration more difficult for all European women, especially young unmarried women, as occurred earlier for Asian women.

Concerns about the sexual morality of female immigrants intersected with concerns over their economic roles in the new industrial economy, as well as with prevailing middle-class views of immigrant women as dependent on male breadwinners to whom they were married. When immigrant women did not conform to such American social norms, they became highly vulnerable to exclusion or deportation proceedings.

Paris was widely viewed as the most active city in fueling international prostitution, a perspective that even some French journalists held to be true. For example, one unnamed French publication ran an article about the methods used in this human trafficking. The author suggested that although French authorities sought to warn women leaving France about the perils they would face, they were powerless to prevent females who were citizens and of age from choosing to make the trip, and underage girls often used assumed names to avoid being caught. The article cited Havana, Manchuria, South Africa, and Cairo as the most common destinations among women leaving France to work as prostitutes.[23]

The French officials with whom Marcus Braun interacted generally opposed enforcing international sanctions against white slavery. They expressed concern that in addition to prostitutes the agreement would prohibit the entry into the United States of a girl or woman "who may have been the mistress of somebody, or perhaps has been living with somebody." M. Hennequin, the French minister of the interior, characterized the law as "outrageous." But in some cases, such as when a young, minor woman living at home was brought to the United States by a well-known "procurer," the French police and authorities were prepared to intervene. For example, a Miss Loth was reportedly abducted from her mother's home in Alfortville, outside of Paris. The alleged abductor, Ferdinand Muller, had reportedly previously taken a Belgian woman to the United States to work as a prostitute. Yet, Braun's investigation of this case also led to tensions with the French, as he reported visiting places where the "gilded youth touches elbow with the various members of the underworld." Rather than existing in separate socioeconomic spheres, where criminals congregate in certain establishments, and more refined citizens in others, he suggested that French society mixed high and low society, both of which partook in vice. That intermingling, he appeared to imply, was evidence of France's moral contamination.[24]

Braun rejected the notion that there was trade comprising a few organizations "having headquarters on both continents for the purpose of exploiting innocent and virtuous women." It was not a highly developed and organized cartel system but rather a decentralized process. He embraced the idea that in most cases the only bond that existed was a shared "esprit de corps . . . which leads kindred spirits, engaged in a nefarious business to consort together at a given spot." Braun found that in each European capital there existed locations "where the pimps and procurers congregate and where they can secure and come into touch with lewd women" and that many sought admission to the United States indirectly through South America or Canada.[25] Therefore, while he conceded that some young European women from good, stable suburban families might fall prey to procurers, most European women who came to the United States and subsequently practiced prostitution freely chose to mingle in the underworld where they met men involved in the promotion of prostitution.

Braun cited Berlin as the "best city in the world" for "pimps and procurers." It was also the sole European city where Braun noted the presence of male prostitutes. That aspect of Berlin's culture and prostitution trade clearly fell outside of Braun's focus. His evidence was highly anecdotal—such as a rumor of a Dresden count and army officer, who had a relationship with a young man whom the count paid $5,000 to leave Germany for the United States. Braun noted that these young male prostitutes were known as "pupen-jungen." He estimated that 30,000 male prostitutes worked in Berlin alone and that they frequented the Union Bar. He characterized the nature of these relationships and interactions as predatory, indicating that these male prostitutes "make it their business to hunt for those unfortunate men, afflicted by 'Homosexuality.'" Here Braun suggests that the male client was the victim and the person exploiting him was the prostitute. That dynamic was a mirror image of the white slavery narrative, where young, innocent European women are exploited by older, often male procurers or clients.[26]

Braun's brief discussion of Berlin's gay prostitution scene suggests he finds it an interesting but not particularly significant discovery that falls outside the purview of his major charge: preventing the importation of female prostitutes to the United States. A Bureau of Immigration and Naturalization note from Daniel Keefe states: "The Inspector appears to have discovered a new species of undesirable immigrant not heretofore met with in the enforcement of the immigration law, and for whose exclusion no specific provision seems to have been made."[27]

Braun further noted that though the city regulated prostitution, bar maids or waitresses were viewed as casual prostitutes who eluded regulations and often migrated to the United States.[28]

As a result of his 1909 European investigation, Braun estimated that there were 50,000 alien prostitutes currently residing in the United States and 10,000 alien procurers and pimps. New York, the largest city and the major port of entry for immigrants, was the center of prostitution in the United States. Another immigration inspector placed that figure much higher, estimating that there were 100,000 alien prostitutes in the United States. Braun asserted that most prostitutes are French, Belgians, and Russian or Polish Jews. He estimated that 75 percent of French and Belgian women arriving in the United States were prostitutes, as were 90 percent of the Japanese female immigrants. Braun claimed that Paris sent more prostitutes to the United States than all other European countries combined. He estimated that in Seattle Jewish women accounted for 70 percent of all prostitutes in the city.[29]

In *The Christian*, an English religious newspaper, it was reported that the Du Fors, a French couple, had been arrested in Chicago and, while on bail, they returned to Paris, where they were arrested, convicted, and imprisoned. The paper reported that the Chicago district attorney had determined that the prosperous couple bought women for £8 and "sold" them for as much as £100 and that they were an integral part of "an organized syndicate with headquarters in Chicago and branch offices established in all our large cities." The reporter continued: "Regularly and systematically, it sends hunters to France, Hungary, Italy, and Canada for victims. . . . They scan immigrants, and seek to trap unprotected girls by speaking to them in their own tongue or by an offer of employment. Then follow in quick succession capture, ruin, slavery—hell!" The reporter concludes by highlighting a meeting of a group of 1,000 Protestant ministers at the Chicago YMCA on February 8, a fitting tribute on the centenary of Abraham Lincoln, the liberator of black slaves.[30] The Du Fors were mentioned briefly in several U.S. deportation cases, probably because their case ultimately revealed connections that led to other investigations.

Progressivism and the Economics of Prostitution

In his report, Daniel Keefe drew extensively on the Braun Report findings. Keefe concluded that European women sought to come to the United States to practice prostitution in part as a result of "the lack of subsequent regulation and sanitary control of such women in the majority of United States cities." The analogies to meat processing and to the Progressive Era's Pure Food and Drug Act are unmistakable. He contrasted that with the situation in Europe, where cities were "infested with women of immoral tendencies, living in poverty and squalor." Therefore, "procurers who desire to secure fresh supplies for their resorts in the United States, are not forced to seduce and debauch innocent women, when with much less exertion, expense and danger, numbers of women can be found ready to accept their terms."[31]

In this context, reformers likened prostitution to any other well-run business that had systemized its supply chain and was deriving benefits from economies of scale. Oil and steel were among the leading sector industries that had benefited from implementing these practices and several American-based global companies increasingly relied on obtaining raw material from abroad. Keefe implicitly argued that the United States' lack of stringent laws against prostitution and lack of public health measures regarding sexually transmitted diseases created a favorable regulatory climate for immigrant women to migrate in order to practice prostitution. In this way, market capitalism encouraged labor migrations and, by extension, a more globalized demand for prostitution.

But he also maintained that European regulation was not very effective, nor did it dissuade many prostitutes from remaining in their occupations, because there were numerous women whom procurers could entice to emigrate. Though prostitution in Belgium, France, or elsewhere was regulated at the local level, Keefe and others expressed their frustration that those nations were reluctant to take meaningful action against the immigration of prostitutes, procurers, or women who were likely to be lured into prostitution.

Emilie Paillet, an alleged French prostitute in San Francisco, was deported in 1908 after a French man named Jules Cerles accused her of being a carrier of a sexually transmitted disease. While in France, Paillet had worked at a cake shop and at a dry goods store in Lille. In contrast to Braun's findings and the narrative arc of *The Christian* article, it appears that Paillet was not motivated by economic desperation, nor was she lured into prostitution by a nefarious procurer or white slave ring. She seemed to have lived a comfortable, if unexciting, suburban life in the outskirts of Paris. It is possible that she sought to move to San Francisco to reconnect with a Parisian man she knew.

The multiple testimonies of relatives, the man, her lover, and others who knew her revealed that her aunt's husband helped her to immigrate to San Francisco. Paillet charged that when her uncle lost work as a carpenter, he pressured her to repay him for her passage. Though her aunt denied it in her testimony, Paillet alleged that her aunt and uncle threatened to turn her into immigration officials if she did not give them money. Paillet denied living in a house of prostitution or earning her living as a prostitute. She admitted only that she lived with Jean Peron, a man whom she had known in Paris and who was not her husband, but denied involvement in prostitution. She maintained that Peron supported her financially.[32]

Following her arrival in San Francisco, she had lived with her aunt and uncle and worked as a servant in a private home, but "kept company with different men and on many occasions remained out all night with these men. . . . She has since been seen a number of times in the company of a notorious procurer and pimp named Louis Bonin." She later told her uncle that Bonin sought to recruit her into prostitution. In the course of her Board of Special Inquiry testimony, in front of five individuals and her attorney, she was asked detailed questions about her personal and sexual history. She admitted to having sexual relations with two other men. An investigator, A. De La Torre, reported that she lived in the New Orleans House, where he saw half a dozen prostitutes and pimps "of the lowest type" leave the building. Though she was represented by an attorney in her appeals hearing and never admitted to engaging in sexual relations for payment, she was unsuccessful in her appeal and was deported to France.[33]

Immigration officials also investigated Russian Jewish women for engaging in prostitution. Russian women were seen as the second most likely group of European immigrant to engage in prostitution. In Chicago, for example, a review of prostitution cases among immigrants found that eleven of the twenty-four cases of immigrants violating the prostitution statute between 1903 and 1907 involved French women, with "Hebrews" (most likely from Russia) representing ten of the cases. John H. Grout, the U.S. consul, reported on prostitution in Odessa, which he termed an "emporium of infamy." He provided an ethnographical explanation for the prevalence of prostitution infused with the vocabulary of eugenics. He argued, "Among the female population is a large percentage with comely faces. Owing to the diversity of the population, there is no really predominant religion, and the tenets of morality do not range high."[34]

In 1908 Lulu Sipher (also known as Lima Lefcovish) and Bessie Green, two Russian Jewish women traveling from Mexico with their alleged procurer, were detained and investigated for violations of Section 3. Sipher had been excluded earlier from the United States at El Paso, so she posed as the niece of Green and Lockfeesh and entered the United States from Mexico at Laredo and allegedly lived in a house of prostitution in Houston. As in the case of most women facing deportation, she was not represented by counsel. She readily admitted living in a house of prostitution. Evidence also suggested that Lockfeesh had been involved in prostitution in South Africa, another alleged international nexus for the prostitution trade. Apparently, there was insufficient evidence to deport Harry Lockfeesh for procurement, though if he was, as alleged, Green's and Sipher's pimp, he too should have faced deportation.[35]

Following Braun's investigation, Helen Bullis was assigned to investigate prostitution in New York City in the Middle and Upper Tenderloin neighborhoods. She documented more than 100 "houses of assignation," apartments, and parlors, as places where prostitutes worked or resided. This culminated in a list resembling a census. She did not note in her list whether the women were immigrants, but she did mention that, though some were long-standing establishments, many of them would change addresses in six months' time. Bullis noted that each house had on average fewer than fifteen "inmates." In the few cases where the proprietor is listed, two are males, but most are female, and are referred to as "Madame."[36]

Though presumably assumed names, women listed on Bullis's census appropriated mainstream, typical first American names of the era—Annie, Helen, May, and Lilly, paired with last names of English origin, such as Palmer, Woods, Walker, and Simmons. If we assume that the prostitutes were European immigrants, they chose socially mainstream names in place of ethnic ones.[37] These women's names would have been fashionable in New York theater and in Hollywood. Indeed since the early era of Hollywood's motion picture industry, immigrants changed their names to downplay their ethnic origins and to appeal to the broadest audience possible. These women selected American names to make them part of mainstream culture, as well as to attract immigrant clientele, who, in turn, sought to become more American by choosing a sexual partner who had a local identity, even when that identity was merely a fictive one.

Soon after this investigation, the Bureau of Immigration marshaled extensive resources to build its case that Albert and Lumbertine Bosny operated a house of prostitution in New York City. It collected testimonies from several female employees. The Bosny case investigation extended to Belgium, where, as in some other European countries, prostitution was legal, requiring licensing and medical inspections. Belgian authorities indicated that the couple had operated an unlicensed "secret house of prostitution" under the guise of a "café-concert" establishment. In fact, the Belgian government refused to become one of the signatories to an international white slavery agreement that would work to reduce the movement of traffic across national boundaries.

The Bosny couple faced deportation at Ellis Island in 1911 after living in New York for several years. The *Morgen Journal* reported this in an article headlined "Williams as a Guardian of Morals" and questioned his dedication of bureau resources and his interference with local authorities while complaining that "he has not enough men to cope with the tremendous flood of immigration." The bureau had in fact dedicated extensive resources and worked with the local police on the investigation to create an airtight case that the couple, Albert and Lumbertine Bosny, participated in an international prostitution ring.[38]

In Belgium, the police had determined that "the husband did not work and the wife was known as a person of light morals."[39] That assertion, repeated later in the report, did not entirely square with the finding that Mr. Bosny was the proprietor of illicit businesses in both Belgium and New York. But, the fact that Albert Bosny depended on his wife's wages clearly rankled those writing the report. In fact, he was denounced as "despicable" for making his living from his wife's work as both a madam and as a prostitute. That raid also coincided with a greater effort among immigration officials to deport not just prostitutes but procurers of prostitutes, who were viewed as part of a European underworld network.

The white slavery investigations suggest that many immigration officials felt that Europeans in France, Germany, Belgium, and Russia were less concerned with morality than were Americans. As immigrant prostitutes, women were viewed as importing these undesirable standards of morality to the United States, often with the assistance of male accomplices. The Immigration Bureau's understanding of the process by which prostitution crossed national boundaries differed significantly from the perceptions of those in women's and religious organizations.

Those reformers who sought an end to "white slavery" saw a more systematic and coordinated process among a group of men who lured innocent, young, usually European women into sexual slavery in a distant country, whether that was the United States, South Africa, or the Middle East. Braun's report implicitly suggested that the United States offered a better economic climate for prostitution to work because of its lack of local health and registration requirements. By contrast, U.S. immigration officials saw dissolute women from European societies, where sexual morality was lax and prostitution readily condoned. But at least in some cases, such as that of Miss Loth and Emilie Paillet, young women from relatively comfortable suburban circumstances, one still a minor, the other a shop assistant, undue pressure from men led them to leave their homes and become involved in prostitution. For young European female immigrants, the path to that life was generally far more complex than either white slavery reformers or immigration officials acknowledged. Yet the prevailing view that continental European societies were permissive and that prostitution was an imported threat to the American moral fabric contributed to a climate that led to the closing of opportunities for all immigrant women and the passage of large-scale immigration restriction laws in the 1920s.

The Differential Regulation of the Southern U.S. Border

A decentralized investigative effort along the Mexican border occurred in several cities and towns where Mexican and European immigrants were actively engaged in prostitution. The Immigration Service did not launch a special investigation, as was the case with Marcus Braun's and Helen Bullis's studies. Instead, the bureau relied on officials already working at immigration stations to submit reports on the prevalence of prostitution on the border, thereby expending few resources on white slavery along the southern border. In addition to Mexican women, French and Eastern European Jewish women were found to have moved to this region in significant numbers to work as prostitutes. The Bureau of Immigration's Braun and Bullis reports on European and New York prostitution concluded that immigrants from France, Russia, and other points in Eastern Europe were among those engaged in the houses of prostitution they investigated in the urban United States. One immigration official concluded that immigrant women older than thirty tended to relocate from the East Coast to the Mexican border and were especially prevalent in mining camps.[40]

In this period, Mexican and European women who engaged in prostitution along this border between the United States and Mexico did not elicit the same level of concern as European prostitutes in New York City, or those in San Francisco and Chicago. Today, of course, Mexican immigration to the United States is highly contested and the border heavily patrolled, but early in the twentieth century, immigration concerns about morality and prostitution were focused on those who were considered permanent immigrants and future citizens. In fact, before 1905 fewer than 3,000 Mexicans were even recorded in official federal immigration aggregate statistics, suggesting that most crossed the border easily and without inspection at border stations, a situation that changed with the establishment of the U.S. Border Patrol in 1924.[41]

The Immigration Service dedicated far fewer of its resources and personnel to investigating the causes of prostitution along the Mexican border and generally seemed less concerned about the threat it posed there. This attitude also markedly contrasted with the bureau's early emphasis on limiting Chinese prostitution, beginning with the 1875 Page Law that made it virtually impossible for an unmarried Chinese woman to immigrate to the United States, because of the supposition that they were being brought to the United States to work as prostitutes. That prohibition, combined with laws barring racial intermarriage, also made it difficult for Chinese immigrants to form families in the United States and led to a highly skewed ratio of men to women that reached 27:1 within the Chinese immigrant community in 1890. By 1882 the Chinese Exclusion Act virtually eliminated immigration from China, with the exception of merchants, students, and a few other categories. By 1907 most Japanese immigration had been curtailed.[42] As a result, employers on the West Coast and in the Southwest increasingly relied on Mexican immigrants as a labor source. Southern and Eastern European immigration to the East Coast reached its height in the first decade of the twentieth century, but those immigrants remained concentrated in the Northeast or Midwest.

There are several explanations for the discrepancy between regulation of prostitution among Europeans in East Coast cities and that along the Mexican border. The focus of immigration regulation remained primarily on Europe because the sheer numbers of immigrants arriving from that continent remained significantly higher than from other regions. Mexicans could migrate on a cyclical basis far more easily than Chinese immigrants, because the continental border was relatively porous and more difficult to regulate than was immigration by sea.

Unfortunately, because immigration officials provide the sources for this situation, the perspectives and voices of the women themselves are virtually impossible to uncover. Newspapers in Mexican border towns did not report on these investigations, nor would the women have likely written about their experiences, even if they were literate. Indeed, in the years before the Mexican Revolution, just 13 percent of Mexican women were able to read and write. In contrast to many of the European women investigated for prostitution, the case files revealed fewer details about the circumstances that led Mexican women into prostitution. Yet, despite these challenges and the biases inherent in government accounts written by officials who were, in the case of the Mexican border investigations, both male and white, these records allow historians to understand some of the women's circumstances, and in a few cases their reactions to deportation, even when mediated by those official government accounts.[43]

Another notable contrast between the European investigations and those along the Mexican border is that in several instances, the male procurers along the southern border faced deportation or arrest for violation of Section 3 of the immigration law. Aside from a few high-profile cases such as the Bosny one, male European immigrants engaged in the prostitution trade as procurers were not routinely arrested, detained, or deported. This was the case even when the man was identified and questioned. Several such Mexican and European men were apprehended as part of the investigations along the southern border.

The fact that relatively few federal resources or personnel were appropriated to investigate prostitution on the border further assured the maintenance of a contingent, productive, and interregional agricultural workforce at a time when the Immigration Service was housed within the Department of Commerce and Labor and southwestern mining and agricultural interests were well represented in Washington. In contrast to Mexican immigrants, who were still viewed as contingent labor and interregional migrants rather than permanent immigrants, Europeans were viewed as future citizens. The fact that Mexican laborers were the likely clients of prostitutes along the border concerned immigration officials less than would have been the case if those clients were native-born or European immigrants. Moreover, the presence of prostitutes "serving" predominantly male, migrant mining camps would seem a less troubling phenomenon than having large numbers of Mexican families relocate to the United States and would have been seen as a fair trade-off for having an inexpensive labor force readily available in major sectors of the U.S. economy. Mexican men, like Italian immigrants, often came to the United States temporarily and without their families to save as much of their wages as possible. In this circular migration pattern, wives or other family members typically remained on their farms in their communities of origin. Wage employment options for women in southwestern mining communities were limited.[44]

The Southwest, having been acquired as an American territory in the mid-nineteenth century, remained sparsely populated, and had not yet been fully incorporated into the American political system or its discourse. By the 1930s, the region would become a major focus of immigration regulation as the Great Depression led to greater concerns about the economic effects of Mexican immigration. Politicians such as Senator Patrick McCarran of Nevada and Congressman Martin Dies of Texas would become active opponents of immigration following their election in the 1930s, and both would later become well known for their staunch anticommunism in Congress. Addressing the influx of prostitution from Europe, and the danger it posed to young immigrant women, was viewed as a more compelling project in the years before major European immigration restriction legislation in the 1920s and the economic crisis of the 1930s.

Investigations in Texas and Arizona

Attitudes toward Mexican women by Anglos along the Texas border at the beginning of the twentieth century are illustrated in an *El Paso Daily Times* article entitled "Wiles of Mexican Girls." The article seems to serve as both a warning and an acknowledgment that Anglo men found Mexican women particularly appealing. A fictive "Mexican girl" was stereotyped as an exotic creature who "loves naturally to dominate and expects man to bow abjectly to the ordeal. She rules him and caresses him into obedience in the same breath. She is haughty with him if the mood strikes her, but flattery is the straw that whisks her off her pedestal."[45] Mexican women are portrayed as an antidote to the "drab Anglo-Saxon." Though not specifically about prostitution, this article suggests that Anglo men objectified Mexican women along the border and certainly cast them as the "other." It further implies that there was a specific demand for Mexican prostitutes among white men on the basis of stereotypes of Mexican women's perceived passion, unpredictability, and cultural differences.

Frank R. Stone of the Immigration Service reported on the local investigation of prostitution in Laredo in 1909. He concluded that most houses of prostitution were operated by Mexican women, *duenas* (or madams), and housed Mexican "inmates," most of whom had resided in the United States for fewer than three years, and many of whom traveled back and forth across the border. In an ironic twist, one such house, Casa Blanca, was occupied by "American" women and was located in the building formerly occupied by the Immigration Service.[46] American railroad workers were also seen as colluding with *duenas* by transporting prostitutes across the border by posing as family units.

Stone's investigation revealed that prostitutes were routinely brought north from Nuevo Laredo. He reported that a constable, Pedro Leas, was responsible for bringing many women into Laredo for prostitution and that he served as the procurer for "some of the most influential and prominent City and County officials," including Laredo's sheriff, Luis Ortiz, who arranged for Leas to bring a young Mexican woman from a prominent family for his "use." Laredo's district attorney knew this family, and he and the mayor returned the woman to Mexico before she was "ruined at that house." In his report, Stone attributed this widespread abuse to the fact that "almost the entire city and County Government are Mexicans . . .

and from the high-handed manner in which they handle State laws here[,] they don't seem to have much respect for the Federal laws." He went on to conclude that most are "dissolute, with little conception to the laws of morality."[47]

It was also alleged that hackmen or *coacheros*, working for procurers, routinely transported women across the border from Nuevo Laredo to houses of prostitution in Laredo. After taking the women into their rooms in houses of prostitution, they would rape them as a type of brutal induction rite, thereby forcing them into lives of prostitution. Though this practice was reported on as a routine event, there seemed to be no subsequent attempt to launch a criminal investigation or effort to learn the identities of the hackmen or their victims.

Pedro Leas and a *duena*, Ruby Brown, were arrested in an effort to disable the major conduits in the cross-border prostitution trade, but no action was taken to stop the sexual violence perpetrated against women working in the city.[48] The situation reported in Laredo involved a much higher level of force and coercion than uncovered by the European and New City investigations. In Immigration Service narratives arising from Marcus Braun's investigation and others, European women were seen as entering prostitution as a result of the influence of a lover, frequenting nightspots in marginal urban neighborhoods, or disputes within their families. This difference might have simply reflected negative stereotypes about Mexican morality among Immigration Service personnel. But if some of these Texas scenarios were accurate, the description of unsuspecting girls brought across the border and coerced into prostitution that embodied the white slavery narrative should have prompted a greater public outcry.

Moreover, in his report Frank Stone seemed to be concerned more with enforcing the letter of the law than its spirit. His interactions with *duenas* led to their assurances that they would seek to employ only those women who had been in the United States for at least three years. Therefore, in these accounts prostitution itself was not viewed as particularly problematic, nor was the exploitation and/or rape of young Mexican women. Rather, the most objectionable aspect was that the houses were operating in violation of federal immigration law, because immigrant women were engaging in prostitution within three years of arrival.

Charles Cornell, the acting immigration inspector stationed in Douglas, Arizona, was far more zealous than Stone in pursuing the male procurers involved in prostitution. These investigations led to the arrest of several men. Cornell also undertook a more thorough investigation of prostitution in the Mexican cities from which prostitutes emigrated, including Juarez, Chihuahua, Nogales, and Sonora. He compiled a list of 150 prostitutes in those Mexican cities and forwarded them to immigrant inspection stations in El Paso, Tucson, and elsewhere in the Southwest. He reported that he had arrested fourteen immigrants for prostitution-related violations of immigration law. Of the twelve females, eleven were deported, and one was imprisoned for violating immigration laws. Both of the male procurers, or pimps, were arrested; one was awaiting trial, and the other was imprisoned. Interestingly, while half of the prostitutes were Mexican, neither procurer was: one was Spanish, and the other French. Additionally, he reported that two male U.S. citizens of Mexican origin were arrested for violation of Section 3 of the immigration law.[49]

Cornell emphasized that several mining camps in Arizona where Mexican workers were employed drew many prostitutes. He asserted that in the mining towns of Clifton and Morenci, prostitutes first accompanied Mexican male workers to the state as "concubines," or common-law spouses, before being deserted and moving into houses of prostitution. He further noted that the pimps resided in other towns to avoid arrest. In fact, these towns are where Linda Gordon situated *The Great Arizona Orphan Abduction*, her study that analyzes how a community controversy reveals the complex dynamics between race, class, religion, and gender in the early twentieth-century Southwest.[50]

Cornell mentions the trend of older European women migrating to the Southwest from New York City and remitting their earnings to their husbands and families who remained in New York. He estimated that more than 95 percent of Jewish prostitutes in Arizona and New Mexico were over thirty. He also suggests that many French prostitutes first entered the trade with promises of marriage or employment once they arrived in the United States.[51]

The Texas investigations also focused to some extent on Jewish and French prostitution in addition to Mexican immigrant prostitution. In San Antonio, Stone discussed the case of Edward Frion, a French "mack" whose wife was practicing prostitution in a crib, a slang term describing a rundown room where prostitutes had sexual relations with customers. He asserted that though the husband was "wealthy and has a fine ranch," his wife "is just a natural born prostitute and can't resist it." He elaborated by noting that this woman makes annual trips to France, which are "not entirely for the good of her health." Although there is no evidence that Stone was a student of European eugenicist ideology, these stereotypes about French women seem directly influenced by Cesare Lombroso's writings on women and prostitution.

In San Antonio, "the acre" was a section of the city where prostitution was prevalent, and the small wooden shacklike structures called cribs were more prevalent than houses of prostitution. Stone noted that city officials were involved in the prostitution business and deemed San Antonio "the rottenest" city he had ever seen. San Antonio's rabbi had worked to end prostitution among Jews in the city, because he saw it as "a disgrace" that reflected poorly on the religious community as a whole. Though Stone acknowledged that "American" women were also working as prostitutes, "their influence is not so concerted and well organized, hence not as efficacious and corrupt as the foreign element."[52]

In an unusually detailed coda to his report, Frank Stone reported that while his investigation was ending in San Antonio, and several women were about to be deported as prostitutes, he spent a great deal of time locating, and finally retrieving, the women's laundry from an African American woman. He paid for this service out of his own funds.

In one of the few instances where prostitutes' perspectives are heard in these Texas and Arizona investigations, he states that "they refuse to pay the bill, saying the Government is responsible for their leaving before their laundry is finished." Here they found a symbolic way to protest their treatment, however quotidian. Yet, in some cases their laundry, or apparel, probably represented a significant portion of their material assets. Perhaps the garments represented their dignity; this was their sole way to demand that the U.S. government treat them fairly. For some, their garments were essential components of their trade and they would need these items should they continue to practice prostitution once they returned to Mexico. Stone concluded that "I believe we owe it to these women to get their laundry for them inasmuch as they are deported without it."[53]

Some case files reveal specific details about how women began work as prostitutes and their life circumstances. Rosa Tijiera was brought into custody for a hearing to determine whether she should be deported to Mexico from Brownsville, Texas, in 1908, because of her entry to the United States without passing inspection. At this point, immigration across the border of Mexico was far less regulated than it would be with the passage of literacy tests and the creation of the Border Patrol in 1924. Immigrants crossing into the United States were required to pass through immigration stations, however. Her true transgression was her occupation as a prostitute. Most notable was the fact that she was born in the United States, and therefore under normal circumstances, should have been treated as a U.S. citizen, and thereby not subject to deportation. But as it happened, she had married a Mexican citizen before passage of the Cable Act, which allowed women to retain or obtain their citizenship status separately from their husbands. Though she had been separated from him for some years, she, like most nonelites living in Mexico, did not obtain a divorce because it was so costly. Therefore, immigration officials determined that she was eligible for deportation. The mother of five children in a household without her husband's income, she admitted practicing prostitution in Matamoras for three months before her arrival in Brownsville. After coming to Brownsville, she returned to Matamoras every few weeks, most likely to see her children.[54]

The case for Tijiera's deportation was made difficult because of the absence of public records in Mexico or in the United States to verify details about her life, as well as the lack of church records documenting some key aspects of her testimony. There was no record of her birth in Cameron County, Texas, baptism record, marriage or divorce record, registration at the American consulate in Mexico, or other documentation of significant life events. Two witnesses who were government officials testified that she was born on a Texas ranch.[55]

Tijiera was socially marginalized in a few ways: by working in an occupation that was viewed as morally reprehensible, by having no citizenship rights apart from those of her estranged husband, and by being rendered invisible in the official records of two separate nations. In essence, until she was detained for possible deportation, she did not exist as a citizen or even as a subject. The record does not indicate whether she was ultimately deported or encouraged to repatriate voluntarily, but she was not represented by anyone at her hearing, which suggests that she was not allowed to remain in the United States.

A similar case was that of Coka Puiento, a Mexican immigrant who in 1909 was suspected of practicing prostitution in Corpus Christi, having crossed the Rio Grande in a rowboat and eluded immigration inspectors. She stated that she had been earning a living as a prostitute for the previous five years and that she was registered as one in Nuevo Laredo. She stated that she had been born in Spain, a fact that she might have asserted as part of a strategy for claiming whiteness, so that she would receive greater consideration by immigration officials.[56]

Sara Servantes and Simon Chavez were detained at El Paso in 1908. Chavez was charged with seeking to import Servantes for immoral purposes, and her two daughters, aged eight and ten, were held in the county jail as "likely to become a public charge" (LPC). It was not clear from the charge whether she would earn her living as a prostitute or whether she was, in the Immigration Service phrasing "a concubine," living with Chavez as a common-law spouse. Ultimately, though immigration officials initially considered using her as a witness against Chavez, she was deported along with her daughters.[57]

In contrast to European immigrants, Mexican men who were connected to prostitution activities, or perhaps simply accompanying a lover or common-law spouse across the border, were far more likely to be detained, arrested, or deported than were European men. Racial bias among members of the U.S. Immigration Service led them to view Mexican men as a greater threat to social stability, even when the practice of prostitution itself was not viewed as problematic along the Mexican border as it was among Europeans in major East Coast cities.

Another significant difference between some of the cases and trends discussed in the prostitution trade among Europeans and Mexicans was that the latter revealed more instances of physical coercion and force. It is certainly troubling to those in the twenty-first century to read accounts that claim that young Mexican women brought into houses of prostitution were routinely raped. It is also disturbing to learn that the immigration inspector who reported on this practice does not seem to have attempted to substantiate them and, if true, to arrest the perpetrators.

Violence against young women along the border between Mexico and the United States remains pervasive. One of the most compelling areas of concern among women's rights activists and scholars today has been that of global human trafficking, especially the practice of sexual exploitation of girls and young women who have few educational or economic opportunities in their rural towns and villages in poor regions, including those in Russia, other parts of the former Soviet Union, and in Asia. Those women migrate to wealthier regions in search of employment, often through the influence or coercive actions of recruiters from organized networks who mislead them.

A major contemporary issue among human rights organizations, such as Amnesty International, has been the murder and disappearance of more than 400 young Mexican women along the Cuidud Juárez–El Paso border since 1993, where Mexican *maquiladoras* employ many women for U.S.-based manufacturers. Human rights groups have documented the inadequate response of government officials from the United States and Mexico to protect these women and solve these cases. As this chapter suggests, the lack of adequate response to widespread violence against Mexican women along this vital border region has parallels to the early twentieth century. Police and immigration officials in Texas border towns had evidence that young Mexican women were being raped after crossing the border and failed to intervene to investigate or prosecute these crimes.[58]

Today, neither Mexican nor American officials have effectively intervened to solve the epidemic number of murders or to ensure that more Mexican women are protected from murder. Although it is possible that the allegations of widespread rape of young Mexican women in San Antonio as a method for forcing them into prostitution were spurious and simply a way to demonize Mexican men as brutal and immoral, the straightforward tone of the report and the fact that this allegation was buried in the narrative rather than emphasized as noteworthy or shocking suggests a second conclusion. In the early twentieth century, there was little outrage in the fact that women, or at least nonwhite women, began their lives as prostitutes by first being subjected to rape. Indeed, the ongoing violence against Mexican women along the Texas border today suggests that the indifference and lack of will among both public officials and the general public to address violence against Mexican women brought to the United States for prostitution has not dissipated.

By comparing these two investigations—of European immigrant prostitutes in major cities with Mexican and European prostitution along the U.S. border with Mexico—one might conclude that "white slavery" more accurately describes the latter situation than the former. But ultimately, while the inhumane and exploitative conditions they were seeking could be found on the southern border, immigration officials were less concerned with prostitution and the welfare of women along this border and thus expended fewer resources to address the issue there. All three investigations demonstrate that locating prostitution and a lack of sexual morality as an external, imported problem enabled the United States to define its citizens and nation as a superior one to that of "Old Europe" and Mexico and their corrupting influence. But such perspectives required that reformers and immigration officials overlook clients and the demand side of the equation. Immigrant women's involvement in prostitution in major American cities as well as in cities and towns along the Mexican border also reveals their limited economic options in the industrial United States. In contrast to men from Mexico or Europe, women had fewer employment opportunities, and domestic service was poorly paid and required extremely long hours. But even those women who brought skills with them, as dressmakers or agricultural producers, faced skeptical immigration officials, who doubted that such women could live on their own wages alone. So they were evaluated and sometimes excluded or deported on the basis of the LPC provision. Thus, women at the borders found themselves closely scrutinized for their economic status and for their sexual morality, which further perpetuated their marginalized status and dependency on male family members.

GENDER, DEPENDENCY, AND THE LIKELY TO BECOME A PUBLIC CHARGE PROVISION

Until the late twentieth century, women have been much less likely than men to immigrate to the United States. In the nineteenth century, that disparity arose from factors including cultural prohibitions against migrating without family members, as well as structural labor and pay inequalities in the U.S. workforce. Those factors led males to immigrate for higher wages and women to remain home to farm or work in their communities. But beginning with the 1875 Page Law that defined Chinese female immigrants as prostitutes, such structural gender inequalities were inscribed in U.S. federal immigration law. By the early twentieth century, single and unaccompanied women immigrants were scrutinized for evidence of prostitution and other non-marital-based sexual activity. With some significant exceptions, men who were suspected of such behavior were not penalized by authorities.

A third way that immigration law restricted women's ability to migrate was through the "likely to become a public charge" (LPC) provision that denied women, even those with occupational skills, the role of independent economic actors. That presumption continued despite the increasing economic opportunities for women in garment industries, department stores, and other sectors. But in contrast to the enforcement of policies concerning sexual morality, there was a major shift in the use of the LPC provision. During periods of economic crisis, beginning with the 1920s agricultural crisis in the Southwest, the definition of economic dependency expanded to include men. At the start of the Great Depression, federal officials used the LPC provision to reduce the number of Mexican men working in the United States and later encompassed Filipinos and other immigrant groups. By the early 1930s, the view that Mexican immigrants were primarily contingent, interregional producers was suspended.

Instead, Mexican laborers were now perceived as potentially dependent on social services and as a net drain on the economy. Although many had been actively recruited by agricultural corporations in the Southwest and West and by industries in the industrial Midwest, they were not perceived as entitled to charitable or government relief. During that transition, the LPC provision provided an existing mechanism to limit immigration from the South and to deport large numbers of Mexicans from the United States. With both Jewish immigrants and Mexicans in the 1930s, the most effective argument against deportation by immigrant advocates was the concept of family reunification and the toll the process had on family members who were U.S. citizens.

The LPC clause had profound consequences for immigrants when it was first implemented and continues to shape federal immigration policy today. In both the first three decades of the twentieth century and during the period from the early 1990s to the present, there were organized efforts to limit immigrants' claims on social welfare benefits motivated by a growing reluctance among state and federal leaders and their constituencies to extend benefits to citizens and noncitizens on an equal basis. The enduring effects of the LPC provision can be seen in California's Proposition 187 and the lesser-known provisions of the 1996 welfare reform act legislation that limited access to social welfare programs of immigrants. Today, it exists in parallel to the country's refugee policy, which emerged in the post–World War II era and exempts certain groups from economic means testing as a condition of entry, though relatively few people are admitted with refugee status.

Although the LPC clause, as written, made no distinctions between male and female immigrants, traditional American notions about gender, work, and the family economy have played a significant role in its interpretation by policy makers and immigration inspectors, even when those norms came into conflict with the cultural and economic traditions of particular immigrant groups. Beginning in the Progressive Era, poverty has often served as a more convenient administrative device for deporting immigrants who were viewed as unfit for future American citizenship. Therefore, the LPC clause and aggregate statistics on causes of deportation often obscure subtler issues concerning racial identities, religion, gender roles, and sexual morality.

Over the years the LPC policy transformed from a provision used to exclude and deport women and vulnerable children to one that was effectively implemented in immigration cases involving men, particularly Mexicans and Filipinos, although immigrant advocacy organizations mitigated some of the harshest aspects of exclusion and deportation laws. U.S. immigration policy involved interactions between local and federal governments, as well as transnational relations, especially those with Mexico and the Philippines. Significant parallels are evident between immigration-related policies in the early twentieth century and those emerging since the early 1990s.

The Historical Origins of the LPC Provision

Before 1882, when the federal government first began the systematic regulation of immigration, poverty among immigrants was a concern of the state, where it arose from English and later colonial-era poor laws. Vagrancy laws had been used widely by local authorities beginning in the colonial era and extended into the Jim Crow era as a way to control free people of color and impoverished people. Such laws would be widely resurrected in the Depression era to control Mexicans and Mexican Americans and to discourage their presence in the United States.

Some early critics spoke out against efforts to conflate immigrants and poverty in the nineteenth century. During times of economic expansion, immigrants were recognized as essential economic actors. In 1876, for example, Hamilton Andrews Hill, a former secretary of the Boston Board of Trade, wrote a report on the relationship between immigrants and "pauperism" in Massachusetts. The pamphlet was written in opposition to a proposal to restore a head tax on immigrants that had been abolished in 1872.[1]

Hill argued that immigrants were essential to economic growth in a rapidly industrializing country and that the state should not put up barriers to entry. Hill took issue with the idea that immigrants were the major source of poverty, arguing that in 1870 Kansas and Nebraska had high percentages of foreign-born residents (24 percent and 35 percent) but low levels of poverty. He noted that the immigrant brought resources, including "hope, enterprise, and courage; but he brings also clothing, tools, and in most instances money." He further asserted that even the impoverished famine-era Irish became productive "producers and consumers, and were able not only to take care of themselves but to remit large sums of money to their friends beyond the sea." He argued that Great Britain, Canada, Australia, and New Zealand, as other settler nations, "were competing actively for the acquisition of the immigrant through financial and land inducements," suggesting that Americans should envision immigrants as central to economic growth.[2]

During the era when a federal immigration policy first emerged, local and state governments and other constituents sought to reduce expenditures by decreasing the number of immigrants requiring charity and medical and institutional care. Because New York was the major port for arriving immigrants, its local and state government officials lobbied strenuously to limit the number of immigrants receiving aid through government institutions. An 1882 immigration law, revised in 1891, stipulated that immigrants deemed "likely to become public charges, persons suffering from a loathsome or contagious disease, persons who have been convicted of a felony or other infamous crime or misdemeanor, involving moral turpitude, polygamists, and also any person whose ticket or passage has been paid for with the money of another" be excluded or deported.[3]

As in the case of pregnant women, the LPC provision arose from state efforts designed to prohibit "paupers" from immigrating to the United States. In 1883 state boards of charities in major East Coast port cities reported on their efforts to monitor the number of impoverished immigrants. Several of these cases pertained to Irish immigrants, who were seeking to flee the milder famine of the 1880s, but whose overall immigration numbers were in steady decline. Other cases concerned Jewish immigrants, who were arriving in the United States in large numbers.[4]

Debates over LPC and Economic Status: Jewish Immigrants in the 1910s and 1920s

The LPC clause was often coupled with a second category in the Bureau of Immigration's Board of Special Inquiry hearings, which determined whether an immigrant would be excluded, deported, or allowed to remain in the United States. This pairing typically occurred with relatively minor and noncontagious physical ailments, such as hernia, conditions that alone would make relatively weak cases for exclusion or deportation. By 1915, 64 percent of immigrants who were debarred or deported from the United States were returned to their countries of origins on LPC grounds.[5]

One immigration official suggested that the LPC provision might be alternatively described as "persons economically unfit," much as other immigrants were excluded on the basis of their physical or mental condition. He asserted that such immigrants posed an "economic menace" to American workers by "degrading our wage-earners and pulling them down to servility or utter dependence." Here, the immigration official fused together a concept of economic eugenics that deemed some immigrants unfit for participation in the American economy, with a more traditional labor critique. Yet, what he actually implied was that these immigrants were all too fit, because they posed a serious competitive threat to native-born workers.[6]

The Hebrew Immigrant Aid Society (HIAS) and other organizations acting as advocates for Jewish immigrants questioned the implementation of the LPC provision. For example, in 1911 Max Kohler, a Jewish community leader writing in the *American Hebrew*, objected to the way that the LPC provision was used to exclude or deport many Jewish immigrants at Ellis Island. Peddlers, tailors, and others were being closely scrutinized despite the fact that those were important and respected occupations among Jews in Eastern Europe and Russia at a time when many other economic options were closed to them. As a 1912 report by the National Jewish Immigration Council noted, some tradesmen were excluded on the basis of minor physical ailments that were deemed likely to prevent them from earning a living.[7]

Anticipating by several decades Joseph Heller's concept of the term Catch-22, Simon Wolf, a Washington lawyer active in Jewish causes, stated in the report, "On the other hand, if they have no trade, they are excluded on account of being paupers. A large number of Russian Jews are tailors, which is but natural, as they have, under the restricted laws of Russia very little chance of adopting trades that would efface them from particular notice, the exclusion of the Ghetto driving many of these people into commercial channels that are peculiarly their own." Wolf argued that "the peddlers were the pioneer merchants of our country at one time; that the one hundred and fifty or two hundred pound pack on the back of the Jews was the department store of the time and they were welcome visitors everywhere." He concluded by noting that, in a country where a rail-splitter and a tailor had become U.S. presidents, "peddlers and their children could achieve as much." The meeting minutes emphasized that in Boston, the LPC charge was not used as extensively as in New York. Yet, because about 75 percent of all Jewish immigrants in that period arrived at Ellis Island, New York became the contested site of discussions about the LPC clause. According to Max Kohler, in 1910 two-thirds of Jewish exclusions were based on the LPC clause.[8]

Jewish advocacy groups also challenged the assertion made by Commissioner of Immigration for Ellis Island William A. Williams. He stated that immigrants could rely only on those who are "legally entitled to support—wives and children" and must remain independent from both government assistance and private charity. They further accused Williams of issuing misleading circulars that did not make it clear to inspectors that "means" can substitute for "cash" upon entry.[9] Charles Duskind, an attorney in New York, wrote to seek clarification on the issue of the LPC provision, stating that the Bureau of Immigration seemed to be excluding not only those reliant on public funds but even those who received aid from private charities.[10] Therefore, the debate in the early twentieth century about the definition of "public charge" presaged more recent controversy about which benefits rendered immigrants dependent on social welfare programs.

In essence this question over the definition of LPC constituted a larger argument among Jewish groups that immigration laws, and enforcement of them, discriminated against Jews and their culture, migration, and employment patterns. Those groups also objected to those laws on the grounds that they perpetuated discrimination in Russia and Eastern Europe, which led Jews to immigrate to the United States in the first place. Kohler argued, "Instead of continuing the time-honored method, which has worked well in hundreds of thousands of cases among Russian Jewish immigrants and others, of permitting the male head of the family to find employment and build a home here, and save enough for his family, he is now likely to be excluded on entry because of uncertainties on these points, unless he brings his family with him at once, in which event, the chances of becoming public charges will be enormously increased."[11] Therefore, Jewish leaders were arguing that the tradition of Jewish families and charitable groups providing assistance to immigrants seeking to establish themselves in the United States was also at stake under these new immigration provisions.

Although Kohler emphasized the effect of the LPC charge on male breadwinners, women were disproportionately deemed LPC in the early twentieth century. That was especially true for women who were unmarried, or those women traveling apart from their husbands or fathers, because such women were viewed largely as economic dependents. This is especially notable in the Jewish immigrant community because unmarried Jewish women in the United States had particularly high rates of employment in the needle trades and other industries, compared to most immigrant and native-born women. Yet, despite the compatibility between many Jewish immigrants' skills and employment opportunities in New York and elsewhere, they were often subject to the LPC charge.[12]

Through its main office in New York and branch offices in several cities, HIAS was particularly active in helping Jewish immigrants to file appeals in Board of Special Inquiry cases. In 1915, for example, HIAS reported that it assisted more than 2,400 immigrants in obtaining a rehearing after being ordered deported. Representatives such as Louis S. Gottlieb, a Washington-based lawyer for HIAS, were often present during appeals involving Jewish immigrants, especially those arriving in New York. Legal representation at these hearings increased the likelihood that immigrants' appeals would succeed.[13]

LPC charges were the most common grounds for exclusion or deportation among the immigrants that HIAS represented. To ensure that they maximized their success rate, the appeals they filed included "affidavits of support," highlighting information on the financial position of the American relatives who were willing to support immigrants and ensure that they would not become dependent on public funds. Those relatives cited for their willingness to post bond were almost exclusively male, whereas many of the relatives appealing the board's decision were females, often widows, teenagers, and adults in their seventies. For example, M.C., an orphaned eleven-year-old girl, arrived from Russia in 1922. Her father had been killed in a pogrom two years earlier, and she maintained that she was poorly treated by her stepmother. The HIAS letter cited the fact that she had two uncles and two male cousins, outlined their income, mortgages, and investments and further noted that all four were U.S. citizens. A week later, HIAS noted that she was admitted temporarily on bond for a six-month period. In some cases, such as with widows and children, discussion of their close relatives with financial means and U.S. citizenship was coupled with references to the immigrant's success in a particular trade, such as dressmaking, and the high prospect of steady employment. Two such cases were successful on appeal.[14]

A similar outcome occurred for a seamstress who had one young child and was pregnant, after having separated from her husband. In his letter seeking an appeal, William Neubau of HIAS stated, "It is most unfortunate that religious differences between the husband and wife, brought about their present separation, and we are strongly of the opinion that a wave of racial discrimination begun about that time may have had a great deal to do with the breaking up of the family ties." He noted that the husband gave permission to the two to immigrate. Another pregnant woman arriving from Romania prior to her husband was denied admission "because the above named alien is pregnant in her seventh month and the Department [doesn't] know whether her husband is admissible, and the alien having a mother residing abroad." Yet her uncle in San Francisco stated that he was willing to support her.[15]

Male heads of households were occasionally excluded solely on LPC grounds, even when they had a trade and male relatives who were United States citizens. In one case that was successfully appealed, a thirty-one-year-old Romanian baker arriving with his wife and two children had been denied entry on LPC grounds alone. They had the misfortune of having been excluded the previous year after the immigration quota had been reached. The fact that the baker's two brothers, at least one of whom was a U.S. citizen, were successful small-business owners in Brooklyn probably helped the family in successfully appealing its case.

Other males found themselves vulnerable to LPC charges. A twelve-year-old boy arriving alone was unsuccessful in appealing his deportation based on LPC charges, though his mother and brother were en route to the United States after his father was killed in a pogrom. Though his uncles in the United States had agreed to support him and to provide him with a "liberal education," and further declared their intent to become citizens, none had yet become one. Though not always the decisive factor, appeals tended to be more successful when relatives were U.S. citizens or army veterans. Thus, HIAS's strategy of emphasizing female immigrants' economic dependence on established male relatives in the United States was often used successfully to gain entry for immigrants facing LPC charges. This situation occurred despite the fact that Jewish women had high rates of workforce participation relative to many other groups. But before the 1930s it remained less common for men than for women to be excluded on LPC grounds.[16]

These cases further illustrate that HIAS was developing a family reunification appeals strategy that anticipated by several decades the provisions contained in the 1965 Hart-Celler Act. Indeed, that family reunification provision has become a hallmark of post–World War II immigration policy. By highlighting the citizenship or veteran status of male relatives already in the United States and establishing their extended families' middle-class credentials, HIAS attorneys were often able to assist immigrants to remain in the country. But the reinforcement of this ideal worked to the disadvantage of those immigrants without family members in the United States. As Linda Gordon has highlighted in *Pitied but Not Entitled*, veteran's status conferred critical entitlement rights to government assistance that was not an available path for women. And the strategy reinforced existing American paradigms of the male breadwinner and the family wage that were already implicit in the enforcement of immigration policy.[17]

HIAS employed a strategically sound approach to the LPC charge by stressing the existing ties to immigrant family members who were living in the United States. The Immigration Service reported that in 1921 Jews arriving in the United States overwhelmingly came to join a close relative, whereas only a third of English, Scotch, and Welch immigrants came to join relatives. The report also noted that one-half of those debarred were "turned back" because they were likely to become public charges. LPC status, the memo stressed, needed to be determined within the United States, where relatives who could assist newly arriving immigrants were located, rather than in Europe. For Jews, more than for others arriving from Europe, claiming a relative who was already in the United States was one way to avoid the LPC charge. Those from Northern and Western Europe were less likely to be viewed as poor and could more easily be admitted as independent economic actors.[18]

The LPC clause would become even more relevant to American immigration policy in the 1930s and 1940s. Following the passage of the National Origins Act of 1924, administrative decisions about admissions shifted from the Bureau of Immigration to the Department of State, which issued visas from U.S. embassies and consulates abroad. Yet, despite this administrative shift, the LPC provision continued to be used in the exclusion of European Jews from entry to the United States in the 1930s and 1940s.[19]

Rehearsal for Repatriation: Mexicans and the LPC Clause in the 1920s

Immigrants from Mexico and other points in the Western Hemisphere were not subject to the immigration restriction laws based strictly on national origins, enacted in 1921 and 1924. Mexicans in the United States were, however, affected by other provisions in immigration law that served as grounds for exclusion and deportation, including the LPC clause, literacy tests, head taxes, medical conditions, and restrictions on undocumented workers. Enforcement of these provisions became widespread following the creation of the federal border control agency in 1924. Moreover, though several efforts were made to further restrict Mexican immigration before the 1930s, such bills were defeated by employers in the Southwest, who relied heavily on labor from Mexico to serve as the engine for economic and financial growth.[20]

Before the 1930s, Mexican immigrants in the United States had routinely faced arrest on charges of violating local vagrancy laws. For example, in Denver Robert F. Reed, the city's chief of police, noted that, although few Mexicans in the United States committed major crimes, they were often arrested on vagrancy violations. Reed noted that when minor crimes had been committed, the police often conducted raids on pool halls that were frequented by Mexicans and when unable to find "the guilty party[,] many people are arrested." Therefore, before the Depression a minority of Mexicans living in the Southwest had already been cast as poverty-stricken and dependent on state and private resources.

In the early 1920s, as the agricultural economy in parts of the Southwest experienced a depression with a significant decrease in crop prices, there were several local controversies about Mexicans who were unemployed or receiving public or charitable assistance. That situation was a regional rehearsal for the deportation raids, nativist backlash, and debates over immigrants' claims on public and private assistance that would emerge during the Great Depression.[21]

Agricultural producers were highly influential in Washington and were able to ensure the continued flow of Mexican laborers across the border to allow for continued economic development. Mexican laborers in Colorado had been actively recruited by sugar beet producers through an exception to the prohibition on the admission of alien contract laborers, a ban that had been the major impetus for the creation of federal immigration laws in the 1880s.[22]

In 1921 H. R. Williams, Denver's chief of police, contacted Vicente Quijena, the Mexican consul in that city. Of the estimated 3,000 to 3,500 Mexican men in Denver, about a 1,000 were unemployed, "roaming the streets, frequenting soft drink establishments and pool halls." Moreover, "There were so many who applied at the City Lodging House that the unemployed white people were obliged to sleep on the floor or be turned away." This comment implied that Mexicans had fewer claims on city services than "white" citizens. Of course, some Mexicans in Denver were naturalized or U.S.-born citizens, whereas not all whites were American citizens.[23]

Single Mexican men were viewed to be more problematic to the social order than those with families. As with the case of Jewish immigrants represented by HIAS and the women immigrating during the wake of the white slavery investigations, migration within family groups was increasingly seen as desirable and as a stabilizing factor among immigrant workers, which would insulate them from poverty and, in some cases, criminal activity. The chief of police asserted that Mexicans were disproportionately responsible for an increase in crimes, including burglaries, holdups, and occasionally murder. The alleged victims appeared to include Anglos, Mexican, Mexican Americans, and, in at least one case, a Chinese man.[24]

In November, the Denver police undertook a raid "on the Mexicans, and 289 arrests were made; 130 of these were sent to court and given hours to leave town, 16 were held for the Government for deportation, and 145 were released."[25] A group of Mexicans identifying themselves as representatives of "the Mexican Colony of Denver" wrote to the Mexican government, lodging a complaint against their treatment by local Denver officials. They stated that "the honest element that goes out looking for work being immediately jailed as 'vags,' which is unjust because the authorities themselves know that there is no work in all the United States." They continued, "That is the reason why we lift our voices to you asking for JUSTICE for the man who is honest and with a family." They indicated that Quijano, the consul in Denver, responded to their complaints: "I can not go against the authorities. If I do so, I will only get their bad will."[26]

By appealing to Mexican officials, these representatives in Denver simultaneously suggested that they were still governed by Mexico, and implying that their unjust and abusive treatment reduced them to second-class status in the United States. But Quijano was not a strong advocate for Denver's Mexican immigrant community in his interactions with the Immigration Service either. W. Mansfield, Denver's inspector in charge stated that Quijano had acknowledged "that many of the Mexicans here were of the very worst type and that they were a menace, and he had endeavored to induce many unemployed Mexicans . . . to return to their homes in Mexico, and he had succeeded in many instances."[27]

A second deportation controversy occurred among Mexican immigrant miners in San Francisco in 1922. *Excelsior*, a Mexico City newspaper, reported that more than 200 immigrants were deported across the Laredo, Texas, border: "Towards the end of March a group of Mexicans were victims of a brutal attack by American authorities from the San Francisco, California jurisdiction." The article noted that they were detained on leaving their work sites and denied the opportunity to contact their family members or withdraw their bank funds. Moreover, the writer mentioned that the deportees were unable to contact Mexican consul Eduardo Ruíz. Ruíz later registered a complaint with the U.S. State Department, but he acknowledged that, even if he had been notified before the action, "there was little he could do to prevent the deportation." The writer concluded, "Our compatriots think that their deportation was caused by the enormous employment crisis in the United States. Thus, they wish to replace their jobs in the mine with American workers. These victims say that the same thing could have happened to the American workers who work in the petroleum camps of Mexico and other places, because the employment crisis exists in Mexico as well."[28] Therefore, the workers were protesting the unilateral deportation policy in an interregional economy in which Mexico also provided employment to U.S. citizens. As in Denver, the Mexican consul in San Francisco was ineffective in successfully protesting the deportations and the treatment of Mexicans during the process.

Immigration authorities disputed that account. J. E. Trout, the Laredo immigration inspector, stated that there was no record of that many deportees returning at that border station; he did acknowledge that there had been a party of twenty-one Mexican immigrants who had been deported at the Laredo station on April 9, 1922. The Immigration Service elaborated on that by claiming that two of that smaller group of deportees had been inmates of an insane asylum in San Antonio.[29]

A 1924 internal memo cited instances of the Immigration Service using the LPC provision along the Mexican border to "clear the records" during a backlog. Immigration inspectors instructed immigrants to return to Mexico, telling them to return for a hearing. If they did not appear within a month, the inspectors classified them as LPC, thereby rendering such immigrants ineligible to return to the United States without Immigration Service permission for another year.[30]

But this group, labeled vagrants or unemployed, remained a very small minority of Mexicans, because of the central position that Mexican workers played in the economic growth of the Southwest and West during the first two decades of the twentieth century. In Colorado, for example, Mexican laborers were crucial to the sugar beet industry, where they worked on half of the land under cultivation, and other agricultural production, and they were also important to the railways and coal mining industry. Previously, beet farmers employed "German-Russian" workers and briefly Japanese laborers. Many Mexicans signed a "family labor contract" that involved several members of the family.[31]

Sugar beet industry representatives reported that Mexicans were excellent workers. The Great Western Sugar Company preferred to employ workers who were with their families rather than single men, perceiving them as more motivated and less prone to crime. They noted that in Wold County, Colorado, those with Spanish surnames were proportionately represented in court cases and as recipients of county poor funds. Moreover, health officials in Colorado reported that there were relatively few Mexicans who were found to have contracted tuberculosis or sexually transmitted diseases. One issue of concern in Colorado was the treatment of children, who were often required by their families to collect coal, and who were not in school full time because the nature of seasonal work meant that their families did not remain in one place. Mortality rates for children of beet workers were very high, as a result of poor living conditions. Among 187 families studied, a total of 443 children had died. The report further noted that Mexican families were often reluctant to request assistance from welfare organizations or government agencies.[32]

The Depression greatly reduced the price of sugar beets and deprived many immigrant laborers of earned wages. Thomas F. Mahony, chair of the Mexican Welfare Committee of the Colorado State Council of the Knights of Columbus, a national Catholic lay organization, wrote a pamphlet urging Mexicans not to migrate to the Longmont area in search of agricultural work. Mexicans, he asserted, were discriminated against in other industries and that employer contracts in the industry were deceptive. He also sent a telegram to William Green, president of the American Federation of Labor (AFL), indicating that the sugar beet industries had cut workers' wages by 25 percent. He noted that this contradicted a statement by Secretary of Labor William Doak that "leading American Industries are maintaining wage scales [in] accordance [with] promises made [at our] conference [in 1929]."[33] Mahony sharply criticized the Works Progress Administration (WPA) for its "starve or work" policy, which, he maintained, required families cut off from rolls to relocate to work in beet fields under "any labor and living conditions and for any wage offered," while simultaneously saving the sugar beet industry substantial labor recruiting costs. He further declared: "It seems to be the interest of the beet sugar industry to have the Spanish speaking people Numerous and Hungry." They will then be "less disposed and able to argue and resist any form of injustice forced upon them." He further noted that earlier efforts to recruit Japanese migrants to the sugar beet industry were largely unsuccessful, because in his view, "They probably got too wise."[34]

Aligned with Father John Ryan, the well-known "labor priest" and major New Deal supporter, Mahony was highly critical of the exploitation of labor by industrial capitalists in Colorado and elsewhere. As well as protesting the exploitation of immigrant laborers by industries in the Southwest and racist hiring practices, Mahony was also a fierce anticommunist and critic of the Mexican Revolution, because of its socialist policies and opposition to the Catholic Church.

The best-known instances of large-scale deportation from the United States occurred during the Great Depression. The LPC provision of immigration policy, coupled with federal, state, and local regulations about eligibility for relief programs, would become central to this deportation situation. Although Mexican immigrants totaled just 1 percent of American population in the 1930s, they composed 46.3 percent of those deported during that decade.[35] But the enforcement of the policy during the 1930s deportation wave changed significantly in that it targeted males to a greater degree than females. Immigrants from Mexico and their children either voluntarily repatriated or were deported, sometimes en masse, from California, the American Southwest, and industrial centers such as Detroit, where workers had migrated in search of higher-paying industrial jobs. In Los Angeles alone, more than a third of the Mexican American population repatriated to Mexico in the 1930s. American citizens were among those who were swept up in deportation raids in workplaces, neighborhoods, and other gathering places and American citizen children of Mexican immigrants, who had little choice but to accompany their parents. In 1930 William Doak erroneously declared that Mexican immigrants in the United States illegally outnumbered those who were in the United States legally. He estimated that 1 million Mexicans were in the United States illegally.[36]

The LPC provision, in particular, provided a mechanism for the large-scale deportation of Mexican citizens and American citizens of Mexican origin during the Great Depression in the 1930s. Other American citizens of Mexican descent who did not have appropriate documentation on hand were deported after being swept up in raids.[37]

National Catholic Welfare Council's Mexican Border Program

Catholics in the National Catholic Welfare Conference (NCWC), an organization that arose from efforts to coordinate the activities of local groups involved in World War I relief efforts, served as advocates for Mexicans in the 1920s and 1930s in ways that paralleled HIAS's work on behalf of its immigrant coreligionists. Both religious organizations stressed the strategy of family reunification. Bruce Mohler, a lay leader, established the NCWC's Bureau of Immigration in 1922. A major initiative of that bureau was to establish new programs in key immigration locations and systemize the administration of existing programs by ethnically affiliated Catholic groups. Because of the large number of Mexicans arriving at the U.S. border by the early 1920s, Catholics increased their presence here rather than focusing their efforts largely on assisting European Catholics arriving at Ellis Island. NCWC workers emerged as active immigrant advocates during the crucial decade of the Great Depression.

Expanding beyond its New York headquarters, the NCWC established an office along the El Paso–Ciudad Juárez border, within a block of the International Bridge. A triweekly clinic providing services to Mexicans also operated on the Juárez side of the border. One of the program's initial accomplishments was to end the practice of line jumping by immigrants paying a three-dollar bribe, which had resulted in "much suffering and actual starvation." By 1931 the NCWC was assisting a total of 26,570 immigrants through its several offices annually.[38]

A major impetus for these NCWC programs was religiously based work, often aimed to counter the influence of Protestant groups, such as the YMCA and Travelers' Aid, groups that Catholics viewed as vehicles for proselytizing newly arriving Catholic immigrants. In 1932 the NCWC noted a distinct downturn in proselytizing along the border with Mexico, "where previously it had been so prevalent." NCWC workers arranged for immigrants who had civil or common-law marriages to obtain sacramental marriage rites. Moreover, the NCWC often assisted priests, seminarians, nuns, and novitiates seeking to visit or train in the United States to navigate the immigration system. It also sought to counter what it perceived as socialist or communist influences in Mexican schools by helping students to attend parochial Catholic schools on the Texas side of the border. To the dismay of NCWC workers, however, many Mexican students opted to attend Protestant schools in Texas.[39]

NCWC workers were highly critical of many elements of immigration law, policy, and enforcement procedures. Those critiques began soon after the bureau's establishment in 1922 when the National Origins Act was passed and intensified during the early 1930s with the mass deportation of many Mexicans. Early on, the NCWC sought to address the racial definitions of Mexicans by protesting when Colorado and Texas officials categorized "the children of Spanish speaking peoples" as either "brown" or black." Through their protests, El Paso's city registrar agreed to "the correction for listing these children as of the 'white' race." They noted that state officials in Texas and the Southwest generally needed to make a distinction between the Mexican "race" and "nationality." A similar debate was also occurring more broadly, in reaction to a federal decision to categorize Mexican Americans as nonwhite in the 1930 U.S. census, but census officials later reversed that decision. Defining Mexican immigrants as "white" provided them with greater social and legal status once in the United States.[40]

The NCWC was especially critical of President Herbert Hoover's intensified campaign to deny immigrants financial assistance, to end immigration, and to deport immigrants. Hoover's policy, articulated on September 8, 1930, of using the LPC provision aggressively was cited as a major problem for immigrant families because of the large numbers of families who were thrown into poverty when their male breadwinners were not allowed to enter the United States or were deported. In 1931 an NCWC administrator stated that the organization "has worked diligently for a solution. The State Department so far has proven obstinate. It may be necessary to apply to President Hoover himself."[41]

Mohler criticized Secretary of Labor Doak's "sensational raids" because investigations were undertaken with slight evidence, including anonymous letters. This led to a situation where "innocent aliens were imprisoned and otherwise subjected to unwarranted embarrassment." The interrogation methods used in the wake of those raids were characterized as "harsh and brutal. Fortunately, our Bureau was able to assist many of these persons out of their difficulties."[42]

Bruce Mohler wrote that the American consuls were "refusing *fireside* relatives with a total disregard for the human elements involved and the tragic consequences of the former Secretary of Labor's drive to establish a record of deportations made it necessary for the Washington Office [of the NCWC] to be continually active in protesting against the many injustices referred for our attention." He further noted that the federal government was particularly "rigid" in its immigration policy before 1933 "in relation to illegal residents, deportations and the restriction in issuance of visas to new immigrants, especially those wishing to join families already here." The report also emphasized that the voluntary return of Mexicans had decreased because conditions in Mexico were "not as favorable as many had thought during the previous year." Repatriation had increased because of both economic depression and "the flagrant lack of social justice as regards the alien resident through discrimination in employment and public relief."[43]

Just as HIAS officials had done in earlier cases, the NCWC employed family reunification arguments and human rights language as effective strategies for opposing Immigration Services' decisions at the border. This approach had an added dimension among Catholics, because of the church's theological opposition to birth control. Moreover, increased Mexican immigration would increase the Catholic population in the United States, especially along the West Coast and in the Southwest. The NCWC noted that it became involved in social service investigations launched by the Department of Labor in cases where families were threatened with separation as a result of deportations and communicated the hardships that such families would endure. Often the deportation case involved "the sole provider of the family," thus impoverishing those family members who remained in the United States. It also worked on family reunification of immigrants awaiting visas from American consuls, including some cases where husbands and fathers had been waiting in foreign countries for years.[44]

Bruce Mohler remarked that in 1933–34 the NCWC had a 93 percent success rate in its appeal decisions. Some of those cases involved immigrants with prior criminal convictions. In fact, the NCWC intervened on behalf of those immigrants who had been involved in relatively minor crimes, especially those who had been convicted while they were young, to assist them to submit a request for pardons or clemency that resulted in a stay of their orders of deportation.[45]

The NCWC also monitored congressional legislation pertaining to immigration and immigrants. Mohler noted that the 73rd Congress added a provision to the National Industrial Recovery Act that allowed for the employment of "aliens who have declared their intentions to become American citizens," a group that had formerly been excluded from eligibility. In this way, NCWC lobbyists paralleled the immigrant advocates of the 1990s who sought to reverse some of the most stringent exclusionary provisions of the 1996 immigration laws barring aliens from social services eligibility. Previously, it had condemned a deportation bill passed in 1929 as "brutal" and "fanatical," with "evil" consequences, because it ignored immigrants' family situations and failed to provide for the eventual possibility of deported immigrants' return or even an appeal process.[46]

In 1932 immigration from Mexico was at a low point. Just 1,514 immigrants were admitted from Mexico, as compared to 7,750 deported to Mexico and 643 people refused entry to the United States. According to the NCWC, that many of its cases along the southern border resulted from situations arising when U.S. Border Patrol officials exceeded their authority.[47]

Medical issues also made migration more difficult. According to the

NCWC, the U.S. Public Health Service physician at El Paso–Ciudad Juárez prevented the border crossing of as many as fifty Mexican immigrants a day, stating that "they were afflicted with syphilis or 'adentitis'" and that the doctor claimed that "he had proof that 95% of the Mexican people were afflicted with venereal disease." The NCWC worked with the Chambers of Commerce in Juarez and El Paso to lodge a complaint against the physician with the U.S. district director of immigration. The report also noted that "adenitis," a swelling of the lymph nodes, was not a condition associated with venereal disease. The fact that the physician claimed falsely that Mexican immigrants were afflicted with sexually transmitted diseases in epidemic proportions had a significant effect on Mexicans seeking to cross the border at El Paso. Had his bias not been detected, the effect would have been larger still.[48]

Another medical deportation case arose when Alfonso Camargo, a Mexican living in Jerome, Arizona, was ordered deported, along with many other Mexicans, because of his indigent status. Upon further investigation, it was determined that he was not subject to deportation because he had resided in the United States for eighteen years, far longer than the three years stipulated by the LPC law. But Camargo was then diagnosed with leprosy and found deportable on medical grounds and was persuaded to repatriate to Mexico voluntarily. The acting supervising inspector in El Paso highlighted the fact that "the alien was not imported under the Department's exceptions" to the ban on contract laborers.[49]

Though rates of leprosy (now Hansen's disease) were higher in Texas than in other states during the 1930s, particularly in regions along the Gulf of Mexico, it does not seem that immigration officials had initially targeted Camargo for deportation on medical grounds. Rather, that diagnosis arose only after the immigrant was determined not to be subject to deportation because of his length of residence.[50]

The New Deal ushered in a more humane immigration process. After Franklin Roosevelt appointed Frances Perkins as secretary of labor and Daniel McCormack became commissioner of immigration, the NCWC became less critical of federal policies along the border with Mexico, noting that "we can look forward to a really humane administration of the immigration laws with due consideration given to social justice for the alien and the welfare of his dependent family." The NCWC indicated that the American consul at Juárez was also more cooperative than in prior years, as a result of NCWC complaints to the State Department about "incorrect rulings" and procedural issues.[51]

The federal government used existing LPC provisions in the 1891 law to limit even further the decreasing number of immigrants who sought admission to the United States. The immigration restriction laws of the 1920s led to a profound decrease of immigrants arriving in the United States from Europe. Although Canadians and Mexicans were not subject to the quota system, in early 1931 the numbers of visas issued to migrants from those two countries decreased by an astounding 75 and 95 percent respectively from the previous year. In March 1931, President Hoover issued an announcement, rather than an executive order, stating that the Immigration Service would enforce those provisions.[52]

By the 1930s, congressional bills such as H.R. 3472 sought to strengthen the LPC provisions of immigration law to make deportation on LPC grounds easier.[53] It sought to build upon the provisions already articulated in the 1917 immigration act that provided for the deportation of immigrants found LPC within three years of entry by making the time period indefinite. Congresswoman Carolyn O'Day of New York, a close friend of Franklin and Eleanor Roosevelt, proposed an amendment to the bill that would extend the period of LPC to five years after entry in which an immigrant seeking voluntary repatriation to return home could do so at government expense.[54]

Popular Nativism

Nativism and anti-immigrant sentiment intensified as the Depression continued. Pressure built from various constituencies, which accused immigrants of depriving "Americans" of access to jobs and charity. The Roosevelt administration received several complaints from white citizens protesting the presence of immigrants during a time of economic distress. Retribution for interpersonal tensions, racism, and nativism, combined with economic deprivation, proved a powerful motivating force for many. A white resident of Port Huron, Michigan, wrote to Franklin D. Roosevelt in 1933 to advocate that he give "our officers more power to clean our city up of Mexicans for we have familys living near me in dangerous people their names is Joseph Rosles and we have too live among so many colored people in affull American Born St[ate] of Michigan St. Clair county[.]" An immigration inspector who followed up on the complaint reported that there had been a neighborhood dispute involving the Rosales and Henshaw children that seems to have precipitated the letter. He concluded that records indicated that the Rosales family was admitted legally and that all but one of their six children was U.S. born. Similarly,

Harold Goodrich of Barstow, Texas, wrote to complain that Mexican immigrants in his town were employed and speculated that they were illegal residents.[55]

A third complaint stated that Japanese employers of Mexican farm laborers were threatening to turn the workers over to immigration authorities if they complained about failure to pay wages on time. Though the San Diego Office of Inspector for the Immigration Service could not document any specific threats, it acknowledged that Stanley Gue, the deputy state labor commissioner, had stated that this was a common practice among Japanese farmers. Ironically, Gue implied that the Japanese farmers themselves should be subject to deportation because they were violating alien land laws, which prohibited Japanese and other Asian immigrants to own agricultural land. Of course, this deportation issue must be seen in the context of virulent anti-Japanese sentiment that permeated California, culminating in legislation such as the Alien Land Laws, and intensified greatly following the outbreak of World War II.[56] Employers routinely used the threat of deportation to intimidate and control workers, to prevent them from reporting labor-related violations to authorities, and to prevent them from organizing labor unions.

Mexican government officials did not object as strenuously to the deportations as it would later protest Jim Crow segregation during World War II. Indeed, the ineffectual response to Mexicans detrimentally affected by the early 1920s agricultural crisis was a harbinger of the consulates' actions during the Great Depression. As historian Jaime Aguila has described, during the 1920s the Obregan government had established two programs associated with its fourteen consular offices in the United States that were designed to assist Mexican citizens avoid workplace exploitation and to address some of their social service needs. They established two organizations: the Comisiones Honorifícas Mexicanos and the Brígadas de la Cruz Azul Mexicana.

During the Great Depression, those Mexican government programs in the United States assisted in the repatriation of large numbers of Mexicans.[57] In fact, the Immigration Service discussed a request by the Mexican Embassy that "Mexican nationals, who would ordinarily be deported to points in Lower California, be sent across the border through more remote points." The San Antonio district director of immigration, William A. Whalen, also asserted that "we are continually apprehending Mexicans who state that they would [rather] be in jail in this country than free in Mexico" because of guaranteed access to food and shelter. He elaborated, recommending that deportations be concentrated at Nogales rather than at Laredo because of the availability of railroad service to the interior provinces.[58]

The Mexican Embassy did send Dispatch Number 413 on May 13, 1931, that enclosed a translated article from *Excelsior*. A major point of the article was that the massive deportations demonstrated the "lack of consideration shown for marriage contracts. Upon being deported to Mexico, Mexicans are separated from their wives, if the latter are Americans." The article continues that it is "an insult, that Mexicans live in a manner irreconcilable with Yankee customs. Neither labor nor marriage contracts are respected, Mexicans being separated from their wives as if they were animals." Indeed, George Harris, the assistant commissioner-general, wrote to the district director of immigration in Los Angeles to ask him to consider these allegations and whether "it is just in every case, and the statements . . . concerning the alleged separations of husbands and wives."[59]

The Mexican government had little power to oppose the repatriation of Mexican citizens or their American-born children because of the relative strength of the American government and its economy. But it is remarkable how unwilling its consular officials were to represent its citizens' interests, given the very rationale of establishing a wide network of consulates in the United States just a decade previously. Moreover, the extent of the Mexican government's close communication and cooperation with immigration authorities in expelling Mexicans from the United States is surprising.

Martin Dies, a Texas congressman and staunch anticommunist who would become involved in the House Committee on Anti-American Activities, articulated his anti-immigrant views in a radio address in 1935. He suggested that the national unemployment crisis was a direct result of the 6 million immigrants "who are deriving their livelihood from jobs which American citizens should fill and could fill if we had the same laws that are in force in other countries. So that from any angle of approach it must be evident to every thinking American citizen that the unemployment problem was transferred to America from foreign lands."[60]

Men of additional ethnic groups, including Filipino immigrants, also faced the threat of deportation in this period. Rather than facing deportation, some immigrants, such as those in Ohio, opted to avail themselves of government incentives to return voluntarily to their homelands so they would not be dependent on local or state assistance. In return for their passage money, they needed to certify that they would not return to the United States. Indeed, the number of immigrants leaving the United States in the 1930s was roughly double the number entering, many of them leaving as a result of deportation or voluntary remigration because of their ineligibility for federal, state, and local assistance programs, including those sponsored by the WPA.[61]

Because most Mexican immigrants were male, this signaled a shift in federal policy, as officials began deporting male immigrants on LPC grounds more systematically during the 1930s. Mexican immigrants were viewed less as productive workers and more as economic dependents. As with many of the immigration policies described earlier, that shift grew from state and local practices that had previously associated the crime of vagrancy with Mexican immigrants.

Filipinos

In addition to the many federal bills addressing immigration during the Great Depression, Congress also addressed the issue of impoverished Filipinos living in the United States during the economic crisis. Filipinos' immigration status was in flux at this time. Many had immigrated to Hawaii and California as agricultural laborers. Following the Spanish-American War in 1898, Filipinos were declared U.S. nationals and were thus the only group exempt from the major ban on Asian immigration. Yet, though they were allowed to immigrate to the United States, they too were barred from obtaining U.S. citizenship. Moreover, few Filipinas came to the United States in this era, leading to the same types of extreme gender imbalances that characterized Asian immigration as a whole. Beginning in 1946, when the Philippines gained political independence under the Tydings-McDuffie Act of 1934, which provided for the country's independence, they would be subject to low quotas of fifty immigrants per year.[62]

As a result of the economic crisis of the early 1930s, an estimated 40,000 to 50,000 Filipinos were "stranded" in the United States without employment, family support networks, or the means to return to the Philippines. The chair of the House committee noted that many Filipinos, who tended to be young, unmarried men, were "walking the streets, some were in jails." Congress debated a proposal to offer voluntary departure to immigrants in that situation on U.S. Navy and Army vessels, which made regular voyages between the United States and the Philippines.[63]

Pedro Guevara and Francisco Delgado, both resident commissioners of the Philippine Islands, provided testimony at the hearing for H.R. resolution 71, a companion bill to H.R. 3472. They stated that it would create ill will among Filipinos to stipulate that those immigrants who availed themselves of the U.S. government program to return migrants to the Philippines would forgo the right to return to the United States in the future. They argued that, practically speaking, with the fifty-person annual quota, few would seek to return in the future, but that an outright ban in the provision would damage goodwill toward the United States.[64]

That assessment by Guevara and Delgado about Filipino reaction led to pointed questions from committee members about whether Filipinos were "ungrateful" to the United States. That rhetoric was a less than subtle invocation of William Taft's paternalism, implied in his phrase "our little brown brothers," used to justify U.S. imperialism in the Philippines following the Spanish-American War. Both representatives stated no. But they did assert that most repatriated Filipinos would have little desire to return to the United States, in part because, as Guevara stated, of the "unfortunate experiences they have had in this country, the distress they have been and are going through." He implied that those occurred as a result of both financial difficulties and racism. He further argued that they would not face continued unemployment once back in the Philippines, because there was little unemployment in the agricultural sectors, only in the cities, and most immigrants "belong to well-to-do families having their own farms." Yet, ultimately a fraction of Filipinos, about 2,200, availed themselves of this provision and returned to the Philippines.[65]

LPC and Recent Immigration Controversies

The use of the LPC charge, first to limit the ability of female immigrants (and orphaned and refugee children) to migrate and later to exclude, deport, or repatriate Mexican and Filipino men in the 1930s, has striking parallels to California's Proposition 187 and the 1996 Personal Responsibility and Work Opportunity Act and Illegal Immigration Reform and Immigrant Responsibility Act (IIRIRA). Both efforts portrayed immigrants as primarily motivated to arrive in the United States to benefit from generous social welfare programs and to drain resources from taxpaying citizens. In both the 1930s and 1990s, the vital role of immigrants in American economic growth by building key infrastructures and performing grueling, poorly paid labor in agriculture, domestic and service sectors, and manufacturing was transformed into a narrative of exploitation and ingratitude by immigrants.

These two laws had important and far-reaching consequences for impoverished Americans generally, and especially women and children.

That legislation further eliminated access to many social welfare benefits among many immigrants who were not U.S. citizens. Benefits included health care programs such as Medicaid and Medicare, as well as other federally funded assistance, including Supplemental Social Security Income benefits and food stamps. Another act received far less attention from the public and the media. Yet the Illegal Immigration Reform and Immigrant Responsibility Act greatly affected immigrants' access to social welfare programs. That legislation followed California's Proposition 187, a referendum that greatly restricted public funds to immigrants and their children. Those initiatives sought to roll back social welfare benefits and educational opportunities provided to poor and other disenfranchised people beginning in the New Deal and continuing into the 1960s Great Society programs. These laws represented a significant shift in attitudes toward immigrants, though it notably exempted many refugees from these federal limits on assistance.

But this sweeping change led to widespread protests by immigrants and immigrant advocates. In response, the federal government changed some key provisions of the 1996 law, and in May 1999 the INS and Department of Health and Human Services (HHS) clarified their interpretation of the effect of the 1996 laws on immigrants' eligibility for public funds. The law stated that aliens would be eligible to receive some federal benefits, including those pertaining to the Children's Health Insurance Program (CHIP), short-term Medicaid (but not nursing or other long-term care), housing subsidies, food stamps, Women, Infants and Children (WIC), and other noncash assistance without jeopardizing their immigration status. The clarification also indicated that enforcement was focused primarily on recent arrivals and those who had not yet obtained permanent residency in the form of a green card. Yet confusion about the impact of the 1996 initiatives remained widespread within many immigrant communities, leading many to forgo assistance despite their eligibility, concerned that the receipt of such benefits would jeopardize their immigration status or that of their family members. In fact, partly as a result of the stigmas and fears created through Proposition 187 and IIRIRA, immigrants and their children, whether citizens or not, are less likely than others in the United States to access welfare benefits for which they are eligible.[66]

Most recently, the Tea Party movement has advanced an agenda of denying birthright citizenship to children of immigrants who are born on U.S. territory. They have employed the rhetoric of "anchor babies," portrayed as a Trojan horse–like plot whereby large numbers of pregnant women cross the Mexican border from Central America to deliver their children in the United States to gain access to generous U.S. government benefits. But the Tea Party's agenda of repealing birthright citizenship will be difficult to translate into federal law, even if the overturning of *jus soli* citizenship has been recently successful in Ireland and other Western democracies. *Jus soli* citizenship has been a long tradition in the United States, encoded in the 14th Amendment, upheld in the *Wong Kim Ark* decision in 1898, and guaranteed to U.S.-born children of those immigrants who were historically ineligible for citizenship themselves.[67]

The increased resistance to extending public funding to impoverished women and immigrants that escalated in the 1980s and 1990s had distinct parallels to debates over the impact of immigrants in the Progressive Era. Just as immigration policies regulating marriage have striking parallels to current federal policy that promotes marriage as a means to economic independence, the LPC provision has links to recent federal social welfare policy. Although the LPC provision was used to exclude or deport both men and women, it had especially profound effects on the ability of single, immigrant women to travel to the United States in search of employment.

In the application of the LPC provision in U.S. immigration regulation, immigrant women were initially assumed to be economically dependent on others, even when evidence suggested otherwise. They risked deportation when their behavior deviated from traditional notions about gender roles and marital relationships, in an era when those social norms were contested among middle-class Americans. In the first three decades of the twentieth century, Jewish immigrants found themselves facing LPC, especially women and children. HIAS effectively represented many immigrants who found themselves stymied by the LPC provision and also lobbied the bureau and published articles on the implications for LPC for the Jewish community. These policies had profound implications for the ability of women to immigrate to the United States. Indeed, some of those policies have parallels to current federal initiatives designed to promote particular types of domestic relationships in a period of rapid social change.

By the early 1930s, under Labor Secretary William Doak in the Hoover administration, the LPC provision became a convenient administrative mechanism within immigration law that could be implemented to deport large numbers of Mexican immigrants, who were predominantly men, from the United States. Before the 1920s, Mexican laborers had been integral to the growth of the agricultural and mining industries in the Southwest and West. Although some Mexicans had been defined as poor, having been arrested for vagrancy by local officials, most were viewed as economically independent actors. With the emergence of an agricultural downturn in the early 1920s, local authorities began casting Mexicans as dependent on local and private charities, and questions about whether Mexican immigrants were entitled to government assistance first emerged. That agricultural recession led to regional rehearsal that began to transform the reputation of Mexican male immigrants from essential but temporary laborers in the booming Southwest economy to a group that was undeserving of economic assistance and prone to poverty. The transformation of Mexican men from essential workers to economic liabilities had crystallized by the beginning of the Great Depression. Filipino men were also vulnerable to being returned to their country on grounds of economic dependency and perceptions of their lack of entitlement to welfare benefits, despite their legal status as residents of a U.S. protectorate. Without actual citizenship, they too were rendered vulnerable during a time of national crisis.

Immigrant advocacy groups, including HIAS and the NCWC intervened, often successfully, on behalf of immigrants facing exclusion or deportation on economic grounds. Family reunification was a strategy that both groups used effectively. In contrast, government officials from Mexico and the Philippines were far less effective in representing the interests of their citizens abroad. Those countries' subordinate status relative to the United States and their workers' nonwhite and contingent role in the U.S. economy rendered them especially vulnerable, relative to other immigrant groups.

Medical issues were a second means of restricting or deporting Mexicans in the 1920s and 1930s. But, because it was more difficult to prove than the LPC charge, it was less frequently invoked. As the next chapter reveals, medical issues often served as proxies for race as a means to exclude or deport immigrants, whether that took the form of a diagnosis that was targeted at Jewish immigrants, a racially differentiated ban on immigrants presenting particular disease symptoms, or concerns about immigrants' requiring state institutional resources. As with the LPC provision, many of these public health concerns were tied to broader labor and economic issues.

LOATHSOME OR CONTAGIOUS

IMMIGRANT BODIES, DISEASE, AND EUGENICS AND THE BORDERS

As the public health field began to emerge in the late nineteenth-century United States, federal government officials began focusing on medical examinations as a crucial aspect of immigration regulation. Tuberculosis and trachoma, a potentially debilitating eye disease, were two of the "loathsome or dangerous contagious" diseases that particularly concerned immigration officials. They located the disease of trachoma in China and determined that the disease was pervasive among Chinese immigrants arriving at the United States' borders. Immigrants from Mexico, Syria, Greece, and other non-Western European regions were also closely examined to determine whether they were carriers. Psychological illness and chronic physical and developmental disabilities also became major concerns. The diagnosis and treatment of such diseases was far less precise than for many medical conditions, and there was greater stigma attached to them than exists today. As with the "likely to become a public charge" (LPC) provision, a major impetus for the medicalization of immigration control stemmed from state budget concerns, especially in New York, where the majority of immigrants landed. Public hospitals and asylums lobbied for exams at the point of entry as a cost-containment measure, similar to those of the past few decades in which states influenced federal-level policies.

The close association between immigrants and contagious disease had been well established in the United States before the era of federal immigration regulation. That link emerged both because immigrants tended to be impoverished and located in overcrowded neighborhoods with poor sanitation and because immigrants were often viewed as importing threats to American society. In the eighteenth and nineteenth centuries, several epidemics, including Philadelphia's 1793 cholera outbreak, disproportionately affected largely immigrant neighborhoods. Later epidemics followed. By 1907 a typhoid outbreak had been attributed to a single immigrant woman, Mary Mallon, an Irish cook in a Long Island household.[1]

Travel across continents can certainly lead to public health emergencies, as demonstrated by the severe acute respiratory syndrome (SARS) virus, which emerged as a health threat in Toronto in 2003 among recent arrivals from Hong Kong. But domestic conditions in hospitals and other settings create environments in which communicable disease spreads rapidly. That provides a partial explanation of how the outbreak occurred in Toronto, rather than in Vancouver or another North American West Coast city along the Pacific Rim, where travel to and from Asia is more frequent.

Beginning with John Higham, several historians have discussed how racial categories shaped the national-origins-based immigration acts of the 1920s. In this chapter, I demonstrate how those racially based constructions led to earlier restrictive laws and policies that discriminated against certain ethnic and religious groups on the basis of scientifically specious concepts about physical disorders and group characteristics. As a result of such policies, the body became increasingly scrutinized for disease and defect at a time when eugenicists seized on such measures as cranial shape and size and categorized peoples according to their physical attributes.[2]

More recently, Alan Kraut, Judith Walzer Leavitt, Alexandra Stern, Natalie Molina, Nayan Shah, Howard Markel, and other historians working at the intersection of medicine, public health, and immigration have analyzed how notions of race and ethnicity have been inextricably linked to the spread of communicable disease and how that, in turn, has influenced public policy.

Mireya Loza and other historians studying the Bracero program have discovered through oral interviews that among the most powerful and painful memories remaining with many Bracero workers is having their unclothed bodies sprayed with DDT upon arrival at the U.S. border. Indeed, photographs of immigrants undergoing medical inspections at Ellis Island have become almost iconic images in historical memories of the U.S. immigration experience.[3]

In his pioneering work about the body and its relationship to the state, Michel Foucault analyzed the ways in which the body contains political implications. Using France as his example, he argued that the state has long used mental and physical health as both a metaphor and criteria for citizenship.[4] As eugenic theories took hold in the United States, concepts of public health encompassed an increasingly broad notion that moved far beyond the idea of preventing the transmission of communicable disease to that of "fitness" for citizenship, a concept that has had significant social, moral, psychological, and physical dimensions.[5] When the federal mechanism allowed for the inspection, exclusion, and deportation of immigrants on the basis of their physical condition, the two trends worked in tandem.

Budget issues figured prominently in discussions of immigrant health. Because immigrants tended to be poor, their presence led to increases in state appropriations for hospitals, asylums, and other institutional and welfare programs. The large increase in immigration in major ports of entry resulted in the expansion of government functions and authority at both the federal and state levels. Officials in New York State and in other major immigrant destinations lobbied strenuously for immigration restriction that would reduce the costs of institutionalization.[6] By 1909, state legislators in Albany increasingly turned their focus to the budget implications of immigrants in various state institutions because New York City was the major U.S. immigration port. Mental health became a particularly important issue among federal immigration officials. Much of their administrative focus concerned the requirement that immigrants who were deported after being declared insane be escorted to their point of origin by a paid companion, which became a much-debated expense.

Immigration officials actually created new disease categories. In this era, classification and categorization were preoccupations of the scientific and medical communities, eugenicists, and Progressive reformers. These categories or typologies clearly shaped the understanding of health and disease as it related to immigration and influenced the ways that particular diseases were perceived in American society. Concern for immigrants' physical conditions was often related to their economic roles and their class status. Two groups, Jews and Syrians, engaged in work as peddlers. In their home countries, and in some rural regions of the United States, peddlers addressed an important need for goods before the emergence of large retail stores and mail-order services. By definition, they were preindustrial, itinerant, and mobile. As the United States became increasingly urbanized and industrialized, demand for their services as middlemen decreased.

In the 1910s the view that some immigrants were unfit for consideration as citizens led to increased immigration restriction laws, first through the implementation of the literacy test in 1917 and restrictions in the 1920s. Immigrants crossing the borders had to demonstrate that they were disease-free, but also that they were morally and socially fit for inclusion in American society. Simultaneously, the borders of physical health, moral and mental health, and social health became increasingly less distinct. In fact, new diseases, such as "poor physique," were being constructed and employed specifically for use in immigration restriction measures. That particular diagnosis was developed at the explicit suggestion of members of the Immigration Restriction League. That category was rooted firmly in eugenics theory and inscribed into immigration policy. In fact, while ultimately adopted, the category confused public health physicians, because it was not a medically accepted diagnosis.

In this era the 1911 Dillingham Commission Report was published under the auspices of the U.S. Senate. Its highly biased classifications of various immigrant groups laid the foundation for a federal immigration policy based on a national quota system that sharply reduced the numbers of Southern and Eastern European and Russian immigrants.[7] The forty-one volume report included a dictionary of races or peoples by anthropologist Daniel Folkmar. With the assistance of his wife, a physician, Folkmar drew extensively on his involvement in the Philippines. He had served as lieutenant governor of a northern region in the Philippine colonial service. In that capacity, he undertook a study of cranial and other physical measurements of Filipino prisoners in 1903, which was exhibited in the 1904 World's Fair in St. Louis.

The dictionary drew heavily upon the increasingly popular eugenics theories of Madison Grant, William Z. Ripley, and other American and European theorists. In England, Sir Francis Galton, inspired by the theories of his cousin Charles Darwin, promoted the idea that the key to social progress lay in improving "inborn qualities" of "human breeding." Giuseppe Sergi and Cesare Lombroso were also active in promoting eugenics in Italy. In an early example of an interdisciplinary field, in the United States the writings of anthropologists, including Franz Boas, melded with scientists, such as Charles Davenport, and other academics.[8]

In 1899 Ripley, an economist who studied at MIT and taught at Columbia, categorized the European population into three major "races": Teutonics, Alpines, and Mediterraneans. Brain size and shape, measured by a cephalic index, along with other physical features, such as build, skin, and eye coloring were what separated one race from another. Ripley served as a member of the U.S. Industrial Commission during the Theodore Roosevelt administration and became influential in federal circles. Ripley, in turn, influenced Grant, who developed the concept of a "master race" and in 1916 published his book *The Passing of the Great Race* and articles in influential mainstream journals of the day.[9] Because of their affiliations with elite universities, their high social status, and their affiliations with the federal government, proponents of eugenicist ideologies were far more influential than immigrant advocates who sought to counter their influence.[10]

By the 1920s leading eugenicists served as advisers to the U.S. government and testified in favor of immigration restriction legislation. Harry H. Laughlin undertook a fact-finding tour of Europe. He began in Brussels at the Solvay Institute at the University of Belgium and the Belgian Eugenics Education Society and visited twenty-five U.S. consulates. He argued that although the United States was founded on an "asylum" principle, many recognized that immigration needed a selecting and sorting process. He also used Sweden and Italy as his case studies of conditions leading to immigration. Laughlin advocated that through its consuls the U.S. Department of State be far more active in determining who is allowed to immigrate to the United States. He further advocated that the Italian and other governments require their emigrants to the United States to provide family information to ensure that immigrants had no heritable disease. He emphasized: "The American people must understand that the European nation, as an exporter, will not have primarily in mind the interests of the American people. Each nation must look out for its own welfare."[11]

Immigrant advocates, including the Hebrew Immigrant Aid Society (HIAS), represented immigrants who were in danger of being excluded upon arrival or deported. They also corresponded with the Bureau of Immigration (the precursor to the Immigration and Naturalization Service, which has been renamed the Bureau of Citizenship and Immigration Services) to address issues of bias. Among the policies that those advocates specifically objected to was the use of "poor physique" or "low vitality" as medically appropriate categories by which to exclude or deport immigrants, especially Russian Jews, a practice that first was inscribed into immigration policy in 1905.

A second controversy in this era occurred over categories describing various European races, derived from the categories on which the Dillingham Report was based. Both Italian American organizations and the Swiss government objected to the way that immigrants from their respective countries were classified. Italian American groups argued that the distinctions made between northern and southern Italians, far from being simply geographical references, were discriminatory and irrelevant. Ethnic classifications such as the "poor physique" category, emerged from the ideologies promoted by immigration restrictionists. Bureau of Immigration records on this topic clearly reveal the ideologies of race and ethnicity that shaped immigration policy in the Progressive Era as well as the efforts of several immigrant advocacy groups to challenge those views.

The practice of classifying Jewish immigrants by their religion, as "Hebrews," rather than by their country of origin led to controversy, as acknowledged by U.S. immigration officials. In 1903 the Department of Commerce and Labor commissioned a report to determine whether Jews were a race, apparently in response to an inquiry by Mayer Sulzberger. Sulzberger, a German immigrant, was a Pennsylvania judge and philanthropist. He was a trustee of the Baron de Hirsch Fund, a vice president of Philadelphia's Jewish hospital, and a founder of the Young Men's Hebrew Association. Simon Wolf, a New York attorney and Jewish activist, had also lobbied the Bureau of Immigration to drop that categorization as inconsistent. In support of his request, he stated that Terence Powderly, the previous commissioner of immigration, had agreed that Jewish immigrants should be classified according to their nationality, not their religion. American Jewish leaders' objections stemmed from their concerns about anti-Semitism and discrimination in Europe and the United States.[12]

That category was based on the popular U.S. practice of referring to "Hebrews" as a race. The Bureau of Immigration had used this designation since 1899, "in compliance with the recommendation of a board established to investigate this question." It was based on William Ripley's *Races of Europe*, a classic in the eugenics canon, which argued that "nationality bears no constant or necessary relation whatever to race." As Benjamin Cable, acting secretary, maintained, "In recording an alien as a Hebrew, it is intended only to indicate that he is of that stock or blood, independent of blood or language."[13]

Jews' religious practices and beliefs certainly set them apart from the majority Protestant population and from Catholics, a growing U.S. demographic especially in the Northeast and Southwest. But it did not fully explain why a religious term was used in place of a geopolitical identity reference. Based on eugenics ideologies and written into immigration policy in 1899, terms "Hebrews" and "Hindoos," used in place of Russia or India, denoted a blend of racial and religious othering that in the latter case was often inaccurate, given that it was sometimes used to describe Sikhs or Muslim Indians.

The dynamics of implementing eugenically influenced immigration restriction laws proved complex. Many of those lobbying for stricter enforcement of immigration laws and the creation of new categories of exclusion were native-born social elites from Boston and other northeastern urban centers. But some of the most important figures implementing immigration policy in this period were immigrants or the children of immigrants. Thus, immigrants and their children, whether as immigrant advocates in their communities or as policy makers or civil servants, had a significant role in shaping immigrant policy in this era. Industrial capitalists and those in agricultural enterprises, on the other hand, had a significant stake in ensuring the steady flow of immigrants who were willing to work for low wages, especially in the rapidly developing Southwest and West Coast.

In her recent book, *Science at the Borders*, Amy Fairchild argues that, contrary to prevailing myths about Ellis Island, few immigrants to the United States were deported on medical grounds. She concludes that deportations on such grounds never exceeded 1 percent of the immigrants arriving in any given year. Fairchild emphasizes that medical inspections were an outgrowth of industrial America's need for productive workers who were physically fit. Although industrial requirements certainly emerged as a major motivation for inspecting immigrants at the border, and her assertions about the small number of medical exclusions are statistically accurate, Fairchild's macrolevel analysis overlooks the myriad ways that other categories of exclusion and deportation, such as the more commonly invoked LPC provision, masked health and other concerns, including racial issues, and the impact that exclusion on medical grounds had on immigrants, potential immigrants, and their communities.

Only by delving into case files and the records of immigrant advocates does one understand how the LPC provision was either used as a surrogate for other concerns or integrated with other issues—such as race—because it was both easier to prove and more acceptable as an exclusion category. Though she ties medical inspection to the imperative of capitalists in establishing an expanding and fit labor force at the turn of the twentieth century, Fairchild does not explore in depth how deportation issues were inextricably linked to other larger social trends and prevailing ideologies in the United States, including those regarding race, gender, and religion.[14]

Certainly, there was a significant role for medical inspectors at the border and at ports of embarkation to prevent the spread of contagious diseases. For example, a cholera outbreak in Russia required quarantine measures of those immigrants originating from Russia to prevent its spread to fellow ship passengers and later to those at the port of disembarkation. In 1907 a group of Russian immigrants in transit to New York on a Cunard ship was held at Trieste and placed in quarantine for five days, and passengers' luggage disinfected. A State Department official in Trieste expressed his concern that the same shipping company failed to quarantine Russians en route to Argentina, who shared a hotel with those bound for the United States. Subsequently, however, the physician agreed to place Russians in quarantine, regardless of their destination.[15]

Trachoma and tuberculosis were two other highly contagious diseases that would have profound consequences if they were not detected. But while those diseases were prevalent among several national populations, they were differentially regulated according to race and ethnicity. Moreover, the crowded and unsanitary conditions aboard steerage served as incubators for scarlet fever, measles, and other communicable diseases that affected children especially. Congressman John Burnett cited official immigration data that indicated that 1,500 children had arrived annually with scarlet fever or measles, most cases having been contracted on board ship, and about 250 had died as a result.[16]

At Ellis Island, two medical inspectors employed by the U.S. Public Health Service reviewed disembarking steerage passengers for "outward signs" of illness, including scalp diseases, glandular inflammation, goiters, and hand and foot defects. The second examined passengers' eyes for trachoma. If any conditions were noted, they were taken aside, placed in an examination room, and given a more thorough physical exam. Those suspected of psychological illness, or imbecility, were asked several questions to evaluate their cognitive abilities. Those presenting with contagious disease or significant psychological conditions were hospitalized. In 1912, 10 percent of new all arrivals to Ellis Island faced Bureau of Special Inquiry hearings and 2 percent were ordered deported.[17]

But two decades after medical issues first arrived at the forefront of immigration law, officials conceded that definitions of disease and the severity of the condition were subjective. In response to inquiries to the Department of State from the Danish government, W. W. Husband admitted to Frank Kellogg, secretary of state, "It would appear to be difficult to lay down any precise rule as to the degree of mental disability necessary

Report of Public Health and Marine-Hospital Service—
Ellis Island, New York, July 1906

Annual Statistics for Ellis Island, Fiscal Year Ending June 1906

Total Certified for Medical Defects: 7,573 aliens

Most Frequent Diagnosis:

Certified for Senility: 1,992

Certified for Hernia: 1,526

Certified for Poor Physique: 315

Certified with Diseases Classified as Dangerous or Loathsome: 976

Certified as Insane, Idiotic, or Epileptic: 189

Certified for Valvular Disease of the Heart: 138

Certified as Mentally Weak or Feeble-Minded: 97

Immigrants Examined for Minor Defects: 29,302

Hospital Admissions: 7,464

Deaths in Hospitals: 327

Births in Hospital: 18

Immigrants Certified with Trachoma—Most Frequent Nativity (836 total)

Italians: 198

Hebrew: 113

Polish: 108

This report provided a breakdown of nativity for trachoma only.

Source: Data from File: 50627/16, RG 85, Entry 9, 1906, NARA.

to cause a decision that such mentally defective alien is of an excludable class."[18]

Hookworm and Trachoma: Debating Diagnoses and Disease

Some diseases, including hookworm and scalp diseases, while contagious, did not merit exclusion or deportation according to the common definition of dangerous or loathsome. Instead, those conditions were associated with poverty and the crowding that arose from transoceanic transportation in steerage class. In fact, immigration officials debated the meaning of medical definitions within immigration policy. The following question arose: if a disease or condition was either loathsome or contagious, but not both, did it constitute grounds for exclusion or deportation? Indeed, the

Bureau of Immigration officials parsed this phrase closely in determining whether a particular illness met either definition. Advances in treatment protocols also affected the classification of particular diseases over time.

Diseases were unevenly diagnosed and associated with particular racial, national, or religious groups. Associating a disease with a specific group stigmatized it further, even when the diagnosis was inaccurate or readily treatable. By the 1910s uncinariasis, or hookworm, became closely associated with Chinese immigrants, even though it was sometimes diagnosed among immigrants from Syria and elsewhere. Federal officials increasingly acknowledged, however, that it was an easily curable disease that might not warrant deportation among those who were diagnosed with it if they agreed to undergo treatment for it immediately after landing. A 1913 Bureau of Immigration study of uncinariasis among Chinese and Japanese immigrants arriving on steamships at the port of San Francisco over a five-month period demonstrated an average certification rate among Japanese of 9 percent and 27.1 percent for Chinese immigrants. This period followed the passage of the Gentleman's Agreement that severely restricted the number of Japanese immigrants allowed into the United States. Decades earlier Chinese immigration had been dramatically reduced and limited to just a few classes, including merchants and students.[19]

By 1922 a Bureau of Immigration memo acknowledged that, with proper treatment, uncinariasis was easily cured within a two- to four-week period. The memo suggested that the medical officers at the port of San Francisco had the authority to treat hookworm at the immigration station but that some Chinese immigrants had been denied the option of treatment because the examiner "indicated that he could not definitely state whether or not the disease would be easily curable, in the given case." The communication further suggested that these cases could be more expeditiously handled by giving "blanket" authority to port officials to allow treatment at area hospitals, if proper bond was furnished to ensure that those immigrants completed their course of treatment. It further noted that hookworm was diagnosed almost exclusively among Chinese immigrants.[20]

In 1925 the commissioner general wrote to Hugh Cumming, the surgeon general of the U.S. Public Health Service, about uncinariasis. He inquired whether it should remain in the "A" category, in the same class of ailments as other more serious diseases. Yet, even after hookworm was reclassified from a serious disease that warranted deportation to a less threatening one that allowed for immigrants to enter if they agreed to immediate treatment, the consequences of being diagnosed at the border remained significant for most immigrants. The bond required for those opting for treatment was set at $2,000 and immigrants would be responsible for paying the hospital fees associated with a prolonged course of treatment. Therefore, immigrants who opted for treatment following their diagnosis for a potentially deportable disease needed to have significant financial means to achieve bail requirements and to pay for hospital treatment. Although hookworm no longer resulted in automatic exclusion, the mandatory and expensive course of treatment meant that disease reclassification had little practical effect for many immigrants who received that diagnosis.[21]

Trachoma was a grave disease that particularly concerned immigration officials, because it could result in blindness. Today, it remains the major cause of blindness worldwide, but because it is treatable with antibiotics, it is now rare in industrialized countries. While trachoma was a serious disease, Europeans were far less likely to be diagnosed with it at the borders than were immigrants from China, Mexico, and the Middle East. Therefore, the physical examination sometimes served as a surrogate for race among non-European immigrants.

At major ports of entry, including Ellis Island and Angel Island, inspectors examined incoming second-class and steerage passengers for signs of trachoma and other diseases that had identifiable physical symptoms. First-class passengers were inspected while still on board ship. Physicians used either their fingers or a buttonhook to turn back passengers' eyelids. If other conditions were detected more informally, the inspector indicated the need for closer inspection with a coded chalk mark on the immigrants' clothing. An estimated 15–20 percent of arriving immigrants were diverted into examining rooms for physicals. They were subject to eye exams, probing by instruments including stethoscopes and thermometers, or, if their mental health was in question, a series of questions and cognitive-based tests.[22] Consequently immigrant officials could reduce the numbers of immigrants from those regions without directly limiting immigration on the basis of racial identities.

Representatives of Jewish immigrants diagnosed with trachoma at Ellis Island requested that the Immigration Service allow them to seek treatment at city hospitals so they could be admitted. Moreover, allowing them to obtain treatment in the city would enable relatives to visit them more easily than would be possible if they remained in Ellis Island facilities. But while this option was a cheaper alternative, Daniel Keefe argued against this change in policy on the grounds that it would encourage "relatives and friends and the steamship lines to bring other diseased aliens here," especially because the facilities were less confining than on Ellis Island. He further posited that by requiring confinement at Ellis Island, immigrants would be motivated to seek treatment before embarkation, though he conceded that there might be exceptions if personal circumstances warranted it. That decision was made soon after HIAS lodged complaints against the quality of hospital food on behalf of a group of Jewish trachoma patients, a move that William A. Williams dismissed as evidence of their "ingratitude" toward immigration officials who decided to allow treatment in lieu of deportation, adding that the trachoma patients "owe their presence here to the mercy shown them by the Department."[23]

Steamship corporations challenged Bureau of Immigration decisions to fine them for transporting immigrants found with trachoma. One such example was that of Annie Berger, who was certified with the disease by Dr. Stoner, the medical examiner at Ellis Island, which "might have been detected at the port of embarkation." Cunard protested the fine of $100. But the question of whether the steamship knowingly transported a passenger with trachoma that had been diagnosed at the port became an issue.

The Department of Commerce and Labor's solicitor characterized Section 9 as "highly penal" and therefore illegal. Section 9 imposed fines on companies in those cases where the secretary of the treasury concluded that the "disease might have been detected by means of a medical examination at the port of embarkation." Bureau officials were highly critical of the solicitor's opinion, because it "tends to break down and destroy the efficiency of Section 9 of the Act of March 3, 1903."[24]

Along the U.S. border with Mexico, physicians inspected immigrants, examining them for symptoms of excludable diseases. In 1908 two young sisters, Margaret and Beatrice Bolado, were excluded from the United States after the physician at the Brownsville immigration station diagnosed them with trachoma. They appealed that decision, on the grounds that two Mexican physicians had stated that they did not have the disease. Consequently, the U.S. ambassador to Mexico intervened and brought the case to the attention of the acting secretary of state, but Secretary Oscar Straus let the excluding decision stand. The Bolado sisters were unusual in that they appealed the exclusion decision and had the financial resources to consult two physicians who offered independent diagnoses from the medical inspector. Most immigrants from Mexico or elsewhere could not contest their diagnosis.[25]

Syrians and the Mexican Border

Abraham Zainey, a Syrian immigrant, who had first been deported in 1906 as a result of a diagnosis of trachoma returned to the United States surreptitiously by crossing from Mexico. He was discovered in a Syrian immigrant community in Providence, Rhode Island, the following year. He had the misfortune of being apprehended following his uncle's death: Zainey's name was published as among the surviving family members when that death notice ran in the New England newspaper, *Al-Hoda*. An immigration official launched a sting operation. Posing as a customer, he discovered Zainey's whereabouts at a photography shop where he had worked. The shop owner said that the boy was currently attending high school in Providence. When immigration officials tracked him down, Zainey told immigration officials that he had been smuggled across the border by Salim Bedowy, who, he reported, was soon due to arrive in Mexico City, where he was assisting three other Syrians afflicted with trachoma to cross the border. Therefore, Bedowy and other Syrians living in Mexico soon became the focus of a wider Immigration Service inquiry.[26]

The concern was that large numbers of Syrians with trachoma were gaining entry to the United States via Mexico. Mexicans were not subject to scrutiny as intense as other groups, in large part because they were viewed as temporary migrants rather than permanent immigrants. Consequently some Syrians, who, like Mexicans, were often darker skinned than Europeans, bought traditional garments and posed as Mexican citizens to elude immigration officials at U.S. border stations. That trend led to an Immigration Service investigation conducted by S. A. Seraphic. He traveled to Tampico, Veracruz, Mexico City, Monterrey, Nuevo Laredo, Matamoros, Porfirio Díaz, Torréon, and Juarez. He found that many Syrians were living in Mexico, working as peddlers. Their original plans to enter the United States were thwarted by their inability to repay their passage to Syrian dry goods operators who were exploiting them, and they were caught in a system similar to debt peonage. In Tampico, for example, Seraphic reported that he found twenty-one Syrians hiding in the rear of a dry goods store run by Syrian Skender Ayar, where they "lived in filth under the most unsanitary conditions." Ayer charged the Syrians exorbitant prices for the goods that they peddled, and they were beholden to

Syrian immigrants in Mexico. (51423/2-A, RG 85, Entry 9, National Archives)

him until they repaid their passage. As he further noted, "The majority of them had unmistakable signs of chronic trachoma in the worst form." At Vera Cruz, eighty Syrian peddlers were living in the back of another dry goods store.[27] Seraphic also reported that at Laredo and elsewhere, Syrians were being treated for trachoma so that they could gain entry to the United States. He also discovered that Greek immigrants were being treated for trachoma in several Mexican towns, having previously been denied entry at the U.S. border.

Syrians, Greeks, and occasionally Italians, dressed in "Mexican costume" blended in with Mexicans crossing the border into the United States. As Mexicans, they were welcome because of the inexpensive labor they could provide. This strategy emerged both informally—as friends and family members informed prospective immigrants about effective means of eluding immigration barriers—and among middle men, such as Skender Ayar, who functioned as "coyotes" for Syrians and others. At Laredo, Seraphic reported that the medical inspector, a Dr. Hamilton, was lax in diagnosing trachoma cases at the border because he was allegedly addicted to drugs or alcohol.[28]

The Syrian interpreter at Laredo was also found to be incompetent and lacking in his knowledge of Arabic. An allegation by Habib Gorrah and his family, Syrian immigrants who appeared to be "of the better class" and showed "no indication whatever of trachoma or any other disease," charged that the interpreter N. T. Abdou at the El Paso–Laredo border had demanded bribes from Syrians crossing the border, including those seeking treatment for trachoma. The inspector in charge launched an investigation, in which he determined that there was sufficient evidence to substantiate the allegations.

For his part, Abdou defended his actions, explaining that Syrians offered him money willingly, "as all Orientals do in such circumstances," and that he cautioned them about deportation if they were found to be contract laborers or living with partners who were not their legal spouses. He essentially claimed that the allegations were a result of cultural misunderstanding and vindictiveness among immigrants, including a woman who was a "victim of polygamy," and that Charles Lyman "was nothing but a Mohammed Soleiman, a Musulman Turk, a polygamist, and a regular beat of Damascus." Abdou further accused them of acting against him because he was a Christian rather than a "true believer in our Prophet Mohammad." But those objections were dismissed, and Abdou was terminated from the Immigration Service. Abdou defended himself by reinforcing immigration officials' negative stereotypes about Middle Eastern immigrants and their presumed relative unfamiliarity with accepted cultural practices, while distancing himself from those who were Muslim. In this particular case, that strategy was ineffective, perhaps because of the number of complaints against him.[29]

Psychological Illness

Several controversies emerged as a result of psychological illness among immigrants. New York State was the site of many debates over the institutional care of immigrants, because Ellis Island was the major port of entry for immigrants and many of them remained in the city. In 1906 immigration officials estimated that more than one-third of all immigrants to the United States were destined to live in New York State. That report further claimed a notable increase over the prior year in the number of excluded "persons afflicted with idiocy and insanity" and a seven-fold increase in those excluded for prior criminal convictions." The report recommended increasing from $100 to $500 the fines imposed on steamship companies for transporting diseased aliens to the United States. Medical inspectors should be hired by those companies at their ports of embarkation.[30]

Although issues of immigration regulation, including exclusion and deportation decisions, were federal ones, the New York legislature introduced legislation to address the costs of institutional care. In 1914 it was estimated that almost a third of the hospital population could be classified "insane aliens." In many ways this issue presaged Proposition 187 and related California legislative initiatives beginning in the 1990s, which arose from taxpayers' unwillingness to fund social services and education for the increasing number of immigrants in that state. That shift in attitude, discussed previously, culminated in the Illegal Immigration Reform and Immigrant Responsibility Act (IIRIRA), which denied eligibility for Medicare and Medicaid to noncitizens in 1996. The New York bill sought reimbursement from the federal government for the cost of caring for psychologically ill immigrants, by establishing better medical examinations and translation services for psychological illness.[31]

Officials debated whether to provide medical treatment to immigrants with psychiatric illnesses at the hospital in Ellis Island or elsewhere. Roger O'Donnell, an immigrant inspector, documented the inadequacy of the psychopathic ward of the Immigrant Hospital at Ellis Island, especially with the presence of insane or violent immigrants. The hospital could adequately care for just three or four severely ill patients at a time, in part because of the lack of skilled attendants. In fact, he noted that occasionally patients assaulted attendants or other patients. Byron Uhl, acting commissioner of immigration at Ellis Island, referred to the assessment report of the ward by the public health officer in charge of the medical division on the island, Dr. L. L. Williams, and then concluded: "The presence in our limited quarters of raving maniacs has a decidedly bad effect upon others who would be, but for these ravings, reasonably tractable." He called for better patient facilities and argued that despite lower costs, continuing with the status quo was "very poor economy."[32]

Immigration officials debated outsourcing psychiatric care to Bellevue Hospital or a sanitarium in Amityville, Long Island. Immigrant officials estimated that the psychopathic ward at Ellis Island could care for twenty-five psychiatric patients for "a short period of time," but to have them hospitalized at Amityville cost six to ten dollars per patient each day. Whether very ill or violent patients should be segregated from others was another area of debate. Bellevue was acknowledged as chronically overcrowded, with up to eighty-five patients in a ward designed to accommodate seventy patients.[33]

Albert Warren Ferris, president of New York State's Office of the State Commission in Lunacy, urged the passage of a federal law increasing appropriations for the institutional costs of deportable aliens with psychiatric illnesses, stating that New York State was housing 200 such patients beyond its capacity. He concluded that "We think that our State should not have to suffer as a result." Though the 1907 Immigration Act that rendered such immigrants inadmissible provided for funds to maintain those immigrants, federal appropriations proved inadequate, given the high numbers of those who were in state care.[34]

Another issue that arose in psychiatric cases was how immigrants who had been deported or excluded at the borders would return to their country of origin and who would pay for such expenses. Such cases illustrated the almost primitive conditions under which many psychiatric patients lived. One controversy emerged after the relatives of a twenty-two-year-old woman, Chaia "Tilly" Ostrovsky, complained that she was treated inhumanely while she was being sent back to Russia. The State Charities Aid Association intervened in her case. She had been locked in a room for nearly five days, and her brother reported that she was "covered with flies and her own filth, and lying on the floor in a semi-conscious condition—the only garment she had on was an undervest." Homer Folks of the State Charities Aid Association attributed Ostrovsky's inhumane treatment to the fact that steamship companies had been given broad authority for the return of mentally ill aliens in 1907.[35] Katherine Tucker, a nurse who visited Ostrovsky concluded that she was in better condition than reported by her family. But Tucker conceded that the crew had prepared Ostrovsky for her visit. Tucker added that "for a girl not in her right mind to be there in the midst of such men, with no one to protect her or look after her, seems to be running a great risk and doing a great injustice."[36]

An Immigration Service investigation, undertaken by Anna Schlesinger, a matron, found similar conditions to those reported by the two charity officials. When Schlesinger visited her, Ostrovsky was sitting on the floor of the cabin, wet, hair uncombed, and improperly clothed and in "a state of mental stupor." A maid or stewardess was said to visit her each half hour, a claim that was unlikely. Despite the investigation's findings,

Acting Commissioner Byron Uhl recommended against the Immigration Service requiring that mentally ill immigrants be accompanied by attendants on their return journey.[37]

The consul general for the Russian Imperial Consulate, however, defended the Russian-American Line, stating that, when purchasing a ticket, Ostrovsky's brother did not mention that the passenger was insane and therefore there was no time to assign attendants to her. He also conceded that she had been locked in her room, justifying it on the grounds that "she seems to have a mania for running out on the deck and disrobing."[38]

The Ostrovsky case also came to the attention of the Council of Jewish Women (CJW), based in New York, which focused on improving measures for the safe transportation of immigrants who were deported on the basis of insanity. Sadie American, executive secretary of CJW, noted that it became active on the issue after receiving "a number of complaints, both of abuse of insane patients on their way to their former homes, as instanced by black and blue marks on their bodies, etc. and also by non-arrival at their homes and the utter disappearance of some cases."[39]

American's letter included a list of deported aliens who were missing, their relatives reporting that they had never reached their final destinations. She further stated: "The Russian Jew is in a condition somewhat different from others, and that repatriation of such persons may entail such suffering, torture and persecution as no humane person wishes to contemplate." American's argument for better safeguards of those deported on grounds of insanity was a political and humanitarian one. In fact, her reference to pogroms and persecution presaged the human rights debates following the Holocaust and European Jewish refugee crisis of the 1930s and 1940s.[40]

Ostrovsky's case was widely publicized in the immigrant community, causing concern among the families of others deported on psychiatric grounds. A Chicago law firm wrote to request information about "what provision is made by the department in caring for the girl in transit and assuring her safe arrival to the town where her parents are and from where she came to this country." In fact, immigration officials wrote in response to the CJW inquiry about two deported immigrants who had vanished before being returned to their destinations that they were unable to determine if they had ever arrived.[41]

Italian government officials also protested U.S. immigration policies pertaining to the return of insane aliens ordered deported. The U.S. Embassy in Rome reported that the Italian Immigration Commission had requested more information on that U.S. policy. In many cases, there were reports of attendants assigned to patients failing to escort them to their final destination. In some cases, this resulted in tragic outcomes. Specifically, the issue arose following the death of a fourteen-year-old Italian boy, Paolo Maltese, who after arriving in Naples was placed in an insane asylum and died just six weeks after leaving the United States. Though many details of his circumstances remain unclear, his case was at the center of disputes over who should have custody of the patient upon landing—the Reggio Commissario or the local police officials. The implication was that the lack of clear authority and of a policy about returned immigrants with psychological disorders contributed to the circumstances of the boy's death.[42]

There was some acknowledgment that psychiatric illness could be temporary. For example, Hilda Mykrs, an immigrant, argued that her condition was hormonally based and claimed that her moods fluctuated with her menstrual cycle, a condition that would today be characterized as premenstrual syndrome. Her second assertion was that her parents were not insane, as originally thought, and so her condition was temporary and not inherited. Nevertheless, her appeal was denied.[43]

Eugenics and the Creation of Disease

During the 1890s and first decade of the twentieth century eugenics theories grew in popularity alongside the development of a federal immigration policy that would culminate in several national-origins bills that sought to change the composition of immigrants from one that was increasingly Asian, Southern, and Eastern European, to one that advantaged those from Northern Europe. Members of the Boston-based Immigration Restriction League (IRL) and others increasingly advanced the notions that recent arrivals from Southern and Eastern Europe were less capable of assimilating into American life than previous groups of immigrants, their behavioral traits posed a threat to society, they were contagious diseases carriers, they were draining state and local resources, and they would weaken the existing racial "stock."[44]

IRL members were drawn largely from the academic community and other elite circles. Henry Cabot Lodge, the U.S. senator representing Massachusetts, was a member. As the number of immigrants arriving from Southern and Eastern Europe continued to increase in the first decade of the twentieth century and threatened the dominance of elites of Anglo-Protestant ancestry in the United States, immigration restrictionists lobbied strenuously for limiting immigration. But these leaders now coalesced around eugenicist ideology, wielding it as a scientific instrument in their attempt to reduce immigration. They also deployed their academic and legislative roles and their social position as experts, along with their position as knowledge producers and the authority gained from scientific positivism, to advance their anti-immigrant agenda. Their training conferred authority on their opinions, despite the fact that it was far afield from medicine or biology.

Eugenics theories were widely advocated and accepted in the United States in this era and influenced ideas and ideologies about race, reproduction and birth control, disability, health care, and education, as well as immigration policies. The "poor physique" category emerged as significant grounds for exclusion or deportation in 1905 in consultation with Robert DeCourcy Ward, a Harvard University climatology professor and a cofounder of the IRL. Ward began a correspondence with immigration officials, including William A. Williams, commissioner of immigration at Ellis Island, in 1905. In his 1904 annual report, Williams had begun to discuss poor physique as a possible category by which to exclude immigrants.[45]

Ward later wrote to Lawrence Murray, assistant secretary of the Department of Commerce and Labor, in response to a *Boston Evening Telegraph* article that detailed how David Murik, a Jewish immigrant returning to Baltimore from a visit to Russia, was excluded from entry because of "poor physique." Murik's three sisters maintained that, though he returned to the United States with less than a dollar in cash, they would provide for him, and HIAS also offered to put up a bond to guarantee he would not be a public charge, but to no avail.[46] Indeed, the formation of the poor physique category was closely linked to the earnings capabilities of arriving immigrants. The diagnosis would be cast as a physical manifestation of the LPC provision. The fact that Ward had no medical training suggests the problematic nature of the category. Unlike trachoma, a highly contagious eye disease often resulting in blindness, or other communicable diseases, "poor physique" was an amorphous diagnosis that covered such diverse conditions as malnourishment, small arteries, poor circulation, deficient muscle development, and "lack of correlation between height and weight."[47]

In his April 12, 1905, letter to Murray, Ward stated, "It has for some time, seemed to me that the most important step which we can possibly take in the matter of a further selection of immigration is to exclude persons of low vitality and poor physique, for in such persons lies the greatest danger to the health and strength of our future American stock. At present I have in hand an amendment to our existing immigration laws which would make it obligatory upon our immigration inspectors to debar aliens certified as being of such poor physique that they would be likely to be public charges."[48] Ward's handwritten amendment adds to the proposed definition "persons physically weak or defective so that they are wholly or partially disabled from manual labor . . . whether the trade or occupations involves hard physical effort or not." Ward advanced the view that even when the "poor physique" diagnosis had no effect on the immigrant's ability to work, it should lead to exclusion or deportation. He argued that this weak condition was hereditary and thus threatening to the future health of the U.S. population.[49]

In 1905 Dr. J. W. Schereschewsky, Public Health and Marine Hospital Service (PHMHS) surgeon at the Baltimore port, arrived at a definition in which he concluded that not only would those of poor physique pass on those traits to their children, but they would do so to an "exaggerated degree." Schereschewsky, who rose to prominence in the emerging field of occupational health, had been educated at Harvard University and later in his career returned there to conduct research on cancer. In order to make the diagnosis carry an implicit and specific threat to public health, poor physique became linked to incipient tuberculosis. "Cases of so called 'chicken breast,' especially those having some of the physical signs of pulmonary tuberculosis, but in which the tubercle bacillus can not be found in the sputum, should be certified under this head." Thus, the definition suggested that those with "poor physique" had the potential of spreading a communicable disease, though there was yet no physical evidence of such a disease.[50]

In 1906 George Stoner, the medical officer at Ellis Island, summarized Schereschewsky's definition of poor physique as "defective physical development, a permanent faulty or reduced condition of the system, a low degree of vitality." But he conceded, "The foregoing is not intended as a complete or satisfactory definition. Indeed such a definition would be difficult to frame. The difficulty arises from the fact that the term does not imply a clinical or pathological entity." In other words, Stoner was skeptical of the diagnosis, which did not seem to have a clear set of symptoms. He concluded that "the medical officers at this station agree . . . [t]hat no specific demonstrable disease sufficient to warrant a certificate exists."[51] Despite significant confusion over the diagnosis, in late 1906, Frank Larned, acting commissioner-general of immigration, noted that the "poor physique" category was "perhaps one of the most important employed."[52]

Even by 1907, uncertainty and debate within the agencies charged with regulating immigration concerning the "poor physique" diagnosis still prevailed. In a letter convening a meeting between Dr. Walter Wyman, the surgeon general of the United States, and the four major East Coast PHMHS officers, Oscar Straus, secretary of commerce and labor, admitted rather candidly, "I am not quite clear in my own mind concerning the character of certain physical ailments with which arriving aliens are afflicted." At that meeting, immigrant officials also debated, but ultimately rejected, a proposal to adopt some of the physical standards used by the U.S. Army, in which those with hernias were often deemed ineligible for service.[53]

Indeed, the poor physique diagnosis was almost always linked to the LPC provision and the concern that those with mild physical defects would be unable to become reliable workers and to support their families. The fact that Jews in this era more often than other groups arrived permanently and within family units probably heightened concerns over their wage-earning potential. Immigrant advocates charged that Jews escaping political and religious persecution in Eastern Europe and in Russia were unfairly being singled out for exclusion and deportation under this policy.

As illustrated in earlier chapters, even when U.S. immigration laws appear to be gender neutral, they were often applied according to prevailing American gender norms. Developing the poor physique diagnosis as a basis for exclusion was one such example. Men's cultural roles as primary breadwinners thus led their bodies to be scrutinized for "poor physique" to a greater degree than women's. Also implicit in the policy was the idea that one's physical condition was central to one's wage-earning potential. But their occupational concentration outside of industries such as construction, mining, and steel production made such conclusions less accurate for Jewish men than for others.[54] In one list of HIAS's "recently appealed cases," five out of eight cases citing "poor physique" were males and all referred to the immigrants' poor economic status or absence of relatives in the United States.[55]

Jewish advocacy groups, most notably HIAS, based in New York objected to this classification, arguing that many Jewish immigrants were being unjustly deported as a result of this diagnosis and that a "poor physique" did not adversely affect an immigrant's ability to work. Instead they countered the assessment of poor Jews as a drain on American society by marshaling evidence of upward mobility and arguing that as a group, Jews were both economically self-sufficient and important contributors to American society.[56]

In a 1911 article published in the *American Hebrew*, Max J. Kohler, an immigration lawyer and American Jewish community leader, argued that the LPC provision was being applied not simply to those who were destitute within three years of arrival but even to those who were deemed "three pounds underweight" in their medical examination. He further maintained that "This works particular hardship upon the Russian Jew, with his deceptive appearance of slight physique, particularly at the end of abnormal conditions attending living in the badly conducted steerage, after being deprived of appropriate food, because of the observance of the Jewish dietary laws."[57] It is unclear from his article whether there was an actual case in which someone faced deportation as a result of being underweight by as few as three pounds, but Kohler's remark refers to the contentious "poor physique" diagnosis. Kohler continued to serve as an advocate for immigrants, and later became active in lobbying Secretary of State Cordell Hull for increased quotas for European Jews seeking to escape Europe during the Holocaust.

Kohler decried the racial categorizations as "probably unconstitutional. . . . The so-called 'race values' of different nationalities are based upon pure, unwarranted assumption, as to which no authorities could agree, even if one could satisfactorily ascertain the average characteristics of any one race." He added that the Immigration Commission's report concluded that "children born not more than a few years after the arrival of the immigrant parents in America develop in such a way that they differ in type essentially from their foreign parents."[58] Thus, he used the Bureau of Immigration conclusions themselves to refute the premise by which the poor physique category became part of immigration policy. He further criticized a proposal to expand the LPC provision to those "who are 'economically undesirable' which phrase is so indefinite that it might be better directly named 'victims of prejudice' and also the exclusion of those unable to pass a physical test equivalent to that required for recruits for our army which absurdly would shut out an overwhelming majority of our own citizens, if applied to them."[59]

Jews were collapsed into one racial group in the immigration records, whereas most other immigrant groups were classified by geographical or linguistic category. Even according to recent scholars of ethnicity, this categorization persists and remains problematic. Certainly there are good reasons for using a religion rather than ethnicity or nationality as an analytic category, given that the historical experience of Jews in particular European countries was radically different from their Catholic and Protestant compatriots. For Jews across Europe and Russia, rates of urbanization, occupational concentrations, and immigration patterns were tied less to their countries of origin than to their religion.

Religious-based classification could assist in cases of religious persecution, but it could also be used to single Jews out, as they were in the enforcement of certain provisions of immigration policy.[60] That was illustrated clearly in the work of Maurice Fishberg, a physician who worked with Jewish immigrants in New York through United Hebrew Charities. His 1911 book, *The Jews: A Study of Race and Environment*, was built on earlier research. In it, he argued for environmentalism rather than genetic determinism in shaping Jewish life. For example, while suggesting that Jews throughout the world tended to be shorter than average, he also concluded that, contrary to prevailing opinion, they tended to be resilient against communicable diseases. That conclusion was important in combating the widespread idea that tuberculosis was epidemic among American Jews. He also suggested they had lower rates of infant mortality than other American immigrant groups.[61]

Yet, while Fishberg used his research to counteract eugenics-based arguments about Jews, William Z. Ripley appropriated some of Fishberg's findings, such as the relatively high intermarriage rates of Jews, to bolster his own claims. Indeed, in a 1908 article Ripley noted with alarm that, according to the 1890 Federal Census, Jews had much lower mortality rates than either many immigrant groups or native-born Americans. He states, "By actuarial computation at these relative rates, starting at birth with two groups of one thousand Jews and Americans respectively [*sic*], the chances would be that the first half of the Americans would die within 47 years; while for the Jews this would not occur until after 71 years. *Social Selection at this rate would be bound to produce very positive results in a century or two.*" While the conclusion that median life expectancy for Jews exceeded the national average by over twenty-four years seems exaggerated, it also contradicted the eugenics-based argument that Jews were physically weaker and prone to illness than the general population. Ripley's work was undoubtedly well known by Ward and other eugenicists. Their fear that Jews, with their high longevity rates, would, in Ripley's words, win "this great ethnic struggle for dominance and survival" might well have motivated eugenicists to lobby so strenuously against their admittance.[62]

By 1913, HIAS was in the process of appealing at least twenty-one deportation cases that were based on medical conditions. Most of these cases referred to "poor physique" and terms such as "malnutrition" and "lack of physical development" and also included references to poverty. Immigration officials criticized HIAS and others for assigning too many immigration assistance agents at Ellis Island and other ports in proportion to other ethnic and religious groups.[63] But it is clear that the advocacy work of immigrant groups such as HIAS was crucial to the successful challenges of some eugenically based and biased diagnoses. Many of those diagnoses were unlikely either to pose threats to public health or to result in immigrants being unable to earn a living. By 1914, one report about "contagious and loathsome diseases," which also listed an array of medical diagnoses ranging from poor physical development, favus, psoriasis, and other noncontagious diseases, concluded, "The number held for 'special inquiry' varies greatly. Where a vessel brings a poor class of immigrants it may reach twenty-five or thirty percent, many of whom must remain here several days."[64] A decade later, this remained the case and provided a further argument for the need for highly restrictive immigration quotas.

H. R. Landis, assistant commissioner of immigration for Ellis Island, gave a speech calling for further restricting immigration. "Ellis Island has long been a part of New York City's protection from foreign invasion. . . . The old days of 5,000 a day are passed. Commissioner Curran has said that he will not undertake to examine more than 2,000 a day; and this number only if they are the so-called Nordics. . . . While a Scandinavian ship may have not more than one-tenth of one percent of its passengers detained, a ship from the Mediterranean may have as high as thirty to eighty-five percent, and that tells the story of why immigration men are in favor of the census of 1890 as a basis for the quotas."[65] Therefore, the ethnic typologies developed by Ripley and others influenced not only the enactment of the national-origins quota as the basis for admission but also the rate of inspections of ships and the likelihood of being diagnosed with a disease that would lead to exclusion or deportation as well.

A related issue was how aging was addressed at the borders. Concurrently with the rise of "poor physique," immigration officials began to classify older immigrants as presenile. That led to at least a few immigrants being deported or excluded. Zelik Woolman and his wife, Sure, were 55 and 59. They were certified for "senility, effecting ability to earn a living," and "senile disability," respectively. Because they had applied for assistance from the Baron de Hirsch Society, their son's submission of an affidavit that he was willing to provide for them in Chicago was unsuccessful. Another case involved Janos Czikai, a forty-eight-year-old Hungarian Magyar man who looked "60 or more" excluded on "presenility" grounds, based on the view that he was no longer fit enough to work at hard manual labor. Indeed, just fewer than 2,000 of the 7,573 arriving immigrants excluded at Ellis Island in 1906 were barred on the basis of a certificate of senility.[66]

Contested Definitions of Race and National Origins

A second controversy over ethnic bias, though one unconnected with physical health, arose as a direct result of the categorization of racial and ethnic typologies. As late as 1934, the Bureau of Immigration was making a distinction between northern and southern Italians. Earlier, a delegate from the Swiss Embassy also wrote to protest the way racial typologies were used in classifying its citizens. It was clear that this classification was a result of the eugenics-based theories espoused by Ripley and others. Frederick Ciampi, writing on behalf of the Italian-American Citizens' Club of Cambridge, Massachusetts, contacted his congressional representative, Arthur Healey, on the matter. Notably, the commissioner of immigration at Ellis Island at the time was Edward Corsi, an Italian American, who had arrived in New York from Italy as a boy. In a letter to Corsi in 1932, another immigration official provided a short history of the bureau's use of this categorization. He traced the decision to Terence Powderly's administration, in 1899, adding: "As you likely know, the statistics of the Immigration Service have differentiated between north and south Italians since 1899, when it was first decided to record arrivals by race. Theretofore all population statistics respecting foreign born in the United States were recorded only by country of birth."[67]

That statement provides an interesting window into the contemporary use of these terms. Though race as it is popularly construed today was, of course, relevant to the commission well before 1899, the term was consistent with the ethnic typologies used in the Dillingham Report. Powderly stated that race would be used "so that from an experience of the distinguishing occupations of each race, its moral, mental, and physical characteristics, and their development under American institutions, a basis may be formed for estimating its effect on the population and industry of the United States." The official argued that the distinction was valid.

"It is remarked by an able and recent writer on racial realities of Europe that Northern Italy was invaded by mostly Nordics, and the northern stream from beyond the Alps continued to flow for centuries, leavening the population of northern and central Italy. Ethnologists tell us that the southern Italians are of Mediterranean origin or stock . . . and that the southern Italians were frequently infused with the Levantine elements. It is believed that even the Italian ethnologists themselves, particularly Sergi, admit the distinction in race between the inhabitants of northern and southern Italy." As historian Peter D'Agostino has discussed, Giuseppe Sergi was an Italian anthropologist who promoted racial classification systems such as the one encoded in immigration policy.[68]

Explaining the classification further, the official cites William Z. Ripley's classification of Europeans into Teutonic, Alpine, and Mediterranean races. Ripley was a Harvard University economist whose original research interests focused on the railroad industry. The official closed his letter by stating that "it would be somewhat revolutionary at this time to combine the two racial divisions of Italy in our figures."[69]

In 1920 the eugenics-based racial classification system came under criticism in Switzerland. Hans Sulzer, a Swiss foreign minister, writing to the U.S. State Department, complained that there was no Swiss category on immigration service forms, but that immigrants from Switzerland were required to categorize themselves by language. He added "It is true that we speak three different languages but it is equally true that the languages do not run at all along racial lines. As a Swiss of that part of Switzerland where a German dialect is spoken, I may say that there is strong feeling against the tendency to be classified as belonging to the German race. We have been separated from Germany for over 600 years and during this time have developed quite different racial features." Interestingly, Sulzer posited that an alternative racial typology be used. "If a discrimination regarding the racial descent of the Swiss is desired, may I not be permitted to suggest that the denominations generally used in Switzerland be adopted. Would it not be possible to establish two Swiss races: The Alemannic Swiss and the Latin Swiss, and, in case of a further division of the latter, separate it into French and Italian Swiss? Such a division seems, however, hardly desirable." By the 1930s, national borders, though far from uncontested, were increasingly the basis for defining immigration quotas. Nevertheless, some eugenics-based classifications persisted.[70]

Many officials administering immigration policy in the Progressive Era had immigrant or second-generation backgrounds. Their intermediary role was akin to that of factory foremen who, as David Montgomery has argued, negotiated the terrain between unions, to which they once belonged, and management, to whom they were now accountable.[71] For example, Edward Corsi arrived as a small boy from Italy; Terence Powderly was the child of Irish immigrants; Oscar Straus, the first Jewish cabinet member and secretary of commerce and labor, immigrated from Germany; and William A. Williams was an English immigrant.

Immigration officials, who had specific, firsthand insights into immigrant life, would not have been particularly fearful of the effect that people from varied cultural values would have on American society. All were nevertheless constrained by the views of influential patricians such as Robert DeCourcy Ward and William Z. Ripley, who perceived themselves as guardians of an Anglo-American culture under threat. The fact that these two men were on Harvard's faculty gave them significant influence in developing a federal immigration policy, despite the fact that their eugenics theories lay far afield from the disciplines in which they trained.

Immigrants and ethnic Americans, both as government officials and as immigrant advocates, had a far more active role in shaping immigration policy in this era than has been acknowledged by most historians. Immigrant communities did not simply accept those federal policies that they perceived to be biased against them. Rather, advocacy groups such as HIAS and the Italian-American Citizens' Club served as advocates for immigrants who found themselves targeted by policies arising from eugenics-based theories. Immigrant advocates represented clients in the Bureau of Immigration's Board of Special Inquiry appeals. They also argued against certain policies in the ethnic press, lobbied their congressional representatives, and took other political action to address perceived biases within an emerging federal immigration policy during the Progressive Era. As we have seen in earlier instances, government officials in particular countries also intervened in cases where their citizens were adversely affected by U.S. laws and policies.

Employment issues also affected the enforcement of immigration laws concerning immigration. Many Jews and Syrians caught at the borders were peddlers. As economic middlemen, they traveled extensively across borders rather than being rooted deeply in one community. As such, they could not be easily contained or monitored, and posed a metaphorical threat to U.S. citizens.

The intersection of public health measures and eugenics ideology at the borders during the first two decades of the twentieth century led to the development of new, nonmedically based diagnoses, such as poor physique and presenility, that were used to keep out those perceived to be physically unfit for strenuous manual labor or those who arrived from regions where the population was deemed unfit for U.S. citizenship. Even in cases where diagnosed diseases were medically well established and highly contagious or posed other threats, they were diagnosed through the prism of racial and ethnic hierarchies that were influenced by eugenics ideology. Medical diagnoses became an effective proxy to regulate immigrants on the basis of racial and religious differences.

Immigration control was not simply a federal function. States, particularly New York, had a vested interest in how health-related immigration policies were implemented, because they shared the costs of medical treatment. Like the LPC provision, these health care costs anticipated similar debates over immigrants' social welfare benefits in the late twentieth century and today. European government agencies also registered their concern about how nationalities were defined and the impact of such decisions on their mobile citizens. The Immigration Restriction League used its privileged position to lobby for stricter immigration laws and policies and to develop new medically excludable categories. Lastly, relatives, alongside groups such as HIAS, the Council of Jewish Women, State Charities Aid, and the Italian-American Citizen's Club, advocated for the humane and just treatment of immigrants.

CLASH OF CIVILIZATIONS
WHITENESS, ORIENTALISM, AND THE LIMITS OF RELIGIOUS TOLERANCE AT THE BORDERS

Muslim and Hindu immigrants and others outside the mainstream Judeo-Christian tradition remained a small minority following the 1882 Chinese Exclusion Act. The ways that religion was regulated at the borders in that early era, however, had significant and long-term implications for the composition of American society and its social institutions. Since the 1965 Hart-Celler law, immigrants to the United States have been increasingly religiously diverse. Nevertheless, those early immigration policies shaped future demographic patterns of immigrants from Asia, the Middle East, and other regions. Moreover, immigration authorities' perceptions of religious minority groups highlight how the federal government's protection of religious freedom has been a relatively recent phenomenon, repeatedly challenged at the state level. As subsequent chapters reveal, constitutional rights, including freedom of religion, are often not extended to immigrants or those seeking admission until a probationary period has passed and they are deemed eligible for citizenship.

Religion's role in shaping definitions of immigrants' admissibility and citizenship suggest a great deal about American belief systems in the early twentieth century. While many newly organized religions grew in popularity as U.S. borders expanded in the nineteenth century, they rarely did so in isolation from global influences. When religious beliefs and cultural practices are closely regulated at the borders, it has major effects on the religious and racial composition of a nation, as well as profound ideological and political implications, even while religious freedom is espoused as a national value.

The federal government's early immigration policy, including specific provisions for exclusion and deportation, clearly outlined a system of racial discrimination. During the past two decades historians have analyzed how this system emerged by examining the impact of the Chinese Exclusion Act; the Gentlemen's Agreement, which severely limited Japanese immigration; ideologies of whiteness that defined subcontinental Indians as inadmissible and ineligible for citizenship; and the deportation of Mexicans in the 1930s. What has not been fully addressed by immigration historians, however, are the specific ways in which deportation and related immigration policies affected the ability of non-Christian groups (and some nonmainstream Christian groups) to migrate to the United States or to remain there.

Like Jews, Indians were classified by the immigration service by their religion, as Hindu, rather than by their nationality, a taxonomy that contrasted sharply with the categories created for most Europeans and other groups. As a result, Indians who were Sikhs, Muslims, Buddhists, or worshipers in other non-Hindu sects, were not recognized separately in the Bureau of Immigration's classification system. Depending on their geographic origins, Muslims from outside the Asiatic Barred Zone, or Asiatic Triangle, were not explicitly denied admission based solely on their racial identities but rather on whether they identified themselves as Muslims. Therefore, Syrian immigrants—who came not from the modern-day nation of Syria, but rather from the region now known as Lebanon—were mainly Christian and remained eligible for admission, whereas many Turkish immigrants faced exclusion. In these cases, religious practices served as a proxy for geographically based exclusions.

Certain immigrants faced barriers in their effort to settle in the United States because their belief systems were deemed incompatible with American values. Indeed, immigrants who professed a variety of religious beliefs or engaged in certain spiritual practices—such as Islam, Hinduism, Mormonism, and Theosophy—were viewed as threats to American society. We have seen how eugenics ideology drove public-health-related deportation decisions about Jews through the "poor physique" diagnosis. In this chapter I analyze the Bureau of Immigration's exclusion and deportation decisions about members of four major groups: European Mormon immigrants, Turkish Muslims, Hindus, and Theosophists. Although cases based on religious considerations are few relative to the number of immigrants facing exclusion or deportation because of "likely to become a public charge" (LPC) or medical grounds, they suggest that religious bias was a more significant factor in early federal immigration than previously recognized.

The belief systems of many Asian, Eurasian, and non-Christian groups were viewed through the lens of Orientalism, a concept articulated by the influential scholar Edward Said. Said argues that after Napoleon's incursion into Egypt in 1798, Europeans (and, subsequently, Americans) promoted a view of the Middle East and Asia that justified European expansionism, colonial rule, and war.[1] "These ideas," wrote Said, "explained the behavior of Orientals, they supplied Orientals with a mentality, a genealogy, an atmosphere; most importantly, they allowed Europeans to deal with and even to see Orientals as a phenomenon possessing regular characteristics."[2] Said argues that although Europeans included India in the framework of Orientalism, that nation posed less of a threat to European rule than did the Islamic world.[3] Immigration and local government officials, as well as the mainstream press and others, used Orientalist-inflected images and rhetoric to defend the exclusion of those who espoused religions that differed from mainstream Judeo-Christian traditions.

Immigration officials characterized some non-Christian groups as cults. In clear contrast to mainstream religious groups, religious leaders were perceived as having undue influence over their adherents. Native-born women were deemed especially vulnerable to their influence.[4] Those early encounters between the state and immigrants associated with Islam, Hinduism, Theosophy, and Mormonism had enduring consequences for their treatment under U.S. deportation law. Deprived of the ability to establish communities, institutions, and gain political influence alongside groups such as Catholics and Jews, they remained marginalized before the 1965 Hart-Celler Act.

The gender relations, familial roles, and sexual practices within those religions, based in theology, lived traditions, or leadership of the religious representatives in the United States, became flashpoints in immigration enforcement. For example, in the Theosophy case, the religious education and custody of Cuban children were at stake. Immigration officials intervened at the behest of Elbridge T. Gerry, the grandson of Madison's vice president and a leading figure in the New York–based, Protestant-oriented child advocacy group that earlier clashed with Catholic leaders over his efforts to proselytize Catholic orphans in his organization's care.

These cases illustrate how the expanding territorial reach of the United States and the liminal nature of religious traditions in more recently established American territories, such as California, Utah, and Cuba, shaped immigration policy and its enforcement. Opinions about what constituted acceptable religious beliefs were more fluid in western states such as California or Utah than in long-standing incorporated regions. But even in western states, controversies emerged there between local citizens and adherents of religions that were non-Christian or were, by U.S. historical standards, recently established.

The United States' growing economic, military, and related interests in Turkey, Cuba, and Asia and elsewhere played a role in determining who from these regions would be allowed into the country and who would be considered a potential citizen. Historian Matthew Jacobson has discussed how racial perceptions and stereotypes served as justification for the U.S. expansionist project and, conversely, the ways that U.S. imperialism influenced ideologies about race and ethnicity in the United States.[5] Immigration enforcement policy sometimes clashed with larger American foreign policy goals, whereas in other contexts it reinforced those goals.

Many federal officials did not acknowledge the inevitable flow of people, ideas, and resources that arose from global expansionism. The globalizing trends that intensified in the decades following the Civil War also extended to religious life. As the United States expanded its global reach by governing new territories and expanding its core markets and trade relations, people from a broader range of countries developed greater familiarity with American culture and products. Consequently, people in Cuba, India, Turkey, and elsewhere sought to migrate to the United States. Simultaneously, a small but growing number of Americans began embracing religious traditions outside of mainstream Christianity. Leaders and followers of those religions who arrived in the United States or returned from abroad encountered federal immigration laws that had been undergoing significant expansion since the last decades of the nineteenth century. Adherents of those religions came into contact with immigration and other officials, who sometimes lacked the basic context in which to understand non-Christian traditions, their institutions, beliefs, and practices. Nor did they always possess the vocabulary necessary to describe those systems.

Mormons, Turkish Muslims, and the Controversy over the Polygamy Clause

As early as 1883, U.S. government officials had discussed the practice of polygamy as a basis on which immigrants might be classified as undesirable, laying the foundation for efforts to exclude some immigrants from the United States. The Church of the Latter Day Saints was a relatively new religious organization that first originated in the United States in the 1820s. Joseph Smith and his followers trekked across the continent, from

New York, to Nauvoo, Illinois, and ultimately to Utah Territory. By the end of the nineteenth century Mormonism became global, taking hold in Switzerland, Great Britain, and elsewhere in Europe. Some European adherents sought to settle in the United States, where there was a significant Mormon population in Utah. Yet, this aspect of globalization soon came into conflict with federal immigration policy, which imposed strict definitions of who qualified for admission.

In 1883 a group of Mormon "proselytizers" arriving from Switzerland became the subject of correspondence among government officials. Much of the discussion between those at the U.S. Consul in Basel and those regulating immigration at the New York Custom House and at Castle Garden centered on whether the Mormons should be excluded as "paupers." As Mormon "proselytizers" seeking converts, and members of a religion that condoned polygamy, this group faced additional scrutiny. The consul's office further characterized this party of about 100 Mormons as among "the most ignorant and degraded classes of the Swiss profile" and as "being imported to the United States to strengthen the ranks of polygamists."[6] Ultimately the commissioner of immigration determined that the Swiss Mormon immigrants "were not paupers and thus could not be returned to Europe."[7]

When this group of Mormons sought to enter the United States, there was not yet a provision for excluding immigrants on the basis of polygamy. But some government officials expressed concern that allowing a substantial number of Mormons to immigrate might strengthen the indigenous Mormon community in Utah and elsewhere.

Debates over polygamy revealed larger concerns about sexuality, marriage, and religious traditions outside mainstream Christianity—whether those traditions were ancient, as Hinduism or Islam was, new, as with Mormon beliefs, or a blend of ancient and new, as with Theosophy. The antipolygamy movement reached its height in the 1880s, just as a comprehensive federal system for regulating immigration emerged. Widespread antipolygamy activism emerged as a response to Utah territory's quest for statehood, but its roots were deeper. Polygamy was linked not only to slavery and despotic rule but also to ancient Muslim traditions that were viewed by many as antithetical to democratic, civilized, and American values and traditions. Senator Justin S. Morrill, in a speech entitled "Polygamy and Its License," defined polygamy as "Mohammedan barbarism revolting to the civilized world." As Said notes, Europeans had viewed Mohammed as "the disseminator of a false Revelation," and "he became as well the epitome of lechery, debauchery, sodomy, and a whole battery of assorted treacheries, all of which derived 'logically' from his doctrinal postures."[8] Because polygamy was acceptable among both Muslims and members of the Church of the Latter-Day Saints, they were linked together as unacceptable religions in the eyes of some Americans.

Antipolygamy reformers condemned Mormon polygamists in the 1870s. In her petition to Congress for woman's suffrage in Utah, Angela French Newman criticized Mormons for exploiting immigrant women who were "wholly ignorant of our language or laws, or the significance of the franchise, with the odor of the emigrant ship still upon their clothing." Though European, such wives were "as far removed from our idea of womanhood as the earth is removed from the sun." Such fear of polygamy gave rise to the inclusion of polygamists as one of the excludable classes of immigrants in the 1891 immigration law.[9]

Although the Church of the Latter-Day Saints was founded in the United States, it became widely categorized as a foreign and barbarian religion because it allowed polygamy. In fact, very few immigrants practiced or accepted polygamy. Antipolygamy activism was not limited to Mormons. Rather, it was translated into anti-Muslim and anti-immigrant sentiment as it became enshrined in immigration law.

As early as 1910, Muslim immigrants arriving in the United States faced exclusion from the country's ports as a result of their religious beliefs. Islam was considered incompatible with American values, based in significant part on immigration officials' perceptions of Muslims as polygamists.[10] That year, forty-three Muslims from the Ottoman Empire, soon to become the Turkish Republic, were barred entry to the United States over a six-month period on LPC grounds, because of their belief in a religion that allowed polygamy. In its enforcement of that policy, the bureau had determined that simply adhering to the tenets of Islam, rather than actually practicing polygamy, served as sufficient grounds for deportation from the United States. The Imperial Ottoman government, communicating through its embassy in Washington, registered a complaint with the U.S. Department of State about its policy toward Turkish immigrants. The American Embassy in Turkey and, in turn, the U.S. Department of State, advocated for a change in enforcement by Bureau of Immigration officials. The polygamy ban was articulated in section 2 of the Immigration Act of 1907, having been originally addressed in the 1891 law.

The law was a culmination of antipolygamy activism in the nineteenth century, which was widely discussed in debates over Utah statehood.[11]

That addition to the class of inadmissible immigrants occurred in reaction to two episodes. The first was a controversy over the 1903 election of Senator Reed Smoot of Utah, a Mormon leader, and his remarks about the practice of polygamy, which had been banned in Utah.[12] A resulting bill proposed by Congressman Charles Snodgrass of Tennessee in 1900 sought to exclude polygamists from eligibility as senators and congressman. The second was President Roosevelt's 1906 State of the Union Address. That year he declared that it was the federal government's role, not the states', to safeguard "the home life of the average citizen," by providing "Congress the power at once to deal radically and efficiently with polygamy."[13]

From 1910 to 1914, the Department of State, under William Jennings Bryan, urged the Bureau of Immigration to clarify its position on polygamy. In 1910 George Horton, the U.S. ambassador to the Ottoman Empire, had initiated an investigation into the bureau's practice in this matter, a process that would endure for four years. The United States had extended most-favored-nation status to the Ottoman Empire, which was in the process of modernizing its infrastructure and offered substantial investment opportunities for U.S. multinational corporations. This controversy occurred in the decade and a half before the transition from the Ottoman Empire, established in A.D. 1300, to the creation of a modern republic under Mustafa Kemal Atatürk following World War I.[14]

The United States had significant economic interests in Turkey, so there was a strong desire on the part of the Department of State to protect that diplomatic relationship and to address any matters that might harm existing negotiations. Horton emphasized the importance of that economic relationship to immigration officials. He cited a few examples: a pending proposal by the Turkish government to increase customs duties by 4 percent; the "desire of the Turkish Government to secure the abolishment of the Capitulations by virtue of which this government and other foreign powers now exercise extraterritorial jurisdiction in Turkey"; a $150 million railway contract to an American company; potential shipbuilding contracts for Turkish naval warships; and a contract to develop a telephone system in Constantinople by a company affiliated with Western Electric. Turkey also had the potential to provide U.S. corporations with access to oil through pipelines from Central Asia and the Middle East. Horton urged a quick resolution to the polygamy contretemps in order to avoid jeopardizing these interests, but the resolution was prolonged.

The controversy over the exclusion of Turkish Muslims first arose in the Turkish press. On February 22, 1910, *Progrès de Salonique* reported that in the previous few months, Turkish Muslims were being excluded from the United States upon arrival, because of provisions in article 2 of the 1907 immigration law. "The measure which [the U.S. government] had just taken against them is consequently unjust and arbitrary and is prejudicial to the rights, honor and dignity of the Moslems and Turks." The article criticized the U.S. government for detaining the immigrants for a week and estimated that about 200 Muslims had been denied admission on the basis of this provision, a figure that was later contested by the bureau. The article argued that the practice of polygamy among Turkish Muslims was rare and growing increasingly less common and was largely confined to high government and religious officials. Moreover, the article noted that this change in enforcement of policy was not a result of a decision by Congress but as a result of the "chief of emigration in the U.S. who applied it without consulting any one." The author criticized the fact that Turkish immigrants had been making an arduous fifteen-day journey only to be turned back at the U.S. port of entry for reasons related to their religious beliefs.[15]

Such negative press in Turkey about U.S. immigration enforcement undoubtedly discouraged some Muslims there from attempting the trip.[16] Moreover, most immigrants from Turkey were male, who arrived without their families, and most intended to work in the United States only temporarily, so their marital status was of theoretical, rather than practical, importance at that point.

During the past decade, much has been written about the influential role of the Muslim and Arab press in shaping global public opinion about American international policies. This controversy is an early example of the importance of the press in creating a perception of Western bias against the Muslim world. It also highlights the Department of State's public diplomacy role and its efforts to soften some of the hard-line policy positions advanced by other branches of the federal government.

In order to smooth diplomatic relations between the United States and predominantly Muslim countries, State Department officials addressed the immigration matter with Bureau of Labor officials. In 1913 George Horton wrote, "The Embassy requests that, in view of the marked difference between the creed of polygamy, which is admitted by the Moslem faith, and the practice of polygamy, this Department uses its good offices to the end that Ottoman emigrants be no longer subjected, upon their arrival in the United States, to measures excluding them from American territory on account of a purely theoretical consideration."[17] Moreover, there was an additional question as to whether the Turkish immigrants had been duly informed of their right to appeal the decision before being returned to Turkey. Concerns arising from this immigration controversy extended to State Department officials stationed at the American Consul in Cairo, though it is unclear to what extent, if at all, immigrants from Egypt were being excluded because of their Muslim beliefs.[18]

In response to pressure from Horton and other State department officials, the bureau developed a scripted questionnaire for use during Board of Special Inquiry hearings that provided careful instructions about addressing polygamy. It was intended to distinguish between those who practiced polygamy (or intended to practice it) and observant Muslims who did not intend to practice polygamy. The latter group would be allowed entry to the United States. After requesting that the immigrant explain his views on polygamy, the immigrant would be excluded if, in the context of "his intent to sojourn or settle in the United States, . . . the alien believes it is right to take more than one wife." If support for, or intent to practice, polygamy while in the United States remained unclear in the immigrant's response, additional questions would be posed. The immigrant would first be asked whether he was aware that there were laws against polygamy in the United States to determine whether "it would be right for you" to have more than one wife while in the United States. Under this new policy, it remained unclear under which circumstances these questions would be posed—whether it would be limited to cases in which an immigrant was Muslim or from various countries with significant Muslim populations, or to all males arriving at U.S. immigration stations.[19]

Under this new line of inquiry, it appears that if an immigrant stated that polygamy was "right" or an acceptable practice, but he had no intent to practice it, that response would still serve as grounds for exclusion. Further, those Turkish immigrants who relied on language interpreters or who knew only basic English would probably miss some of the nuances implicit in those questions. The questionnaire about polygamy arose in part because at least one Turkish Muslim immigrant was excluded after affirming that polygamy was an acceptable practice within Islam. The transcript of Bou Haikel Darwish's testimony reveals that in response to the question "Do you believe it is right for one man to have more than one wife at the same time?" He responded, "Yes. It is legal to marry seven." The follow-up question was, "But do you personally believe it to be right?" Darwish responded "Yes." Based in part on his responses, Darwish was returned to Turkey.

Though Charles Nagel cited this answer as evidence that Darwish believed in polygamy, one could argue that he was simply affirming that, as a Muslim, this practice was deemed acceptable within his religion's belief system.[20] It remains uncertain whether the newly elaborated polygamy policy did, in fact, clearly distinguish between an immigrant's support of the basic tenets of Islam and his actual intent to maintain or enter into marriage with more than one woman while in the United States.

A similar case arose in Boston when Ismal Mustafa, a widower, and his three-year-old daughter, Haydish, arrived from Marseilles in 1913. He sought entry at the port of Boston with the intention of moving to the industrial city of Lowell to find employment as an ironworker, with the assistance of a half brother who lived there. Mustafa was excluded after his first hearing. He then spoke to a lawyer and appealed the ruling. The commissioner-general concluded that he had changed his story about polygamy in order to be admitted. Initially he did state that he believed in the practice of polygamy, at least in theory. Mustafa was first asked "if it would be right" to have more than one wife while in the United States. The exchange proceeded as follows:

> A. "Yes, sir; but as long as there is one child living I don't like to take another wife."
> Q. If you didn't have this child, do you believe in plural marriages?
> A. Yes, I would if I didn't have this child and my first wife was alive, I would have taken another wife.
> Q. As we understand it, you believe that you are at liberty, according to the Mohammedan Religion, to have four wives?
> A. Yes, if I had money enough to support them.[21]

During his appeal, Mustafa stated that he did not believe in polygamy and later elaborated that: "My decision is that I am not going to take another [wife] while I am alive."[22]

As a result of the continuing controversy about Turkish exclusion issues, Bureau of Immigration officials determined that the polygamy clause was just one strategy to exclude or deport Muslims. As Commissioner-General Albert Caminetti noted, "Frequently, also, persons rejected on this ground [polygamy] could just as well be rejected on some other, such as likely to become a public charge or physically defective."[23] Caminetti offered a solution that would appease the Department of State by using equally effective, but nonreligious, grounds on which to exclude Turkish immigrants from the borders.

By 1914, Turkish Muslims continued to be excluded from the United States because of their religious beliefs rather than their actual practice of polygamy. Immigration officials had excluded nine Turkish immigrants at the Boston port who arrived on two vessels in January of that year, and they were ordered to be returned to Turkey. Youssouf Zia, the ambassador representing the Imperial Ottoman Embassy in the United States, wrote to Secretary of State William Jennings Bryan in protest. He reminded him that Turkey had been granted most-favored-nation status and that there were explicit clauses in the treaties between the two countries that secured the right of Ottoman subjects to immigrate to the United States. He then protested the U.S. government's continued policy of excluding "those Ottoman subjects who profess Mohammedanism. In the absence of a discriminating clause that might justify this action of the authorities concerned and in view of the principle of freedom of conscience accepted by every State, I place sufficient reliance upon your Excellency's well known sense of justice and equity to entertain the hope that you will issue to the said authorities instructions strictly to observe existing treaties."[24]

The Bureau of Immigration defended its actions to State Department officials on several counts. First, it argued that the numbers of immigrants who had been excluded and returned to Turkey was relatively small. In the year ending June 30, 1909, the Bureau of Immigration had denied admission to twenty-four "polygamists," only two of whom were from Turkey. The majority were from East India, with two each from England, Holland, and Syria. But by 1910, the total number of Turkish immigrants excluded on grounds of polygamy had increased to 69. In defending its policy, the bureau pointed out that 864 Turkish immigrants had been admitted that year, so the excluded number was only a small fraction of that total. Bureau officials continued to assert that excluded Muslims were those professing their belief in polygamy and that Turkish immigrants were not being singled out. Moreover, the officials stated that many of those who had been excluded on grounds of polygamy had also been excludable on additional grounds, most commonly those based on their being contract laborers or their likelihood of becoming a public charge.[25]

During the Turkish Muslim polygamy debate, there was also some discussion about the prevalence of polygamy in India. Immigration policies that directly or indirectly influenced immigration were often closely intertwined with racial issues, especially in relation to Hindus and Muslims. Indians were largely excluded on the basis of their racial classification, upheld in the 1923 *Thind* case, a U.S. Supreme Court decision. In that case, Bhagat Singh Thind was determined to be ineligible for U.S. citizenship, because of his racial identity as an Indian from the Asian subcontinent. The *Thind* decision stemmed in part from the 1917 law creating an Asiatic Barred Zone, a region defined as east of the Caucasus, the Ural River, and the Ural Mountains. Immigrants from within those regions would be excluded from entry to the United States. The argument used in deciding the scope of citizenship relied significantly on the question of whether immigrants were eligible for admission. But it also stemmed from the earliest naturalization law, enacted in 1790, that limited citizenship to immigrants who were white. Prior to *Thind*, several Indians, Chinese, Syrians, and Armenians had been granted citizenship, because courts varied widely in their interpretation of which groups were white.[26]

In one sense it was ironic that Thind—a Sikh, World War I veteran, and University of California at Berkeley graduate—and his lawyers advanced the argument in the case that ethnographers had concluded that Indians were part of the original Aryan or Caucasian race. Thus, to argue their case that Indians should be eligible for citizenship, Thind and his lawyers employed the very racial taxonomies that had been used so extensively in the 1911 Dillingham Commission Report to support the 1920s immigration quotas and other racial-based restrictions. They turned those racial classifications on their head by arguing that Indians, not northern Europeans, were the authentic Caucasians or Aryans. Despite these arguments, Thind lost his case, and, by extension, Indians remained ineligible for U.S. citizenship because of the existing American racial definitions embedded in immigration law.[27]

The discussion about polygamy among Indian immigrants revealed that Bureau of Immigration officials were unfamiliar with the religious practices of some of the major religious groups there. For example, the commissioner of immigration of the port of San Francisco stated that at that port it was standard practice to ask "Hindoo aliens" about their belief in the practice of polygamy and that "the invariable answer has been that they neither believe or practice the same." He added that the bureau's "Hindoo interpreter Mr Madge" had advised him that "the Indians that come here are of two religious beliefs, to wit—Singhs [Sikhs] or Hindoo Buddhists, whose teachings are against polygamy, and the Mohammedans, whose religious belief favors polygamy." He further noted that "only the princes and wealthy Indians of Mohammedan belief actually practice polygamy, as the others find it sufficiently hard to support one wife and one set of children in their own country." Of course, rather than just two groups, Mr. Madge had named four major religious groups in India, each with highly distinct traditions.[28] Further, his assessment that immigrants from India stated that they did not practice polygamy contrasts with the bureau's statistics for 1909, in which sixteen of twenty-four immigrants excluded on grounds of polygamy were from East India. Assuming that immigrants practicing polygamy were not all arriving at ports other than San Francisco, this illustrates the significant variability in the way that immigration officials enforced the polygamy ban.[29]

Another deportation controversy occurred in 1913, when Moola Singh and seventy-two other Sikhs (or Hindus) from India residing in the Philippines were deported on LPC grounds upon their arrival in Seattle. The bureau denied their appeal by responding that the single question in the case was whether the immigrants had been denied a hearing. It further cited five federal cases where LPC legislation was upheld—involving three Chinese and two Japanese immigrants.[30]

Many of the religions that were less familiar to Americans differed in significant ways in their leadership structure and gender roles from mainstream Protestant denominations, or even Catholicism. They found new adherents among mainstream American Christians, especially those who tended to be affluent or well educated. Though women also formed a majority of worshipers within many American religious groups, the gender roles and leadership positions within these less familiar groups struck many Americans as unusual at a time when women's rights were shifting in significant ways. Women in these religious groups assumed roles as charismatic leaders, were more active than men, or had differing marital obligations or practices. Such issues led these religions to be viewed as controversial among those charged with immigration law enforcement. By 1910, provisions in immigration law were used to exclude or deport immigrants whose religion allowed the practice of polygamy, whether they were Mormons or Muslims and whether they practiced or intended to engage in polygamy as individuals.

Swami Yogananda Encounters the Board of Special Inquiry

In the 1920s Swami Yogananda, a celebrated Hindu leader later given the honorific title Paramahansa, arrived in the United States. He was an Indian master, or swami, whose mission was to live and teach in the West. Today, he is considered a pioneer by many American practitioners of yoga and meditation. Born Mukunda Lal Ghosh, to well-to-do Bengali parents, he had graduated from the University of Calcutta and studied with Sri Yukteswar Giri, who eventually assigned him to lecture in the West.[31]

Yogananda's mother had a significant influence on his spiritual life. That spiritual relationship might explain why American women in particular would later be drawn to his religious leadership. A striking and attractive figure, with long flowing hair that fell well past his shoulders, he dressed in the traditional garments worn by many Indian religious leaders. He was acquainted with India's nationally revered poet Rabindranath Tagore and in 1935 he met with Mahatma Gandhi at Maganvadi, his ashram near Wardha, at the height of the Indian independence movement.

Paramahansa Yogananda's autobiography, published in 1946, has recently been reissued to an American audience that is increasingly interested in learning more about Hinduism and yoga.[32] W. Y. Evans-Wentz, an American anthropologist on the faculty of Jesus College, Oxford University, wrote the forward to the book's original edition. Though Evans-Wentz's early research was focused on Celtic fairy tales and folklore, he later translated *The Tibetan Book of the Dead* into English and, after living in India for some years, he eventually became a Buddhist monk. Evans-Wentz, like Yogananda, was an early figure in interpreting Eastern belief systems for audiences in the United States and Europe. The *Tibetan Book of the Dead* remains popular among those interested in Buddhism.

Yogananda had other important supporters outside of India. He dedicated his autobiography to Luther Burbank, a friend who was a well-known botanist and preservationist in California. Burbank had served as a character reference for Yogananda, presumably in response to some of the skepticism or condemnation Yogananda encountered on his tour of the United States. In Burbank's open letter, dated December 22, 1924, he stated, "The Swami's idea of right education is plain commonsense, free from all mysticism and non-practicality; otherwise it would not have my approval."[33]

Hinduism is actually not a single, unified religion, but rather comprises a variety of smaller sects that share similar traditions and beliefs. Indians who adhere to this tradition make up about 80 percent of the population of modern India. They believe that humans have four basic goals in life: wealth (*artha*), pleasure or happiness (*kama*), duty or virtue (*dharma*), and liberation from the cycles of existence (*moksha*). Within Hinduism, yoga, a system of meditation and exercise, centered on breathing, is a path to knowledge through spiritual wisdom.[34]

When Yogananda arrived in the United States to lecture about Vedic teachings and to establish centers throughout the United States, relatively little was known about Eastern spirituality. A few decades before his arrival, another Indian religious leader, Swami Vivekananda, had participated in the World's Parliament of Religions at the 1893 Chicago World's Fair to educate westerners about Hinduism. During the nineteenth century there was a growing fascination with Hinduism and other Eastern religions among writers and other intellectuals, including Henry David Thoreau and Walt Whitman in the United States. But most Americans knew very little about religions other than Christianity. Because so few Indians lived in the United States in the nineteenth century, Americans had few opportunities to learn about the religion from adherents themselves. In fact, just over 2,000 Indians were counted in the U.S. Census. In contrast, as a result of Britain's colonial rule of India, and its extensive administrative structure there, there was more cultural exchange between those two countries.[35]

Yogananda originally traveled on a British passport to the United States in 1920, in order to attend an ecumenical conference of world religions in Boston, the International Congress of Religious Liberals, a similar meeting to the World's Parliament of Religions in Chicago. After traveling widely on his U.S. lecture circuit, Yogananda eventually established the Self Realization Fellowship. By the 1930s the organization had more than 150,000 members and had established twenty-five centers located throughout the United States. The fellowship was also known as the Yogoda Sat-Sanga Society, but the group generally used the westernized name in its publications and other printed materials. The major center was located in Encinitas in the greater Los Angeles area. Yogananda's first spirituality book, *Whispers from Eternity*, was published in 1929.

Allegations of financial and moral improprieties led to a 1935 Bureau of Special Inquiry hearing on his return to the United States. But this was far from Yogananda's first encounter with immigration or other U.S. government officials. Indeed, he found himself subject to continual scrutiny by state and federal officials from 1926 to 1936. The members of the Bureau of Special Inquiry interviewed several people who testified on his behalf and others who complained about his behavior. Specifically, the hearing revealed that he was viewed as having an undue influence on wealthy women, some of whom suggested that he acted with impropriety toward them and that he demanded that his adherents cater to his every need. Other issues arose because of a dispute with a former protégé who moved to the United States with him from India.[36]

Foreign-born Christian ministers and other religious leaders were routinely allowed to enter the United States. In fact, they were specifically exempt from restrictions on alien contract labor. The fact that Yogananda had not graduated from a traditional theological seminary created an immigration problem for him. That point became a line of questioning used in his Bureau of Inquiry hearing. Whether it had been appropriate for him to represent himself as a "professor" was another issue of contention raised in his Bureau of Special Inquiry hearing. Professors and ministers were those allowed greater freedom to immigrate to the United States. For example, those two categories were among the classes of workers exempted from the contract labor law under the Immigration Act of February 20, 1907.[37] Because he was not affiliated with a particular seminary or university in the United States, his status became a source of debate. One immigration official stated that to qualify for admission as a professor, an immigrant must have been teaching at a university or seminary for two years prior to entry. The controversy stemmed in part from the supposition that theology and religion were taught in a university or seminary setting. Indeed, religious education through seminaries was not part of the training of religious leaders in India. That Yogananda subsisted on a relatively modest income rather than drawing a traditional annual salary produced skepticism among Bureau of Immigration officials, whose questioning revealed them to be perplexed by his lack of understanding about his own finances.[38]

In 1926 members of the Cleveland Better Business Bureau sent a telegram to the Immigration Bureau and Department of State asking whether there was a record of lawful entry of "a man purporting to be an Indian Swami going under name Swami Yogananda. . . . Please wire place of entry date of entry and profession claimed." In 1929 Yogananda was stopped at the Guadalajara immigration station while seeking to renter the United States after a brief visit to Mexico. Adele Calhoun, the manager of the Los Angeles office of the State of California's Division of Immigration and Housing, also lodged complaints about him with the Bureau of Immigration. Specifically, she questioned whether he "is a fit person to re-enter the United States under the garb of a spiritual teacher."[39] That phrasing suggested that Calhoun and others perceived him to be a charlatan or a huckster.

By 1935 the bureau acknowledged that Yogananda had been under investigation for some time. He was viewed as the leader of a society "which preys upon the weaknesses of women, [yet] we have been unable to penetrate deeply into its mysteries or to secure evidence to warrant the institution of deportation proceedings against any of its alien leaders and members."[40] Much of the evidence raised in Yogananda's hearing and in correspondence among immigration and other government officials was acknowledged to be hearsay and rumor.

The concern that Yogananda was preying on white women and perhaps engaging in sexual relationships with them had a particular resonance in California, a state where antimiscegenation laws had been strictly enforced against relationships between whites and Asians, including Japanese, Chinese, and Filipinos. Indeed, such laws remained in existence and were enforced until 1948. Other laws enacted in this era sought to limit ownership of agricultural land to U.S. citizens because of the fear that Asians were dominating the agricultural economy. One 1933 court decision allowed a Filipino man and a white woman to marry after Filipino organizations argued that Filipinos were not Mongolian but rather Malay, a category not covered by the antimiscegenation law.[41] Gender ratios among Asian immigrants were heavily skewed toward men. That imbalance was a byproduct of the Page Law and subsequent efforts to limit permanent immigration, by making it difficult to establish nuclear families. As was the case in the South among African Americans and whites, while interracial relationships between white men and Asian women were accepted, the reverse was not the case. On occasion, such interracial relationships led to physical violence by white men who intervened to stop them.[42]

Hilda Concorde Brodeur Allen, a disillusioned member of the fellowship, stated in a letter to the Sri Ramakrishna mission in Calcutta her belief that Yogananda "demands blind faith from his followers and to feed this demand, he has created what I shall term a group mind or consciousness which saturates the very air we breathe and envelops each member in a sort of mesmeric clutch so that there exists but one main idea or objective—namely, to worship him."[43] Allen was a New Englander who received a convent education in France. She moved to England and married an Englishman, but they eventually separated. A few years later she recalled that when she returned to the United States, she was particularly drawn to Vedanta philosophy in part because of her "French temperament and natural spontaneity."[44]

In her late thirties, Allen moved to California to live as a "disciple" in Yogananda's center for six years. In her narrative about her relationship with Yogananda, she implies that the two of them had a sexual relationship and that other women at the Center became jealous of her relationship with him. She relates her belief that "I was destined to become the mother of a divine child by S.P. [Swami Paramahansa] and unable to uncover the meaning of my strong impulse, I went to him and tearfully told him about it." According to Brodeur, he dissuaded her from her desire to have him father her child, arguing that it would divert her from her spiritual growth and devotion. She implies that soon after that incident they embarked on a consensual sexual relationship that later became acrimonious because of his interest in other women. Later, she asserted that Yogananda's behavior was inappropriate. Although this relationship might have been inconsistent with the ideals of celibacy that Indian swamis advocated, Yogananda was neither the first nor the last religious figure to influence his female followers to his advantage, nor to expect them to devote themselves to his needs.

Earlier, Ettie Bletch, an unmarried woman from Cleveland, had joined Yogananda and Richard C. Wright, his personal secretary, on his travels, including his trip to see Mahatma Gandhi in Wardha, India. In Yogananda's autobiography, he describes her briefly as "an elderly lady from Cincinnati" who was one of his earliest American followers. The relationship between Bletch and Yogananda was used to illustrate his inappropriate behavior toward women, but there was little evidence to suggest that she was unduly influenced by him.[45]

The other controversy centered on Yogananda's financial situation. Perry Rogers, an assistant to Yogananda, was interviewed by the bureau about Yogananda's financial circumstances and practices, but he offered no tangible evidence supporting a case for deportation, apart from expressing his view that swamis are "'leeches' on society." Others who knew Yogananda, but who were not members of the fellowship, defended his character against criticism and recommended that he be allowed to remain in the United States. He also had a financial dispute with a follower who had left the fellowship.[46]

Many of Yogananda's immigration problems centered on the skepticism with which immigration officials and other Americans viewed non-Christian belief systems. The questions posed by the immigration officials revealed the difficulty they had in interpreting his work and background within the context of traditional, mainstream Christianity. Immigration officials lacked the basic religious vocabulary to interview him effectively about his experiences and to understand his responses. Terms such as minister, preacher, seminary, and church lack precise equivalents in non-Christian religions. In fact, the records reveal that simply using a religious and honorific title was viewed somewhat suspiciously because his religious title and adopted name were referred to as his alias, in contrast to his legal name at birth.

Some of the cultural confusion is evident in the following amusing exchange during his 1926 Bureau of Special Inquiry hearing.

> Q. To what religion did you belong before you joined and organized this new Church?
> A. In India the same only the name is different. It is called Yogoda Satsanga. That is the Indian name for Self Realization Fellowship.
> Q. Well if there was a religion why did you have to organize a new one?
> A. As a branch of the one that is in India.
> Q. Before your master organized this church, did it exist?
> A. How could it exist before he organized it [?].[47]

Ultimately, after the Bureau of Special Inquiry interviewed Yogananda and several witnesses, it voted two to one to allow him to remain in the United States. Yogananda continued to live and teach in California until his death in 1952. He attracted followers who were searching for meaning and community but who looked for it outside of Western religious traditions. Later he became popular with those in the movie business and other wealthy Americans. For example, Doris Duke, heir to the tobacco fortune, became an acquaintance and member of the society that Yogananda founded.[48]

Katherine Tingley, Theosophy, and the Cuban Children Case

The Universal Brotherhood immigration case of 1902, which centered on a major American branch of Theosophy, shared several important characteristics with the Yogananda case. Both cases concerned a religious group whose members had established a significant estate in Southern California and were led by a charismatic leader who was greatly influenced by Eastern religious beliefs and who emphasized mysticism. The United Brotherhood was an organization based on the Theosophical principles of Helena Blavatsky, a Russian immigrant living in London, and an American, Henry Steel Olcott. The two had met in Vermont when they became involved in a society of Spiritualists, which they both ultimately found unsatisfying. Theosophy, or "divine wisdom," emphasized many Indian sacred texts, such as the Vedas and Upanishads, but its leaders did not view Theosophy as directly arising from Hinduism or Buddhism. Instead, they believed that ancient Theosophical beliefs influenced Hinduism and Buddhism. Beginning in 1878, Blavatsky and Olcott had spent several years in India to learn about Hinduism and Buddhism.[49]

In contrast to most European and American religions at the time, women constituted a significant percentage of Theosophy's leaders and adherents. Both Yogananda and Blavatsky sought to make their religions appealing to Americans. Like Yogananda's adherents, many members of the Universal Brotherhood were elite and wealthy, and in that era Theosophy was a transnational movement that was simultaneously gaining popularity in Asia, Europe, and the United States. As with the Yogananda controversy, the immigration case also emerged as a result of charges arising from disaffected members who accused their former leader of being authoritarian and egocentric. Both cases centered on alleged financial and other improprieties of its leaders and the fact that their behavior did not adhere to expected gender and other religious norms. Yet, though race and nationality were both factors in the controversy, in contrast to Swami Yogananda, the religious leaders involved in the Universal Brotherhood case—as well as the founder of the religious organization itself—were white and either American or European.

Theosophy was rooted in Buddhist and Hindu theology and emphasized mysticism. Blavatsky wrote extensively about Theosophical issues in her most famous book *The Secret Doctrine* and several other books, such as *Isis Unveiled*. Blavatsky had established the practice of Theosophy with men from established Anglo-American families, including Henry Steel Olcott, as well as with William Q. Judge, an Irish immigrant living in New York. Writers and intellectuals such as W. B. Yeats found Theosophy particularly appealing. After Blavatsky's death, there were several schisms that occurred within the movement, as it splintered into various branches—one was based in Point Loma, California, on a site overlooking the Pacific.

Michael Ashcraft, a religious historian, argues that Theosophy was associated with millennialism and served as an appealing alternative to Christianity for many mainstream Protestants in the United States. California, he notes, had a much lower percentage of Protestants than on the East Coast, where the majority of the American population belonged to Protestant denominations. In contrast, just 14 percent of Californians identified themselves as Protestant, and the majority was not active in any religious community. Therefore, this less traditional religious environment was an ideal location for Theosophy and other religions to flourish.[50]

Point Loma, 1919. (Prints and Photographs Division, Library of Congress)

Katherine Wescott Tingley led the Theosophy branch established at Point Loma. Tingley, born in 1847 in Newbury, Massachusetts, was one of several leaders vying to succeed Blavatsky after her death. Tingley, along with others in the Theosophical movement, formed the United Brotherhood, an organization that remained separate from that of Annie Besant and William Judge, who formed the Theosophical Society, known as Adyar, after the location of the Theosophical organization headquarters in India. Theosophical leaders including Henry Olcott, Countess Wachtmeister, and Annie Besant publicly criticized the United Brotherhood and Tingley's leadership of the group. Robert Crosbie, an initial ally of Tingley, later broke from her organization and established another group, the United Lodge of Theosophists.[51]

In her youth Tingley led a typical life for a nineteenth-century upper-middle-class woman in New England, where her father owned a lumber company and hotel. She was raised as a Congregationalist and, as a young woman, established a society to visit hospitals and prisons and was active in mission work. Hardly conventional for a nineteenth-century woman of her socioeconomic status, however, was the fact that she had been divorced twice before her marriage to Philo Tingley in her early forties. Her husband moved to Point Loma with her but maintained a low profile in the organization. Tingley's willingness to flout convention in her personal relationships was probably a major factor in drawing her to Theosophy. In 1894 she joined the Theosophical Society, which sought to develop a following throughout the world.[52]

A widely publicized immigration case emerged shortly after questions arose about Tingley's leadership in the New York newspapers by disaffected members of her society in Point Loma, California. The immigration investigation arose as a result of Point Loma society's school, which actively recruited students from abroad, including Cuba. The *Los Angeles Times*, purchased by Harry Chandler and Harrison Gray Otis in 1882, was particularly disdainful of her in its extensive coverage of her activities.[53] In fact, as a result of their sensationalistic coverage of the Brotherhood and her role as a leader, she won a libel suit against the newspaper, along with a modest settlement of $7,500.[54]

Tingley presided over a large estate that included the Lotus School, a boarding school that enrolled children from throughout the world. Children had become increasingly important in the activities of the United Brotherhood, and orphans and other disadvantaged children were among the residents at Point Loma. The children of members of the United Brotherhood were often intentionally separated from other children, who remained under the care of other adults on the estate. The organizations' emphasis on a particular diet and manner of dress, in loose gowns and uniforms, also became an object of fascination among journalists who covered Tingley and her religious organization.[55]

Theosophy's challenge to the primacy of the nuclear family in the decades following the Victorian era and Point Lomas's accumulation of substantial resources from some elite members generated a great deal of hostility. Controversies arose when members of a family challenged the right of the school to prevent parents from seeing children, especially when the parents were estranged from each other. The *Los Angeles Times* reported that because children lived separately from their parents, "Tingley Had Scorn for 'Mother Love.'"[56] A second controversy emerged when George Patterson, the son of Harriet Thurston, an elderly member of the Point Loma community, contested his mother's will. Thurston had bequeathed Tingley an estimated $300,000.[57] That Theosophy was not rooted exclu-

Katherine Tingley, ca. 1919. (Prints and Photographs Division, Library of Congress)

Children at Point Loma, 1919. (Prints and Photographs Division, Library of Congress)

sively in a Christian tradition but was heavily influenced by Asian religions was yet another source of discomfort among Tingley's critics.[58]

Dr. Gertrude Wyckoff Van Pelt, a physician who had emerged as a leader in the Universal Brotherhood organization, made a trip to Cuba in 1902 on Tingley's behalf. On her return to the United States, she brought with her a second group of Cuban children to be enrolled in the school. Van Pelt was a remarkable figure. She was born in Elizabeth, New Jersey, in 1856. After obtaining her undergraduate education at Cornell, she entered the Woman's Medical College of Philadelphia in 1886. There she wrote a thesis on obstetrics. Later she published a medical textbook on diseases of the stomach and trained in Paris at the end of the nineteenth century. She was also a member of the Massachusetts Medical Society.

Van Pelt might have developed an interest in Theosophy through a fellow student at the Women's Medical College. Anandibai Joshee, who graduated with Van Pelt in their class of thirty-three women, was lauded as the first Indian woman to attend medical school in the United States. It is possible that Van Pelt was first exposed to India and Hinduism in that context, and her interest later drew her to Theosophy. After becoming involved in Theosophy, Van Pelt continued publishing but switched her focus from medical research to Theosophical subjects.[59]

The major immigration case involving Tingley's leadership and Theosophy occurred in 1902, four years after the Spanish-American War. Cuba had come under the close control of the United States after Spain was effectively expelled from the island, and Cuban officials supported U.S. sugar and tobacco interests. Tingley and other Theosophists had been involved in war relief efforts in Cuba. Following four centuries of Spanish rule, the Catholic Church held a virtual monopoly over organized Cuban religious life. Now that rule had ended. Tingley viewed Cuba, newly associated with American expansionism, as a new frontier for Theosophy. She sought to expand her schools internationally, including in London and in Santiago.

After the Spanish-American War, Tingley saw the opportunity to spread Theosophy to a new population in much the same way that American and European Christians had viewed China and Japan as a region ripe for religious expansionism in the mid- to late nineteenth century. In several significant ways, Tingley's plan to create new Raja Yoga centers paralleled American capitalists' drive to develop new markets in Cuba, the Philippines, and other newly acquired territories. In fact, U.S. officials established vital military and naval bases in both countries, along with establishing an American-based educational system in the Philippines, which ultimately led to English becoming a lingua franca among those receiving a formal education.

By 1902, Tingley had become the subject of a series of sensationalistic articles in the *Los Angeles Times*. The notoriety that arose from that press coverage led to an investigation of the Cuban children's immigration status. The fact that the religious organization was led by a powerful, twice-divorced woman was certainly a factor in the negative *Los Angeles Times* coverage. The Point Loma community was referred to as the "spookery," its adherents "spooks," and Tingley herself was derided as a "High Priestess," "Purple Mother," and the "Purple She."[60] Passages such as this one about the benefits of railroad expansion in Southern California which included gratuitous remarks about Tingley were typical of the attitudes toward the Point Loma Theosophists: "The only dangerous obstacle we see . . . is that Mrs. Katherine Tingley might, for some esoteric reason or other forbid the work. She might, perhaps, fear that the construction of such a steel belt around the world would interfere with the transmission of esoteric electrical influences between the Mahatmas who roost on the high tableland of Central Thibet, and the spooks who stroll around at midnight in their nightgowns."[61]

In the course of the Bureau of Special Inquiry hearing, Dr. Van Pelt maintained that the Lotus School's work with children in Cuba originated when Katherine Tingley visited Cuba "under the direction of President McKinley; her work was recognized by the Government, and she became known to a great many people there; they all loved her."[62] At that point, the Lotus School had an enrollment of about 150 students, 35 of whom were from Santiago, Cuba. The *Los Angeles Times* criticized Tingley's work in Cuba but was equally critical of Cubans themselves. Using language typical of those who sought to colonize, it complained, "Cuba is acting toward the United States like a spoiled child; and that is what comes from coddling. And when she gets in trouble again, it is to this country that she will look for succor, with the surety of finding it. How sharper than a serpent's tooth it is to have a thankless republic sitting out there in drink and making faces at us."[63]

Most of the children who were traveling with Van Pelt from Santiago, Cuba, to California via Ellis Island were under twelve and from poor families. Van Pelt asserted that the parents of the children had urged her to take their children to the United States so that they would be educated and that they had given her their legal consent to do so. Van Pelt further claimed that she had brought the children to the United States with the approval of Alderman Bacca from Santiago, as well as having had received legal authorization from their families.[64] The attorney representing Tingley and Van Pelt, D. Emery, argued in an immigration hearing that Van Pelt had received permission from the children's parents, who had signed documents that were notarized by an attorney and brought to the American consul in Cuba.[65]

The children's deportation hearing occurred following their debarkation at Ellis Island. Elbridge T. Gerry, the founder of the Society for the Prevention of Cruelty for Children had filed a complaint with immigration officials. When the children arrived at Ellis Island with Dr. Van Pelt, they were detained on grounds that they were likely to become public charges. Gerry had been a major figure in the child-saving movement of the nineteenth century, a largely evangelical Protestant movement that sought to place impoverished, homeless, and orphaned children in Christian homes. William A. Williams, the commissioner for immigration for Ellis Island, was also involved in the case, one of several highly publicized controversies that occurred during his tenure. The case emerged in large part from the negative publicity from the series of articles in the *Los Angeles Times*, which were used extensively in the Board of Special Inquiry hearing.[66]

Religious conversion became a significant source of controversy. Most of the children had been raised as Catholics, and one was Presbyterian. Van Pelt's attempt to enroll them in a school run by adherents of Theosophy was portrayed in the immigration hearing as an attempt at religious conversion. But each of the children interviewed stated that their parents had arranged for them to go to California, obtain an education, become fluent in English, and return to Cuba permanently. That Gerry's intervention should lead to objections that Catholic children were being converted to Theosophy was ironic, given that Protestant "child-saving" organizations had long been accused by Catholic leaders of removing Catholic children from orphanages or poor homes in New York and placing them with Protestant families.[67]

Sensationalistic accounts of life at Point Loma, along with allegations regarding the past sexual history of Katherine Tingley, were entered into evidence at the Bureau of Special Inquiry appeal hearing to determine the fate of the Cuban children. Edward Parker and others testified that Tingley's brother was reputed to be a notorious gambler and accused Katherine of being a neglectful wife and parent. He also testified at the Bureau of Special Inquiry hearing that she was rumored to have been, beginning in her hometown of Newburyport, Massachusetts, at the age of twelve, a promiscuous character who had broken up at least one home, drank liquor, refused to pay her debts, and that she had been involved in other "notorious" activities.[68]

Van Pelt, who had appealed the case on behalf of the Point Loma society, arranged for others in the United Brotherhood to provide testimony on Tingley's behalf. Her supporters included Mr. A. G. Spalding, whose family manufactured tennis and other sporting equipment. Spalding and his wife, Elizabeth, were long-term members of the United Brotherhood. Spaulding assured immigration officials that the students' educational and living expenses would be provided for at the school and added that his own children were enrolled there.[69]

The appeal was denied, and the children were ordered returned to Cuba. Ultimately, however, the secretary of treasury, L. M. Shaw, soon moved to intervene in the case. The Bureau of Immigration took the case under review.[70] Frank Sergent made a visit Point Loma to inspect the school and the facilities on the compound. He concluded that the facilities were acceptable, and there was "nothing about it which was likely to injure the morals of the Cuban youngsters." Sergent recommended that the students be allowed to travel there for their education. As a result, the children were released and allowed to proceed to Point Loma as planned. His visit sparked renewed controversy in the *Los Angeles Times*. One article implied that he was biased toward Tingley, while local members of the Society for Prevention of Cruelty to Children were denied a similar opportunity to inspect the school, having been stopped at the "Egyptian gates" of the compound.[71] That description embodied the Orientalism articulated by Said. In the years following the hearing, additional Cuban students were recruited to Point Loma. In 1906 Tingley visited Cuba to inspect the Raja Yoga centers in Santiago and work on her plans to establish others in Havana.[72]

Federal immigration authorities regulated the practice of new religious traditions in the United States by monitoring the flow of peoples who espoused those beliefs in ways that rendered it more difficult for the diffusion of beliefs to occur. By interrogating immigrants in some groups about their religious beliefs in ways that differed from those in more mainstream groups, the U.S. government's early regulation efforts effectively hampered the development of new religious communities in the United States. This religious diffusion was a direct result of American and European global economic and territorial expansionism and the cultural exchange that was a natural outgrowth of that process. But for many in the public and within the federal government, the importation of unfamiliar beliefs across U.S. borders was perceived as a threat to American social norms.

Among Muslims and others associated with polygamy, Hindu groups, and Theosophists, gender roles and behavior became highly contentious. Local officials, religious leaders, and the press highlighted the exoticism of these religions and called for the U.S. Immigration Bureau to intervene to protect existing religious and cultural norms. The impact that these religions had upon supposedly vulnerable women was another significant concern. Race had an important impact on larger public perceptions about these religious traditions, even when most of the leaders and adherents in those communities were white. Therefore, Mormons were equated with Muslims because of their shared belief in polygamy and, by implication, exploitation of women. Theosophy became Oriental because of its associations with Hinduism, Buddhism, and non-Western dress, as well as its perceived threat to the Victorian family structure.[73] The feminization of religion, as exemplified by Yogananda's strong following among women and by Katherine Tingley's and Gertrude Van Pelt's leadership roles, also drew scrutiny among those in the public and in the press.

Historians have examined how many racialized provisions in U.S. law have been rectified since the passage of the 1965 Hart-Celler Act, but few have studied the early mechanisms that excluded or deported immigrants on the basis of their religious beliefs. But as this chapter illustrates, the enforcement of policies based on religious traditions and practices have had long-term implications for the development of American religious life. Those facing bias because of widespread unfamiliarity or discomfort with their religious traditions do so in part because these religious communities have emerged as relatively recent features of American life and, rather than being diffused widely, have remained concentrated in certain cities and regions of the country. Though never as numerous as those excluded or deported on racial, LPC, or medical grounds, the ways that immigrants were affected in these three major cases demonstrate how immigration authorities challenged the right of some religious adherents to practice their religion freely and to benefit from the cultural interactions that were an outgrowth of American expansionism and globalization that intensified in the late nineteenth century.

The United States' increased global political and economic power intensified cultural exchanges far beyond Europe, and led to greater familiarity with American institutions, values, and opportunities. That resulted in greater immigration from such regions, including India, Cuba, and Turkey, where the U.S. presence became a familiar one. But many Americans were unprepared for the immigration that resulted from American expansionism, leading to greater conflicts about religious values at its borders.

DEPORTATION BASED ON POLITICS, LABOR, AND IDEOLOGY

In the wake of World War I and the Russian Revolution, immigrants in the United States faced intense scrutiny about their political activities, beliefs, and especially their labor activism. Deportation became a critical mechanism used to control and discourage political dissent. Higher levels of deportations have tended to occur following national crisis and insecurity—World War I, the Great Depression, the Cold War, and most recently 9/11. World War I led to a major suspension of civil liberties throughout American society, most notably with the enactment of the Espionage Act of 1917, Sedition Act of 1918, and the Alien Law of 1918. Those laws, though directed primarily toward immigrant radicals, created an opening to limit protections to noncitizens following the war. World War I provided a context in which corporations could condemn strikes and strikers as antithetical to patriotism, successfully fusing the imperatives of industrial production with nationalist ideology. An understanding of the rise of state mechanisms, including the FBI and its precursor, to deport immigrants who were considered ideological threats provides significant insight into the ways that control of immigrants expanded well beyond regulation at the point of entry to the policing of immigrants' daily activities sometimes decades after their arrival.[1]

Beginning with William Preston's *Aliens and Dissenters: Federal Suppression of Radicals, 1903–1933*, most accounts of U.S. political and labor deportation efforts have focused on Russian and Eastern European communists and anarchists, and with the notable exception of Emma Goldman, on men. But politically motivated deportation efforts continued on a smaller scale in the decades between the Palmer Raids and the McCarthy era, as illustrated by the Marcus Garvey, Claudia Jones, and Harry Bridges cases.

The lack of attention to Garvey's and Jones's cases by historians emanates in part from a narrow definition of political activism and ideology. But by broadening the definition of politics to include social movements that focus on racial equality and labor rights, we can understand that federal authorities were concerned about immigrants beyond communists and anarchists. Immigration Service and Justice Department officials characterized the ideologies that some immigrants brought across borders as threats to the political and industrial system in the United States.

The Palmer Raids have particular salience for understanding current removal procedures in the post-9/11 period. Attorneys for the Department of Justice, for example, have cited the deportations following those raids to bolster their contention that closing deportation hearings to the public are not without precedent. A well-known directive from Immigration Judge Michael Creppy, issued on September 21, 2001, stated that "special issue" deportation hearings would exclude family and friends. This decision was soon challenged. The Palmer Raids serve as an earlier example of how in an era of perceived national emergency and in cases of a threat against national security, open deportation hearings were prohibited. Another parallel between 9/11 and the Red Scare was that in each case federal legislation was passed to extend the powers granted to the federal government for an indeterminate period, without a clear beginning and end point, as is the case during a conventional war such as the U.S. Civil War.[2]

Immigrants, many of whom were not yet citizens, were particularly vulnerable to deportation because of the lack of full constitutional protections afforded them. The 1919 deportation of Emma Goldman, Alexander Berkman, and almost 250 others from New York to Russia on the *Buford*, nicknamed the "Soviet Ark," has been well documented. Other immigrants faced deportation in that era, including Louis Wirth, a German immigrant who would later become a major figure in American sociology and a faculty member at the University of Chicago.

The Palmer Raids, undertaken by Attorney General A. Mitchell Palmer, led to what Louis F. Post, the dissenting assistant secretary of labor, later termed a "deportations delirium." Palmer undertook the action after several bombs were sent through the federal mail system and another damaged Palmer's house. These bombs were never traced to a particular group or individual. By the early 1920s, the Bureau of Immigration had issued 6,328 warrants of arrest to immigrants who were charged with deportable offenses. Ultimately, 1,119 of those warrants were sustained, and those immigrants were ordered deported.[3] Later in the 1920s anticommunist and antianarchist sentiment subsided, but the pressure to deport communists and anarchists mounted again in the 1930s, when the Committee on Immigration and Naturalization held hearings on the International Workers of the World (IWW), a radical union headed by Bill Haywood that was especially active in the West. In 1912, the IWW had organized large strikes among textile workers in Lawrence, Massachusetts, and elsewhere in the Northeast. Samuel Dickstein of New York chaired that committee and worked closely alongside members Martin Dies, a fervent anticommunist congressman from Texas, and Albert Johnson, cosponsor of the earlier national-origins legislation.

The federal deportation mechanism became an effective strategy for curtailing the importation of ideas and activists who worked on behalf of grass-roots social or political change. Since the Civil War, the United States economy had benefited from labor migrations from Europe, Mexico, and Asia, which fueled its industrial, agricultural, and geographic growth. U.S. corporations imported raw materials from those global regions and marketed finished products there. But the importation of social movements and ideologies from those regions, whether political, religious, labor, or economic, posed a danger that required curtailment at the border. Deporting immigrant activists became an important capability of the bureaucratic infrastructure to monitor and control immigration. It occurred in tandem with the emergence of visa and passport control at points of departure, which Aristide R. Zolberg has termed the "remote control" process of regulating immigration.[4]

Just before the first Red Scare, an incident occurred in Bisbee, Arizona, that is central to the narrative of the history of western labor and the Progressive Era. In 1917 the Bisbee Deportation, as it is known, was a roundup and removal of immigrant workers from a location rather than a physical expulsion from the United States, as the more common use of the term deportation suggests. Nevertheless, because it occurred shortly before the Red Scare, targeted immigrant laborers, and sought to vanquish a radical labor movement, the Bisbee incident shares several similarities with the traditional deportation process as one in which the state physically removes immigrants from a nation.

Bisbee was a copper mining company town. Its largest employer, Phelps Dodge, owned the stores and newspaper and provided housing and much of the town's infrastructure. The long-standing union, the International Union of Mine, Mill, and Smelter Workers (formerly affiliated with the Western Federation of Miners) organized in Bisbee in 1916. But mine workers viewed that union as ineffective, so the IWW began a successful organizing campaign there.[5]

Before the strike, Harry Wheeler, the sheriff of Cochise County, Arizona, drew a distinction between the rights afforded to U.S. citizens and those who were aliens. He pledged to "protect all men in the constitutional rights as citizens of this state and of the United States of America and all aliens in peaceful pursuit of their daily labor or vocations." His view of immigrants' rights was a narrow one, focusing solely on their right to continue working in the United States or freedom to contract, in contrast to broader political and other rights accorded to U.S. citizens. He cast the strikers as disloyal and unpatriotic for their disruptive potential to the copper industry. He stated that he was prepared to deputize "every able-bodied loyal American in Cochise county" to preserve peace and order.[6]

The United States' entry into the war made it possible to cast strikers as unpatriotic because copper was a strategic resource necessary to industrial production. G. W. Dowell, manager of the Copper Queen Branch of Phelps Dodge, portrayed the strike as nothing less than political treason. L. C. Shattuck of the Shattuck Arizona Copper company condemned the imminent strike as "a nation-wide conspiracy by enemies of the United States government to restrict [or cut off] the copper output required to prosecute the war."[7]

The following day, a group of around 1,000 "of the leading business men and citizens of this district" formed a Citizen's Protective League. As the strike proceeded into July, the rhetoric escalated. During a meeting of 500 citizens in Globe, a resolution was passed declaring the IWW to be a "public enemy," denouncing the strike tactics as "terrorism," and calling for the suppression of public assemblies organized by the IWW.[8]

The Bisbee strike and subsequent roundup and removal garnered national attention. The *Los Angeles Times*, a probusiness newspaper owned by the Chandler family, condemned the IWW workers as agitators who are "for the most part foreigners; and the hatred towards our government may be traced in many of them to jail sentences following such indiscretions as theft and burglary." More than 200 armed guards carried out the removal of workers and others from Bisbee. Two people were killed in the process—a shift boss at the mine and a miner, who was thought to have fired the fatal shot. Many of the men who were deported from Bisbee neither were members of the IWW nor were they striking, but some had refused to cross the picket line. The telegraph office was shut down to prevent strikers and those sympathetic to them from contacting government authorities or relatives.[9]

Police rounded up the protesting miners and brought them to Hermanas, an isolated town where they were stranded. They were then moved to the town of Columbus, where they were held against their will from July 14 to mid-September.[10] Of the 900 workers who were forcibly removed from Bisbee, many were immigrants. More than one-quarter of the workers were from Mexico, where most workers in the state originated. Though Mexicans did not have a major reputation for radical labor activism in the United States in this era, they formed a substantial portion of the mine workers in the Southwest. Among Europeans, many were either from Finland (seventy-six) or from the countries that until recently composed the former Yugoslavia: Serbia, Bosnia, Croatia, and Montenegro (eighty-six). These European regions were adjacent to Russia, then in the throes of revolution. Many Finns arriving in the United States in this era brought with them radical views about labor.[11] Few among those deported returned to Bisbee. In fact, some were ultimately deported from the United States to their countries of origin, although it remains unclear how many.[12]

President Woodrow Wilson appointed a commission, led by Secretary of Labor William B. Wilson, to investigate the Bisbee Deportation. Commission members acknowledged significant problems with the raid. But the Department of Labor justified some of the actions as an outgrowth of wartime contingencies. As the report asserted, "Battles are fought not only between armed men but between the factories, workshops, and mines of the contending nations. Consequently upon the outbreak of hostilities it became one of our first concerns to keep in motion the wheels of our industrial machine."[13]

Bisbee shared many of the attributes of other politically motivated deportation efforts that occurred between World War I and World War II. Immigrant-led movements to improve the lives of working Americans were sometimes charged with being unpatriotic or, in some cases, treasonous. Constitutional protections, including free speech and other guaranteed rights, were denied to immigrants and in some cases suspended for U.S. citizens. Under Palmer, J. Edgar Hoover was successful in usurping the deportation function from the Department of Labor when immigrant activity was defined as political. In 1940 the federal immigration regulation function, which was defined as a labor issue from its 1882 inception, would in its entirety migrate to the Department of Justice, where it remained until 2002. National security concerns became a pretext for government efforts to expel social activists, even though their aim was primarily directed toward peacefully addressing social and economic disparities.

The Palmer Raids and the Rise of the FBI

Immigration deportation efforts between World War I and the late 1950s coincided with the rise of the FBI as one of the most powerful agencies within the federal government. J. Edgar Hoover was central to the surveillance that led to the deportation of political and social activists, and he worked to ensure that the Bureau of Investigation (BI), later the FBI, removed control over the deportation process of political activists from immigration officials in the name of national security. Although Hoover is best known for his role in the McCarthy era, and his subsequent wiretapping of the Kennedy brothers and Martin Luther King Jr., his enormous influence within the domestic intelligence sphere dates back to the Palmer Raids. His surveillance of political activists and other well-known figures in American life seems to have been fueled by a volatile mixture of self-righteous morality, jealousy, racial prejudice, sexual repression, and a desire to accumulate power.[14]

Hoover usurped political deportations from Bureau of Immigration control, though it remained an administrative rather than a criminal procedure. The Bureau of Investigation pursued aggressively those it deemed political agitators and later handled the deportation hearings of many immigrants who were detained for violation of Section 22. J. Edgar Hoover was committed to the deportation of Berkman and Goldman and intervened personally to ensure that the federal government acted quickly. He also ensured that Goldman's bail was set at $15,000, a very high sum for that era. Hoover dispatched agents to Rochester and Chicago to interview Goldman's family members and others to determine whether she was a U.S. citizen.[15]

Hoover targeted mainly communists and anarchists but also leaders of popular grass-roots social movements, such as the Caribbean immigrants Marcus Garvey and Claudia Cumberbatch Jones, a communist and labor activist. Hoover viewed Garvey's popular United Negro Improvement Association (UNIA) as a destabilizing force, because of Garvey's strong critique of racism, the economic system, and his movement's potential to gain a large membership base throughout the United States and internationally. Therefore, because it was a grass-roots movement, it shared some similarities with communist activism, though Garvey argued that communism had been an ineffective movement. In fact, Garvey had initially tolerated Wilfred Domingo's socialist perspectives, which were increasingly evident in the UNIA publication, *Negro World*. But Garvey soon drove his old friend out of UNIA when socialist papers began commenting favorably on Domingo's views, and Garvey decided that Domingo was a liability. Ironically Garvey and Alexander Berkman were incarcerated in the same prison—the Federal Penitentiary in Atlanta—while serving sentences for relatively minor crimes (urging noncompliance with conscription laws and mail fraud, respectively), and each faced immediate deportation charges upon his release.[16]

A major issue in court cases and other debates about the deportation of communists, anarchists, and members of the IWW was whether these organizations advocated or supported the overthrow of the U.S. government through the use of force or violence. After the Socialist Party split in 1919, communists formed two organizations in the United States, the Communist Labor Party of America and the Communist Party of America, drawing heavily from those active in the Socialist Party. Although membership in the Socialist Party itself was not a violation of 1917 immigration law that expanded the class of deportable immigrants to include political radicals, those immigrant socialists whose membership chapters voted to affiliate with one of two communist parties found themselves at risk for deportation.

Several legal scholars, including Judge Learned Hand, Zechariah Chafee, and George Anderson, argued that the Communist Party did not advocate the use of violence and thus its members were not subject to deportation simply because they were members of the party. In Sam Nelson's case, Hand concluded: "The only thing that I can derive from the record is that [Nelson] believes that there is an irreconcilable conflict between employer and employee and he believes that fruits and even instruments of production belong to the worker."

A relevant question in such deportation proceedings and court cases became whether the immigrant advocated sabotage or the willful destruction of property. That question presented a much lower threshold than whether one advocated the use of force to overthrow the federal government.[17] The IWW came under intense scrutiny following its successful 1912 strike in Lawrence, Massachusetts.

Family reunification issues become a widely employed argument against political deportation, as it did for many other types of cases. For example, Louis Post addressed the procedure's effect on mixed citizenship status families. He specifically stated that in cases in which "the alien is the father of children born in the United States, and therefore constitutional American citizens, and who are dependent upon and receive from him parental support, every fair doubt regarding membership within the purview of the statute will be accorded."[18]

In addition to Louis Post, several other individuals and organizations protested the effect of the Palmer Raids on the immigrant community. The Foreign Language Information Service (FLIS), an immigrant advocacy organization that emerged from the Committee on Public Information, an organization led by George Creel, mobilized public support for World War I. A FLIS administrator registered a strong complaint to Robert Scott, secretary to A. Mitchell Palmer. He compared the physical aftermath of the widespread raids on the offices of radical organizations to "a Belgian house after a Hun raid." He contended that immigrants had a legitimate argument when they asserted that "they are being treated no better than they used to be under the old tyrannical regime in their own country. Their lives and property are in danger."[19]

In his book, *Freedom of Speech*, Zechariah Chafee, a First Amendment scholar on the Harvard Law School faculty, argued that a major constitutional distinction existed between a belief in communism, socialism, or anarchism, which was protected by the law, and advocating the overthrow of the U.S. government by force. Those beliefs, he asserted, were clearly protected, and any attempts to deport immigrants because of their membership in radical political parties or labor unions was unconstitutional. In fact, many of those charged with deportable offenses after the widespread raids in New England were ultimately released, with the claim, "The Communist Party does not advocate 'force and violence.'"[20]

Chafee criticized A. Mitchell Palmer for his statement, "The best way to keep order was to attack the spreaders of agitation by means of the deportation statute." Chafee further called for the American people "to be startled out of their complacent acquiescence in these raids by the confinement of hundreds of their fellow citizens in jails, without the slightest charge of crime or possibility of such charge under any law of the United States."[21]

Chafee noted that some of those detained were U.S. citizens. For example, Peter Frank of Massachusetts was required to submit proof of his U.S. citizenship, even though he was born in the U.S. and had always resided within the country. Chafee argued that the Deportation Act of 1918 would not be limited to communists, but could be employed to break up many other organizations.[22] He emphasized that there was a vast chasm between "the ballot and the bomb," asserting that a "general strike may be more effective against a government than an armed rebellion." Another of his objections to the deportation raids was the widespread assumption of guilt by association.[23] Chafee's arguments also reflected the Jeffersonian view that rebellion against the prevalent government was not inherently dangerous, noting that the United States was founded on such an act.

In addition to constitutional scholars and jurists, others protested the broad powers that the Sedition and Espionage acts gave federal authorities in their efforts to deport politically active immigrants. A. J. Liebling, a New York journalist, noted that the deportation laws passed in this era were crafted so broadly that "an alien who dropped a penny in the hat passed around by an Unemployed Council speaker or who bought a copy of the *Daily Worker* could, in the heat of any industrial dispute, be deported."[24] Other critics noted that language barriers had led some immigrants to add their names to communist or anarchist party membership lists without understanding the significance of their actions.

Emma Goldman and Alexander Berkman

The best-known deportation case in the United States involved anarchists Emma Goldman and Alexander Berkman who, by the time of their deportation to Russia in 1919, were leading radicals who has established political journals and lectured widely. Goldman arrived in New York City from St. Petersburg, Russia, as a young woman, after living briefly in Rochester. She came to the United States to escape an unhappy family life, wishing especially to gain independence from her authoritarian father. Many of her family members eventually immigrated to New York State. She became drawn to anarchism while a factory worker and was influenced by Johann Most, a German American anarchist, and others. In addition to her political activism on free speech and antiwar issues, her work as a nurse and midwife led her to advocate for women's access to contraception, sexual equality, and other feminist beliefs. By 1906, she had founded *Mother Earth* magazine and lectured widely to support its publication. She forged a long political and personal partnership with Alexander Berkman, a fellow anarchist, who edited the *Blast* from offices in the same building.[25]

Berkman had become notorious for his attempt to assassinate Henry Clay Frick, Andrew Carnegie's business partner, during the Homestead strike at Carnegie Steel in Pittsburgh in 1892. He was convicted and served a fourteen-year prison sentence. Goldman was not with Berkman in Pittsburgh, nor was she implicated in planning the event. But she too had a criminal record. In 1893, she was arrested and sentenced to a year in prison after her conviction on an incitement-to-riot charge for a New York speech she gave to a group of unemployed people during the severe economic depression that year. She had been arrested several other times in the years leading up to her 1917 trial.[26]

Although the pair would not be deported until 1919, their public opposition to federal registration and conscription laws once the United States entered World War I in 1917 ultimately led to their expulsion from the United States. Beginning in January 1917, Bureau of Investigation and other agencies placed Goldman and Berkman under close surveillance in their public and private activities relating to their antiwar positions.[27]

It was in 1907 that Goldman's political beliefs first brought her under close federal scrutiny and rendered her vulnerable to deportation. In November, U.S. commissioner for immigration Oscar Straus had written to Robert Watchhorn, commissioner of immigration at Ellis Island, recommending that Goldman face a Board of Special Inquiry hearing because, as an anarchist, she was a member of the classes deportable under in the 1903 and 1907 immigration acts. Ultimately, Straus decided not to pursue deportation, because of Goldman's twenty-two-year U.S. residency and the legal ambiguity of the term "alien."[28]

In late June 1917, Goldman and Berkman chose to represent themselves at trial following their arrest. They were charged with advocating that American men refuse to comply with the conscription law requiring draft registration. Berkman and Goldman argued that the law was unconstitutional because it violated the provision against "involuntary servitude." They freely acknowledged having organized against the conscription law, published articles criticizing it, and mailing letters denouncing it. Lincoln Steffens and John Reed were among the well-known witnesses providing testimony.[29]

The prosecution, led by Harold Content, assistant U.S. attorney, argued that Goldman and Berkman had conspired to incite the public to violate federal law, bringing into evidence their publications *Mother Earth* and the *Blast*, their establishment of an organization known as the No-Conscription League, and transcripts of their public lectures, including one on May 18 at Harlem River Park and Casino. At that protest, soldiers and sailors disrupted the meeting. Goldman and others involved in the No-Conscription League had initially planned a public meeting of mothers of draft-age sons, but they later expanded it to include a broader audience.[30]

The prosecutor sought to establish that Goldman advocated violence in her speech and that Goldman and Berkman used the mail to advocate that people resist registering for the draft. Yet none of the several witnesses called to testify about the Harlem River Park speech recalled Goldman advocating the use of violence. The witnesses also emphasized that it was a peaceful protest, with the exception of the group of soldiers who disrupted her lecture. Though government agents testified that she did make such statements, Berkman effectively challenged the accuracy of their transcriptions. Another line of questioning concerned whether the lecture was billed as a "no-conscription" or "no-registration." If the prosecution could prove the latter, it would suggest that the pair had explicitly advocated that individuals violate the law. Though both Goldman and Berkman spoke during the trial, and Goldman's lecture was the focus of the trial, Berkman clearly dominated the defense. The jury convicted them. Their attorney, Harry Weinberger, soon appealed their case to the Supreme Court, citing the unconstitutionality of the draft law. But the Supreme Court heard a group of ten cases about the draft, known collectively as the Selective Draft Law cases, and upheld the law.[31]

Immediately following their release from prison in 1919, Goldman and Berkman faced deportation proceedings at Ellis Island. By then, the Palmer Raids and Red Scare were at their height. Several additional laws had been enacted related to U.S. entry into World War I. In 1918, the Immigration Act expanded the list of deportable offenses to include advocating anarchy, and efforts to deport Berkman and Goldman were mobilized. A deportation warrant for Goldman was issued in St. Louis on September 5, 1919. Her "advocating and teaching anarchy" and the "overthrow of the government by force or violence," in violation of the provisions of the 1918 immigration law, became the grounds for her deportation.[32] As in the earlier case against Goldman, though there was ample evidence to prove that she advocated anarchy, no one could establish that she ever publicly advocated the use of violence. Indeed, it was her critique of the government's use of violence that formed the basis of her embrace of anarchy and opposition to conscription during World War I.

Several well-known Americans rose to Goldman's and Berkman's defense. Those providing evidence included Alice Stone Blackwell, a social activist and suffrage leader. Blackwell wrote to Anthony Caminetti, commissioner-general of immigration, protesting Goldman's deportation.

She and Goldman had been friends for years. Blackwell's family included Lucy Stone, the nineteenth-century suffragist, several abolitionists, and the first female physician in the United States. Blackwell emphasized that, although both advocated social change, they disagreed strenuously about anarchism and its tactics. Blackwell characterized Goldman as sincere and honest. The two had discussed the use of violence. Blackwell stated that Goldman confided in her that on multiple occasions she had dissuaded others in the anarchist movement from turning to violence. Blackwell concluded by arguing that "it seems to me a serious mistake in policy to deport a woman who is really a restraining influence among [radical anarchists]. All the restraining influences are especially needed at this time when the minds of so many persons are in a nervous, inflammable, and unbalanced state." Therefore, Blackwell characterized her friend as a moderating force in the movement and argued that her deportation would have a negative impact as a result. Berkman, in contrast, had acknowledged using violence, most notably in his attack on Henry Clay Frick. Though Goldman was not implicated in that crime, it is likely that she supported Berkman's plan.[33]

Weinberger continued to represent the pair. He once again filed a lawsuit on their behalf. Because deportation was still considered an administrative, not criminal, procedure, little could be done to overturn the process. Berkman, for his part, refused to participate in his deportation hearing. Just before his release from the Federal Penitentiary, he issued a public statement dated September 18, 1919, providing his rationale for refusing to participate in his deportation hearing. He declared: "My social views and political opinions are my personal concern. . . . Free thought, necessarily involving freedom of speech and press, I may tersely define thus: no opinion a law—no opinion a crime. For the government to attempt to control thought, to proscribe certain opinions or proscribe others, is the height of despotism." Because Berkman was not a U.S. citizen, it was not clear which rights he was guaranteed under the U.S. Constitution.[34]

The defense strategy hinged greatly on Goldman's citizenship. If Weinberger could establish Goldman's U.S. citizenship, she could not be deported. Weinberger managed to have the issue brought before the Southern District of New York on a writ of habeas corpus while the two were in federal custody awaiting their deportation case and while he addressed Goldman's citizenship issue.[35]

Berkman had no such recourse. Berkman had remained a citizen of Russia, and because of his conviction in the Henry Frick case, his deportation case was more straightforward. Goldman argued that she had attained U.S. citizenship through her 1887 marriage to Jacob Kerstner in Rochester. She produced evidence that the U.S. Department of State had issued her a passport in 1908 as Kerstner's wife, recognizing her U.S. citizenship. Kerstner's citizenship had later been revoked through denaturalization, and therefore the government asserted that she too had lost her citizenship by virtue of her marital status. Before 1922, women's citizenship status in the United States was tied to their husband's. Weinberger argued that she had never been notified of this change in Kerstner's status and that the revocation of his citizenship did not affect her status. A secondary argument was that she had received U.S. citizenship through her father while still a minor.[36]

These legal strategies were notable because they emphasized Goldman's subordination to the two men in her life: her father and her husband. These indirect sources of citizenship and rights through male relatives were the very forms of gender subordination that she was seeking to abolish through her writings and activism. Though these activities were the cause of her deportation, the most effective legal strategy she could use was to reinforce those dependent ties to male relatives. Therefore, even a radical advocate of anarchism, free love, and women's rights used a variant of the family reunification strategy—a dependence argument—to fight her deportation. In her case, however, it ultimately failed. The fact that Berkman dominated the testimony of their first trial also suggested the limits of women's power in the political and ideological spheres.

Goldman's defense was stronger than Berkman's because of her claim to U.S. citizenship and the fact that her prior conviction did not involve violence. But she had been a target of the Bureau of Investigation since its inception, and the agency marshaled significant resources to argue that her case for U.S. citizenship was tenuous. The related issue of free speech was never resolved. In contrast to Berkman, whose major focus was anarchism, Goldman advocated many ideologies that were considered radical—anarchism, but also pacifism, women's rights, and free love. She advocated these in many well-attended rallies and lectures and in her writing.

Despite her claims to derivative U.S. citizenship through both her father and her marriage, and despite testimony from Blackwell and other character witnesses confirming that she opposed the use of violence, she was ordered deported. The free speech question—whether there was a right to espouse a radical political ideology—remained unresolved. It continued to concern those involved in deportation issues in the 1930s. Ultimately the McCarran Act, or Internal Security Act (ISA), passed in September 1950, resolved the issue by declaring that there existed no legal right to espouse radical beliefs, such as those associated with communism. Though a decade earlier the Smith Act had forbidden membership in organizations that advocated the overthrow of the federal government and required immigrants to register with the federal government, the McCarran Act recognized no distinction between freedom of ideology and conspiracy to overthrow the U.S. government.[37]

Although the Goldman and Berkman case was widely publicized and was undoubtedly the best-known political deportation case to occur in the aftermath of World War I, many ordinary immigrants and radical activists faced deportation hearings as well. Federal officials conducted raids in cities including New York, Hartford, Chicago, and Boston.

One of the major episodes in the Palmer Raids occurred in Hartford, Connecticut, where forty-seven men had been arrested without warrants, and fifty additional people were arrested for simply visiting those friends in jail. This group, which was eventually transported to Deer Island Prison in Massachusetts, was not released for five months. Government officials reported that at the prison "conditions were unfit and chaotic," aliens were held "practically incommunicado," with "inadequate heat or sanitation." Moreover, there was "dire confusion" between immigration and Department of Justice officials. The conditions led to at least one suicide. Notably, English colonists had held Amerindians on that same site on Deer Island in 1676 during King Philip's (or, more accurately, Metacomet's) War in New England. Later, it became the landing spot in Boston Harbor for the large numbers of Irish immigrants fleeing the Irish famine, some of whom were quarantined there because of illness. Thus, more than 300 years after King Philip's War, Deer Island was still used to contain those deemed dangerous to the polity. Today, it is best known as a major water treatment site.[38]

By November 10, 145 people had been arrested in Hartford, which exceeded by a substantial margin the 30 arrested in New York raids.[39] Immigrants in smaller industrial centers such as Bridgeport, Ansonia, Manchester, New Britain, and Waterbury, were also targeted in the raid. Those towns tended to be populated by significant numbers of Russian and Eastern European immigrant workers. They worked in the munitions, brass, tool, and metalworking industries that were crucial to American economic production and particularly to the World War I defense industry. Several immigrants were targeted for their affiliation with the Union of Russian Workers; sixty members of that union were brought into custody.[40]

Federal agents working for the Bureau of Investigation arrived in Hartford and soon announced that they had discovered drawings of 1915 model .30-caliber machine guns in a locked chest at the Union of Russian Workers' Market Street headquarters. BI agents determined that the drawings had been removed surreptitiously from the Colt Firearms Factory in Hartford. This provided federal authorities with evidence that the group promoted violence and thus rendered members vulnerable to deportation under the recent legislation.[41]

Editors at the *Hartford Courant* supported the federal government's role in the Red Scare and its raids and deportations of immigrants. Very little about those captured in the November raids was published, other than their affiliation with the Union of Russian Workers, and in some cases the towns in which they resided. The newspaper did not include a complete list of names in its coverage of the raids and related events. Presumably at least some of those arrested had spouses and children, but it was not clear what the effect the raids had on these families.[42]

In Chicago, several immigrants were arrested during the Palmer Raids and became subject to deportation. With the assistance of their attorneys, Louis Wirth's and Selma Nelson's deportation orders were ultimately canceled. Wirth was twenty-two years old and a recent graduate of the University of Chicago, where he wrote a thesis on communism and studied economics and sociology. He would later become a leading sociologist. He had immigrated to the United States from Germany as a boy, joining an uncle in Omaha where he attended public school. Wirth had never become a U.S. citizen, and thus his political activities put him at risk for deportation. Several people testified to his community involvement and his talent as a scholar, including Robert Park, the pioneering University of Chicago sociologist who undertook important research on race and immigration in the United States.[43]

Wirth admitted attending Communist Party meetings and reading widely on communism as part of his college studies. His roommate, Joseph Schaffe, served as temporary secretary of the Central Branch of the Communist Party of America in Chicago. Wirth stated that he was opposed to the use of "all forms of violence and unlawful means." But J. Edgar Hoover argued in a memo to Anthony Caminetti, commissioner-general of immigration, that the "provision of the Act of October 16, 1918, does not require that the alien who is a member of such an organization shall in addition to being a member of the same also actually believe in the principles advocated by the organization." Wirth was also charged with being an anarchist, which is difficult to reconcile with communist principles. He stated that he did not join the party, did not have a membership card, and that his roommate had paid the fifty-cent dues on his behalf.[44]

Wirth also maintained that "being a student of economics, he reads every available publication on that subject, and has attended radical meetings at various places."[45] He did not disavow communism in its entirety, instead focusing on his opposition to violence. When asked: "Do you believe in the principles as outlined in the Manifesto and Program of the Communist Party of America and Communist International?" He hedged: "I cannot say I do believe in them."[46]

Wirth's strong connections at the University of Chicago and in the Progressive reform community in the city contributed to his ability to appeal his deportation order and to remain in the United States. Wirth was active in many Chicago organizations, and some of that work could be viewed as patriotic. He had worked with disabled soldiers in the Red Cross, and in the Office of Personal Service, helping boys in the juvenile detention system. Testimony from his supervisors, including Miriam Low and his sociology professor Robert Park, seemed to have assisted him in his defense. They served as character witnesses. Low described his "excellent conduct, as well as his honesty, integrity, and obedience to the rules and regulations of the organizations."[47] Park argued, using his sociological perspective, that political radicalism was essentially "a sort of intellectual growing pain" or a normal developmental phase of those from sixteen to thirty.[48]

Some immigrants faced deportation when the American Socialist Party in which they were active dissolved and their local branches merged with the Communist Labor Party (CLP). Selma Nelson, a twenty-nine-year-old woman, had arrived in Chicago after immigrating to the United States in 1912 from Latvia, then part of Russia. She faced deportation, along with her husband, John, on the basis of her initial membership in the Socialist Party, after she had signed an application to join the CLP. Nelson was one of relatively few women to face deportation in the wake of the Palmer Raids. Although Emma Goldman was the best-known immigrant to face deportation in this era, her fame made her exceptional. More often, men were detained for deportation because of their workplace activism.

Nelson described herself as a housewife and was expecting her first child at the time of her detention. She spent five days in custody before being released. Interestingly, she responded to a question about her entry to the United States that her maiden name was Johnson, an unusual surname for a Latvian woman. There are two explanations for her response. First, as a Latvian, she might have Anglicized her last name before arriving in the United States. It is also possible that she misunderstood the question, because her attorney's last name was Johnson. She stated that her knowledge of English was limited and that she read books in Lettish. The hearing transcript reveals her limited knowledge of English. Moreover, though Nelson regularly attended Socialist Party meetings and paid membership dues, she was not particularly active in the CLP. She was told that she did not have to pay membership dues because she had been "in good standing in the Socialist Party."[49]

Nelson admitted that she had joined the Communist Labor Party, alongside her husband, when her Socialist Party chapter voted to form an alliance with it. She was also charged with being an anarchist who "believes in and advocates the overthrow by force or violence of the Government of the United States." But never in her deportation hearing testimony did she admit to advocating or believing in the latter, nor did the government provide evidence that membership in the CLP was synonymous with advocating violent means of political change. It is notable that, though she described herself as a housewife, she said that she joined the Socialist Party because it "is a working party, and because I am a working woman, that is the reason I joined."[50] Both Nelson and Wirth were asked during their deportation hearings whether they had read the Third International Manifesto. Nelson stated that she had not, while Wirth had asserted that his interest in communism was academically motivated. Ultimately, Nelson's deportation order was canceled after she was released on $10,000 bail.[51]

The Palmer era deportation effort was launched by the attorney general's office, rather than by the Immigration Service, which had previously handled all deportation proceedings. Nelson's case was administered by a "special employee" of the Bureau of Investigation of the U.S. Department of Justice.[52] Though the federal immigration function would be moved from to the Department of Justice in 1940, it was still housed in the U.S. Department of Labor.

The Supreme Court never issued a decision on the constitutionality of the arrest and deportations arising from the Palmer Raids. Yet some jurists did weigh in on the tactics used. After listening to fifteen days of testimony, Judge George W. Anderson of Boston wrote in his opinion in the *Colyer v. Skeffington* hearing on a habeas corpus petition filed on behalf of 112 prisoners. The immigration deputy acknowledged that some of the immigrants had been imprisoned prior to warrants being issued. Judge Anderson ultimately concluded that nearly 1,000 immigrants had been denied due process.[53] Both Judge Felix Frankfurter and Professor Chafee of Harvard filed amicus briefs in the case. Anderson also concluded that there was scant evidence to suggest that the Communist Party intended to overthrow the U.S. government using force or violence.[54]

The *Colyer* case was a pivotal deportation case after the Palmer Raids. William Thomas Colyer and his wife, Amy Colyer, faced deportation for their activism in the Communist Party in Boston. W. T. Colyer, a British subject who had lived in the United States since 1915, was deported on April 11, 1922. He was held at the detention center at Deer Island, Massachusetts, in 1920.[55] After losing their appeal in the First Circuit Court, the Colyers considered bringing their case to the Supreme Court, but ultimately decided not to appeal their case further. The court asserted, "Deportation, when ordered by the proper executive officer of the Government, is not visited upon the alien for any crime; and the fact that the reason assigned for his deportation may constitute a crime under the local law does not make the hearing upon deportation a trial in a criminal case, to be conducted under the rules of evidence that apply to such a trial."[56] In addressing the issue of whether membership in the Communist Party could be construed as supporting violence, several passages were quoted. Those included: "Communism does not propose to 'capture' the bourgeoisie parliamentary state, but to conquer and destroy it."[57]

Amy Colyer remained forthright in expressing her beliefs in radical political change. At her hearing, she refused to speak until her attorney was present, despite the inspector's assurances that she could speak without legal representation. The hearing was postponed until several weeks later. She also declined to provide answers to inquiries about her husband's occupation and the exact reasons for their move to the United States, though she stated that she typed the articles he submitted to magazines. She acknowledged her membership in a socialist organization in London and her membership and office holding in the Central Branch of the Communist Party in Boston. She further refused to discuss the identity or activities of others in the organization.[58]

Unlike Selma Nelson, Amy Colyer acknowledged having read the *Communist Manifesto* and agreed with many of its principles. Though Colyer, too, declared that she was a housewife, it was clear that Colyer was more involved in party politics than was Selma Nelson. She served as her husband's intellectual partner and edited his writing. To a question about the U.S. Constitution in which she was asked: "Do you understand the form of government that you are enjoying in the United States?" she retorted: "I am not enjoying it, but I think I understand it." She further asserted that her deportation violated constitutional rights to "Free Speech, war to be declared by Congress, [and] the right of those arrested to a speedy trial." Colyer boldly implied that the Palmer era raids and deportation hearings constituted an undeclared war.[59]

Colyer renounced her intent to become an American citizen, although her husband had earlier applied to do so; therefore, by extension she was in the process of becoming one as well. She also boldly asserted about the Socialist Party: "That organization is being persecuted and you are going after perfectly innocent people. I don't wish to disgrace myself by helping you to spy on innocent people."[60]

Another vital exchange occurred over the meaning of the following passage: "The revolutionary era compels the proletariat to make use of the means of battle, which will concentrate its entire energies, namely mass action, with its logical result, direct conflict with the governmental machinery in open combat." Palmer and other officials cited this statement to bolster their position that communism advocated force. The quote was drawn from the Trotsky's manifesto of First Congress of the Communist International in Moscow in 1919. Amy Colyer maintained that those were metaphorical references to battle and combat, and she noted that the movement possessed no arms in which to undertake violence.[61] Other documents, including the party's constitution and minutes of meetings were used as exhibits in the Colyer deportation case. A blank membership form was found in their Wellesley home, along with other communist documents.[62]

Even when immigrants or other noncitizens were not targeted for deportation, they feared that they would become vulnerable under the Espionage Act and other curtailments on freedom of expression. As during the later McCarthy era, the Palmer Raids had a chilling effect on debates on many political topics, not simply those pertaining to radicalism. In Hartford, an Indian speaker, S. N. Ghose, declined to address several questions following his lecture on the relationship between India and England and the negative effects of colonial rule. In refusing to address those issues, he specifically cited the recently enacted Espionage Act.[63]

A major revelation in the *Colyer* case was testimony that the Department of Justice had compiled a list of 46,000 U.S. citizens who were deemed to be radicals. This fact bolstered Chafee's arguments that denying immigrants significant constitutional rights would lead inexorably to the curtailment of U.S. citizens' rights. That position anticipates recent debates about the Patriot Act and other federal policies following 9/11. Since 9/11, deportations have increased dramatically, while public perceptions about the impact of immigration have become far more critical. David Cole and other constitutional scholars have argued that denying rights to immigrants and other noncitizens on U.S. soil or in U.S. custody ultimately leads to the curtailment of the rights of citizens. In fact, these developments have had a major impact on discussions about the role of habeas corpus rights for U.S. citizens and intensified racial profiling of Arab American and Hispanic citizens, who are perceived as aliens in the United States.

Caribbean Activists: Marcus Garvey and Claudia Cumberbatch Jones

Alternative economic views and labor activism also fueled deportations of two Caribbean immigrants during the late 1920s, an era that has been viewed as a relatively uneventful one from a political perspective. U.S. immigration had slowed considerably from outside the Western Hemisphere in response to the effectiveness of the national-origins laws that significantly restricted the number of immigrants from many regions, especially Southern and Eastern Europe. But it is not surprising that two Caribbean activists should be targeted for deportation, since West Indians had been cast as dangerous revolutionaries and a threat to the institution of slavery before the Civil War, as typified by Toussaint L'Ouverture's leadership of the 1791 Haitian Revolution.[64]

In 1927 Marcus Garvey, the charismatic and controversial leader of the Harlem-based United Negro Improvement Association (UNIA) was deported to Jamaica, his country of origin, after having been convicted and imprisoned for mail fraud in connection with his business. Though he had taken steps toward naturalization, he had never obtained U.S. citizenship. Efforts by UNIA supporters to grant him a presidential pardon failed. After Garvey had served part of his five-year sentence in an Atlanta penitentiary, President Calvin Coolidge granted him clemency, and the remainder of his sentence was commuted. Having been refused an executive pardon, which would have erased his criminal record, his conviction on mail fraud charges led immediately to his deportation order.

Relative to the immigrant population as a whole, few Jamaicans or other people of African descent had voluntarily immigrated to the United States by the time that Garvey arrived in the country. A sizable number of West Indians had been brought to New Orleans as slaves. Caribbean immigrants arrived in greater numbers after World War II. One notable exception was in Harlem, where there was a West Indian immigrant community by the early 1920s, and that community allowed UNIA to thrive as a pan-African, transnational movement.[65]

J. Edgar Hoover, who had overseen many of the Palmer era deportations less than a decade earlier, also launched this effort, after having overseen the initial investigation of Garvey's activities in 1917. In fact, during the November 1919 Palmer Raids, Hoover emphasized that his investigations had unearthed "222 foreign language newspapers which have openly advocated changes in the governmental system by violence and preached sedition." He also characterized some black newspapers as "particularly insolent." Clearly Garvey's paper was one of those.[66]

NAACP leaders and others in mainstream racial organizations criticized Garvey and his leadership style. Many viewed him as compromising their efforts to demonstrate the accomplishments and merits of highly educated professional African Americans, whose deft leadership would be critical to achieving racial equality. Therefore, Garvey's popular movement, his lack of U.S. citizenship, his racial identity, and his alienation from the mainstream civil rights movement combined to make him particularly vulnerable to charges of fraud, harsh sentencing, and finally deportation.[67]

Black elites such as W. E. B. Du Bois and other intellectuals found Garvey to be an embarrassment and an impediment to their strategy to achieve racial equality. A large and imposing figure, Garvey dressed in garish uniforms, punctuated by an elaborate, Napoleonic-style hat. He drew further attention by leading large parades down Amsterdam Avenue. His perplexing associations with hate groups and others who believed in racial inferiority further alienated many in the NAACP. He forged relationships with the Ku Klux Klan and other southern-based white supremacist groups, a position that seemed in direct opposition to his emphasis on the importance of economic self-reliance among African Americans. Garvey interacted with eugenicists, including Madison Grant, who promoted a branch of scientific racism that led to widespread sterilization among African Americans. Grant and his allies advocated a "Back to Africa" movement, echoing the nineteenth-century African colonization movement that stressed the inability of North Americans of African descent to

Marcus Garvey, 1926. (Prints and Photographs Division, Library of Congress)

assimilate into mainstream society. Garvey's Back to Africa movement, by contrast, was fueled by his pessimism that those in the African diaspora would ever receive equal opportunity in majority-white societies. Eugenicists supported similar efforts because of their belief in the genetic inferiority of African Americans. Garvey's alliances with eugenicists and other white supremacists rightly disturbed those in the early twentieth-century civil rights movement.[68]

Garvey's failure to align with the mainstream civil rights movement was not the reason, however, that Hoover and others monitored him for decades and advocated for his deportation. Rather, it was his leadership of a very popular social movement that emphasized black empowerment. Despite tensions with Du Bois and other African American leaders, Garvey was extremely popular among working-class Harlemites, and his movement grew rapidly into more than 500 chapters across the United States, including many in the rural South.

Over the past decade, there has been a resurgence of interest in the Garvey movement. That trend largely arises from the interest in transnationalism and the focus on grass-roots organizing efforts. Though there had been some scholarly interest in Garvey in the 1960s, in the ensuing decades U.S. historians largely overlooked both Garvey and UNIA. Recently, there has been a reexamination of the roots of the post–World War II civil rights movement, along with a renewed interest in the history of the Pan-African movement and in the international dimensions of the U.S. civil rights movement. As a result, historians have begun to reengage with the Garvey movement. In particular, historians have focused on the impact of UNIA on the rural South and in African countries before independence. Previously, UNIA was largely portrayed as a movement rooted in the urban North. But southerners who were involved in the post–World War II civil rights movement often point to the influence that UNIA had on their parents and other civil rights activists in the previous generation.[69]

Unlike most Red Scare targets, Garvey was not involved in political or labor movements such as communism, anarchism, or the International Workers of the World. In fact, Garvey was a proponent of business entrepreneurship and capitalism. But his popular grass-roots social movement threatened the social order by its potential to challenge existing racial and class relations in the Northeast and elsewhere.

E. David Cronon, who wrote the first full-length academic study of Garvey, characterized his Pan-African movement as the largest and most powerful organization of African Americans to date. UNIA launched a black cruise ship line, the Black Star Line, the Negro Factories Association, and the Black Cross Nurses Association. As part of its emphasis on improving African American self-images, UNIA even supported the development of a line of African American dolls.[70]

Garvey and other officers in UNIA were active in political movements in Europe and Africa. While Garvey was in prison, UNIA officers corresponded with members of the African National Congress, based in Johannesburg, the political party established in the mid-1920s to challenge apartheid and other policies that denied significant rights to black, Asian, and biracial South Africans. In 1927 the ANC newspaper *Abantu-Batho* published an article condemning Garvey's conviction and imprisonment in the United States. Garvey also spoke positively of the ongoing Irish independence movement and its leaders and the quest for self-determination.[71]

Several studies of Garvey and his larger grass-roots movement that spread throughout the United States and elsewhere, including Ghana, discuss his imprisonment on fraud charges, but significantly less has been published about his deportation. Scholars have not fully analyzed the federal government's decision to grant Garvey an early release rather than a pardon. Yet, such a decision was highly significant, because a pardon would have protected him from deportation.

Garvey's international reputation and his often-critical opinions of U.S. foreign policy issues seem to have rendered him a more threatening activist in the view of federal officials. Recently some valuable primary materials on Garvey have been published. They reveal that Garvey was subject to an extensive investigation by the Bureau of Investigation as a "Negro agitator."[72]

Though deportation efforts occurred only after Garvey's criminal conviction in 1927, the executive branch of the U.S. government had him under surveillance since the Red Scare. Some of his claims in articles published in the UNIA newspaper, *Negro World*, in late 1918 seem to have precipitated the initial BIA investigation. In one he concludes his discussion of the peace talks between the United States and Japan and League of Nations organization efforts by noting, "We hope Japan will succeed in impressing upon her white brothers at the Peace Conference the essentiality of abolishing racial discrimination."[73]

D. Davidson, the BI investigator, infiltrated UNIA meetings. He reported that at a well-attended meeting in Harlem Garvey announced that one million African Americans would soon be mobilized, "combined with Japan, to take up arms for social equality." At that same meeting, A. Philip Randolph and Ida Wells-Barnett were chosen as delegates to represent "negroes at the Versailles conference." According to Davis, Garvey had predicted that the next war would be "between the negroes and the whites." Rather than simply a rhetorical flourish, Garvey's statement seems prescient in retrospect, given the major race riots that would occur in Chicago, Tulsa, and several other cities during the Red Summer of 1919.[74]

Marcus Garvey, 1924. (Prints and Photographs Division, Library of Congress)

During wartime, labor activism was cast as unpatriotic. So too was a popular movement organized around racial equality and economic empowerment. Rumors arose that "agents of the Central Powers were circulating among the Negro people of the United States." Two African American military officers, Major Walter Loving and Charles Holston Williams, were recruited by the Military Intelligence Branch of the U.S. Army to undertake surveillance in Harlem and in other black communities and to report on the activities of Garvey and other leaders.[75]

Garvey's conviction and his deportation, which removed him from the center of the UNIA movement, effectively led to the organization's demise. The fact that he was charged and deported almost immediately after his release further demonstrate that the process of deportation was not always distinct from the criminal justice system. In fact, immigrant noncitizens increasingly face both criminal convictions, followed by deportation.

Advocating radical changes to race relations and economic equality and racial pride as expressed in Garvey's Pan-African nationalist movement, symbolized by the now widely recognized tricolor flag of red, white, and green, left him vulnerable to deportation in ways that were similar to immigrants who advocated communism and anarchism. To charge Garvey with a crime and to force his removal from the United States, where UNIA was based, led to the rapid decline in UNIA membership and, ultimately, to the demise of the movement itself. His reputation would be rehabilitated and the movement revived to some degree only with the African and Caribbean independence movements of the 1950s and 1960s.[76]

Garvey and his movement had a complex relationship to American communism. Communist support for his movement and the confluence of membership among southern African Americans are in some ways ironic, given that in his writings he was quite critical of communism in effecting social change: "Our modern systems of Government have partly failed and are wholly failing. We have tried various forms, but none has measured up to the Ideal State. Communism was the last attempt, and its most ardent advocates have acknowledged its limitations, shortcomings and impossibility."[77] His arrest, nevertheless, prompted an outcry from members of the Communist Party of America, another marginalized movement that was perceived as threatening. After UNIA's decline, some southern UNIA members joined the American Communist Party, viewing it as the only acceptable alternative for significant political change.[78]

Garvey posed a similar threat to that of Paramahansa Yogananda. Each man was a charismatic leader in a transnational movement, one religious and another socioeconomic, that was increasingly popular with Americans. Both had a commanding physical presence and dressed distinctively in outfits that highlighted their lack of conformity to mainstream American cultural norms and traditions. Yogananda was particularly popular with women, which local authorities and immigration officials viewed as problematic; Garvey's movement appealed to rural and working-class African Americans who were not the focus of the early African American organizations, whose intentional strategy was to build a class of well-educated elites. Garvey's relationship with Amy Jacques, the assistant who later became his second wife, was also the subject of surveillance by the BI. In fact, BI officials considered arresting Garvey for violations of the Mann Act, which forbade bringing women across state lines for prostitution or other immoral purposes.[79]

Each of these two imported movements had the potential to restructure existing social relations within the United States in ways that would be unfamiliar to its political leaders. Each was led by a nonwhite leader whose country of origin had been fundamentally reshaped by British colonization. The deportation mechanism offered an effective and speedy means to curtail the popularity of the movement by physically removing its leader from the United States.

Like Garvey, Claudia Cumberbatch Jones was a Caribbean immigrant activist in New York. She too was a Pan-African activist involved in many transnational networks, especially those based in London. While living in the Notting Hill neighborhood of London, she interacted with Kwame Nkrumah and other future leaders of the African independence movement. She organized the now renowned Notting Hill Ethnic Festival. Like Garvey, she was incarcerated in an American prison prior to facing deportation. Marcus Garvey and Claudia Jones were also linked through the activism of Garvey's first wife, Amy Ashwood Garvey, a friend of Jones's.[80] In contrast to Garvey, however, Jones was a feminist and a member of the Communist Party. Until the publication of Carole Boyce Davis's biography in 2007, relatively little had been written about Jones, a significant figure in radical circles. Jones emigrated from Port of Spain, Trinidad, to the United States with her aunt and three sisters in 1924 and later attended high school in New York City. Early in her life, she was involved in two mainstream civil rights groups, the NAACP and the Urban League, before becoming involved in leftist and labor organizations. Like Maida Springer, who also had Caribbean roots, she was active in radical labor circles. Both women had arrived in Harlem as girls. Springer had accompanied her family from Panama, where her father had earlier migrated from the Caribbean in search of employment. But, though Springer was a leftist labor activist, she never joined the Communist Party. Jones was active in the defense of the Scottsboro Boys in 1931 and later joined the staff of the *Daily Worker*. As a result, Hoover began surveillance on her organizing activities. As a longtime resident who planned to remain in the country, she sought U.S. citizenship. Because of her affiliation with the Communist Party, however, her citizenship application was denied, thus rendering her vulnerable to deportation.[81]

Jones was noted in the African American press for her youth and energy. A 1939 headline in the *Chicago Defender* announced "Girl Heads Communists in New York State," reporting that the "lovely" twenty-three year old had been elected by acclaim. But she was also active in mainstream racially based groups, such as the National Council of Negro Women. Like Emma Goldman, she knew Elizabeth Gurley Flynn, and both of them were among those convicted in 1955 for their roles in the Communist Party. Moreover, like Goldman, her political and personal relationships were intertwined—Jones had been romantically involved with Howard "Stretch" Johnson, a fellow Communist.[82]

Jones did not face deportation until the 1950s, decades after Garvey, Goldman, and Colyer, but her case had its origins in the laws and policies emerging from the first Red Scare of the late 1910s and early 1920s. In 1940 Howard W. Smith introduced in Congress an amendment to Section 20 of the Immigration Act of 1917. The Alien Registration Act was popularly known as the Smith Act. It rendered illegal groups that advocated the overthrow of the U.S. government and required all adult aliens to register with the federal government. In 1950 the Internal Security Act, or McCarran Act, was passed. It outlawed membership in the Communist Party. Decades earlier, Zechariah Chafee and other legal scholars had argued that a belief in communism and membership in the party was not tantamount to advocating the overthrow of the U.S. government through the use of force. But increasingly, such efforts to distinguish the belief in communism as separate from advocating the overthrow of the U.S. government failed. The two were now conflated in law, despite vigorous arguments on this issue during the first Red Scare. U.S. naturalization applications continue to ask about Communist Party affiliation, though it no longer results in automatic denial of U.S. citizenship, in part because of the ubiquity of party membership in China and elsewhere.[83]

Claudia Jones (second row, first from left) with fellow Smith Act defendants before U.S. Federal Court building, 1953. (Claudia Jones Photograph Collection, Photographs and Prints Division, Schomburg Center for Research in Black Culture, The New York Public Library, Astor, Lenox and Tilden Foundations)

Jones was convicted under the Smith Act and sentenced to federal prison in Alderson, West Virginia. She recounts that while in prison she learned how to weave place mats and won a blue ribbon at the local fair for her skills. She was released early on the basis of good behavior. Before her deportation to England under the McCarran Act, she wrote a letter to "Comrade [William Z.] Foster," which she referred to as her "autobiographical (personal, political, medical) history." Her very short essay in the form of a letter reveals her wry sense of irony blended with a trenchant social critique. She began with a short discussion of her middle-class farm family's fortunes being hurt by the declining price of cocoa on the world market and its decision to migrate as a way to regain their economic status. But she related that they "suffered not only the impoverished lot of working class native families, and its multi-national popu-

Unidentified event attended by (left to right) Claudia Jones, Paul Robeson, Amy Ashwood Garvey, Eslanda (Essie) Robeson, and unidentified couple, ca. 1959. (Claudia Jones Photograph Collection, Photographs and Prints Division, Schomburg Center for Research in Black Culture, The New York Public Library, Astor, Lenox and Tilden Foundations)

lace, but early learned the special scourge of indignity stemming from Jim Crow national oppression."[84]

Many of Jones's childhood memories were centered on race. She chose a Chinese girl as her running mate in a school election and resisted the pressure of her teachers to select a replacement. The team won by a significant majority. She also recounted the controversy that arose when she donated blood to an Italian girl at Sea View tuberculosis sanitarium, as well as the poor treatment she and other African American students faced in school.

Jones held a negative view of the impact of immigration to the United States on the lives of Caribbean immigrants and other nonwhites. Despite their belief that their lives would improve once in the United States, the members of her family did not prosper. Her mother, a garment worker,

Claudia Jones seated at her desk reviewing a copy of the *West Indian Gazette*. (Claudia Jones Photograph Collection, Photographs and Prints Division, Schomburg Center for Research in Black Culture, The New York Public Library, Astor, Lenox and Tilden Foundations)

died of spinal meningitis at age thirty-seven, her health, from Jones's perspective, compromised by poor working conditions and the stress of immigration. After high school graduation, Jones sought work in a laundry, then a factory, and finally a shop. By the Depression, she applied for work with the Federal Theatre Project, but decided to take a much less lucrative job with the *Daily Worker*. She too suffered from chronic health problems, receiving treatment for coronary disease as a young adult.

It was the confluence of her family's experience with racial discrimination and harsh working conditions that led to her social activism and later to her commitment to communism. But that, too, was not a panacea in the long term. Like many other African Americans, she clashed with Earl Browder, the party's U.S. leader and wrote about her differences in articles for *Political Affairs*. After her deportation, she settled in Notting Hill and was instrumental in establishing the famed ethnic festival there, as well as a newspaper for Caribbean immigrants. Like Garvey, she died in London following her deportation, but not before making an impact on her new society and contributing to a larger transnational network of social and political activists.

Harry Bridges

Alfred Renton Bridges, known as Harry, was born in 1901 to a middle-class family near Melbourne, Australia. His early life offered no indication that he would become a major labor radical in the International Longshoreman's and Worker's Union (ILWU). Bridges's biographer, Robert Cherny, suggests that his witnessing high rates of injuries among dock workers fueled his commitment to the union and sparked his lifelong commitment to activism. After traveling to India and England, Bridges first came to the United States in 1920, soon settling in New Orleans and later moving to San Francisco, and joining the IWW. Ironically, he left the IWW after he became concerned that membership in it would make him vulnerable to deportation. He worked closely with the Communist Party as a leader in the ILWU. In 1937 the ILWU joined the newly created CIO under his leadership.[85]

The Bridges case became one of the most controversial deportation cases in the twentieth century. There were two attempts by the federal government to deport him—one in 1934 and, after that effort failed, a second in 1940. In 1934, shortly following his appointment as the Joint Strike Committee chair for a major maritime strike, immigration officials on the West Coast reported to the Immigration Service in Washington that he associated with Communist Party members. This evidence was bolstered by the discovery of a membership card bearing the name "Harry Dorgan," the last name being the maiden name of Bridges's mother. Carol Weiss King, a New York University Law School graduate, was Bridges's attorney. King first became active in deportation issues during the 1920s, when she defended immigrants facing deportation in the aftermath of the Palmer Raids. Her biographer notes immigration law was a particularly challenging field in this era, since at that time there had been few Supreme Court rulings on deportation and little scholarship on immigration law.[86]

A group of conservative members of Congress, led by J. Parnell Thomas of New Jersey, took the unusual step of threatening Secretary of Labor Frances Perkins with impeachment if she did not carry out Bridges's deportation order. Perkins responded to that pressure by appointing a special officer to hear Bridges's case. He was James Landis, the newly appointed dean of Harvard Law School and a veteran of the Security and Exchange Commission (SEC). Landis maintained that the deportation process should be covered by the Sixth Amendment and that aliens should be able to subpoena witnesses. Landis's assertion that immigrants or other noncitizens should be covered by the Sixth Amendment during their deportation hearings was an important one, given that the process was an administrative one, not a criminal proceeding.[87]

The charges in the 1934 case were dropped after Landis wrote a highly critical report on the evidence and witnesses in the case. The retroactivity of the law is another issue that arose in the case. Landis argued that it was unconstitutional to deport Harry Bridges and other immigrants on the basis of their affiliation with a group that occurred before the federal ban on membership of that group. Landis further agreed that several government officials had conspired against Bridges, including those employed by the Immigration Service and the Portland Police Department.

The Bridges case broke down over more mundane matters, including the credibility of the witnesses called to testify against him. Bridges himself never conceded that he was ever a member of the Communist Party. After Landis's report was released, Perkins canceled the deportation order.[88]

But the controversy was not over. In 1940 the House took another unusual step when it passed a bill mandating that Bridges be deported, but the effort was defeated in the Senate. The INS ordered him deported a second time. Bridges's lawyer filed an unsuccessful motion to dismiss charges on the grounds of double jeopardy. The second case resulted in a deportation order. But ultimately the Supreme Court overturned that decision in *Bridges v. Wixon* (1945).[89]

Efforts to deport Bridges were abandoned by the late forties, and he remained in the United States, obtaining his U.S. citizenship in 1946. He died in San Francisco in 1990. When the Soviet archives were opened to international scholars after 1989, historians found evidence suggesting that Bridges had, in fact, been active in the Communist Party.[90]

Bridges benefited from widespread publicity, his attorney's prior experience with Palmer Raid defendants, the move toward protecting immigrants' rights under the New Deal, and the relative lack of political power among conservatives in the decade preceding the Cold War and the rise of McCarthyism. He obtained U.S. citizenship as the Cold War began. That offered him greater protection; while denaturalization was used as a strategy against naturalized Americans during the McCarthy era, it was a more onerous process than deportation.

Though the United States had benefited from territorial and corporate expansionism in the late nineteenth century, its leaders were far less comfortable with the importation of new ideas and movements from regions beyond Western Europe. Politics, in the form of communism, socialism, and labor radicalism were the major focus of deportation efforts during the post–World War I Red Scare. But political activism was not the only perceived organized threat to the social structure in the 1920s and 1930s. Popular transnational social movements, including those advocating economic and racial justice, were viewed as destabilizing factors in the United States. Between World War I and World War II, the federal government used the deportation mechanism to squelch dissent among immigrant activists who promoted ideologies that were deemed contrary to the American mainstream.

That group included communists and anarchists, whose treatment in the aftermath of the Palmer Raids has been well documented, but also labor activists and others who advocated a more equitable workplace and society. In addition to the high profile cases of Emma Goldman, Alexander Berkman, and Harry Bridges, many average workers in New England, Chicago, and elsewhere were arrested and faced deportation for their political beliefs. Although Marcus Garvey, and to a lesser extent, Claudia Jones, are recognized for their public roles, significantly less has been written about the events surrounding their deportation. Expressing political beliefs outside the mainstream no longer received constitutional protection. To support communism or anarchism was to advocate violent revolution. Once the Smith Act was enacted, the mere belief in communism when expressed publicly was formally rendered illegal. This effort coincided with the rise of domestic government surveillance within the Department of Justice, which would assume the immigration regulation function entirely by 1940.

Noncitizen immigrants were denied constitutional rights to freedom of expression, the full rights to their religious beliefs, and the ability to organize social and economic movements, especially when those ideologies have been transnational in origin. Yet, such limitations did not go unchallenged. Legal activists, including Louis Post, Zechariah Chafee, James Landis, and Carol Weiss King demonstrated the unconstitutionality of the process. Ultimately, J. Edgar Hoover's determination to eradicate political radicalism, combined with his unchecked use of intimidation and success in increasing the scope and power of the FBI, limited the efficacy of those reasoned arguments. As the next chapter discusses, immigrants in the United States have also been rendered politically vulnerable because of the legal ambiguity of their relationship to the Constitution, international human rights law, and the deportation mechanism, which is defined as an administrative, not a criminal procedure.

IMMIGRANTS' RIGHTS AS HUMAN RIGHTS

The rights of immigrants in the United States have been debated vigorously since the late nineteenth century. Until they are afforded constitutional protections extended to all U.S. citizens following their naturalization, immigrants' relationship to the U.S. Constitution and to the laws governing citizenship of their countries of origin remain particularly ill-defined and ambiguous. As discussed in previous chapters, several groups of immigrants have, over the course of American history, been expressly banned from obtaining U.S. citizenship. Asians and others defined as nonwhite, for example, were systematically barred from U.S. citizenship before 1952. Similarly, before 1922, American women who married non-U.S. citizens relinquished their U.S. citizenship. Therefore, while such residents could choose to live permanently in the United States, many could not claim the same rights accorded to most U.S. citizens. Recent debates over the federal detention of noncitizens, including immigrants, have also had significant implications for terror suspects held outside the United States, including those in Guantánamo Bay.

This chapter argues that debates about immigrants' rights in the United States, especially in the context of deportation, are vital to understanding the historical origins of international human rights policies that emerged following World War II. Moreover, these questions have saliency for the rights of all noncitizens in the United States, including those affected by the events of 9/11. As we have seen, immigrant noncitizens could not always exercise First Amendment rights. Several immigrant groups faced exclusion or deportation as a result of their religious beliefs or particular practices associated with them. Since the Red Scare, immigrants who advocated political or social ideologies deemed radical were closely monitored and subject to deportation. Beyond constitutional protections, accorded in many circumstances to "persons" rather than to citizens, the administrative process of deportation has itself raised human rights concerns among immigrant advocates and legal scholars.[1]

Immigrants and the U.S. Constitution

Immigrants who are excluded or who face deportation in the United States are subject to administrative law procedures. In some cases, however, such as those of Marcus Garvey and Emma Goldman, immigrants are subject to deportation on the basis of their prior criminal convictions, a situation that has become increasingly common in recent decades. That fundamental fact has crucial implications for deportees' rights. Until the 2010 *Padilla v. Kentucky* Supreme Court ruling, immigrant noncitizens who face deportation, but not criminal charges, were not clearly covered by the Sixth Amendment to the U.S. Constitution and related protections guaranteed to those charged with crimes, including the right to a speedy trial. During the course of U.S. deportation history, administrative proceedings have limited basic rights, such as the ability to cross-examine witnesses, or the option to petition for a pardon.[2]

In those cases where the process occurs outside of the criminal justice system, deportation is not considered a criminal measure in the same sense as is imprisonment. Nevertheless, the deportation process shares several similarities with criminal proceedings. The immigrant is often detained, sometimes for a substantial length of time, and undergoes interrogation. A warrant is issued in the case of deportation proceedings, just as in the case of a criminal arrest, and the immigrant can either be released on bond or be detained while awaiting a hearing.

Deportation hearings were first brought before the Bureau of Immigration's Board of Special Inquiry. In 1922 that board, along with the agency regulating immigration, was moved to the Department of Labor, becoming the Board of Review. By 1940 the Board of Review was transferred to the Department of Justice and became the Board of Immigration Appeals, an administrative body that was separated from the Immigration and Naturalization Service. During the 1980s, immigration judges were removed from the INS and became a distinct unit within the Department of Justice.[3]

Historically, most immigrants facing deportation had no legal representation, largely because they were unable to afford counsel. We have seen the ways in which particular nations, through their international consulates and embassies, as well as the U.S. Department of State, have intervened in some high-profile deportation cases and particular U.S. immigration policies. But those remained exceptional cases. In other cases, such as that of Russian Jews and other political refugees, their motivation to immigrate was to escape state persecution. Therefore, they had no government recourse but effectively existed between two states and received the full protection of neither.[4]

Until the post–World War II era, immigrants and other aliens had limited recourse for challenging immigration-based decisions through the U.S. court system. Historically, the exclusion and deportation function was interpreted to fall under the plenary power doctrine, meaning that it was not subject to appeal or review by the judiciary branch. Until the late nineteenth century, it remained unclear whether the federal government possessed the authority to regulate immigration, and the power was not enumerated in the U.S. Constitution. In fact, as illustrated in chapter 3, several states did regulate immigration before 1882, focusing particularly on paupers and health concerns. By 1849, in the *Passenger* cases, the Supreme Court suggested that it considered immigration a federal matter.

As emphasized in prior chapters, immigrant advocates and the press, especially the immigrant press, have been at the forefront of many immigrant exclusion or deportation decisions that have been viewed as unduly harsh toward individuals. We have seen how some of the most compelling cases in the public's view have involved issues perceived as intrusions into family life or neglecting to provide individuals with refugee status on humanitarian grounds. Whether objecting to deportation on grounds that it would result in the separation of spouses from each other, infant children from their mothers, or excluding Jews seeking refuge from pogroms, press coverage has in some cases led to a positive outcome for immigrants facing exclusion or deportation. That function has been critical because the judicial branch has demonstrated a reluctance to act because of the plenary powers doctrine. In the absence of active review by the judiciary, popular opinion and media attention have sometimes served as a check on administrative decisions. This has been especially evident when family unification issues were at stake.

During the nineteenth century, the immigration regulation function was interpreted as one of the Constitution's sovereign powers. That principle arose in part from the view that immigration has implications for foreign relations, a power reserved for the federal government. Therefore, immigration regulation was viewed as a congressional and executive prerogative and the judiciary should therefore refrain from intervening in the process. Judges have argued that because aliens are citizens of other countries, decisions involving their rights have significant foreign policy implications that are best left to those branches. Moreover, the Civil War and subsequent constitutional amendments further solidified federal power, especially in the realm of citizenship and other constitutional rights, and led to greater consolidation of the immigration regulation function.[5]

As noncitizens, nonnaturalized immigrants have been variously defined as aliens, denizens, subjects, or quasi citizens. In that context, their ambiguous rights placed immigrants alongside African Americans, indigenous peoples, and residents of U.S. territories and protectorates such as Hawaii, Puerto Rico, and Guam. As legal historian Daniel Kanstroom has emphasized, Indians, along with these other groups, were found to be "perpetual inhabitants with diminutive rights."[6] Legal scholars have noted that when immigration cases did come before the courts, they were often debated on procedural rather than constitutional grounds. Noncitizen immigrants have, however, been deemed by the courts to have vital rights, including that of due process, in matters other than immigration.[7]

Several cases in the first decades of federal immigration regulation shaped the contours of immigrant rights in exclusion and deportation processes. The Chinese Exclusion Act of 1882, which placed a decade-long ban on the immigration of Chinese laborers, was among the first federal immigration laws. Congress periodically renewed and extended such legislation to prohibit most Chinese migration. Those exclusion laws soon generated several major Supreme Court cases establishing the plenary power doctrine in this era. Chinese immigration was regulated under a set of laws separate from European immigration laws. Nevertheless, those rulings had broader consequences for the rights of immigrants in the United States. As Hiroshi Motomura argues, these early court cases largely reflect a classical view of immigration—as a contractual relationship between the newcomer and a nation, and as a process granting privileges rather than conferring individual rights.[8]

In the 1889 *Chae Chan Ping* case, one of the Chinese exclusion cases, for example, the Court affirmed that the federal government maintained "sovereign powers" over immigration. Chae Ping lived in the United States, and traveled to China, having obtained a reentry certificate upon his departure. Before his return to the United States, Congress imposed new restrictions on Chinese immigration. Chae Ping found himself excluded from the United States, and his reentry certificate had been voided, because of the 1883 Scott Act, barring Chinese laborers from returning to the United States. Chae Ping was represented by nationally recognized attorneys, who were retained on his behalf by the Chinese Six Companies, a San Francisco–based ethnic community group.

The plaintiff's argument that Chae Ping's reentry was a right, rather than a privilege, was unsuccessful. The court decided that his reentry certificate did not protect him from changes in the law. Chae Ping was ultimately deported on September 2, 1889. Neither the plaintiff's argument nor the decision explicitly addressed the racialized and discriminatory nature of the exclusion laws. This was partially related to the plenary power act that reserved for Congress the right to oversee immigration. The interpretation of the Fifth Amendment as extending equal protection guarantees against the federal government came only later.[9]

The *Yick Wo v. Hopkins* case in 1886 had some positive implications for immigrants' rights. In that case, the U.S. Supreme Court determined that the Fourteenth Amendment applied to all persons without respect for their nationality. *Yick Wo v. Hopkins* would again be employed in segregation cases during the 1960s. Ruling in 1892 six years later in another exclusion case, *Nishimura Ekiu v. U.S.*, Judge Horace Gray stated in his opinion that the judiciary could not order the entry of aliens who were neither citizens nor residents and that "the decisions of executive or administrative officers, acting within the powers expressly conferred by Congress, are due process of law," thereby reinforcing the plenary powers doctrine in immigration cases. The judge rejected the plaintiff's claim that her exclusion, based on the public charge provision, despite her possession of twenty dollars upon entry, was unfair and violated her individual constitutional rights, upholding the plenary power doctrine.

In the 1896 *Wong Wing v. U.S.* case, the court heard the arguments of the appellant. Wong was determined to have immigrated to the United States in violation of Chinese Exclusion Law and sentenced to sixty days of hard labor as a punishment after T. E. McDonough, deputy collector of customs, arrested him in Detroit. He brought suit, arguing that he was being unlawfully detained. He further argued that his punishment conflicted with the Fifth and Sixth Amendments, because he was denied the right to have his case heard by a grand jury, a speedy and public trial, in the district in which the crime was alleged to have been committed. According to legal scholar John S. Richbourg, the case was significant: "A resident, alien born, is entitled to the same protection under the laws that a citizen is entitled to. He owes obedience to the laws of the country in which he is domiciled, and, as a consequence, he is entitled to the equal protection of those laws." Yet, though Wong was not required to serve his original sentence, he was, nevertheless, deported to China.[10]

Deportation and exclusion, like a double helix, run in separate lines but cross at critical points. In the nineteenth century, the rights of excluded immigrants, denied initial admission to enter the country, and those facing deportation proceedings after residing in the United States, were not always distinct. Over time, judicial decisions began to reflect greater distinctions between the exclusion and deportation process. Ultimately, each process evolved to encompass a particular set of rights. That reasoning derived from the concept that once the immigrant had established himself or herself in the community, he or she was entitled to greater due process than those who were excluded (or rendered inadmissible) and were defined as never having landed in the United States. The latter "territorial standing" concept was often a rhetorical one, because immigrants might be physically present in the United States while in temporary detention or paroled as they awaited their hearings. Moreover, some exclusion cases arose in which the immigrants could not secure entry into another country, as the *Mezei* case illustrates. Since 1996, however, exclusion and deportation processes have once again moved toward consolidation under the administrative immigrant "removal" process but not as a constitutional matter.

The Oppenheimer Report

In addition to court rulings that shaped the parameters of immigrant's rights during detention, exclusion, and deportation proceedings, several vital public debates arose about the rights of noncitizens in the deportation process during the 1920s and 1930s. Many of these centered on the inherent contradictions that arise when immigrants are accused of violating federal immigration laws but are not guaranteed each of the protections afforded to citizens through the federal court system.

Just before the large-scale deportation of Mexicans and other immigrants in the United States, major studies of the U.S. deportation process were undertaken by four attorneys and scholars: Reuben Oppenheimer, Jane Perry Clark, Norman Alexander, and William Van Vleck. Though historians have generally marked the end of the Progressive Era with America's entry into World War I, several recent studies have convincingly argued that the Progressive movement retained its influence well into the 1920s. This is one such example. These deportation studies were very typical of Progressive Era investigations that identified a problem, undertook careful studies, marshaled evidence and statistics, and offered recommendations for policy changes. The difference is that by the 1920s, the political climate had become inhospitable to such reform efforts.[11]

In 1931 Baltimore lawyer Reuben Oppenheimer authored a congressional report on immigration deportation proceedings for the Wickersham Commission. His study was included in the National Committee on Law Observance and Enforcement Report, a large-scale examination of the criminal justice system in the United States. Oppenheimer, a Baltimore native, later became a Maryland Court of Appeals judge. A graduate of Johns Hopkins University and Harvard Law School, he was active in several Jewish organizations, including the American Jewish Committee, the Jewish Welfare Fund of Baltimore, and the Baltimore Jewish Council. Previously, he had focused on family and juvenile law for the Children's Bureau. His long-standing ties to Jewish advocacy groups undoubtedly increased his awareness of immigration issues, which were widely discussed in Jewish publications in the early twentieth century.[12]

One of Oppenheimer's major conclusions was that the deportation process created a harmful conflict of interest because it involved the collapsing of investigatory, prosecutory, and judgment functions under one agency: "The inspector in charge is in reality a prosecuting official. His main interest is in seeing that the case of his office, which often he himself has prepared, is substantiated."[13] Oppenheimer suggested that an independent panel be established outside of the Department of Labor to hear and adjudicate cases.[14]

Oppenheimer's groundbreaking report outlined many of the legal issues and challenges facing immigrants who encountered the deportation process. But it has been largely overlooked by historians, because the Wickersham Commission concentrated primarily on investigating the narcotics and alcohol trade. Nevertheless, his study provided a valuable critique of the deportation process, even though few of his proposed reforms were implemented. In addition to Wickersham, the commission included Roscoe Pound, dean of Harvard Law School, and a sole female panelist, Ada Comstock, who would later serve as president of Radcliffe College.[15]

The report opened with a short history of early U.S. immigration law. Oppenheimer emphasized that debates over the ways in which immigrants and United States citizens were treated under law occurred well before the federal government systematically regulated the flow of immigration. The issue first emerged in the early nationalist period with the

Portrait of Judge Reuben Oppenheimer (1897–1982), by Selma Levy Oppenheimer. Collection of the Maryland State Archives.

Alien and Sedition Acts. Those acts were part of a larger rift between Federalists, led by President John Adams and Alexander Hamilton, and Republicans such as Thomas Jefferson and James Madison. The Republicans' support of the French Revolution led to Federalists' efforts to limit the political influence of European immigrants who might ally with the Republicans by significantly increasing the number of years of residency required for citizenship and making it easier to deport those who were seen as political radicals. Oppenheimer quoted James Madison on the hardships of deportation for those who have settled in the United States and become integrated into their new communities.[16]

Oppenheimer reached the conclusion that the deportation process, which concerned some of "the most important of human rights" needed significant reform and that "unconstitutional, tyrannical, and oppressive" methods were sometimes used. Citing Justice David Brewer in the *Fong Yue Ting v. U.S.* (1893) Supreme Court decision, he emphasized the gravity of the impact of the alien, who "is forcibly taken away from home, and family, and friends, and business, and property, and sent across the ocean to a distant land." He further noted that deportations affected family members, who were often U.S. citizens, and also that once an immigrant was deported, he or she was ineligible to return to the United States, a policy that has since been modified.[17]

Oppenheimer emphasized that most deported immigrants were not convicted criminals but had violated immigration law on a technicality. Because of the significance and irrevocable nature of the deportation act, he recommended that a presidential pardon be allowed in certain cases. In keeping with his interest in the rights of children, he noted that a minor child, even one who was a U.S. citizen, usually had no choice but to accompany a parent or parents who had been ordered deported. It was unlikely that he or she would return to the United States before reaching adulthood.[18]

The process of deportation also had significant constitutional implications, through the possible curtailment of personal liberty. He argued that "unlawful searches and seizures may be perpetrated; rights of lawful assembly and free speech may be infringed." He further highlighted the fact that the hearings were not public. He was highly critical of deportation raids, which occurred widely during the Red Scare of the late teens, and would occur again largely within Mexican communities shortly following the publication of his report in the 1930s.[19]

Oppenheimer noted that "the rights given by the Federal laws to the administrative agency are tremendous in scope. The very investigations to see whether suspected persons are subject to deportation by their nature, involve possible interference of the gravest kind with the rights of personal liberty." He provided as specific examples unlawful searches and seizures, free speech, and the right to assembly.[20]

In reviewing the immigration regulation, inspection, and deportation process, Oppenheimer carefully examined the Bureau of Immigration's administrative structure. He reported that the immigration inspectors were not trained nor did they undergo a character investigation. Though applicants needed to pass a short written exam, there were no educational requirements.[21]

Much of the inspectors' information arose from correspondence, often sent anonymously by someone acquainted with the immigrant. That gave rise to a concern that the government would use deportation as a blunt instrument in a personal vendetta. For immigrants, the threat that an employer, neighbor, or spurned lover would turn them into the authorities, whether real or false, was potent. The concern that they might be turned in for having committed deportable offenses often silenced immigrants and certainly led many of them to refrain from exercising many rights guaranteed to U.S. citizens, such as free speech, the right to association, and other actions that might engender retaliation.[22]

In 1907 the Immigration Bureau issued a regulation telling inspectors "not to lend their aid in causing the arrest of aliens upon charges arising out of personal spite or enmity, unless the truth of such charges is clearly established." By 1911 the policy that discouraged the use of information gained through spite or retribution by immigrants' acquaintances was no longer in force.[23]

Public and private organizations, such as hospitals or charity providers frequently provided immigrant officials with information leading to deportation. Another of Oppenheimer's concerns was that some judges set sentences for aliens to ensure that they were subject to deportation. For example, an alien sentenced to a term of just over a year would be deportable, whereas a sentence of just under a year might spare an immigrant from deportation charges.[24]

Oppenheimer identified several basic procedural issues and inconsistencies that could unduly influence the outcome of a hearing. For example, sometimes the immigrant inspector took notes, or when a stenographer was employed, the inspector requested that parts of the hearings not be recorded. The inspector had a great deal of latitude in determining whether a translator was needed.[25]

Oppenheimer further outlined several fundamental violations of immigrants' rights in his 1929 investigations. In fewer than half of all documented cases were immigrants informed at the beginning of their hearing that "anything they said could be used against them in subsequent proceedings" and that they could decline to provide an answer to avoid self-incrimination, and few in actuality refrained from answering questions. As uniformed officers, immigrant officials intimidated many immigrants from "countries where authority speaks with even a stronger voice than it does in the United States, and where failure to answer inquiries from Government officials would involve much more serious consequences." He added that immigrant officials singled out Mexicans as being especially "anxious to give out responses which they think are expected."[26] Despite the fact that deportation was an administrative, not a criminal, process, Oppenheimer noted that the methods of immigration officials sometimes were "inquisitorial" and that cross-examination could be undertaken with "the vigor of an unrestrained prosecuting attorney." Immigrants were sometimes asked highly personal questions, especially about their sexual histories, even when unrelated to the grounds for deportation but designed to intimidate the immigrant.[27]

Oppenheimer concluded that immigrants retained legal counsel in just one-sixth of the 453 cases he reviewed in 1929. For Mexicans, that rate was significantly lower: about 1 or 2 percent. Although financial considerations figured largely in this situation, he found that in some cases immigration inspectors discouraged the use of attorneys during hearings.[28] Mexicans, he noted, were also more likely than other immigrants to be deported on grounds of moral turpitude simply because they had entered into common-law marriages rather than those sanctioned by the state. He noted that even immigrants in long-term, exclusive partnerships in Texas, a state where common-law marriages were recognized, were deported.[29] Oppenheimer's report suggested that in those cases where immigrants did receive legal counsel, they were more likely to win their cases on appeal than those without legal representation.

Oppenheimer's study was prescient in many ways. In fact, he identified many of the procedural and legal issues that would later be articulated in international human rights law following the establishment of the United Nations and the ratification of the Universal Declaration of Human Rights. His approach was influenced by Progressive Era reform movements and the idea that groups of socially marginalized people deserved greater rights and that systematic investigation and publicizing the findings would create the context for change.

Oppenheimer's investigation generated significant opposition. The report's critical findings led two members of the Wickersham Commission to withhold their endorsement of Oppenheimer's conclusions.[30] Henry W. Anderson objected to the view that "the officers administering the law are often guilty of lawless invasion or disregard of the fundamental rights of the persons concerned." Kenneth Mackintosh, a Washington State judge, also challenged the investigation, declaring that it exaggerated the level of negligence in the administration of immigration law.[31]

After the Wickersham Report was made public, William Doak, the newly appointed secretary of labor, strenuously objected to the conclusions published in conjunction with Oppenheimer's study. The Wickersham Commission Report, as well as its recommendations for reforming immigration policies and procedures, was ignored by those in the Herbert Hoover administration. In effect, the intensive investigation to which Oppenheimer had devoted so much of his energy was shelved. The vital immigrant rights issues that he raised were never completely resolved, although some of his policy recommendations were raised by a committee established by Frances Perkins following her appointment as secretary of labor in the Roosevelt administration.[32] Therefore, although Oppenheimer's report led to some reforms in immigration deportation procedures during the 1930s under Perkins, many of the fundamental questions about noncitizens' human and legal rights issues were never resolved.

Just one year following the release of Oppenheimer's report, William C. Van Vleck, dean of the George Washington University Law School, wrote a study on the process of immigration regulation, *The Administrative Control of Aliens: A Study in Administrative Law and Procedure*. That study included both review of immigration records and observation of procedures used in the implementation of various procedures. Several of his conclusions were similar to those of Oppenheimer. He noted that most immigrants had no financial ability to retain legal representation and that immigration officials sometimes asked leading questions during deportation hearings or raised issues unrelated to the case.[33]

In his study of immigration laws, also undertaken shortly after the Wickersham study, Norman Alexander concurred with many of Oppenheimer's criticisms of the deportation process, including the problematic issue of the exclusion and deportation process occurring without the constitutional protections of rights afforded by the separation of powers. He noted that "there is a marked tendency at the present time to adopt a more liberal view toward alleged encroachments by one branch of the federal government on the domains of the other." He concluded that the situation illustrated "the wide powers and broad discretion that Congress must bestow upon immigration officials without delegating any legislative functions."[34] He added: "From the time the alien embarks from a foreign port until he departs from this country the hand of the administrative officer may reach out and not release his grasp until the alien is once again in the land of his birth or has become a citizen here."[35]

Alexander emphasized the need for more rules regarding the type of evidence allowed in a deportation hearing and limits on the use of *ex parte* or confidential evidence. He added that immigrants should be informed of the evidence being used by government officials in their cases. Alexander also argued that the perceived fairness of these proceedings had vital implications in international affairs. He stated, "Just as injudicious legislation by Congress has led to international friction, so a discriminatory policy pursued by administrative officials might provoke international controversies."[36]

A young scholar undertook another study of immigrant rights in the deportation process in the early 1930s. Jane Perry Clark Carey was a faculty member at Barnard College in New York. As a female political scientist, she was a pioneer in that field. She had received her Ph.D. from Columbia after graduating from Vassar College. In her dissertation, she analyzed the U.S. deportation process. Published in 1931, the investigation remained the single full-length monograph on the topic until recently. Later, she published research on American federalism, on the Soviet Union, and on the Middle East, as well as a book on Greek politics, co-written with her husband and fellow political scientist, Andrew Galbraith Carey. She also worked for the federal government on the issue of displaced persons in the immediate post–World War II era and served as a consultant for the UN High Commissioner of Refugees in the early 1950s.[37] Carey's interest in deportation issues, and later her research on federalism, undoubtedly led to her focus on refugee policy in a global context. Carey's sample was culled from deportations occurring between July 1925–January 1926 and January–July 1930. She addressed only cases that resulted in actual deportations, rather than those successfully appealed, and her study was limited to Europeans.

Carey placed U.S. deportation in the broader context of the Anglo-American legal tradition. She notes that an early immigration deportation case occurred in London in 1440, with "no cause laid against him but only he is a stranger born." That practice carried over to the English colonies, where as early as 1639, Plymouth colony sent its paupers to Europe, a practice of "removal" that became widespread in the colonies until the American Revolution. She characterized the 1917 revisions to deportation law as a "crazy-quilt' that was "barely intelligible even to the initiate." The continual revisions to the time frames affecting deportability on various grounds (e.g., three or five years following entry, or indefinitely), was particularly confusing. Moreover, Carey states, "Judicial interpretation too has sailed a devious course, often it seems, without chart or compass and in apparent disagreement as to the route.[38]

Strange Passage, the Depression, and New Deal Policies

In January 1931, in the early years of the Great Depression, the Hoover administration conducted one of the most notorious deportation raids in U.S. history. William Doak ordered a major federal operation targeting the 100,000 immigrants that he argued were deportable, because of violations of immigration laws. The raid focused on Los Angeles County, a metropolitan region that was second only to Mexico City in the size of its Mexican population. Doak ordered that immigration agents from other cities be brought in to help execute the raid. By publicizing those arrests, he sought to intimidate immigrants into leaving the United States rather than subjecting themselves to deportation.[39]

The Doak Raid became the subject of *Strange Passage*, a fictional account of a deportation party traversing the country by train in the 1930s. Theodore Irwin published his book a few years after the Oppenheimer Report was released. Irwin illustrates the effects of the deportation raids in the early Depression years as experienced by a group of immigrants on a train that departed from the West Coast to Ellis Island, where they were to be placed on steamships returning to their countries of origin. The novel's literary merit, which includes a stilted love story at its center, is significantly outweighed by its social critique.

Irwin, who had earlier published articles on lynching for the *American Mercury* and on free speech in *Public Opinion Quarterly*, was active in the American Civil Liberties Union. Irwin discusses the stories that led the dozen main characters to be ordered deported and the stereotypes and prejudices that they encountered from immigration officials and others.[40]

Irwin sets much of his book on Ellis Island. One immigrant awaiting deportation observes sardonically that the Statue of Liberty has its back to them. Another character questions why Americans support stricter immigration quotas and deportation drives: "There are three million square miles of land here, which should give a living to ten times the population today."[41]

Twenty-first-century readers would find it curious that although Mexicans constituted the group most affected by deportation raids during the early 1930s, Irwin's fictional group was largely comprised of European immigrants, alongside a Syrian and West Indian. His location in New York, and his work with the ACLU and those in political circles there, as well as the numerical weight of European immigrants in this era, probably all influenced that omission.

In the concluding chapter of his novel, Irwin makes reference to the Wickersham Commission Report and Secretary of Labor Frances Perkins's vow to implement reforms to the system of immigration deportation and conditions at Ellis Island, thereby creating a "New Deal for the alien." Those reforms were to include the cessation of raids, illegal administrative actions, and warrantless arrests. Perkins also disbanded the Section Twenty Four Squad that enforced the alien contract laws. At Ellis Island, immigrants were allowed access to telephones to contact their attorneys, and armed guards were no longer stationed there.[42]

Irwin discusses how the Immigration Service highlighted that it suspended deportation of "aliens of good character particularly those who have American-born wives and children on humanitarian grounds, thus sparing their families a great deal of hardship." Both Irwin and the immigration officials he portrays are very skeptical of these reform efforts. An immigrant official argued that although the commissioner sought to portray the humanitarian elements of the reforms, many in the service perceived them as primarily cost-cutting measures. By deporting fewer people, they saved $120 per person, which was important, given that congressional appropriations for immigration had been decreased by $1 million. By allowing aliens with U.S. family members to remain as breadwinners, fewer wives and children would rely on public funds.[43]

Irwin's novel portrays an immigration official as stressing that in response to the Wickersham Commission Report, the Department of Labor eased some of its restrictions on visitors who were deemed radical. For example, the Immigration Bureau lifted a ban allowing political radicals to visit the United States. Political radicals and activists, such as British Communist leader Tom Mann, Emma Goldman, and Henri Barbusse, were no longer barred from speaking in the United States.[44]

Some of the issues raised by Oppenheimer, Clark, Irwin, and others were revisited following Franklin Roosevelt's election. As the New Deal began Frances Perkins, a Progressive reformer, was appointed Secretary of Labor, the first woman to serve as a U.S. cabinet member. She appointed a commission to review some of the issues surrounding immigration policy, including those raised in the Oppenheimer report. The fifty members of the Ellis Island Committee were a notable group and represented industrialists, Progressive reformers, immigrant advocates, clergy, physicians, and others. As one might expect, many were New York State Democratic delegates. The chairman, Carleton H. Palmer, headed the Squibb Corporation; Mrs. Vincent Astor, Mrs. Marshall Field, Mrs. Charles Dana Gibson, and Mrs. Daniel O'Day were the wives of the railroad magnate, the department store owner, the well-known illustrator, and a Rockefeller business partner. Read Lewis worked with Josephine Roche and Marion Schisby in the Foreign Language Information Service. Max Kohler was the attorney and immigrant advocate affiliated with HIAS, and Roger Williams Straus, was the son of Oscar Straus, the former Department of Labor secretary. Franklin Kirkbride and Israel Goldstein were religious leaders.[45] James W.

Gerard was the ambassador to Germany in the Woodrow Wilson administration and a mining financier.

But a few committee members were skeptical of liberalizing immigration policies. For example, Dr. Foster Kennedy, an Irish-trained physician at Cornell University, was a major proponent of eugenics theory. He advocated euthanasia and sterilization for those who had certain psychiatric illnesses or were developmentally disabled, referring to them as "nature's mistakes."[46]

Family unification issues were at the heart of the reforms that the members of the commission proposed. Most significantly, they proposed that the "likely to become a public charge" (LPC) provision be amended so that if spouses or children sought to join a spouse or parent who was already in the United States, they could do so once they secured a bond of $500 or more. They also advocated relaxing the entry ban on those having committed a crime of moral turpitude more than five years before entry if they were married to a U.S. citizen and are "otherwise a person of good moral character."[47]

Some revisions to immigration policy occurred in the area of medicine and diagnostic categories. One notable change was that although immigrants with more than one episode of psychiatric illness would be excluded, those who experienced an isolated episode could be reviewed by the medical board at the port of entry to determine whether they should be admitted. Additionally, it was decided that some forms of epilepsy would be grounds for exclusion, whereas others were not.[48]

The committee also concluded that immigrants should not be deported "for *mere* belief" in socialism, anarchy, or other radical ideologies. That vital distinction had earlier been raised unsuccessfully in many of the protests against immigration deportations in the wake of the Red Scare, including during Emma Goldman's and Alexander Berkman's deportation hearings. Ultimately, that particular recommendation was not adopted in response to the Ellis Island Commission's recommendations, however. In fact, during the Cold War the Supreme Court in the *Heikkila v. Barber* and *Shaughnessy ex re Mezei* cases upheld the decisions to deport the two immigrants on the basis of their prior party affiliations.[49]

In addressing immigrant rights during the detention and deportation process, the report highlighted issues pertaining to the physical grounds, facilities, and social services at Ellis Island. In typical Progressive Era fashion, the idea that one's physical surroundings could improve the health and welfare of immigrants underpinned those suggested improvements.

The report noted that Ellis Island was not simply a temporary way station for immigrants entering the United States, but by the 1930s its facilities held 150–200 immigrants for up to months at a time while awaiting deportation.[50] Lastly, committee members addressed the widely varying definitions about what constituted the LPC provision. The report called for a uniform standard to be adopted.[51]

During World War II, immigration slowed considerably in part because of the dangerous conditions at sea. In the 1940s, the issue of global migrants largely centered on the development of refugee policies for the millions of Jews fleeing Nazi Europe and the many other displaced persons. As occurred in World War I, immigrant officials were reluctant to deport immigrants under such unstable and potentially dangerous conditions. Moreover, there were fewer immigrants to deport. Immigration to the United States had decreased significantly—first through the national-origins legislation enacted in the 1920s, then though the worldwide depression, combined with large-scale deportation and voluntary repatriation efforts of that decade.

Cold War Era Deportation Decisions

Following World War II, the Cold War led to a second Red Scare that constricted the rights of citizens and noncitizens alike. As had occurred in the aftermath of World War I, J. Edgar Hoover and the FBI again fueled much of the hysteria over national security and the threat from outsiders, especially immigrants. By the beginning of the twentieth century, immigrants facing deportation were guaranteed hearings and protected by the due process clause, whereas those who were excluded were not.

Legal scholar Charles Weisselberg provides two examples of how excluding immigrants without a hearing deprived immigrants of vital opportunity to obtain a fair decision. The first is the case of Ellen Knauff, a German-born Czech woman who married an American citizen following World War II, when she was employed as a civilian worker in the U.S. Army in Germany. Arriving in the United States with her husband, she planned to apply for U.S. citizenship under the provisions of the 1945 War Brides Act. But she was excluded and detained at Ellis Island and denied a hearing for security reasons, a decision that was deemed consistent with the 1941 Security Act. This was an unpopular decision and received a great deal of press coverage. She petitioned to challenge her exclusion order, issued by the attorney general. In its 1950 decision *U.S. ex rel Knauff v. Shaughnessy*, the U.S. Supreme Court upheld a district court and Second

Circuit Court decision to deny relief, reiterating the view that admission is a privilege, not a right, and affirming the plenary power doctrine.[52]

The initial exclusion decision turned on information alleging that while working for the U.S. government in Europe, Knauff had passed secret information to Czech officials, though the evidence for those allegations was slim. A public outcry against the Knauff decision ensued. Several members of Congress worked to pass a private bill on her behalf to enable her to remain in the United States. Justice Robert H. Jackson, of the U.S. Supreme Court, who had dissented in the early decision, issued a stay of her exclusion. Her husband met with the attorney general, who ordered immigration officials to reopen her case, which was heard by the Board of Special Inquiry. Knauff was ultimately paroled from Ellis Island and afforded a Board of Special Inquiry exclusionary hearing. After hearing evidence against her, including the testimonies of three witnesses, she produced evidence that she had no access to confidential information and that she had left the division before the date that witnesses claimed she had passed on information. She was ordered excluded. But although the board ruled against her, she appealed that decision, and her exclusion was ultimately reversed. She remained in the United States permanently.[53]

Weisselberg emphasizes that Knauff's hearing was critical to her obtaining justice. In most exclusion cases at that time, immigrants were not granted hearings and so could not defend themselves effectively. It was as a result of extensive and sympathetic press coverage, and the fact that she was married to an American citizen while both were serving on behalf of the American government in postwar Europe, that she gained the opportunity to obtain a hearing that ultimately exonerated her.[54] Knauff, like others, benefited greatly from the high value placed on family reunification in immigration policy.

Shaughnessy v. United States ex rel. Mezei was a second pivotal case for immigrant rights in the post–World War II era. That ruling concerned Ignatz Mezei, an immigrant who had moved to the United States in 1923. In 1948, he traveled to Romania to visit his gravely ill mother but was denied entry there. Upon his return to the United States, he was excluded on the basis of national security issues and detained at Ellis Island, because of his activities during the 1930s with an organization that was associated with communism, and the fact that he was absent from the country for an extended period. Yet, he did not have a significant role in it. He was unable to gain permission to enter other countries to which he applied for visas and was detained by immigration officials for almost two years.

Ellen Knauff, after hearing the news that she would not be deported. AP Wire photo, published in the *Detroit News* on November 3, 1951.

The 1953 *Mezei* Supreme Court decision upheld his exclusion. Despite having lived in the United States for more than two decades, by being excluded rather than ordered deported, Ignatz Mezei was treated as if he had never set foot on American soil, a concept that Weisselberg calls the "entry fiction." The court further rejected challenges based on the First Amendment and other grounds. Nevertheless, Mezei was ultimately paroled, because no other country would agree to accept him. The decision not to give him permission to reenter the United States would have effectively resulted in his indefinite, and theoretically permanent, detention at Ellis Island without legal recourse.

Two cases, *Gegiouw v. Uhl* in 1915 and *Heikkila v. Barber* in 1953, had additional implications for immigrant rights during U.S. deportation proceedings. The *Gegiouw* case concerned a group of Russian immigrants who were excluded on LPC grounds because the labor market in its destination city—Portland, Oregon—was viewed as "overstocked." Max Kohler, a lawyer and immigrant advocate, served on the legal team that argued the case, while Justice Oliver Wendell Holmes wrote the decision. Kohler argued that aliens are entitled to due process both under the Fifth Amendment and under Section 25 of the immigration law, and so it was a denial of due process to deny them a hearing for "controverted facts." The court overturned the decision to exclude the immigrant, because it was determined that the acting commissioner could not make exclusion decisions based on local, as opposed to national, factors.

The *Heikkila v. Barber* case hinged on whether the Internal Security Act of 1950, which rendered membership in the Communist Party grounds for deportation, was unconstitutional and whether Heikkila could seek judicial review of the decision. The majority decided that Section 19 (a) of the Immigration Act of 1917 did not allow an alien to seek relief in the courts from the attorney general's decision, because the 1917 act rendered that ruling final. Ultimately, it concluded, an immigrant could invoke only habeas corpus to challenge an order of deportation.

Recent Controversies

Between the early 1960s and the 1990s, deportation rates and controversies subsided. Some of the most racially discriminatory features of earlier immigration laws were addressed. Chinese (and soon other Asian) immigrants were no longer barred from naturalization, and family reunification provisions led to a wider global representation of immigrants. Still, racially biased policies and quotas that privileged Europeans over those from other global regions continued to exist in immigration legislation until 1965. The growth of the postwar economy and population led to a surge in military production, construction, and consumer demand. That expansion resulted in the extension of the Mexican Bracero program until the 1960s. Once again Mexicans were recruited for low-wage agricultural positions, this time under the formal auspices of the federal government. Modern civil rights activism and resulting legislation also affected U.S. immigrants. For example, César Chávez, Dolores Huerta, and others brought greater attention to Mexican American rights and broader unionization efforts among those who had been previously excluded from the AFL-CIO. A domestic shortage of nurses, physicians, and engineers led to the immigration of a group of highly skilled Asian immigrants from the Philippines and India. As a result of these circumstances, political representation and influence in ethnic communities increased into the 1970s, while international human rights and refugee policy also flourished during the Cold War, though heavily skewed by strategic and ideological concerns.[55]

But the close of the Cold War marked a return to a deportation-focused agenda. The expansion of the Republican Party's law-and-order platform, the success of the Reagan agenda and the fracturing of the New Deal coalition, the veiling of racial rhetoric in opposing illegal immigration, and deindustrialization led to a rise in deportations by the 1990s. Successful legal challenges led to the weakening of affirmative action policies. These trends reversed several of the gains in immigrant rights and status since the early 1960s.[56]

Though the increase in deportation of immigrants has escalated since 9/11, this trend actually dates from the 1990s. The Illegal Immigration Reform and Immigrant Responsibility Act (IIRIRA) welfare provisions in 1996 responded to California's Proposition 187 that rendered noncitizens ineligible for social benefits until it was overturned. This section addresses two interrelated deportation trends occurring since 1995: the racially motivated, economically based popular efforts against increasing numbers of Mexican and Central American immigrants migrating to the United States and working in construction, service, and agricultural sectors; and fears about crime and national security that culminated in the detention and deportation of immigrants from the Middle East and other regions.

Heightened public concern over crime led to the enactment of laws and policies such as the three strikes provision and mandatory sentencing guidelines that resulted in stricter immigration regulation in the area of deportation policy. Ironically this trend occurred during a period in which major violent crime declined sharply, largely as a result of robust economic growth. For immigrants, these stricter laws and enforcement mechanisms led to a spike in removals (formerly deportations), most often for minor and misdemeanor offenses, after the definition of aggravated felony was expanded to include fifty classes of crimes, including, in some cases, shoplifting.[57]

The law also applied those definitions retroactively. In many cases, young adults who had lived in the United States since infancy were threatened with deportation for nonviolent crimes and were faced with returning to a country where they had no immediate families or community ties. In others, parents of American citizens who had committed a minor offense in their youth were threatened with deportation several years or even decades later. Those immigrants are denied the right to counsel during the Bureau of Immigration Appeals process. The law further enabled the federal government to deport those immigrants while their cases are pending. Those two features of the deportation laws signal a departure from earlier procedures.[58]

Within the United States, these policies have had a chilling effect on Middle Eastern immigrants and their communities since 9/11. When the federal government requested that all Arab and Middle Eastern immigrant men voluntarily register with the Immigration and Naturalization Service, 13,000, or 16 percent of those who complied, later faced deportation, even though they had no ties to terrorist organizations. Of the 82,000 men who registered with the federal government and many more who have been scrutinized at airports or border points since 9/11, 11 at most have been accused of having links to terrorist organizations, but even that number might be high. In fact, many of those facing deportation after cooperating with the federal government had visa violations that arose from governmental delays in processing their applications or simply from a failure to submit a timely change of address form to the INS. Once the number of Middle Eastern and Arab immigrants deported exceeded 1,000, the federal government refused to make public further information on how many Arab and Middle Eastern immigrants have been detained or deported.[59]

Additionally, the 1996 Antiterrorism and Effective Death Penalty Act (AEDPA), together with the IIRIRA, limited habeas corpus rights for noncitizens, a trend that has escalated in the wake of 9/11. In fact on January 11, 2007, President George W. Bush's attorney general, Alberto Gonzáles, asserted in a Senate Judiciary Committee hearing that habeas corpus was not a right protected under the U.S. Constitution. This statement was a particularly dramatic example of how laws and court decisions that initially limit the rights of noncitizens can eventually be extended to curtail the rights of U.S. citizens.[60]

In the past decade removals or deportations have also once again been employed as a strategic labor management tactic by corporations in a national climate where unions have seen a major decline in membership and the federal government has continued to rule against unionization rights. As discussed earlier, that strategy was employed during the post–World War I Red Scare and Bisbee deportations and again in the 1930s and during the McCarthy era. In Tar Heel, North Carolina, for example, Smithfield Foods, whose workers were seeking to organize with the United Food and Commercial Workers Union, ICE conducted a raid that targeted immigrants active in unionization efforts.[61]

The deportation process has depended on cooperation with state and local authorities, though those relationships are fraught with tension and competing agendas. Over a century after the first federal immigration laws were enacted, debates over whether states, counties, or localities can legislate, regulate, or enforce immigration provisions continue to arise on a regular basis. Despite the fact that immigration regulation had been deemed a federal power in the nineteenth century and that the federal framework for immigration control was established in 1882, states had never fully ceded that right to the federal government.

Since then, local, county, and state governments have increasingly passed legislation and enacted policies that have collided with federal legislation. In Virginia, for example, officials in Prince William County, a rapidly growing region with an increasing Latino population, unanimously passed a resolution in 2007 requiring that immigrants' legal status be determined by new police procedures, such as checking drivers' documentation during routine traffic violations, whether or not there is probable cause to believe that they are not legal residents of the United States. The measure also seeks to exclude undocumented immigrants from receiving county services. Interestingly, in public debates about the policy, the county sheriff suggested that the policy could not be realistically enforced without a huge increase in personnel and related budget expenditures. Despite increasing the role of local police in stopping and checking documents, the number of serious crimes committed by immigrants was low. In 2008 undocumented immigrants accounted for just 2 percent of major violent crimes in Prince William County. Comparisons with prior years are not possible, because that was the first time that data were tabulated by immigration status.[62]

Residents in neighboring northern Virginia counties have also engaged in intense debates over whether day laborers should be provided with a dedicated site from which to obtain short-term employment. It remains unclear whether these laws can withstand judicial scrutiny, because as recently as the 1990s California's Proposition 187 was declared unconstitutional because it conflicted with the federal government's power to regulate immigration.[63] But in 2011 the U.S. Supreme Court upheld controversial Arizona legislation imposing sanctions on employers hiring undocumented immigrants. Moreover, depending on the levels of police training, whether or not community policing approaches are used, local attitudes toward immigrants, and criminal procedural processes, local and county laws have the potential to give rise to systematic racial profiling. In fact, officials in adjoining Fairfax County determined that the county should focus enforcement efforts on "illegal behavior, not immigration status," except in cases where the federal government mandated that status be determined before providing services or benefits.[64]

New York State and Maryland legislatures debated whether to continue allowing immigrants to obtain driver's licenses regardless of their status. Following 9/11, the federal government had established the Real ID program that required states to tighten restrictions on issuing drivers' licenses as an antiterrorism measure. As a result of heated controversy about the program, however, Janet Napolitano, DHS secretary, pledged to modify it. In 2006 Hazleton, a town of about 23,000, located in an isolated coal-producing region of Pennsylvania, passed the Illegal Immigration Relief Act, a law penalizing businesses for hiring or renting property to workers who are undocumented. At that time more than 100 municipalities were considering similar ordinances. The rationale for this act was that crime had increased as a result of immigration. But evidence reveals that crime levels decreased at the time that the Hispanic population grew in the city. Though struck down in federal court, in light of the 2011 Supreme Court Arizona immigration decision, the case has been remanded.[65]

The sharp rise in deportations over the past decade has led to human rights violations—including indefinite detention and harsh imprisonment—and has led the United Nations to criticize the treatment of those awaiting deportation. The inhumane detention conditions endured by many immigrants have had severe and sometimes fatal consequences. Immigrants are often detained in overcrowded, understaffed prisons, for indefinite periods. The majority of those affected by these severe detention conditions are Mexican and other Central Americans who have not been associated with terrorist activities.

In 2007 the *New York Times* published a front-page article about the increase in deaths among immigrants and other aliens held in U.S. detention facilities. Nina Bernstein, its author, noted that since 2004 at least 62 detained immigrants have died while in U.S. custody. Two years later, officials released information that the number of such deaths had been higher than previously reported—since 2003 it had surpassed 100. Many had medical conditions that were not adequately treated while they were held in federal custody. They were among over 27,500 immigrants in the past several years who have been held in detention while awaiting a decision by the Department of Homeland Security about whether they would be removed (formerly deported). Immigrants and asylum seekers are housed in a variety of facilities—those run by the Department of Homeland Security's ICE, county jails, and privately operated institutions.[66]

A 2009 Migration Policy Institute report found that immigrants were detained for an average of eighty-one days while awaiting the outcome of their deportation cases and that some without criminal convictions were detained for more than a year. The majority of those detained did not have criminal records; 78 percent were from Mexico, other countries in Central and South America, or the Caribbean. Most were housed in local or state jails. Additionally, the 1996 Illegal Immigration Reform and Immigrant Responsibility Act (IIRIRA) made detention mandatory for some asylum seekers who lacked proper documentation until they could establish a credible case for their fear of persecution.[67]

Immigrant detention is the subject of a larger UN study on the human rights of migrants. The *Times* article further noted that, although the federal government had adopted detention standards in 2000, in contrast to rules governing the treatment of criminal inmates, such guidelines were not legally enforceable because, unless they face criminal prosecution as well as deportation, detained immigrants are covered by administrative law, but not the constitutional protections that accompany criminal procedures.[68] These detention conditions have become increasingly salient because of the sharp increase in immigrants facing deportation in the past two decades. In 2007, 319,000 aliens were removed from the United States, the fifth year of continuous increase. A third of those actions was expedited removals and involved no hearing. In 2002 the number of removals totaled 165,168. In recent years, Mexicans have accounted for the vast majority of immigrants removed from the United States, with just under 209,000 in 2007, trailed by Hondurans and Guatemalans.[69]

In contrast to several groups, including women, African Americans, and gays and lesbians, who have experienced a net progression toward attaining a greater number of civil rights during the second half of the twentieth century, such pattern has not clearly emerged for immigrants. Certainly, although many of the racial exclusion features of immigration laws have been addressed since World War II, policies often remain differentially enforced by country of origin, or have differential effects based on economic status or political exigencies, which often serve as proxies for race. Moreover, though nonnaturalized immigrants usually retain citizenship in their countries of origin, it remains rare for those countries to intervene in individual deportation cases, though we have seen how they intervene in policy matters that affect significant numbers of their citizens.[70]

Immigrant political mobilization efforts, however, were much more widespread, visible, and effective than in the past. In response to the punitive measures in proposed federal immigration reform legislation in 2006, major protests were organized in Washington, Los Angeles, New York, and elsewhere. Immigrants were influenced by strategies implemented by the modern civil rights movement, women's movement, and gay and lesbian rights efforts. They also benefited from the increase in mixed-status households in the United States. An individual who is undocumented might have a spouse, child, parent, or other relatives who are U.S. citizens, so the demarcation between "legal and "illegal" (or irregular) populations is blurred.

The Hispanic vote was a vital bloc in the 2004 and 2008 presidential elections, and neither Republicans nor Democrats wished to alienate this swing group, which has become essential to Electoral College victory. Although some Hispanic voters who were U.S. citizens supported stricter immigration measures, they were not in the majority. Because many nonimmigrants have faced discrimination, such as through racial profiling, many second- and third-generation Hispanics recognize that harsh immigration policies had the potential to adversely affect themselves, local businesses, and their communities. Moreover, the rise of mixed-status families among Hispanics in particular mean that immigration-related policies often have significant impact on all members of those communities.

U.S. immigrants are not entitled to vote before their naturalization, though they had been granted voting rights by several localities in the nineteenth century. Although the right to vote is correctly viewed as both an obligation and a privilege conferred by democratic citizenship, the absence of voting rights leaves immigrants vulnerable—there is no natural political constituency to ensure that deportation proceedings are fair. Yet, though immigrant noncitizens have very limited political rights, they maintain some obligations typically associated with citizenship—for example, they are subject to the draft and must pay taxes and social security.[71]

Until immigrants have been in the United States long enough to be eligible to apply, they remain in legal limbo. Although one might argue that immigrants are by definition living in the United States by choice, some are unable to return to their countries of origin, whether from fear of persecution or because family ties keep them in the United States. Immigrant children must rely on their parents to apply for citizenship on their behalf, and some U.S. citizen children are obligated to accompany their immigrant parents who are deported, because they cannot remain in the United States by themselves. Historically, as a result of racial exclusion and gender norms, many people could not choose U.S. citizenship, or found that eligibility for either entry or citizenship depended greatly on their marital status.

Alexander Aleinikoff, a legal scholar who studies immigrants' relationship to constitutional law, notes that the Bill of Rights does not limit rights on the basis of citizenship but uses "person" extensively. Aleinikoff and other legal scholars suggest that the plenary power doctrine, in which the courts defer to Congress and the executive branch in matters of immigration, is outmoded. He maintains that the widespread rationale that immigration does not belong in the court system because of its vital foreign policy implications is not a sufficiently strong defense of the doctrine.[72]

Broader Implications for Nonimmigrant Aliens

Historical debates over which rights are accorded to noncitizens in the United States, including those who were political dissenters, have implications that extend to recent debates over the treatment of detainees at Guantánamo Bay, suspects held in undisclosed locations abroad under extraordinary rendition, Middle Eastern immigrants detained indefinitely in American jails for visa violations, and other noncitizens. There are certainly distinctions between the rights accorded those noncitizens residing in the United States and the rights of those classified as enemy combatants—whether in Guantánamo Bay, territories such as Iraq and Afghanistan (where the United States is involved in war or military actions), or those detained by U.S. allies. But the rights accorded both to noncitizens in the United States and to those in territories controlled by the United States since 9/11 and as a result of antiterrorism policies have long-term implications for American citizens as well, as Georgetown University law professor David Cole and others have argued. In other words, the treatment of aliens or noncitizens serves as an entering wedge to defining and limiting U.S. citizens' rights.

In a particularly controversial decision, the Bush administration defined detainees arrested during military operations in Afghanistan and Iraq as "enemy combatants," rather than as political prisoners. Therefore, those detainees are not covered by Geneva Convention mandates. Yet, since 2001 the Supreme Court has ruled in several instances that Guantánamo detainees must be accorded greater rights. Later, American citizens arrested both in the United States and abroad for activities related to Al Qaeda–sponsored training camps were also classified as enemy combatants, a decision that has significant implications for the civil liberties of U.S. citizens. Finally, in 2009, following a campaign pledge, President Barack Obama signed an Executive Order closing Guantánamo Bay Prison and in June the first of those prisoners was brought to the United States to await trial. The plan sparked immediate opposition from Republicans and Democrats alike and the closure has been delayed indefinitely.

There are several instances where immigrants and other noncitizens were detained for substantial periods as a result of basic errors or overzealousness. In 2001 Purna Raj Bajracharya, a Nepalese tourist with limited knowledge of English, found himself incarcerated in solitary confinement for three months, and forced to remove his clothes, because in preparing to return to Nepal, he had aroused suspicion when videotaping some New York skyscrapers to show his relatives. His incarceration occurred after he was interrogated by the FBI without a translator present. Bajracharya's name was not found on any terrorist-related databases, and like most Nepalese, he was a Buddhist, not a Muslim. But Bajracharya was released only after spending many months in a federal detention center, in part because his access to legal assistance, translators, and publicity was curtailed. He was never charged with a crime and was eventually allowed to return to Nepal voluntarily, although he was escorted to his plane in shackles and in prison attire. Under immigration law, Bajracharya's overstaying his tourist visa would be grounds for his deportation, but his treatment in jail far exceeded the penalty for that violation and constitutes a major breach of his human rights. Although the inspector general's office determined that such detainees were being mistreated, such cases are not being prosecuted because the witnesses were being deported immediately following their mistreatment.[73]

Bush administration officials justified these actions by defining the war on terror broadly enough so that it was not limited to certain nations and their citizens or by a time frame, as wars have been conventionally demarcated. After holding those detainees in custody for more than two and a half years without charges or hearings, and without access to legal representation, the Supreme Court ruled under *Hamdi v. Rumsfeld* in June 2004 that detainees were entitled to trials and could not be held indefinitely.[74] Those in the Bush administration, especially Attorney General John Ashcroft, relied heavily on the provisions of immigration law in the United States, because they do not provide the full constitutional rights accorded to U.S. citizens through the criminal court system. As Cole points out, under criminal law, people cannot be held for more than forty-eight hours without charges, and their hearings cannot be held in secret, thereby ensuring that no one can trace who or how many are being held. Under immigration law, however, persons can be held in custody without charges for a "reasonable" period, thereby extending the period of detention, and allowing for preventative detention, which is otherwise difficult to sustain under the Constitution. In June 2001, in *Zadvydas v. Davis*, the Supreme Court ruled that federal statutes do not authorize indefinite detention in cases in which removal is not foreseeable and is subject to federal review.[75]

By analyzing which rights have been extended to immigrants and other noncitizens and which were withheld, we can better understand the meanings of American citizenship, the legal privileges it confers, and ongoing debates over which human rights exist independently of one's legal status, citizenship, or nationality. It also provides greater context to the history of the development of international human rights law and theories, especially following World War II and the ratification of the United Nations Declaration of Human Rights.[76]

Questions about the constitutional rights of noncitizens, whether resident aliens or others, who are suspected of violating immigration laws or criminal laws also have vital implications for enemy combatants who have been imprisoned in military facilities in Iraq or Afghanistan, placed in Guantánamo, or transported to countries in Eastern Europe and the Middle East under extraordinary rendition.

The Bush administration's decision to classify those individuals as enemy combatants rather than as prisoners of war was a monumental one. Defining opponents and terror suspects as enemy combatants allowed the administration to circumvent the Geneva Convention and its clear statement of what constitutes the acceptable treatment of captured prisoners. Specifically, methods of torture, such as water boarding, sexual abuse and humiliation, and other inhumane practices have been both sanctioned and implemented at Abu Ghraib, Guantánamo, and the many still undisclosed locations where enemy combatants were taken under extraordinary rendition. In his book, *Ghost Planes*, Stephen Grey emphasizes that many suspects were transported to "black sites" without charges and access to legal representation and tortured. In some cases young children of those suspects were also transported in jets to other countries allowing torture under extraordinary rendition. One suspect, who was later released, spoke of prisoners assigned color-coded clothing indicating whether or not they had been charged with a crime.[77]

The definition of enemy combatants was ultimately expanded to include U.S. citizens who had been involved in religious activities that were associated with training camps or were determined to become involved in terrorist organizations or plots. For example, a year after 9/11, six men in Lackawanna, New York, were arrested for alleged involvement in terrorist activities. They grew up in a Yemeni immigrant community outside Buffalo, and most were born in the United States. They pled guilty to attending an Al Qaeda training camp, in large part because they were faced with being detained in a secret military prison without a trial or access to legal representation for an indeterminate period. Neal Sonnett, chair of the American Bar Association's Task Force on Treatment of Enemy Combatants, asserts, "The defendants believed if they didn't plead guilty, they'd end up in a black hole forever."[78]

Moreover, until some significant Supreme Court decisions ruled otherwise, suspects were allowed to be held indefinitely at those detention sites. Many suspects were later released and it became clear that they had committed no crimes. In December 2007, the Supreme Court heard a consolidated case, *Boumediene v. Bush* and *Al Odah v. U.S.*, about a group of Algerian Guantánamo detainees who had been in U.S. custody since 2002. In the case, the Supreme Court heard arguments about the legitimacy of military tribunals that were created in 2006 to address issues arising from previous Supreme Court rulings on Guantánamo. The Bush administration argued that detainees at Guantánamo do not have habeas corpus rights, in part because Guantánamo lies outside U.S. law. But those earlier rulings suggest that the Supreme Court considers the naval base at Guantánamo to be covered by the U.S. Constitution. In June 2008 the Supreme Court decided in a 5–4 opinion that the prisoners in Cuba were covered by habeas corpus, given that Guantánamo was within de facto sovereign territory of the United States. Consequently, the Military Commissions Act of 2006 was a violation of those rights.[79]

If detainees are not protected by the U.S. Constitution while under military detention, it remains unclear what rights they are entitled to and what country has jurisdiction over them—Algeria, Cuba, or Bosnia, or the nation in which they were arrested? The Bush administration has defined their status not as prisoners of war, but as enemy combatants, thus depriving them of rights accorded under the Geneva Convention or other international bodies. So the case raises the question of what rights they have and whose rights. If not covered by U.S. laws, what country or governing body has jurisdiction over them?

There is a provision under the U.S. Constitution for the suspension of habeas corpus, but only when "unless in cases of rebellion or invasion the public safety may require it." There are distinct parallels to the notion of "territorial standing" that was used to distinguish the rights of aliens who had been admitted and were being deported, and the lesser rights accrued to those who might physically be detained on U.S. soil but face exclusion.

A specific issue in this case is whether detainees should have access to the evidence and the identities of the witnesses used in their trials by military commissions. These three-person tribunals were established in 2006 in response to an earlier Supreme Court ruling in *Rasul v. Bush* that declared that prisoners could not be held indefinitely without trial. Yet since that 2004 decision, just 38 of the 534 Guantánamo detainees were declared not to be enemy combatants. These military tribunals do not allow defendants to be represented by counsel during the entire process and do not have the power to free the detainee if he is not convicted. Each detainee is assigned "a personal representative," but unlike an attorney, that representative is expected to provide any intelligence information received through conversations to the military. Thus far, most Guantánamo detainees have not been charged with a crime, and none has been convicted.[80] A notable strategy in the hearing was the statement by Seth Waxman, the lawyer for the detainees, that not only had they been detained in isolation for six years but many of them had been "plucked from their wives and children." That statement was designed to appeal to the humanity of the detainees, a strategy that has often been effective in garnering public and media support for immigrants in detention in the past.[81]

The treatment of noncitizens and U.S. citizens who have been deemed enemy combatants since 9/11 has demonstrated the erosion of civil liberties during the ongoing war on terror. This war differs from previous ones in that it is being waged not only in Afghanistan and Iraq but against alleged terrorists throughout the world, most of whom are not acting as soldiers or agents of a particular state. Prisoners of war have been redefined as enemy combatants so as to elude the provisions of the Geneva Convention. In contrast to earlier wars, where the enemy was defined as a citizen of a nation against whom the United States was at war, these enemy combatants have been defined as terrorists, whether they are citizens of Iraq or Afghanistan, citizens of many other nations who are often U.S. allies, or U.S. citizens or immigrants to the United States.

By analyzing which rights have been extended to immigrants and which were withheld, we can better understand the meanings of American citizenship, the legal privileges it confers, and ongoing debates over which human rights exist independently of one's legal status, citizenship, or nationality. Those debates provide greater context to the history of the development of international human rights law and theories. Recognizing that immigrants have never been afforded the same rights as U.S. citizens under the Constitution, several scholars, attorneys, and activists in the 1920s and 1930s articulated an early framing of universal human rights principles that guide the appropriate treatment of global migrants. Those critics espoused the Enlightenment-influenced ideals that humans had rights independent of their nationality or those granted by the political regime under which they resided. Consequently, they argued, migrants should be accorded certain basic rights by the U.S. government, such as the right to legal representation, the separation of administrative functions from judicial ones in deportation, and the right to humane conditions and limited length of detention while awaiting the outcomes of their deportation cases.

Following the gains of the modern U.S. civil rights movements in the 1950s and 1960s, including the Civil Rights Act, immigrants and their advocates have been more successful in political mobilization efforts, including by opposing criminalization provisions of the 2006 immigration reform bill. More recently, detention issues have been addressed in the 1990 Convention on the Protection of the Rights of All Human Migrants and Members of Their Families. According to the resulting document, "Migrant workers and their families shall have the right to equality with nationals of the State concerned before the courts and tribunals." But the implementation of that process has been uneven and inconsistent.[82]

In the United States, such a process remains elusive. There remain two systems of justice: one for U.S. citizens and another for noncitizens. Nevertheless, the major national protests in 2006 illustrate that immigrants have claimed human rights and civil rights language to argue for improved treatment in the United States under immigration laws and policies.

In 2009 Janet Napolitano of the Department of Homeland Security released information on her agency's plans to reform the process of detaining immigrants awaiting asylum or removal hearings. If they take effect, the majority of detained immigrants, who are not accused of criminal activity, would no longer be imprisoned in jails or penitentiaries. Addressing some of the criticisms contained in the Migration Policy Institute (MPI) report and other immigrant and human rights investigations, this plan addresses the growing number of immigrants incarcerated, the increased death rate in detention, and the high cost of imprisoning noncriminals. In fact, ICE records reveal that the number of noncriminally convicted alien detainees declined in the last quarter of 2009.[83] But despite these efforts to improve detention conditions, there remains relatively little public policy dialogue on significantly reforming the process of immigrant removal.

CONCLUSION

Current debates over immigration, including deportation, have strong historical roots, originating with European poor laws. Modern implementation of immigrant regulation depended on the emergence of a large federalized bureaucracy. American attitudes toward race, gender, religion, politics and labor issues, and health and fear of contagions all shaped how Congress enacted immigration legislation and immigrant officials implemented it. The presence of immigrants helped to define U.S. citizenship. But immigrants and their advocates, both in the United States and abroad also had a significant role in the deportation process, even when they were not successful in their ultimate goals. Dialogue about immigrant rights in the United States also shaped our modern concept of human rights.

This book has illustrated the ways that Congress, the Department of State, and U.S. immigration officials also recognized that the nation-state was far from static, both in the United States and around the world. While rooted in the nation-state, deportation was a transnational process. In enforcing immigration, both policy officials and politicians acknowledged the malleability of the state, its definition, its borders, and the often bilateral or multilateral constituents concerned with immigration issues. As a result of American expansionism following the Spanish-American War in 1898, for example, the Philippines was for a time exempt from the U.S. ban on immigration from Asia. The United States recognized the Irish Free State when it emerged briefly from Great Britain and later became the Republic of Ireland. Turkey became a desirable trading partner. And increasingly dual citizenship, though not formally recognized by the United States except in a few cases, became widespread. Some Cubans, whose interactions with the United States were intensive after 1898, sought to benefit from educational opportunities in the United States. U.S. government agencies understood that immigrants' political identities were not always reducible to the nation-state, but that very fact was perceived as a threat. Federal agencies, first in the BI (later the FBI), employed surveillance and immigration enforcement measures against socialists, anarchists, communists, and pan-African activists. Whether in the form of new religious practices and concepts, or social or political ideologies and trends, transnational movements could be suppressed at the borders by immigration and other officials by making leaders vulnerable to scrutiny, deportation proceedings, or criminal charges. So deportation, while bound by the laws and policies of a particular state, is a global process.

My research emphasizes that immigrants and their advocates were active agents in the shaping of immigration policies, and that their voices have grown more effective since the 1980s. Though not always successful, immigrant advocacy groups, along with attorneys representing immigrants in appeals and in Supreme Court decisions, affected positive outcomes for immigrants, among them Caterina Bressi, Ellen Knauff, Sarah Kevin, and Louis Wirth. New Deal–era activists and officials addressed some of the most punitive features of exclusion and deportation policies. In recent decades, however, law and order policies calling for strict immigration enforcement have collided with the need for inexpensive labor to fuel economic growth in construction, service, and other sectors and the growing influence of Hispanic voters, who tend to oppose highly restrictive laws and are neither solidly Democratic nor Republican. Over the past century, the United States has demonstrated significant legislative and administrative power to regulate immigration, but that function has not always been effectively implemented. Moreover, immigrants from the Western Hemisphere were not subject to numerical quotas until after World War II.[1]

Since the 1980s issues of immigration and deportation have been major concerns of many other liberal democratic states, including those across Europe. Just as in the United States, that immigration flow has led to many cultural and social tensions, often of a religious nature. That widespread growth in immigration and deportation policies has led to much scholarship on the role of the state in global migrations. As liberal democratic countries have become increasingly diverse, their populations became more highly skilled, and indigenous birth rates dropped. As Europe prospered in the World War II era, immigrants from neighboring nations were increasingly replaced by more migrants from non-European countries. Another reason for the growth in longer-distance migration arose from the establishment of the Common Market in 1957 and the European Union in 1993, which has since expanded to twenty-seven members. EU citizens migrate, work, and live within the larger membership zone with fewer restrictions than previously—they are no longer defined as migrants.[2]

The migration policies of the United Kingdom, the modern world's most significant empire before the decolonization movement following

World War II, took a fundamentally different shape than in the United States, Australia, and Canada. Unlike each of those three nations, land was scarce, population density was high, and industrialization and urbanization had accelerated in the early nineteenth century, beginning with textile production. Consistent with the very rationale for mercantilism and colonial expansion, most agricultural production occurred in British colonies, rather than in the home territory, and industry was actively discouraged in those regions.

The global reach of empire allowed for significant internal migration when the Irish supplied labor in London, Manchester, and Liverpool. A significant noncolonial immigration occurred in the nineteenth century, as German and later Eastern European and Russian Jews settled in Britain, both permanently and temporarily. But, in part because the cost of travel was prohibitive for most, Asian, African, and Caribbean subjects did not migrate in large numbers to Britain until after World War II. From the British Nationality Act in 1948 until 1962, the 800 million citizens of New Commonwealth countries (e.g., India, Pakistan, Bangladesh, and Jamaica) shared the same British citizenship and migration rights as Old Commonwealth countries (e.g., Canada, New Zealand, and Australia). Jamaicans saw their rights to immigrate to the United States severely restricted by the McCarran Walter Act in 1952, so Britain became a logical alternative. As Randall Hansen illustrates, several members of British Parliament expressed their reluctance to enact restrictive migration affecting Old Commonwealth countries, and most assumed those societies would provide most of the immigrants to the United Kingdom. But in 1962 significant immigration restriction provisions were enacted.[3]

As many liberal democratic societies were increasing their immigration levels from prior limits, Britain's 1962 immigration law severely restricted immigration quotas. Christian Joppke characterizes the post–World War II United Kingdom as a "zero-immigration country." That transition occurred, he argues, because of public anti-immigration sentiment that rendered politicians who supported immigration vulnerable in elections and because of the weak court system relative to Parliament. Racial clashes in the late 1950s also contributed to restrictionist policies. When 200,000 New Commonwealth Asians sought entry to the United Kingdom after being expelled from newly independent Kenya in 1962, they were refused entry despite their status as British nationals. While immediate family members were exempt from immigration quotas under the U.S. Hart-Celler Act in 1965, British law did not provide for secondary or family migration. Joppke discusses how this led to "asymmetrical treatment of husbands and wives," with the presumption that men, but not women, were economic migrants.[4]

In 1971 immigration to Britain was restricted based on a "patriality" principle, limited to those with a parent or grandparent born in the United Kingdom. The law also provided for greater deportation powers. By 1981 the principle of *jus soli* had been modified to deny citizenship to those born in the United Kingdom to temporary migrants and non-British citizens. Thus, New Commonwealth groups who had more recent experience and fewer familial ties within Britain, including those from Asia, Africa, and the Caribbean, would be severely disadvantaged relative to others. By 1988, the obvious gender biases were removed from family migration policy, but controls on marriage migration were tightened, thereby disadvantaging later arrivals who had deferred family reunification. Simultaneously, it expanded European Union nationals' rights.[5]

The Netherlands, and France, have for centuries experienced migration to and from neighboring European countries (such as Belgium and Italy), as well as a significant Jewish diaspora population spurred by the Spanish Inquisition. Since World War II, those countries began to see many more migrants from its former colonies following decolonization in Africa, Asia, and the Caribbean. As in the United Kingdom these former colonial subjects from Sri Lanka, Suriname, Algeria, Morocco, and elsewhere obtained rights to dual citizenship. While often viewed with hostility and subject to discrimination in Europe, they were generally not subject to deportation. During the Nicholas Sarkozy administration, the French government proposed DNA testing to limit the number of family members eligible to migrate to France. This effort was largely directed at its North African population. Questioning the veracity of familial claims recalls the nineteenth century "paper sons" controversy among Chinese immigrants to the United States.[6]

Many European countries have experienced regular immigration flows from nearby European countries, including those from Poland and Russia. Under Bismarck, Germany began to regulate immigration among Poles. During the Holocaust, immigrant laborers in Germany and its territories were replaced by forced laborers, especially Jews, and prisoners of war who supplied industrial, service, and agricultural labor and often perished or were killed in concentration camps. In post–World War II Germany, migrants typically came from Greece and Turkey rather than from its former colonies in Africa and elsewhere. Though 12.6 million immigrants settled in West Germany from 1950 to 1993, German politicians denied that it was a nation of immigrants, and integration was not part of its self-definition, in part because of its goal of German reunification and the effects of the 1973 oil crisis on unemployment rates. Though Turkish immigrants to Germany were often permanent, as guest workers their immigrant status remained temporary. Germany denied *jus soli* citizenship to those born within Germany to noncitizen parents until 2000, when a law made Turkish immigrants and their children eligible for German citizenship, though under restrictive conditions, including six years of school attendance in Germany. Upon reaching adulthood, dual-national children who chose German citizenship had to renounce their other citizenship. Those who do not wish to renounce citizenship could opt for a "pink card" that offers partial rights to immigrants.[7]

Germany also maintained a highly decentralized system of state-based immigration enforcement relative to the federalized United States and other industrialized countries. But in 1973 its deportation power was limited in a Constitutional Court ruling. Following 1989 German reunification, East Germans arrived in many German cities to fill low-wage jobs, but those workers were not immigrants but new citizens.

Other European nations, especially Spain and Italy, have seen an influx of African immigrants during a time of economic growth. Between the 1990s and the global financial crisis of 2008, Ireland transformed itself from a country of long-term out-migration to one of net in-migration. In the 1990s Irish citizens returned to their country of origin due to dramatically improved employment opportunities, while Europeans from the European Union, especially Poles, and West Africans arrived in Ireland. The reception to those immigrants was particularly negative. In the past decade, the Irish government has also suspended its practice of conferring *jus soli* citizenship upon birth to those born in Ireland to non-EU citizens, while simultaneously extending citizenship rights to descendants of Irish-born immigrants living abroad.[8]

These public reactions to immigrants are particularly ironic for Irish and Italians, whose long legacy of widespread poverty led them to migrate in large numbers to the United States, Canada, Australia, and elsewhere beginning in the mid- nineteenth century. As economic migrants, they established chain migration networks, and their remittances were central to the prosperity of their communities. But negative sentiment by the majority population in many European countries has given rise to an increase in deportations. For example in 2008, 66,275 immigrants were removed or voluntarily deported from the United Kingdom, which represented a 5 percent increase from the previous year. In 2009, with its unemployment exceeding 17 percent, Spain recorded the highest rate of deportations in Europe.[9]

Latin America, including Argentina and Brazil, were also significant forces in attracting global migrants. Like the United States, Brazil sought alternate sources of labor for its expansive agricultural sector, mining, and other industries following the abolition of slavery. Spanish, Portuguese, and Italian migrants in particular were vigorously recruited as laborers for grain and coffee production, and their voyage was often subsidized. Jews also came in significant numbers at the turn of the twentieth century; Japanese laborers were also drawn to Peru, Brazil, and other South American countries.[10]

Deportation and immigration policy are subjects that have been increasingly addressed by political scientists, in addition to historians, sociologists, and anthropologists. Political theorists and comparativists studying international migration and the inherent tensions between national sovereignty and human rights claims tend to classify scholars into two groups. The first are statists, those who argue that the nation-state and its attendant interest groups (or clients) and legal systems have a significant influence on global migration patterns and the incorporation of immigrant groups into society and political life. That concept originated with the Westphalian model of territorial sovereignty, in which states are understood to exist on a free and equal basis, with ultimate authority over those within its geographical boundaries. Scholars promote a convergence thesis that posits that many liberal democratic states have imposed similar measures to regulate and incorporate immigrants. But they differ in their assessment of how effective states have been in regulating immigration in the past few decades, citing the pervasiveness or irregular migration. James Hollifield, for example, argues that "Competing interests in pluralistic societies lead to policy-making gridlock which, in the face of ever stronger economic incentives, permits immigration to continue in one form or another." He suggests that the nation-state is still central to immigration restriction, explained best through a theory of complex interdependence, rather than an international migration regime in which international organizations constrain a particular nation's sovereignty and autonomy.[11]

The second group, globalization or decline-of-citizenship scholars, in contrast, argue that a state's ability to impose migration control has decreased significantly as a result of international human rights and the related rise of international governing bodies. Citizenship (and, as a result, territorial sovereignty) has therefore become less geographically bounded because of an unprecedented flow of goods, services, and peoples across borders. That perspective is influenced by Immanuel Kant's concept of a universal "right of sojourn" and Hannah Arendt's concept of "statelessness" and the limits of the nation-state to protect human rights. Therefore, a particular nation-state is rendered less able to control immigration or to define citizenship.[12]

While I agree that the increase in irregular migration and the more pervasive concept of dual nationality suggest that notions of political and national identity are increasingly flexible, and less bound to one set of laws, and that migration is not always within the ability of the state to regulate effectively, the nation-state, its geographical borders, and its policies have remained powerful determiners of an immigrant's rights before, during, and after migration and are essential to the act of expulsion. Similarly, Seyla Benhabib's understanding of immigration's relation to the nation-state is neither purely statist or globalization driven. In developing her argument for "cosmopolitan federalism," she states, "Permanent alienage is not only incompatible with a liberal-democratic understanding of human community; it is also a violation of fundamental human rights." She asserts that "policies regarding access to citizenship ought not to be viewed as unilateral acts of self-determination, but rather must be seen as decisions with multilateral consequences that influence other entities in the world community. Joseph Carens also advances the view that the length of residence and subsequently membership in a political community should have an impact on an immigrant's deportability to avoid just a status of permanent alienage.[13]

As a historian I recognize that globalization is far from a recent phenomenon, and that the state's role in shaping immigration remains significant, especially through the process of deportation. Some elites with dual citizenship, especially those with the right to move easily within the EU, work in professional and multinational settings where a demand for their skills and expertise pose few barriers to travel and where their identities, interests, language, and associations are not locally or regionally bound. At the other end of the spectrum are those who are trafficked across borders or arrive as irregular migrants, such as the estimated 8 million who now live in the United States. But most global migrants are limited by visas, work permits, security measures, and financial constraints. As chapter 7 detailed, the plenary powers doctrine and the administrative control of immigration law severely limited the extension of constitutional rights to noncriminal immigrants facing deportation. Although refugee policy is globally driven and overseen by international bodies and foreign policy agendas, and while treaties such as NAFTA continue to influence immigration policy, in the United States the role of international bodies and courts in regulating immigration is limited relative to Europe.

The effects of the recent global financial crisis on immigration in the United States and elsewhere remain to be seen. As occurred during the Great Depression, the rate of immigration from Mexico has decreased since 2008. Financial remittances returned to families of immigrants have also decreased because of the sharp decline in construction, manufacturing, travel, and other labor sectors where immigrants are concentrated. Though immigration reform became a less pressing issue than health care and banking reform, the stimulus plan, and other public policy issues, it will have to be returned to the congressional agenda.

APPENDIX A

Excerpts of Major U.S. Legislation Pertaining to Immigration Deportation Policy

Legislation from 1790 to 1900

ALIENS ACT OF JUNE 25, 1798 (1 STATUTES-AT-LARGE 570)
Represented the first federal law pertinent to immigration rather than naturalization. Provisions:

a. Authorized the president to arrest and/or deport any alien whom he deemed dangerous to the United States.
b. Required the captain of any vessel to report the arrival of aliens on board such vessel to the collector, or other chief officer, of the Customs of the Port.

This law expired two years after its enactment.

ALIEN ENEMY ACT OF JULY 6, 1798 (1 STATUTES-AT-LARGE 577)
Provided that in the case of declared war or invasion the president shall have the power to restrain or remove alien enemy males of fourteen years and upward, but with due protection of their property rights as stipulated by treaty.

NATURALIZATION ACT OF APRIL 14, 1802 (2 STATUTES-AT-LARGE 153)
Provisions:

a. Reduced the residence period for naturalization from fourteen to five years.
b. Established basic requirements for naturalization, including good moral character, allegiance to the Constitution, a formal declaration of intention, and witnesses.

STEERAGE ACT OF MARCH 2, 1819 (3 STATUTES-AT-LARGE 488)
First significant federal law relating to immigration. Provisions:

a. Established the continuing reporting of immigration to the United States by requiring that passenger lists or manifests of all arriving vessels be delivered to the local collector of customs, copies transmitted to the secretary of state, and the information reported to Congress.

Source: U.S. Bureau of Citizen and Immigration Services, "Historical Immigration and Naturalization Legislation," http://www.uscis.gov, accessed June 30, 2009.

b. Set specific sustenance rules for passengers of ships leaving U.S. ports for Europe.
c. Somewhat restricted the number of passengers on all vessels either coming to or leaving the United States.

ACT OF MAY 26, 1824 (4 STATUTES-AT-LARGE 36)
Facilitated the naturalization of certain aliens who had entered the United States as minors, by setting a two-year instead of a three-year interval between declaration of intention and admission to citizenship.

ACT OF FEBRUARY 22, 1847 (9 STATUTES-AT-LARGE 127)
"Passenger Acts," provided specific regulations to safeguard passengers on merchant vessels. Subsequently amended by the Act of March 2, 1847, expanding the allowance of passenger space.

PASSENGER ACT OF MARCH 3, 1855 (10 STATUTES-AT-LARGE 715)
Provisions:

a. Repealed the Passenger Acts (see the 1847 act) and combined their provisions in a codified form.
b. Reaffirmed the duty of the captain of any vessel to report the arrival of alien passengers.
c. Established separate reporting to the secretary of state distinguishing permanent and temporary immigration.

ACT OF FEBRUARY 19, 1862 (12 STATUTES-AT-LARGE 340)
Prohibited the transportation of Chinese "coolies" on American vessels.

ACT OF JULY 4, 1864 (13 STATUTES-AT-LARGE 385)
First congressional attempt to centralize control of immigration. Provisions:

a. Authorized the president to appoint a commissioner of immigration to serve under the authority of the secretary of state.
b. Authorized immigrant labor contracts whereby would-be immigrants would pledge their wages to pay for transportation.

On March 30, 1868, the Act of July 4, 1864, was repealed.

NATURALIZATION ACT OF JULY 14, 1870 (16 STATUTES-AT-LARGE 254)
Provisions:

a. Established a system of controls on the naturalization process and penalties for fraudulent practices.
b. Extended the naturalization laws to aliens of African nativity and to persons of African descent.

ACT OF MARCH 3, 1875 (18 STATUTES-AT-LARGE 477)
Established the policy of direct federal regulation of immigration by prohibiting for the first time entry to undesirable immigrants. Provisions:

a. Excluded criminals and prostitutes from admission.
b. Prohibited the bringing of any Oriental persons without their free and voluntary consent; declared the contracting to supply "coolie" labor a felony.
c. Entrusted the inspection of immigrants to collectors of the ports.

CHINESE EXCLUSION ACT OF MAY 6, 1882 (22 STATUTES-AT-LARGE 58)
Provisions:

a. Suspended immigration of Chinese laborers to the United States for ten years.
b. Permitted Chinese laborers already in the United States to remain in the country after a temporary absence.
c. Provided for deportation of Chinese illegally in the United States.
d. Barred Chinese from naturalization.
e. Permitted the entry of Chinese students, teachers, merchants, and those "proceeding to the United States . . . from curiosity."

On December 17, 1943, the Chinese exclusion laws were repealed.

IMMIGRATION ACT OF AUGUST 3, 1882 (22 STATUTES-AT-LARGE 214)
First general immigration law, established a system of central control of immigration through state boards under the secretary of the treasury. Provisions:

a. Broadened restrictions on immigration by adding to the classes of inadmissible aliens, including persons likely to become a public charge.
b. Introduced a tax of fifty cents on each passenger brought to the United States.

ACT OF FEBRUARY 26, 1885 (23 STATUTES-AT-LARGE 332)
The first "Contract Labor Law." Made it unlawful to import aliens into the United States under contract for the performance of labor or services of any kind. Exceptions were for aliens temporarily in the United States engaging other foreigners as secretaries, servants, or domestics; actors, artists, lecturers, and domestic servants; and skilled aliens working in an industry not yet established in the United States.

ACT OF FEBRUARY 23, 1887 (24 STATUTES-AT-LARGE 414)
Amended the Contract Labor Law to render it enforceable by charging the secretary of the treasury with enforcement of the act and providing that prohibited persons be sent back on arrival.

ACT OF OCTOBER 19, 1888 (25 STATUTES-AT-LARGE 566)
First measure since the Aliens Act of 1798 to provide for expulsion of aliens—directed the return within one year after entry of any immigrant who had landed in violation of the contract labor laws (see acts of February 26, 1885, and February 23, 1887).

IMMIGRATION ACT OF MARCH 3, 1891 (26 STATUTES-AT-LARGE 1084)
The first comprehensive law for national control of immigration. Provisions:

a. Established the Bureau of Immigration under the Treasury Department to administer all immigration laws (except the Chinese Exclusion Act).
b. Further restricted immigration by adding to the inadmissible classes persons likely to become public charges, persons suffering from certain contagious disease, felons, persons convicted of other crimes or misdemeanors, polygamists, and aliens assisted by others by payment of passage, and forbade the encouragement of immigration by means of advertisement.
c. Allowed the secretary of the treasury to prescribe rules for inspection along the borders of Canada, British Columbia, and Mexico so as not to obstruct or unnecessarily delay, impede, or annoy passengers in ordinary travel between these countries and the United States.
d. Directed the deportation of any alien who entered the United States unlawfully.

ACT OF MARCH 3, 1893 (27 STATUTES-AT-LARGE 570)
Provisions:

a. Added to the reporting requirements regarding alien arrivals to the United States such new information as occupation, marital status, ability to read or write, amount of money in possession, and facts regarding physical and mental health. This information was needed to determine admissibility according to the expanding list of grounds for exclusion.
b. Established boards of special inquiry to decide the admissibility of alien arrivals.

Legislation from 1901 to 1940

ACT OF APRIL 29, 1902 (32 STATUTES-AT-LARGE 176)
Extended the existing Chinese exclusion acts until such time as a new treaty with China was negotiated, and extended the application of the exclusion acts to insular territories of the United States, including the requirement of a certificate of residence, except in Hawaii.

ACT OF FEBRUARY 14, 1903 (32 STATUTES-AT-LARGE 825)
Transferred the Bureau of Immigration to the newly created Department of Commerce and Labor, and expanded the authority of the commissioner-general of immigration in the areas of rule making and enforcement of immigration laws.

IMMIGRATION ACT OF MARCH 3, 1903 (32 STATUTES-AT-LARGE 1213)
An extensive codification of existing immigration law. Provisions:

a. Added to the list of inadmissible immigrants.
b. First measure to provide for the exclusion of aliens on the grounds of proscribed opinions by excluding "anarchists, or persons who believe in, or advocate, the overthrow by force or violence the government of the United States, or of all government, or of all forms of law, or the assassination of public officials."
c. Extended to three years after entry the period during which an alien who was inadmissible at the time of entry could be deported.
d. Provided for the deportation of aliens who became public charges within two years after entry from causes existing prior to their landing.
e. Reaffirmed the Contract Labor Law (see the 1885 act).

ACT OF APRIL 27, 1904 (33 STATUTES-AT-LARGE 428)
Reaffirmed and made permanent the Chinese exclusion laws. In addition, clarified the territories from which Chinese were to be excluded.

NATURALIZATION ACT OF JUNE 29, 1906
(34 STATUTES-AT-LARGE 596)
Provisions:

a. Combined the immigration and naturalization functions of the federal government, changing the Bureau of Immigration to the Bureau of Immigration and Naturalization.
b. Established fundamental procedural safeguards regarding naturalization, such as fixed fees and uniform naturalization forms.
c. Made knowledge of the English language a requirement for naturalization.

IMMIGRATION ACT OF FEBRUARY 20, 1907
(34 STATUTES-AT-LARGE 898)

A major codifying act that incorporated and consolidated earlier legislation:

a. Required aliens to declare intention of permanent or temporary stay in the United States and officially classified arriving aliens as immigrants and nonimmigrants, respectively.
b. Increased the head tax to four dollars (established by the Act of August 3, 1882, and raised subsequently).
c. Added to the excludable classes imbeciles, feeble-minded persons, persons with physical or mental defects that may affect their ability to earn a living, persons afflicted with tuberculosis, children unaccompanied by their parents, persons who admitted the commission of a crime involving moral turpitude, and women coming to the United States for immoral purposes.
d. Exempted from the provisions of the contract labor law professional actors, artists, singers, ministers, professors, and domestic servants.
e. Extended from two to three years after entry authority to deport an alien who had become a public charge from causes which existed before the alien's entry.
f. Authorized the president to refuse admission to certain persons when he was satisfied that their immigration was detrimental to labor conditions in the United States. This was aimed mainly at Japanese laborers.
g. Created a Joint Commission on Immigration to make an investigation of the immigration system in the United States. The findings of this commission were the basis for the comprehensive Immigration Act of 1917.
h. Reaffirmed the requirement for manifesting of aliens arriving by water and added a like requirement with regard to departing aliens.

WHITE SLAVE TRAFFIC ACT OF JUNE 25, 1910
(36 STATUTES-AT-LARGE 825)

The Mann Act. Prohibited the importation or interstate transportation of women for immoral purposes.

ACT OF MARCH 4, 1913 (37 STATUTES-AT-LARGE 737)

Divided the Department of Commerce and Labor into separate departments and transferred the Bureau of Immigration and Naturalization to the Department of Labor. It further divided the Bureau of Immigration and Naturalization into a separate Bureau of Immigration and Bureau of Naturalization, each headed by its own commissioner.

IMMIGRATION ACT OF FEBRUARY 5, 1917
(39 STATUTES-AT-LARGE 874)
Codified all previously enacted exclusion provisions. In addition:

a. Excluded illiterate aliens from entry.
b. Expanded the list of aliens excluded for mental health and other reasons.
c. Further restricted the immigration of Asian persons, creating the "barred zone" (known as the Asia-Pacific triangle), natives of which were declared inadmissible.
d. Considerably broadened the classes of aliens deportable from the United States and introduced the requirement of deportation without statute of limitation in certain more serious cases.

ACT OF MAY 22, 1918 (40 STATUTES-AT-LARGE 559)
"Entry and Departure Controls Act," authorized the president to control the departure and entry in times of war or national emergency of any alien whose presence was deemed contrary to public safety.

QUOTA LAW OF MAY 19, 1921 (42 STATUTES-AT-LARGE 5)
The first quantitative immigration law. Provisions:

a. Limited the number of aliens of any nationality entering the United States to 3 percent of the foreign-born persons of that nationality who lived in the United States in 1910. Approximately 350,000 such aliens were permitted to enter each year as quota immigrants, mostly from Northern and Western Europe.
b. Exempted from this limitation aliens who had resided continuously for at least one year immediately preceding their application in one of the independent countries of the Western Hemisphere; nonimmigrant aliens such as government officials and their households, aliens in transit through the United States, and temporary visitors for business and pleasure; and aliens whose immigration is regulated by immigration treaty.
c. Actors, artists, lecturers, singers, nurses, ministers, professors, aliens belonging to any recognized learned profession, and aliens employed as domestic servants were placed on a nonquota basis.

ACT OF MAY 11, 1922 (42 STATUTES-AT-LARGE 540)

Extended the Act of May 19, 1921, for two years, with amendments:

a. Changed from one year to five years the residency requirement in a Western Hemisphere country.
b. Authorized fines of transportation companies for transporting an inadmissible alien unless it was deemed that inadmissibility was not known to the company and could not have been discovered with reasonable diligence.

IMMIGRATION ACT OF MAY 26, 1924 (43 STATUTES-AT-LARGE 153)

The first permanent limitation on immigration, established the "national origins quota system." In conjunction with the Immigration Act of 1917, governed American immigration policy until 1952 (see the Immigration and Nationality Act of 1952). Provisions:

a. Contained two quota provisions:
   1. In effect until June 30, 1927—set the annual quota of any quota nationality at 2 percent of the number of foreign-born persons of such nationality resident in the continental United States in 1890 (total quota: 164,667).
   2. From July 1, 1927 (later postponed to July 1, 1929) to December 31, 1952—used the national origins quota system: the annual quota for any country or nationality had the same relation to the 150,000 total as the number of inhabitants in the continental United States in 1920 having that national origin, based on the continental U.S. population in 1920.

      Preference quota status was established for unmarried children under twenty-one; parents; spouses of U.S. citizens aged twenty-one and over; and for quota immigrants aged twenty-one and over who are skilled in agriculture, together with their wives and dependent children under age sixteen.
b. Nonquota status was accorded to wives and unmarried children under eighteen of U.S. citizens; natives of Western Hemisphere countries, with their families; nonimmigrants; and certain others. Subsequent amendments eliminated certain elements of this law's inherent discrimination against women, but comprehensive elimination was not achieved until 1952 (see the Immigration and Nationality Act of 1952).
c. Established the "consular control system" of immigration by mandating that no alien may be permitted entrance to the

United States without an unexpired immigration visa issued by an American consular officer abroad. Thus, the State Department and the Immigration and Naturalization Service shared control of immigration.

d. Introduced the provision that, as a rule, no alien ineligible to become a citizen shall be admitted to the United States as an immigrant. This was aimed primarily at Japanese aliens.
e. Imposed fines on transportation companies who landed aliens in violation of U.S. immigration laws.
f. Defined the term "immigrant" and designated all other alien entries into the United States as "nonimmigrant" (temporary visitor). Established classes of admission for nonimmigrant entries.

ACT OF MAY 28, 1924 (43 STATUTES-AT-LARGE 240)
An appropriations law, provided for the establishment of the U.S. Border Patrol.

ACT OF MARCH 31, 1928 (45 STATUTES-AT-LARGE 400)
Provided more time to work out computation of the quotas established by the Immigration Act of 1924 by postponing introduction of the quotas until July 1, 1929.

ACT OF APRIL 2, 1928 (45 STATUTES-AT-LARGE 401)
Provided that the Immigration Act of 1924 was not to be construed to limit the right of American Indians to cross the border, but with the proviso that the right does not extend to members of Indian tribes by adoption.

REGISTRY ACT OF MARCH 2, 1929 (45 STATUTES-AT-LARGE 1512)
Amended existing immigration law authorizing the establishment of a record of lawful admission for certain aliens not ineligible for citizenship when no record of admission for permanent residence could be found and the alien could prove entrance to the United States before July 1, 1924 (subsequently amended to June 3, 1921, by the Act of August 7, 1939—53 Statutes-at-Large 1243). Later incorporated into the Alien Registration Act of 1940.

ACT OF MARCH 4, 1929 (45 STATUTES-AT-LARGE 1551)
Provisions:

a. Added two deportable classes, consisting of aliens convicted of carrying any weapon or bomb and sentenced to any term of six months or more, and aliens convicted of violation of the prohibition law for which a sentence of one year or more is received.

b. Made reentry of a previously deported alien a felony punishable by fine or imprisonment or both.
c. Made entry by an alien at other than at a designated place or by fraud to be a misdemeanor punishable by fine or imprisonment or both.
d. Deferred the deportation of an alien sentenced to imprisonment until the termination of the imprisonment.

ACT OF FEBRUARY 18, 1931 (46 STATUTES-AT-LARGE 1171)
Provided for the deportation of any alien convicted of violation of U.S. laws concerning the importation, exportation, manufacture, or sale of heroin, opium, or coca leaves.

ACT OF MARCH 17, 1932 (47 STATUTES-AT-LARGE 67)
Provisions:

a. The contract labor laws were applicable to alien instrumental musicians whether coming for permanent residence or temporarily.
b. Such aliens shall not be considered artists or professional actors under the terms of the Immigration Act of 1917, and thereby exempt from the contract labor laws, unless they are recognized to be of distinguished ability and are coming to fulfill professional engagements corresponding to such ability.
c. If the alien qualifies for exemption under the above proviso, the secretary of labor later may prescribe such conditions, including bonding, as will ensure the alien's departure at the end of his engagement.

ACT OF MAY 2, 1932 (47 STATUTES-AT-LARGE 145)
Amended the Immigration Act of 1917, doubling the allocation for enforcement of the contract labor laws.

ACT OF JULY 1, 1932 (47 STATUTES-AT-LARGE 524)
Amended the Immigration Act of 1924, providing that the specified classes of nonimmigrant aliens be admitted for a prescribed period of time and under such conditions, including bonding where deemed necessary, as would ensure departure at the expiration of the prescribed time or upon failure to maintain the status under which admitted.

ACT OF JULY 11, 1932 (47 STATUTES-AT-LARGE 656)
Provided exemption from quota limits (i.e., give nonquota status) to the husbands of American citizens, provided that the marriage occurred prior to

issuance of the visa and prior to July 1, 1932. Wives of citizens were accorded nonquota status regardless of the time of marriage.

ACT OF JUNE 15, 1935 (49 STATUTES-AT-LARGE 376)
Designated as a protection for American seamen. Repealed the laws giving privileges of citizenship regarding service on and protection by American vessels to aliens having their first papers (i.e., having made declaration of intent to become American citizens).

ACT OF MAY 14, 1937 (50 STATUTES-AT-LARGE 164)
Made deportable any alien who at any time after entering the United States:

a. as found to have secured a visa through fraud by contracting a marriage that, subsequent to entry into the United States, had been judicially annulled retroactively to the date of the marriage.
b. Failed or refused to fulfill his promises for a marital agreement made to procure his entry as an immigrant.

ACT OF JUNE 14, 1940 (54 STATUTES-AT-LARGE 230)
Presidential Reorganization Plan. Transferred the Immigration and Naturalization Service from the Department of Labor to the Department of Justice as a national security measure.

ALIEN REGISTRATION ACT OF JUNE 28, 1940
(54 STATUTES-AT-LARGE 670)
Provisions:

a. Required registration of all aliens and fingerprinting those over fourteen years of age.
b. Established additional deportable classes, including aliens convicted of smuggling, or assisting in the illegal entry of other aliens.
c. Amended the Act of October 16, 1919, making past membership—in addition to present membership—in proscribed organizations and subversive classes of aliens grounds for exclusion and deportation.
d. Amended the Immigration Act of 1917, authorizing, in certain meritorious cases, voluntary departure in lieu of deportation, and suspension of deportation.

ACT OF JULY 1, 1940 (54 STATUTES-AT-LARGE 711)
Amended the Immigration Act of 1924, requiring aliens admitted as officials of foreign governments to maintain their status or depart.

Legislation from 1941 to 1960

NATIONALITY ACT OF OCTOBER 14, 1940 (EFFECTIVE JANUARY 13, 1941, AS 54 STATUTES-AT-LARGE 1137)
Codified and revised the naturalization, citizenship, and expatriation laws to strengthen the national defense. The naturalization and nationality regulations were rewritten and the forms used in naturalization proceedings were revised.

PUBLIC SAFETY ACT OF JUNE 20, 1941 (55 STATUTES-AT-LARGE 252)
Directed a consular officer to refuse a visa to any alien seeking to enter the United States for the purpose of engaging in activities that would endanger the safety of the United States.

ACT OF JUNE 21, 1941 (55 STATUTES-AT-LARGE 252)
Extended the Act of May 22, 1918, giving the president power, during a time of national emergency or war, to prevent departure from or entry into the United States.

ACT OF DECEMBER 8, 1942 (56 STATUTES-AT-LARGE 1044)
Amended the Immigration Act of 1917, altering the reporting procedure in suspension of deportation cases to require the attorney general to report such suspensions to Congress on the first and fifteenth of each month that Congress is in session.

ACT OF APRIL 29, 1943 (57 STATUTES-AT-LARGE 70)
Provided for the importation of temporary agricultural laborers to the United States from North, South, and Central America to aid agriculture during World War II. This program was later extended through 1947, then served as the legal basis of the Mexican "Bracero Program," which lasted through 1964.

ACT OF DECEMBER 17, 1943 (57 STATUTES-AT-LARGE 600)
Amended the Alien Registration Act of 1940, adding to the classes eligible for naturalization Chinese persons or persons of Chinese descent. A quota of 105 per year was established (effectively repealing the Chinese exclusion laws—see the Act of May 6, 1882).

ACT OF FEBRUARY 14, 1944 (58 STATUTES-AT-LARGE 11)
Provided for the importation of temporary workers from countries in the Western Hemisphere pursuant to agreements with such countries for employment in industries and services essential to the war efforts.

Agreements were subsequently made with British Honduras, Jamaica, Barbados, and the British West Indies.

WAR BRIDES ACT OF DECEMBER 28, 1945
(59 STATUTES-AT-LARGE 659)
Waived visa requirements and provisions of immigration law excluding physical and mental defectives when they concerned members of the American armed forces who, during World War II, had married nationals of foreign countries.

ACT OF JULY 2, 1946 (60 STATUTES-AT-LARGE 416)
Amended the Immigration Act of 1917, granting the privilege of admission to the United States as quota immigrants and eligibility for naturalization races indigenous to India and persons of Filipino descent.

ACT OF AUGUST 9, 1946 (60 STATUTES-AT-LARGE 975)
Gave nonquota status to Chinese wives of American citizens.

ACT OF MAY 25, 1948 (62 STATUTES-AT-LARGE 268)
Amended the Act of October 16, 1918, providing for the expulsion and exclusion of anarchists and similar classes, and gave the attorney general similar powers to exclude as the secretary of state had through the refusal of immigration visas.

DISPLACED PERSONS ACT OF JUNE 25, 1948
(62 STATUTES-AT-LARGE 1009)
First expression of U.S. policy for admitting persons fleeing persecution. Permitted the admission of up to 205,000 displaced persons during the two-year period beginning July 1, 1948 (chargeable against future year's quotas). Aimed at reducing the problem created by the presence in Germany, Austria, and Italy of more than 1 million displaced persons.

ACT OF JULY 1, 1948 (62 STATUTES-AT-LARGE 1206)
Amended the Immigration Act of 1917. Provisions:

a. Made available suspension of deportation to aliens even though they were ineligible for naturalization by reason of race.
b. Set condition for suspension of deportation that an alien shall have proved good moral character for the preceding five years, and that the attorney general finds that deportation would result in serious economic detriment to a citizen or legal resident and closely related alien, or the alien has resided continuously in the United States for seven years or more.

CENTRAL INTELLIGENCE AGENCY ACT OF JUNE 20, 1949 (63 STATUTES-AT-LARGE 208)
Authorized the admission of a limited number of aliens in the interest of national security. Provided that whenever the director of the Central Intelligence Agency, the attorney general, and the commissioner of immigration determine that the entry of a particular alien into the United States for permanent residence is in the interests of national security or essential to the furtherance of the national intelligence mission, such alien and his immediate family may be given entry into the United States for permanent residence without regard to their admissibility under any laws and regulations or to their failure to comply with such laws and regulations pertaining to admissibility. The number was not to exceed 100 persons per year.

AGRICULTURAL ACT OF OCTOBER 31, 1949
(63 STATUTES-AT-LARGE 1051)
Facilitated the entry of seasonal farm workers to meet labor shortages in the United States. Further extension of the Mexican Bracero Program.

ACT OF JUNE 16, 1950 (64 STATUTES-AT-LARGE 219)
Amended the Displaced Persons Act of 1948. Provisions:

a. Extended the act to June 30, 1951, and its application to war orphans and German expellees and refugees to July 1, 1952.
b. Increased the total of persons who could be admitted under the act to 415,744.

INTERNAL SECURITY ACT OF SEPTEMBER 22, 1950
(64 STATUTES-AT-LARGE 987)
Amended various immigration laws with a view toward strengthening security screening in cases of aliens in the United States or applying for entry. Provisions:

a. Present and former membership in the Communist Party or any other totalitarian party or its affiliates was specifically made a ground for inadmissibility.
b. Aliens in the United States who, at the time of their entry or by reason of subsequent actions, would have been inadmissible under the provisions of the Internal Security Act were made deportable regardless of the length of their residence in the United States.
c. The discretion of the attorney general in admitting otherwise

inadmissible aliens temporarily, and in some instances permanently, was curtailed or eliminated.

d. The attorney general was given authority to exclude and deport without a hearing an alien whose admission would be prejudicial to the public interest if the attorney general's finding was based on confidential information the disclosure of which would have been prejudicial to the public interest of the United States.
e. The attorney general was given authority to supervise deportable aliens pending their deportation and also was given greater latitude in selecting the country of deportation. However, deportation of an alien was prohibited to any country in which the alien would be subject to physical persecution.
f. Any alien deportable as a subversive criminal or member of the immoral classes who willfully failed to depart from the United States within six months after the issuance of the deportation order was made liable to criminal prosecution and could be imprisoned for up to ten years.
g. Every alien residing in the United States subject to alien registration was required to notify the commissioner of immigration and naturalization of his address within ten days of each January 1 in which he resided in the United States.

ACT OF MARCH 28, 1951 (65 STATUTES-AT-LARGE 28)

Provisions:

a. Gave the attorney general authority to amend the record of certain aliens who were admitted only temporarily because of affiliations other than communist.
b. Interpreted the Act of October 16, 1918, regarding exclusion and expulsion of aliens to include only voluntary membership or affiliation with a communist organization and to exclude cases where the person in question was under sixteen years of age, or where it was for the purpose of obtaining employment, food rations, or other necessities.

ACT OF JULY 12, 1951 (65 STATUTES-AT-LARGE 119)

Amended the Agricultural Act of 1949, serving as the basic framework under which the Mexican Bracero Program operated until 1962. Provisions:

a. The U.S. government is to establish and operate reception centers at or near the Mexican border; provide transportation, subsistence, and medical care from the Mexican recruiting centers to the U.S. reception centers; and guarantee performance by employers in matters relating to transportation and wages, including all forms of remuneration.

b. U.S. employers pay the prevailing wages in the area, guarantee the workers employment for three-fourths of the contract period, and provide workers with free housing and adequate meals at a reasonable cost.

ACT OF MARCH 20, 1952 (66 STATUTES-AT-LARGE 26)

Provisions:

a. Amended the Immigration Act of 1917, making it a felony to bring in or willfully induce an alien unlawfully to enter or reside in the United States. However, the usual and normal practices incident to employment were not deemed to constitute harboring.
b. Defined further the powers of the Border Patrol, giving officers of the Immigration and Naturalization Service authority to have access to private lands, but not dwellings, within twenty-five miles of an external boundary for the purpose of patrolling the border to prevent the illegal entry of aliens.

IMMIGRATION AND NATIONALITY ACT OF JUNE 27, 1952 (INA) (66 STATUTES-AT-LARGE 163)

Brought into one comprehensive statute the multiple laws that, before its enactment, governed immigration and naturalization in the United States. In general, perpetuated the immigration policies from earlier statutes with the following significant modifications:

a. Made all races eligible for naturalization, thus eliminating race as a bar to immigration.
b. Eliminated discrimination between sexes with respect to immigration.
c. Revised the national-origins quota system of the Immigration Act of 1924 by changing the national-origins quota formula: set the annual quota for an area at one-sixth of 1 percent of the number of inhabitants in the continental United States in 1920 whose ancestry or national origin was attributable to that area. All countries were allowed a minimum quota of 100, with a ceiling of 2,000 on most natives of countries in the Asia-Pacific triangle, which broadly encompassed the Asian countries.
d. Introduced a system of selected immigration by giving a quota preference to skilled aliens whose services are urgently needed in the United States and to relatives of U.S. citizens and aliens.

e. Placed a limit on the use of the governing country's quota by natives of colonies and dependent areas.
f. Provided an "escape clause" permitting the immigration of certain former voluntary members of proscribed organizations.
g. Broadened the grounds for exclusion and deportation of aliens.
h. Provided procedures for the adjustment of status of nonimmigrant aliens to that of permanent resident aliens.
i. Modified and added significantly to the existing classes of nonimmigrant admission.
j. Afforded greater procedural safeguards to aliens subject to deportation.
k. Introduced the alien address report system whereby all aliens in the United States (including most temporary visitors) were required annually to report their current address to the INS.
l. Established a central index of all aliens in the United States for use by security and enforcement agencies.
m. Repealed the ban on contract labor (see Act of March 30, 1868) but added other qualitative exclusions.

ACT OF SEPTEMBER 3, 1954 (68 STATUTES-AT-LARGE 1146)
Provided for the expatriation of persons convicted of engaging in a conspiracy to overthrow or levy war against the U.S. government.

Legislation from 1961 to 1980

ACT OF SEPTEMBER 26, 1961 (75 STATUTES-AT-LARGE 650)
Liberalized the quota provisions of the Immigration and Nationality Act of 1952:

a. Eliminated the ceiling of 2,000 on the aggregate quota of the Asia-Pacific triangle.
b. Provided that whenever one or more quota areas have a change of boundaries that might lessen their aggregate quota, they were to maintain the quotas they had before the change took place.
c. Codified and made permanent the law for admission of adopted children.
d. Established a single statutory form of judicial review of orders of deportation.
e. Ensured a minimum quota of 100 for newly independent nations.
f. Called for the omission of information on race and ethnic origin from the visa application.

g. Strengthened the law against the fraudulent gaining of nonquota status by marriage.
h. Authorized the Public Health Service to determine which diseases are dangerous and contagious in constituting grounds for exclusion.

ACT OF OCTOBER 24, 1962 (76 STATUTES-AT-LARGE 1247)
Provisions:

a. Granted nonquota immigrant visas for certain aliens eligible for fourth preference (i.e., brothers, sisters, and children of citizens) and for first preference (i.e., aliens with special occupational skills).
b. Called for a semimonthly report to Congress from the attorney general of first preference petitions approved.
c. Created a record of lawful entry and provided for suspension of deportation for aliens who have been physically present in the United States for at least seven years in some cases and ten years in others.

ACT OF DECEMBER 13, 1963 (77 STATUTES-AT-LARGE 363)
Extended the Mexican Bracero Program one additional year to December 31, 1964.

IMMIGRATION AND NATIONALITY ACT AMENDMENTS OF OCTOBER 3, 1965 (79 STATUTES-AT-LARGE 911)
Provisions:

a. Abolished the national origins quota system (see the Immigration Act of 1924 and the Immigration and Nationality Act of 1952), eliminating national origin, race, or ancestry as a basis for immigration to the United States.
b. Established allocation of immigrant visas on a first come, first served basis, subject to a seven-category preference system for relatives of U.S. citizens and permanent resident aliens (for the reunification of families) and for persons with special occupational skills, abilities, or training (needed in the United States).
c. Established two categories of immigrants not subject to numerical restrictions:
    1. Immediate relatives (spouses, children, parents) of U.S. citizens, and
    2. Special immigrants: certain ministers of religion, certain former employees of the U.S. government abroad, certain persons who lost citizenship (e.g., by marriage or by service in foreign armed forces), and certain foreign medical graduates.

d. Maintained the principle of numerical restriction, expanding limits to world coverage by limiting Eastern Hemisphere immigration to 170,000 and placing a ceiling on Western Hemisphere immigration (120,000) for the first time. However, neither the preference categories nor the 20,000 per-country limit were applied to the Western Hemisphere.
e. Introduced a prerequisite for the issuance of a visa of an affirmative finding by the secretary of labor that an alien seeking to enter as a worker will not replace a worker in the United States nor adversely affect the wages and working conditions of similarly employed individuals in the United States.

FREEDOM OF INFORMATION ACT OF JULY 4, 1966
(80 STATUTES-AT-LARGE 250)
Provisions:
a. Established that the record of every proceeding before the Immigration and Naturalization Service in an individual's case be made available to the alien or his attorney of record.
b. Required that public reading rooms be established in each central and district office of the INS, where copies of INS decisions could be made available to the public.
Effective July 4, 1967.

ACT OF OCTOBER 20, 1974 (88 STATUTES-AT-LARGE 1387)
Repealed the "Coolie Trade" legislation of 1862. Such legislation, passed to protect Chinese and Japanese aliens from exploitation caused by discriminatory treatment from immigration laws then in effect, had become virtually inoperative because most of the laws singling out Oriental peoples had been repealed or modified.

ACT OF OCTOBER 30, 1978 (92 STATUTES-AT-LARGE 2065)
Provided for the exclusion and expulsion of aliens who persecuted others on the basis of race, religion, national origin, or political opinion under the direction of the Nazi government of Germany or its allies.

Legislation from 1981 to 1996

ACT OF OCTOBER 2, 1982 (96 STATUTES-AT-LARGE 1186)
Greatly limited the categories of aliens to whom the Legal Services Corporation may provide legal assistance.

IMMIGRATION REFORM AND CONTROL ACT OF NOVEMBER 6, 1986 (IRCA) (100 STATUTES-AT-LARGE 3359)

Comprehensive immigration legislation:

a. Authorized legalization (i.e., temporary and then permanent resident status) for aliens who had resided in the United States in an unlawful status since January 1, 1982 (entering illegally or as temporary visitors with authorized stay expiring before that date or with the government's knowledge of their unlawful status before that date) and are not excludable.
b. Created sanctions prohibiting employers from knowingly hiring, recruiting, or referring for a fee aliens not authorized to work in the United States.
c. Increased enforcement at U.S. borders.
d. Created a new classification of seasonal agricultural worker and provisions for the legalization of certain such workers.
e. Extended the registry date (i.e., the date from which an alien has resided illegally and continuously in the United States and thus qualifies for adjustment to permanent resident status) from June 30, 1948, to January 1, 1972.
f. Authorized adjustment to permanent resident status for Cubans and Haitians who entered the United States without inspection and had continuously resided in the country since January 1, 1982.
g. Increased the numerical limitation for immigrants admitted under the preference system for dependent areas from 600 to 5,000 beginning in fiscal year 1988.
h. Created a new special immigrant category for certain retired employees of international organizations and their families and a new nonimmigrant status for parents and children of such immigrants.
i. Created a nonimmigrant Visa Waiver Pilot Program allowing certain aliens to visit the United States without applying for a nonimmigrant visa.
j. Allocated 5,000 nonpreference visas in each of fiscal years 1987 and 1988 for aliens born in countries from which immigration was adversely affected by the 1965 act.

IMMIGRATION ACT OF NOVEMBER 29, 1990 (104 STATUTES-AT-LARGE 4978)

A major overhaul of immigration law:

a. Increased total immigration under an overall flexible cap of 675,000 immigrants beginning in fiscal year 1995, preceded by a 700,000 level during fiscal years 1992 through 1994. The 675,000 level to consist of 480,000 family-sponsored, 140,000 employment-based, and 55,000 "diversity immigrants."

b. Revised all grounds for exclusion and deportation, significantly rewriting the political and ideological grounds. For example, repealed the bar against the admission of communists as nonimmigrants and limited the exclusion of aliens on foreign policy grounds.
c. Authorized the attorney general to grant temporary protected status to undocumented alien nationals of designated countries subject to armed conflict or natural disasters.
d. Revised and established new nonimmigrant admission categories:
    1. Redefined the H-1(b) temporary worker category and limited number of aliens who may be issued visas or otherwise provided nonimmigrant status under this category to 65,000 annually.
    2. Limited number of H-2(b) temporary worker category aliens who may be issued visas or otherwise provided nonimmigrant status to 66,000 annually.
    3. Created new temporary worker admission categories (O, P, Q, and R), some with annual caps on number of aliens who may be issued visas or otherwise provided nonimmigrant status.
e. Revised and extended the Visa Waiver Pilot Program through fiscal year 1994.
f. Revised naturalization authority and requirements:
    1. Transferred the exclusive jurisdiction to naturalize aliens from the federal and state courts to the attorney general.
    2. Amended the substantive requirements for naturalization: state residency requirements revised and reduced to three months; added another ground for waiving the English-language requirement; lifted the permanent bar to naturalization for aliens who applied to be relieved from U.S. military service on grounds of alienage who previously served in the service of the country of the alien's nationality.
g. Revised enforcement activities. For example:
    1. Broadened the definition of "aggravated felony" and imposed new legal restrictions on aliens convicted of such crimes.
    2. Revised employer sanctions provisions of the Immigration Reform and Control Act of 1986.
    3. Authorized funds to increase Border Patrol personnel by 1,000.

4. Revised criminal and deportation provisions.

h. Recodified the thirty-two grounds for exclusion into nine categories, including revising and repealing some of the grounds (especially health grounds).
i. Waived the requirement that workers with expertise in these fields were needed by an employer in the United States.

VIOLENT CRIME CONTROL AND LAW ENFORCEMENT ACT OF SEPTEMBER 13, 1994 (108 STATUTES-AT-LARGE 1796)

Provisions:

a. Authorized establishment of a criminal alien tracking center.
b. Established a new nonimmigrant classification for alien witness cooperation and counterterrorism information.
c. Revised deportation procedures for certain criminal aliens who are not permanent residents and expanded special deportation proceedings.
d. Provided for expeditious deportation for denied asylum applicants.
e. Provided for improved border management through increased resources.
f. Strengthened penalties for passport and visa offenses.

ANTITERRORISM AND EFFECTIVE DEATH PENALTY ACT OF APRIL 24, 1996 (110 STATUTES-AT-LARGE 1214)

Provisions:

a. Expedited procedures for removal of alien terrorists.
b. Established specific measures to exclude members and representatives of terrorist organizations:
    1. Provided for the exclusion of alien terrorists.
    2. Waived authority concerning notice of denial application for visas.
    3. Denied other forms of relief for alien terrorists.
    4. Excluded from process aliens who have not been inspected and admitted.
c. Modified asylum procedures to improve identification and processing of alien terrorists.
    1. Established mechanisms for denial of asylum to alien terrorists.
    2. Granted authority to inspection officers to both inspect and exclude asylum applicants.
    3. Improved judicial review process to expedite hearings and removal (if necessary) of alien terrorists.
d. Provided for criminal alien procedural improvements.

1. Provided access to certain confidential immigration and naturalization files through court order.
2. Established a criminal alien identification system.
3. Established certain alien smuggling-related crimes as RICO-predicate offenses.
4. Granted authority for alien smuggling investigations.
5. Expanded criteria for deportation for crimes of moral turpitude.
6. Established an interior repatriation program.
7. Allowed for deportation of nonviolent offenders prior to completion of sentence of imprisonment.
8. Authorized state and local law enforcement officials to arrest and detain certain illegal aliens.
9. Expedited process of criminal alien removal.
10. Limited collateral attacks on underlying deportation order.
11. Established deportation procedures for certain criminal aliens who are not permanent residents.

PERSONAL RESPONSIBILITY AND WORK OPPORTUNITY RECONCILIATION ACT OF AUGUST 22, 1996 (110 STATUTES-AT-LARGE 2105)

Provisions:

a. Established restrictions on the eligibility of legal immigrants for means-tested public assistance:
    1. Barred legal immigrants (with certain exceptions) from obtaining food stamps and Supplemental Security Income (SSI) and established screening procedures for current recipients of these programs.
    2. Barred legal immigrants (with certain exceptions) entering the U.S. after date of enactment from most federal means-tested programs for 5 years.
    3. Provided states with broad flexibility in setting public benefit eligibility rules for legal immigrants by allowing states to bar current legal immigrants from both major federal programs and state programs.
    4. Increased the responsibility of the immigrants' sponsors by making the affidavit of support legally enforceable, imposing new requirements on sponsors, and expanding sponsor-deeming requirements to more programs and lengthening the deeming period.

- b. Broadened the restrictions on public benefits for illegal aliens and nonimmigrants.
  1. Barred illegal, or "not qualified aliens," from most federal, state, and local public benefits.
  2. Required INS to verify immigration status in order for aliens to receive most federal public benefits.

ILLEGAL IMMIGRATION REFORM AND IMMIGRANT RESPONSIBILITY ACT OF SEPTEMBER 30, 1996 (110 STATUTES-AT-LARGE 3009)

Provisions:

- a. Established measures to control U.S. borders, protect legal workers through worksite enforcement, and remove criminal and other deportable aliens:
  1. Increased border personnel, equipment, and technology as well as enforcement personnel at land and air ports of entry.
  2. Authorized improvements in barriers along the southwest border.
  3. Increased antismuggling authority and penalties for alien smuggling.
  4. Increased penalties for illegal entry, passport and visa fraud, and failure to depart.
  5. Increased INS investigators for worksite enforcement, alien smuggling, and visa overstayers.
  6. Established three voluntary pilot programs to confirm the employment eligibility of workers and reduced the number and types of documents that may be presented to employers for identity and eligibility to work.
  7. Broadly reformed exclusion and deportation procedures, including consolidation into a single removal process as well as the institution of expedited removal to speed deportation and alien exclusion through more stringent grounds of admissibility.
  8. Increased detention space for criminal and other deportable aliens.
  9. Instituted three- and ten-year bars to admissibility for aliens seeking to reenter after having been unlawfully present in the United States.
  10. Barred reentry of individuals who renounced their U.S. citizenship in order to avoid U.S. tax obligations.
- b. Placed added restrictions on benefits for aliens:
  1. Provided for a pilot program on limiting issuance of driver's licenses to illegal aliens.

2. Declared aliens not lawfully present ineligible for Social Security benefits.
3. Established procedures for requiring proof of citizenship for federal public benefits.
4. Established limitations on eligibility for preferential treatment of aliens not lawfully present on the basis of residence for higher education benefits.
5. Provided for verification of immigration status for purposes of Social Security and higher educational assistance.
6. Tightened the requirement for an affidavit of support for sponsored immigrants, making the affidavit a legally binding contract to provide financial support.
7. Provided authority of states and political subdivisions of states to limit assistance to aliens in providing general cash public assistance.
8. Increased maximum criminal penalties for forging or counterfeiting the seal of a federal department or agency to facilitate benefit fraud by an unlawful alien.

c. Miscellaneous provisions:
1. Recodified existing INS regulations regarding asylum.
2. Provided that the attorney general's parole authority may be exercised only on a case-by-case basis for urgent humanitarian reasons or significant public health.
3. Created new limits on the ability of F-1 students to attend public schools without reimbursing those institutions.
4. Established new mandates for educational institutions to collect information on foreign students' status and nationality and provide it to INS.
5. Tightened restrictions regarding foreign physicians' ability to work in the United States.
6. Added new consular processing provisions and revised the visa waiver program.

APPENDIX B

Aliens Removed or Returned, Fiscal Years 1892 to 2008

Year	Removals[1]	Returns[2]	Year	Removals[1]	Returns[2]
1892	2,801	NA	1926	31,454	NA
1893	1,630	NA	1927	31,417	15,012
1894	1,806	NA	1928	30,464	19,946
1895	2,596	NA	1929	31,035	25,888
1896	3,037	NA	1930	24,864	11,387
1897	1,880	NA	1931	27,886	11,719
1898	3,229	NA	1932	26,490	10,775
1899	4,052	NA	1933	25,392	10,347
1900	4,602	NA	1934	14,263	8,010
1901	3,879	NA	1935	13,877	7,978
1902	5,439	NA	1936	16,195	8,251
1903	9,316	NA	1937	16,905	8,788
1904	8,773	NA	1938	17,341	9,278
1905	12,724	NA	1939	14,700	9,590
1906	13,108	NA	1940	12,254	8,594
1907	14,059	NA	1941	7,336	6,531
1908	12,971	NA	1942	5,542	6,904
1909	12,535	NA	1943	5,702	11,947
1910	26,965	NA	1944	8,821	32,270
1911	25,137	NA	1945	13,611	69,490
1912	18,513	NA	1946	17,317	101,945
1913	23,399	NA	1947	23,434	195,880
1914	37,651	NA	1948	25,276	197,184
1915	26,675	NA	1949	23,874	276,297
1916	21,648	NA	1950	10,199	572,477
1917	17,881	NA	1951	17,328	673,169
1918	8,866	NA	1952	23,125	703,778
1919	11,694	NA	1953	23,482	885,391
1920	14,557	NA	1954	30,264	1,074,277
1921	18,296	NA	1955	17,695	232,769
1922	18,076	NA	1956	9,006	80,891
1923	24,280	NA	1957	5,989	63,379
1924	36,693	NA	1958	7,875	60,600
1925	34,885	NA	1959	8,468	56,610

Year	Removals[1]	Returns[2]	Year	Removals[1]	Returns[2]
1960	7,240	52,796	1985	23,105	1,041,296
1961	8,181	52,383	1986	24,592	1,586,320
1962	8,025	54,164	1987	24,336	1,091,203
1963	7,763	69,392	1988	25,829	911,790
1964	9,167	73,042	1989	34,427	830,890
1965	10,572	95,263	1990	30,039	1,022,533
1966	9,680	123,683	1991	33,189	1,061,105
1967	9,728	142,343	1992	43,671	1,105,829
1968	9,590	179,952	1993	42,542	1,243,410
1969	11,030	240,958	1994	45,674	1,029,107
1970	17,469	303,348	1995	50,924	1,313,764
1971	18,294	370,074	1996	69,680	1,573,428
1972	16,883	450,927	1997	114,432	1,440,684
1973	17,346	568,005	1998	174,813	1,570,127
1974	19,413	718,740	1999	183,114	1,574,863
1975	24,432	655,814	2000	188,497	1,675,876
1976	38,471[3]	955,374	2001	189,026	1,349,371
1977	31,263	867,015	2002	165,168	1,012,116
1978	29,277	975,515	2003	211,098	945,294
1979	26,825	966,137	2004	240,665	1,166,576
1980	18,013	719,211	2005	246,431	1,096,920
1981	17,379	823,875	2006	280,974	1,043,381
1982	15,216	812,572	2007	319,382	891,390
1983	19,211	931,600	2008	358,886	811,263
1984	18,696	909,833			

Source: U.S. Department of Homeland Security, Enforce Alien Removal Module (EARM), February 2009, and Enforcement Case Tracking System (ENFORCE), December 2008.

Notes:

NA = not available.

[1] Removals are the compulsory and confirmed movement of an inadmissible or deportable alien out of the United States based on an order of removal. An alien who is removed has administrative or criminal consequences placed on subsequent reentry owing to the fact of the removal.

[2] Returns are the confirmed movement of an inadmissible or deportable alien out of the United States not based on an order of removal. Most of the voluntary returns are of Mexican nationals who have been apprehended by the U.S. Border Patrol and are returned to Mexico.

[3] Includes the fifteen months from July 1, 1975, to September 30, 1976, because the end date of fiscal years was changed from June 30 to September 30.

NOTES

Introduction

1. Transcript, "Annapolis, Maryland, Immigration Raid," news story, WAMU Radio, aired July 14, 2008, Lagan Sebert, reporter.

2. Ibid. On law and order issues in the early 1980s, see Weaver, "Frontlash: Race and the Development of Punitive Crime Policy."

3. Transcript, "Annapolis, Maryland Raid," WAMU.

4. On intersectionality, see Crenshaw, "Demarginalizing the Intersection of Race and Sex" and "Mapping the Margins: Intersectionality, Identity Politics, and Violence against Women of Color"; McCall, "The Complexity of Intersectionality," chart, 171. This concept emphasizes the accumulating effects that categories such as race, gender, class, and sexual orientation have on people's experiences.

5. Mexican Americans were categorized differently by race both over time, by locality, by class position, and under federal law. In 1930 the U.S. federal census classified Mexican Americans as nonwhite but then rescinded that decision prior to the 1940 census. In recent decades, Hispanics can choose among given racial identifications, and since 2000 can opt for more than one racial category. See Rodriguez, *Changing Race*; Haney-López, *White by Law*; Hernández, *Migra!: A History of the U.S. Border Patrol*; Gomez, *Manifest Destinies*.

6. See United States, "Annual Report of the Commissioner-General of Immigration" (1895–1904). The U.S. government reclassified many groups by race in 1899 and grouped immigrants by nationality in several various ways in this period. Immigration totals for groups do not always correlate to others in various tables in a given year. For example, there are separate categories for Turkey in Asia and Turkey in Europe, but it remains unclear how they were differentiated. As I began my research I planned to draw more fully on these data. In these early years, however, the reporting and categorization of the data are inconsistent enough to warrant their use only for general trends and broad comparative purposes, not for more detailed comparisons. Percentages need to be viewed in the context of small total numbers for some groups.

7. Ibid.

8. See INS Web site, appendix I. "Immigration and Naturalization Legislation," http://www.ins.gov/graphics/aboutms/statistics/statyrbook96/appendix.pdf, accessed June 20, 2002.

9. When I began this project, I had planned to undertake a systematic sampling of immigration case files. But I soon realized that such a methodology would be impossible because of the lack of comprehensive finding aids for the case records I use and the significant number of missing case and administrative files in the collection. There is an old basic index card entry system for the case records on microfilm.

10. U.S. Department of Homeland Security, *Yearbook of Immigration Statistics: 2008*, 100, table 36; United States, "Annual Report on Immigration" (1906), 10–11, 14; (1927); and (1926), 29.

11. U.S. Department of Homeland Security, *Yearbook of Immigration Statistics: 2008*, 100, table 36.

12. U.S. Department of Homeland Security, Bureau of Immigration and Customs Enforcement, "Endgame." Also see Leal, "Deporting Social Capital: The Removal of Salvadoran Migrants from the United States."

13. In *A Nation by Design*, Aristide Zolberg argues that, although relatively little federal immigration legislation was enacted before the late nineteenth century, the founders did have an impact on immigration and key early national and antebellum legislation and judicial rulings pertaining to shipping, railroads, landownership, business, and banking profoundly shaped future immigration trends and policies. On visas, see 244 and 264.

14. See, for example, the essays in the forthcoming book, *Shifting Control: Gender and Migration Policy, 1917–2010*, coedited by Marlou Schrover and Deirdre M. Moloney.

15. An excellent example of this new scholarship is illustrated by the 2009 conference "Deportation and the Development of Citizenship," organized by the Department of Migration and Refugee Studies at Oxford University, which brought together scholars from several countries working on the legal, historical, policy, and activist aspects of related migration and refugee issues, including the denial of asylum claims and an analysis of what occurs to migrants who return to their countries of origin following removal. http://www.rsc.ox.ac.uk/PDFs/programmeconferenceondeportation developmentcitizenship.pdf, accessed January 10, 2010.

16. On the American, or Know-Nothing, Party of the 1850s and Denis Kearney's Workingman's Party, see Anbinder, *Nativism and Slavery*, and Chan, *Asian Americans*.

17. See, for example, Foner, *Reconstruction*; Sullivan, *Lift Every Voice*; Bay, *To Tell the Truth Freely*.

18. See INS Web site, Appendix I, "Immigration and Naturalization Legislation," http://www.ins.gov/graphics/aboutms/statistics/statyrbook96/appendix.pdf, accessed June 20, 2002.

19. Roger Daniels's research is one notable exception. See, for example, *Guarding the Golden Door* and "No Lamps Were Lit for Them."

Two recent books published on immigration regulation in this period examine it through the lens of the broader history of Ellis Island and Angel Island. In *Angel Island* Erika Lee and Judy Yung also make an important contribution by analyzing Filipino immigration, which remains an understudied ethnic group in the field of immigration history. In *American Passage* Vincent Cannato addresses the relationship between eugenics, the controversies in Ellis Island administration, including those arising during William A. Williams's tenure, and the impact of quota laws.

20. Several laws enacted during the 1920s sought to reduce significantly the number of immigrants admitted to the United States. Those laws did not address immigration within the Western Hemisphere. In 1921 a temporary law confined the number of immigrants from each country affected to 3 percent of those residing in the United States according to the 1910 federal census, for a maximum of 355,000 European immigrants each year. That law was replaced by a permanent law in 1924. After much debate, that law reduced the total annual quota to 150,000 and linked the percentage from each country to the census of 1890. A third system emerged in 1927, a national-origins plan

linking the quotas for each country to the population of America in 1920 (when the population was more diverse than it had been in 1890), and the quotas would be determined by a special board. Moreover, the decision about admitting immigrants would shift to the consuls abroad rather than at the ports of entry. Efforts to change the 1927 system arose in 1929 but were ultimately unsuccessful. With the exception of the Filipinos and some minor exceptions often based on occupation, Asians had been systematically excluded from entry to the United States through the Chinese Exclusion Act (in 1882 and renewed in 1902), the Gentleman's Agreement (1907–8), and the creation of the Asiatic Barred Zone (in 1917). For simplicity, I refer to these three laws collectively as the national-origins laws, because they make nationality the most significant basis for determining eligibility to immigrate. See Divine, *American Immigration Policy*, especially 5–47. Though markedly dated, there are relatively few more recent comprehensive histories of U.S. immigration policy.

21. Hughes and Cain, *American Economic History*.

22. Ibid.

23. Smith, *A Historical Guide to the U.S. Government*. Though scholars and the public have generally associated "illegal immigration," with the post-Watergate era and with border crossing from Mexico and other points from the South, in *Impossible Subjects*, Mae Ngai argues that illegal immigration figured prominently much earlier in the century in immigration law, policy, and discourse.

The racial and ethnic typologies that were highlighted in the Dillingham Report persisted in the American mainstream long after the Progressive Era. In his book, *The Living Races of Man*, for example, Carleton S. Coon discusses various races as having distinct differences rooted in biology. The research for Coon's project received funding from the National Science Foundation and the U.S. Air Force. In recent decades most American social scientists and historians have argued that racial and ethnic groups are socially constructed rather than rooted in genetic and other biological differences.

24. Rodgers, *Atlantic Crossings*.

25. Higham, *Strangers in the Land*; Divine, *American Immigration Policy*.

26. Vecoli, "Contadini in Chicago"; Bodnar, *The Transplanted*; Yans-McLaughlin, *Family and Community*.

27. Skocpol, Evans, and Rueschemeyer, *Bringing the State Back In*; Ngai, *Impossible Subjects*; Zolberg, *A Nation by Design*; King, *Making Americans*.

28. R. Chin, *The Guest Worker Question*; Schrover, "Family in Dutch Migration Policy, 1945–2005"; Rygiel, *Destins immigrés: Cher, 1920–1980*; Rosenberg, *Policing Paris*; McKeown, *Melancholy Order*; E. Lee, "The Yellow Peril"; Chang, "Circulating Race and Empire." Yukari Takai is currently working on a history of immigration policy along the Canadian and United States borders. Takai, "Navigating Transpacific Passages."

29. Lombroso and Ferraro, *Criminal Woman*, 171. See chapter 22 in particular. D'Agostino, "Craniums, Criminals," 328; Higham, *Strangers in the Land*; Stern, *Eugenic Nation*.

30. Higham, *Strangers in the Land*.

31. Over the past decade or so, several scholars have examined issues that address the Chinese Exclusion Act directly or indirectly. They include E. Lee, *At America's*

Gates; Gyory, *Closing the Gate*; Peffer, *If They Don't Bring Their Women Here*; McKeown, *Chinese Migrant Networks*; Hsu, *Dreaming of Gold, Dreaming of Home*; Salyer, *Laws Harsh as Tigers*. My emphasis is on the role of Chinese exclusion on legal precedents involving immigrant rights and its impact on Mexican immigration patterns and racially differential diagnosis of public health with respect to Chinese and other immigrants. Carey, *Deportation of Aliens*. Kanstroom, *Deportation Nation*.

32. Gardner, *Qualities of a Citizen*; Luibhéad, *Entry Denied*; Canaday, *The Straight State*.

33. Ngai, *Impossible Subjects*; Kanstroom, *Deportation Nation*; Gardner, *Qualities of a Citizen*; Luibhéad, *Entry Denied*.

34. Kanstroom, *Deportation Nation*.

35. See E. Lee, *At America's Gates*, and Peglar-Gordon, *In Sight of America*.

36. Ruiz, *Cannery Women, Cannery Lives*, 19; L. Gordon, *The Great Arizona Orphan Abduction*, 101–7, 311; Peck, *Reinventing Free Labor*, 168, 188, 199.

37. From a forum discussion on whiteness that presents Arnesen's critique, several additional historians' comments, and a response by Arnesen, see "Scholarly Controversy: Whiteness and the Historians' Imagination." Hasia Diner published a short essay on whiteness scholarship, "The World of Whiteness," that is largely critical of the field for restating arguments of previous immigrants rather than raising innovative points, ignoring tensions within immigrant groups, and depriving immigrants of agency. Surprisingly, though a pioneer in the history of female immigrants to the United States, she does not discuss the lack of attention to gender.

38. Jordan, *White over Black*.

39. D'Agostino, "Craniums, Criminals"; Lombroso and Ferraro, *Criminal Woman*.

40. Skocpol, Evans, and Rueschemeyer, *Bringing the State Back In*.

41. Moch, *Europeans on the Move*, 9, 31, 48.

42. Tavan, *The Long Slow Death of White Australia*, 7–8.

43. Ibid.

44. A dissertation by Christopher G. Anderson, "Restricting Rights, Losing Control," provides a comprehensive historical overview of that policy.

45. Ibid., 193–96.

46. Johnson, *The Voyage of the Kogmagata Maru*. Thanks to Shobita Parthasarathy for information on this.

Chapter 1

The author wishes to thank Jean Allman and Antoinette Burton, until recently the editors of the *Journal of Women's History*, and its two anonymous reviewers for their helpful comments on this chapter as well as Suzanne Harris of the National Archives, Marian Smith, senior historian of U.S. Citizenship and Immigration Services, an agency within the Department of Homeland Security (formerly the Immigration and Naturalization Service, or INS), and audience members of the 2004 European Social Science History Conference at Humboldt University in Berlin, where this research was first presented.

1. Memos, April 16, 1913, February 11, 1911, and May 24, 1909; Daniel D. Davies to Commissioner-General of Immigration, April 16 and 22, 1909, File: 51777/231-A, RG 85,

National Archives and Records Administration, Washington, D.C. (hereafter NARA). Landis later served as the first commissioner of organized baseball in the United States following the Chicago Black Sox Scandal.

In this chapter, I use many case files involving exclusion and deportation from Entry 7 of RG 85 of the National Archives. I also use administrative files from Entry 9 that contain a great deal of correspondence among immigration and other government officials. The investigation into white slavery, led by Marcus Braun, is one of the major issues generating numerous administrative files. Many of the particular cases discussed in this article are Board of Special Inquiry cases that determined whether there were sufficient grounds for deportation, and the files include correspondence between Bureau of Immigration officials and sometimes with other government officials, as well as information on whether the immigrant was successful in the appeal or was returned to her country of origin. In some instances, these files contain interviews with the immigrant herself and also include interviews with witnesses. Attorneys occasionally represented these women, but in most of these cases, they had no legal representation. The Board of Special Inquiry hearing was an administrative, not a judicial, proceeding.

The National Archives case files for this early era are not well indexed by name, subject, or date. Many of the files cited in the index are missing. Therefore, a systematic sampling approach to deportation case files in this era is not feasible. Deportation involves an action against an immigrant who has lived in the United States and is later accused of violating one or more provisions of immigration law. In some cases, such as enforcement of the "likely to become a public charge" (LPC), immigration officials had to prove that the circumstances of an immigrant's dependence on public assistance arose from conditions existing before his arrival. The statutes of limitation on the various grounds for deportation were often subject to revision. Debarment or exclusion refers to actions taken against an immigrant at the border or upon debarkation from a ship at the port of entry. Another challenge in using a statistical analysis of gender as a major variable is that aggregate annual immigration statistics compiled in the Annual Reports of the commissioner-general of immigration in the early era do not break down reasons of exclusion or deportation by gender, nor do they provide a breakdown of gender within data by countries of origin. Moreover, many immigrants facing deportation proceedings chose to depart voluntarily and therefore are not included in the deportation statistics.

2. Several scholars address the debates arising over citizenship in the Progressive Era. They include R. Smith, *Civic Ideals*; Gerstle, *American Crucible*; Jacobson, *Barbarian Virtues*; King, *Making Americans*. Candice Bredbenner's *A Nationality of Her Own* discusses the importance of citizenship among immigrant women in particular.

On materialism, see, for example, L. Gordon, "Putting Children First," 63–86.

3. Archdeacon, *Becoming American*, 115.

4. On the Page Law, see Hirata, "Free, Indentured, Enslaved"; Yung, *Unbound Feet*; Peffer, *If They Don't Bring Their Women Here*. Other recent scholarship on Chinese immigration and the effects of the Exclusion Act include E. Lee, *At America's Gates*; Gyory, *Closing the Gate*; Chan, *Entry Denied*; McKeown, *Chinese Migrant Networks*; Salyer, *Laws Harsh as Tigers*.

5. United States, "Annual Report on Immigration" (1916).

6. Ibid., (1916), xiii; (1904), 11; (1910), 11; (1920), 10–11. Evans, "'Likely to Become a Public Charge,'" 153–61. On immigrant gender ratios over time, see Gabaccia, "Women of the Mass Migrations," 91–92. I discuss the LPC charge more extensively in chapter 3.

7. State of Pennsylvania, "The Second Immigration Report of the Board of Commissioners of Public Charities for the Year Ending June 30, 1884," 17, File: 834; Report from Frederick Busch, September 14, 1883, File: 1075, RG 85, Entry 7, NARA.

8. As with any group of official case files, the immigrant woman's perspective is not always included in the record. Even when she provides a deposition, testimony, or letters, it is through a process that is mediated by government officials. There are very few, if any, sources to document broadly immigrant women's experiences with deportation or exclusion outside the context of official proceedings. Therefore, these files offer an important source for studying nonelite women. For more on the challenges of using government or social service case files in historical research, see Iocovetta and Mitchinson, *On the Case*.

9. Rockman, *Welfare Reform in the Early Republic*.

10. For more on women's immigration and work patterns in this era, see Gabaccia and Iacovetta, *Women, Gender, and Transnational Lives*, and Gabaccia, *From the Other Side*.

11. The LPC issue is examined more fully in chapter 3.

12. Memos to Acting Secretary, signed by Daniel J. Keefe, August 9 and 10, 1909, File: 52533/34, RG 85, Entry 9, NARA.

13. Memo to Acting Secretary, signed by Daniel J. Keefe, August 10, 1909, File: 52533/35, RG 85, Entry 9, NARA.

14. Memo to Acting Secretary, signed by Daniel J. Keefe, undated, File: 52533/36, RG 85, Entry 9, NARA.

15. Memo, signed by Frank Larned, undated; Memo, signed by N. M. Smith, January 29, 1912; Letter from Thomas Kirk, to Commissioner-General of Immigration, January 20, 1912; Note from George Brooks, undated; Transcript of Caroline Stewart Butler interview hearing, January 12, 1912, File: 53444/8, RG 85, Entry 9, NARA.

16. Memo to Acting Secretary, signed by Daniel J. Keefe, undated; Gideon Travis to Commissioner-General of Immigration, January 9, 1912, and notation, January 11, 1912, File: 53444/3, RG 85, Entry 9, NARA.

17. For more on race suicide fears, see King and Ruggles, "American Immigration, Fertility, and Race Suicide."

18. Memo, "In re what effect the common-law marriage of an alien woman to a citizen of the United States has with respect to the citizenship of her minor child," by H. B. Collins, February 23, 1921, File: 55301/548A, RG 85, NARA. The Cable Act allowed most married women to retain their citizenship status, but there were some exceptions, such as when a woman married a man "ineligible for citizenship" or lived with her non-American husband outside the United States for a period exceeding two years. Such exceptions were addressed by Congress in the early 1930s. On the evolution of citizenship laws pertaining to married women, see Bredbenner, *A Nationality of Her Own*. On the history of marriage and marital laws in the United States, see Cott, *Public Vows*, and Hartog, *Man and Wife in America*.

19. Memos, February 20, 1908, July 25, 1909, and January 23, 1909; Charles Earl to

John Sargent, March 17, 1908; Testimony transcripts of Kogero Sumida, February 11, 1908, and of Natsu Takaya, February 14, 1908, File: 51777/52, RG 85, NARA.

20. At this time most Syrian immigrants were Christian rather than Muslim, and the borders of that region differed significantly from what they are today.

21. F. H. Larned, Acting Commissioner-General, to H. E. Cook, July 27, 1908; Harold Cook to F. P. Sargent, July 20, 1908, File: 51777/232, RG 85, NARA.

22. Memo, April 27, 1914, signed by Acting Commissioner Uhl, File: 53770/128, RG 85, NARA.

23. Memo from Everett Wallace, October 25, 1910, File: 53019/144, RG 85, NARA.

24. Daniel Keefe to J. H. Whitely, October 31, 1910; J. H. Whitely, to Commissioner-General of Immigration, October 25, 1910; Brown McDonald to Commissioner-General of Immigration, October 20, 1910, File: 53019/148, RG 85, NARA.

25. See the references in n. 24 above.

26. See the references in n. 24 above.

27. See the references in n. 24 above.

28. See Orloff, "Women Immigrants and Domestic Violence."

29. United States, "Annual Report on Immigration" (1908), 8. Unfortunately, the Bureau of Immigration does not report aggregate data on grounds for deportation by gender, though prostitutes are defined as female.

30. Hart H. North to Commissioner-General of Immigration, February 8, 1908, File: 51777/42, RG 85, NARA.

31. *American*, May 9, 1913; *Tribune*, May 19, 1913; *New York Staatszeitung*, May 6 and 7, 1913, Clippings regarding the Annie Hof case, William A. Williams Papers, Folder 6, Box 3, New York Public Library.

32. Diner, *Erin's Daughters in America*.

33. Delaney, *Demography, State and Society*, 57–69.

34. J. Lee, *Ireland, 1912–1985*.

35. A broader discussion on how the moral turpitude and related clauses in deportation policy affected women is discussed in Moloney, "Women, Sexual Morality, and Economic Dependency."

36. Memo to Secretary from Daniel O'Keefe, March 12, 1913; Patricia O'Brien to H. B. Wilson, March 17, 1913; Memo to Commissioner-General of Immigration from William A. Williams, May 5, 1915, File: 53625/492, RG 85, NARA.

37. Clipping, *Fair Play*, September 7, 1912, Folder 2, Box 3, William A. Williams Papers. For more on Terrell's case, see Memo for the Acting Secretary, October 5, 1912, File: 52271/59, RG 85, NARA.

38. Carey, *Deportation of Aliens*, 448–49.

39. In Ireland today, the children of immigrants are no longer automatically granted Irish citizenship (a concept known as *jus soli*) because they are born in Ireland, a constitutional change that occurred in 2004 with the Irish Nationality and Citizenship Act. That change places Ireland in line with other European Union countries. Simultaneously, the Irish government is extending citizenship eligibility under certain circumstances to the great-grandchildren of those born in Ireland who are living abroad. See *The New York Times*, February 25, 2008, and www.citizensinformation.ie/categories, accessed March 6, 2010.

40. See, for example, Katherine Boo, "The Marriage Cure," *New Yorker*, August 18, 2003.

Chapter 2

1. Research from this chapter was originally presented at history conferences and a public lecture: the Social Science History Conference, Chicago, November 16, 2007; the European Social Science History Conference, Lisbon, February 2008; and the University of Houston, March 2008. The author wishes to acknowledge the helpful suggestions of her conference co-panelists and members of both audiences, as well as Debra Bergoffen and Paula Gilbert for their editorial advice. Portions of this chapter appeared in "Women, Sexual Morality, and Economic Dependency" and in Bergoffen, Gilbert, Harvey, and McNeeley, eds., *Confronting Gender Global Justice*.

Immigrant women who were excluded or deported from the United States in these years generally found that immigration officials used provisions of the LPC clause rather than those of prostitution because it was generally easier to prove. In the first two decades of the twentieth century, women of all nationalities constituted about a third of all immigrants arriving in the United States, but they were proportionately more likely than men to face LPC charges, especially if they were unmarried and traveling outside a family structure. In contrast, from 1892 to 1920, the numbers of immigrant women excluded from the United States on the basis of prostitution went from 80 in 1892 to a high of 510 in 1917. In six of those years, no immigrants were excluded for prostitution. The mean number of immigrant women excluded annually for prostitution in the years from 1892 to 1920 was 131. The number of immigrant women deported on grounds of prostitution (after having resided in the United States) also remained low, generally fewer than 200 per year before 1920.

2. Carey, *Deportation of Aliens*, 233.

3. Anna R. Igra's work addresses efforts among Jewish organizations in Russia, England, and New York City to assist deserted wives and to prevent Jewish female immigrants from engaging in prostitution. See "Likely to Become a Public Charge."

4. Peiss, *Cheap Amusements*.

5. On women's organized efforts against white slavery and promotion of port protection programs, see chapter 3 of my book, *American Catholic Lay Groups*. On prostitution and white slavery, see Rosen, *The Lost Sisterhood*, 113. See also Walkowitz, *Prostitution and Victorian Society*.

6. S. Cohen, *Folk Devils and Moral Panics*.

7. Peck, "White Slavery and Whiteness"; Diffee, "Sex and the City"; Foner, *Free Soil, Free Labor*; Roediger, *The Wages of Whiteness*, especially 73–87.

8. See Walkowitz, *Prostitution and Victorian Society*; Rosen, *The Lost Sisterhood*; Addams, *A New Conscience*.

9. Addams, *A New Conscience*, 18–19.

10. Ibid., 28, 33–34.

11. Ibid., 167–72, 64–70.

12. Ibid., 119, 169–70.

13. Beer and Joslin, "Diseases of the Body Politic."

14. The precursor to the INS, which has itself been renamed the U.S. Citizenship and Immigration Services, is now an agency within the Department of Homeland Security. Daniel T. Rodgers discusses how American Progressive reformers were heavily influenced by European efforts in *Atlantic Crossings*. Many spent time in Europe to learn about various reform efforts. As Allen F. Davis discussed in *Spearheads for Reform*, Jane Addams and other American settlement house pioneers were inspired by London's Toynbee Hall.

On Harry Laughlin, see U.S. House of Representatives, "Europe as an Emigrant-Exporting Continent and the United States as an Immigrant-receiving Nation," 1231–1437.

15. Memo, "in re report of immigrant inspector Marcus Braun, summarizing the results of his investigation of the 'White Slave' traffic in Europe," October 12, 1909, File: 524841-H, RG 85, Entry 9, NARA.

16. Report to Commissioner-General of Immigration, from Marcus Braun, October 2, 1909, File: 52484/1-G, RG 85, Entry 9, NARA; Memo, "in re report of immigrant inspector Marcus Braun," October 12, 1909; Keire, "The Vice Trust"; Turner, "Daughters of the Poor."

17. Guy, *Sex and Danger in Buenos Aires.*

18. F. R. Stone to Commissioner-General of Immigration, June 7 and 28, 1909, File: 5248418-A, RG 85, Entry 9, NARA. On Cesare Lombroso's theories of criminality and prostitution, see Lombroso and Ferraro, *Criminal Woman*, especially chap. 22.

19. Braun Report, October 2, 1909, File: 52484/1-G, RG 85, Entry 9, NARA; Memo, "in re report of immigrant inspector Marcus Braun," October 12, 1909.

20. See the references in the preceding n. 19 above.

21. Marcus Braun to Commissioner-General of Immigration, June 23, 1909, and September 16, 1909, Files: 524841/D and F, RG 85, Entry 9, NARA.

22. Files: 52484/3, 524841-C, and 524841/11A, RG 85, Entry 9, NARA.

23. Article enclosed in correspondence from Congressman William Bennett to Charles Nagle, Secretary of Commerce and Labor, March 7, 1910, File: 524836, RG 85, Entry 9, NARA. The document enclosed is a typescript translation of a French article in an unnamed newspaper.

24. Marcus Braun to Commissioner-General of Immigration, September 16, 1909, File: 524841-F, RG 85, Entry 9, NARA.

25. "Participants in the 'White Slave' Traffic in United States," [Report, circa 1909], File: 524841-H, RG 85, Entry 9, NARA.

26. Marcus Braun to Commissioner-General, August 2, 1909; Daniel Keefe to Acting Secretary, August 23, 1909, File: 524841-E, RG 85, Entry 9, NARA.

27. See the references in n. 26 above.

28. Files: 524841-G and 524841-E, RG 85, Entry 9, NARA. These were the only references to nonheterosexual prostitution that I read in these many reports, though it is certainly possible that other examples exist in the many case files on this topic.

29. "Participants in the 'White Slave' Traffic in United States."

30. News clipping, "An Awful Revelation," *The Christian* (Great Britain), February 11, 1909, File: 524832, RG 85, Entry 9, NARA.

31. Mara Keire also traces how the language and concepts used to describe prostitution evolved from one of sin and salvation in the nineteenth century to one of international cartels and antitrust issues by the Progressive Era. Keire, "The Vice Trust."

32. File: 5177761, RG 85, Entry 7, NARA.

33. Ibid.

34. File: 52483/12, RG 85, Entry 9, NARA.

35. Files: 517737, 517773/7-A, and 517773/7-B, RG 85, Entry 7, NARA.

36. See the references in n. 35 above.

37. Robert Watchhorn to Daniel Keefe, April 6, 1909. File: 524843, RG 85, Entry 9, NARA.

38. File: 53019/138B, RG 85, Entry 9, NARA; Bosny Report, Box 5 (on microfilm), William A. Williams Papers.

39. See the references in n. 38 above.

40. On the New York investigation, see File: 524841/F. On the Mexican Border, see Files: 52484/8-A, 52484/8-B, and 52484-C, RG 85, NARA.

41. United States, "Annual Report on Immigration" (1895–1904).

42. Chan, *Asian Americans*, 106.

43. Mexican literacy figure is from Sánchez, *Becoming Mexican American*, 27–28. The corresponding figure for men was 33 percent. Literacy rates varied significantly by region and class, but it is unlikely that prostitutes had particularly high literacy rates in this era.

44. Ibid., 41.

45. *El Paso Daily Times*, January 30, 1908. The author wishes to acknowledge Jaime Aguila for directing her to this source.

46. F. R. Stone to Commissioner of Immigration, June 25, 1909, File: 5248418-A, RG 85, Entry 9, NARA.

47. Ibid.

48. Ibid.

49. Charles Cornell to Commissioner-General of Immigration, December 26, 1909, File: 524848-C, RG 85, Entry 9, NARA.

50. Ibid.; L. Gordon, *The Great Arizona Orphan Abduction*.

51. Charles Cornell to Commissioner-General of Immigration, December 26, 1909, File: 524848-C, RG 85, Entry 9, NARA.

52. Stone to Commissioner, June 7 and 28, 1909, File: 5248418-A, RG 85, Entry 7, NARA.

53. Ibid.

54. Memo to F. W. Berkshire, to Charles Earl, Acting Secretary of Commerce and Labor, February 23, 1908; Warrant for Tijiera, February 25, 1908; Testimony of hearing, February 29, 1908; Memo to Murray from F. H. Sargent, March 6, 1908, File: 51777/56, RG 85, Entry 9, NARA.

55. See the references in n. 54 above.

56. E. B Holman to F. P Sargent, February 25, 1908; Deportation Warrant, July 1, 1907, File: 51777/34, RG 85, Entry 7, NARA.

57. Luther C. Steward, Acting Supervising Inspector, to Daniel Keefe, Commissioner-General of Immigration, letter and reply from Keefe, both April 23,

1909; Steward to Keefe, April 12 and 16, 1909, and Keefe's reply, April 17, 1909; F. H. Larned to Steward, December 3, 1908; FVB, Supervising Inspector, El Paso, to Keefe, November 27, 1908; Acting Commissioner-General to Steward, November 18, 1908; Steward to Commissioner-General of Immigration, November 18, 1908, File: 52241/20, RG 85, Entry 7, NARA.

58. Amnesty International, "Report on Women of Juarez and Chihuahua."

Chapter 3

1. Hill, *An Inquiry into the Relations of Immigration to Pauperism.*

2. Ibid.

3. Shenton, "Ethnicity and Immigration," 263. On welfare and welfare reform issues, see Mink, *The Wages of Motherhood* and *Welfare's End.* Linda Gordon discusses how the resistance to providing poor women with social benefits existed in marked contrast to attitudes toward male veterans, including those arising from the New Deal and Great Society, in *Pitied but Not Entitled.*

4. "Registers of Letters Received, Docket of Cases, 1882–1887," vol. 1, RG 85, Entry 1, NARA.

5. See, for example, Carey, *Deportation of Aliens*, 102–4, and "Extracts from Minutes of Second Annual Meeting of National Jewish Immigration Council Held February 18, 1912, at the Clara de Hirsch Home, 225 East 63rd Street, New York," File: 53173/12, RG 85, NARA; Evans, "'Likely to Become a Public Charge.'"

6. United States, "Annual Report on Immigration" (1910), 5.

7. "Extracts from Minutes . . . February 18, 1912"; Max Kohler, "Immigration and the Jews of America," *American Hebrew*, June 27, 1911; both in File: 53173/12, RG 85, Entry 9, NARA.

8. Kohler, "Immigration and the Jews of America."

9. Ibid.

10. "Hearing in the Commissioner's office, Ellis Island, N.Y., September 27, 1909, upon complaint concerning the method of executing the Immigration Laws," File: 52600/13A, RG 85, Entry 9, NARA.

11. Ibid.

12. See, for example, Glenn, *Daughters of the Shtetl.*

13. "Synopsis of the Report of the Activities of our Society for the Year 1915," microfilm, Reel 24, HIAS Ellis Island Records, YIVO Institute for Jewish Research.

14. Historians using HIAS records from this period must not publish names of immigrants involved in these cases without individual permission from their families. So I have used only initials to identify them. On MC's case, see letter William Neubau to Commissioner of Immigration, July 12, 1922, and reply [G/JP, handwriting illegible] to William Neubau, July 16, 1922. On cases involving EC and children and RC and daughter, see William Neubau to Commissioner of Immigration, January 3, 1922 and September 2, 1922. On EC's successful appeal, see telegram to R.B. from HIAS. On RC's appeal, see Ellis Island Representative to Louis Gottlieb, September 4, 1922, microfilm, Reel 4, HIAS Ellis Island Records. On veterans' greater access to social welfare benefits, see L. Gordon, *Pitied but Not Entitled.*

15. On HD's case, see William Neubau to Commissioner of Immigration, Octo-

ber 6, 1922, and November 21, 1922; Louis Gottlieb to William Neubau, November 29, 1922. On SD's case, see William Neubau to Commissioner of Immigration, October 6, 1922, and Gottlieb to Neubau, October 13, 1922, microfilm, Reel 5, HIAS Ellis Island Records.

16. William Neubau to Commissioner of Immigration, July 15, 1922; telegram to HDD from HIAS, July 28, 1922, microfilm, Reel 5. On the twelve-year-old boy, see William Neubau to Commissioner of Immigration, March 9, 1922, and telegram to CR from HIAS, March 17, 1922, microfilm, Reel 2, HIAS Ellis Island Records.

17. L. Gordon, *Pitied but Not Entitled.*

18. "Miscellaneous Statistics from W. W. Husband," February 9, 1922; Immigration and Refugee Services of America, Folder 23, Box 50B, Immigration History Research Center, University of Minnesota. The number of immigrants reported in this summary was low (262 "Hebrews" and 209 from England, Scotland, and Wales from January to July 1, 1921). This must have been a sample statistic.

19. Evans, "'Likely to Become a Public Charge,'" 223–25.

20. Gonzáles, *Mexicanos*, 135–38, 147. Sociologist Cybelle Fox's research on social welfare and immigration in this era intersects with mine. See her book *Three Worlds of Relief.*

21. On the agricultural depression in the United States during the 1920s, see, for example, Goldberg, *Discontented America.*

22. W. W. Husband to Congressman John C. Box, April 13, 1921, File: 55091/6, RG 85, Entry 9, NARA.

23. Chief of Police, Denver [H. R. Williams], to Vicente Quijano, January 13, 1921, File: 55091/6, RG 85, Entry 9, NARA.

24. Ibid.

25. Ibid.

26. Undated Document [circa 1921], "Copy of a Complaint Presented by the Mexican Colony of Denver to the Mexican Government," File: 55091/6, RG 85, Entry 9, NARA.

27. W. R. Mansfield to Commissioner-General of Immigration, December 6, 1921, File: 55091/6, RG 85, Entry 9, NARA.

28. *Excelsior*, April 15, 1922. Translated from Spanish.

29. J. E. Trout to Supervising Inspector, May 24, 1922, File: 55091/6; Assistant Secretary, Immigration Service to the Secretary of State, June 9, 1922, RG 85, Entry 9, NARA.

30. Clyde Campbell to Commissioner-General of Immigration, October 24, 1923, File: 52730/40-B, RG 85, Entry 9, NARA.

31. Thomas Mahony, "The Problem of Our Spanish Speaking Migratory Laborers," August 8, 1939, Folder 3, Box 2, Thomas F. Mahony Papers, University of Notre Dame.

32. C. V. Maddux and C. W. Doherty, "Report of Addresses Given at the First City Conference on Denver's Social Problems," June 6, 7, 8, 1928; Thomas Mahony, "Address at the National Conference of Catholic Charities," November 12, 1929, Thomas F. Mahony Papers.

33. Telegram to William Green from Thomas F. Mahony, April 3, 1931, Thomas F. Mahony Papers.

34. Thomas F. Mahony, "The Problem of Our Spanish Speaking Migratory Agricultural Laborers," the National Conference of Catholic Charities, August 8, 1939, Thomas F. Mahony Papers.

35. Balderrama and Rodriguez, *Decade of Betrayal*, 67.

36. Doak figure cited in J. C. B. Brodie to Jason Buchanan, February 5, 1936, File: 44739/674A, RG 85, Entry 9, NARA.

37. Balderrama and Rodriquez, *Decade of Betrayal*.

38. National Catholic Welfare Conference(NCWC), Annual Report, 1922–23, NCWC Papers, American Catholic History Research Center and University Archives, Catholic University, Washington, D.C.; NCWC, Annual Report, 1931–1932, NCWC Papers.

39. NCWC, Annual Report, 1932–1933, NCWC Papers.

40. NCWC, Annual Report, 1929–30. The U.S. Bureau of the Census made a decision to categorize Mexican Americans as nonwhite in the 1930 census but reversed the decision and returned to classifying Mexican Americans as whites in the 1940 census. On the classification of Mexicans in the federal census, see Merchant, Gratton, and Gutmann, "Race and Deportation: Mexicans in the 1930 and 1940 Censuses." State censuses were less uniform in their racial classification of Mexican Americans.

41. NCWC, Annual Report, 1930–1931.

42. NCWC, Annual Report, 1931–1932.

43. NCWC, Annual Report, 1932–1933 (emphasis added).

44. NCWC, Annual Report, 1933–34.

45. Ibid.

46. NCWC, Annual Report, 1929–1930.

47. Ibid.

48. NCWC, Annual Report, 1931–1932.

49. S. C. Wilmot [?] to Commissioner-General of Immigration, July 19, 1921, File: 55091/6, RG 85, Entry 9, NARA.

50. J. Taylor, Vitek, Enriquez, and Smedley, "A Continuing Focus of Hansen's Disease in Texas."

51. Ibid.

52. Carpenter, "The New Immigration Policy and the Labor Market," 720.

53. "Report of Addresses Given at the First City Conference on Denver's Social Problems," June 6, 7, 8, 1928.

54. U.S. House of Representatives, "To Provide for Removal at Government Expense of Certain Financially Distressed Aliens Who Apply for Permission to Return to Their Native Country."

55. Clyde B. Cross to Acting Inspector in Charge, INS, Port Huron, Michigan, September 21, 1933, and Mrs. H. Henshaw to Franklin D. Roosevelt, July 31, 1933; on Texas, Harold W. Goodrich to Office of the Attorney General, Washington, July 28, 1933, File: 55639/616A, RG 85, Entry 9, NARA.

56. Herbert C. Gerrish to Inspector in Charge, October 30, 1933, File: 55639/616A, RG 85, Entry 9, NARA.

57. On the Mexican government's diplomatic actions during World War II, see

Guglielmo, "Fighting for Caucasian Rights." On the era before the Depression, see Aguila, "Mexican/U.S. Immigration Policy prior to the Great Depression," especially 216–19, and González, *Mexican Consuls and Labor Organizing.*

58. William A. Whalen to Commissioner-General of Immigration, October 21, 1930, File: 55608/126, RG 85, Entry 9, NARA.

59. Enclosure to Dispatch 413, May 13, 1931, from the Embassy of Mexico; Translation of *Excelsior*, May 11, 1931; George Harris to District Director of Immigration, June 9, 1931, File: 55739/674, RG 85, Entry 9, NARA.

60. Dies speech in "Congress Speaks," NBC Broadcast, May 6, 1935, text reprinted in *Congressional Record*, May 10, 1935.

61. Balderrama and Rodriguez, *Decade of Betrayal*, 53–54; Sánchez, *Becoming Mexican American*, 210.

62. Posadas, *The Filipino Americans*, 16, 23; Ngai, *Impossible Subjects*, 120–25.

63. H.R. Res. 71, February 6, 1935, Companion Bill to H.R. 3472.

64. Ibid., 19.

65. Ibid., 12; Posadas, *The Filipino Americans*, 24.

66. On the impact of the 1996 act and Proposition 187 on immigrants in particular, see Century Foundation, "Immigration Reform," Report, (2000), 30–31. In 1997 some federal benefits, such as food stamps and SSI, were reinstated for elderly and disabled immigrants who were already in the United States, but not for those arriving in the future. By 1999 the Department of Health and Human Services and the INS issued a more comprehensive ruling that clarified the "public charge" definition. See United States, "HHS Joins the INS and State Department in Clarifying 'Public Charge' Guidance," May 26, 1999; National Immigration Law Center, "New INS Guidance on Public Charge." On immigrants' accessing and use of benefits, see Haskins, Greenberg, and Fremstad, "Federal Policy for Immigrant Children."

67. *Time*, June 11, 2010, http://www.time.com/time/nation/article/0,8599,1996064,00.html#ixzz18aPWdJ5h, accessed December 17, 2010. Kanstroom, *Deportation Nation*, 128–32.

Chapter 4

1. Leavitt, *Typhoid Mary*.

2. Higham, *Strangers in the Land.*

3. Loza, "The Bracero Project."

On the topic of immigrants, bodies, and disease, see, for example, Kraut, *Silent Travelers*; Markel, "When Germs Travel"; Shah, *Contagious Divides*; Fairchild, *Science at the Borders*; Molina, *Fit to be Citizens?*.

Kraut addresses health issues of Jewish immigrants and the work of Maurice Fishberg in chapter 6 of his book. For general background on the eugenics movement in the United States and England, see Kevles, *Genetics and the Uses of Human Heredity*; Gilman, *Disease and Representation*; Foucault, *The History of Sexuality*; Gould, *The Mismeasure of Man.*

4. Foucault, *The History of Sexuality*; Gould, *The Mismeasure of Man.*

5. Eugenics is a topic that has recently undergone a resurgence of interest among historians. See, for example, Stern, *Eugenic Nation*; Dorr, *Segregation's Science*; Dowbig-

gin, *Keeping America Sane*; D'Agostino, "Craniums, Criminals"; King and Hansen, "Eugenic Ideas, Political Interests and Policy Variance."

6. New York State, Senate Resolution, February 16, 1914, File: 52730/3-C, RG 85, Entry 9, NARA.

7. As was noted earlier, several laws enacted during the 1920s sought to reduce significantly the number of immigrants admitted to the United States. Those laws did not address immigration within the Western Hemisphere. In 1921 a temporary law confined the number of immigrants from each country affected to 3 percent of those residing in the United States according to the 1910 federal census, for a maximum of 355,000 European immigrants each year. That law was replaced by a permanent law in 1924. After much debate, that law reduced the total annual quota to 150,000 and linked the percentage from each country to the census of 1890. A third system emerged in 1927, a national-origins plan, which linked the quotas for each country to the population of America in 1920 (when the population was more diverse than it had been in 1890) and the quotas would be determined by a special board. Moreover, the decision about admitting immigrants would shift to the consuls abroad rather than at the ports of entry. Efforts to change the 1927 system arose in 1929, but were ultimately unsuccessful. With the exception of the Filipinos and some other categories, Asians had been systematically excluded from entry to the United States through the Chinese Exclusion Act (renewed in 1902), the Gentleman's Agreement, and the creation of the Asiatic Barred Zone (in 1907). For simplicity, I refer to these laws collectively as the national-origins laws, because they make nationality the most significant basis for determining eligibility to immigrate. See Divine, *American Immigration Policy*, especially 5–47.

8. Compomanes, "Images of Filipino Racialization"; Parenas and Fowler, *Anthropology Goes to the Fair*.

9. Higham, *Strangers in the Land*, 150–54.

10. On Grant and the rise of the eugenicist movement, see Spiro, *Defending the Master Race*.

11. U.S. House of Representatives, "Europe as an Emigrant-Exporting Continent and the United States as an Immigrant-Receiving Nation," quotation, 1262.

12. Undated Report, on Department of Commerce and Labor letterhead, c. 1903, File: 52363/25, Entry 9, RG 85, NARA; Joseph Jacobs, "Sulzberger," Jewish Encyclopedia, 1901–1906, http://www.jewishencyclopedia.com/view.jsp?letter=S&artid=1160, accessed June 2009.

13. Isi Fischer to William Taft, May 16, 1911; Benjamin Cable to Isi Fischer, May 29, 1911; Simon Wolf to George Cortelyou, October 13, 1905, RG 52363/25, RG 85, Entry 9, NARA.

14. Fairchild, *Science at the Borders*, 4–7.

15. George Hotschick to Assistant Secretary of State, November 22, 1907, File: 51814/6, RG 85, Entry 9, NARA.

16. John Mann, unpublished article manuscript, December 1914, File: 53371/74, RG 85, Entry 9, NARA.

17. Ibid.

18. W. W. Husband to Frank B. Kellogg, April 27, 1926, File: 52730/40C, RG 85, Entry 9, NARA.

19. Samuel W. Backus to Commissioner-General of Immigration, October 25, 1913, File: 54261/184, RG 85, Entry 9, NARA.

20. Memo from Assistant Commissioner-General (Watchhorn), June 6, 1922, File: 54261/184, RG 85, Entry 9, NARA.

21. Commissioner-General to Hon. Hugh Cumming, September 24, 1925, File: 54261/184, RG 85, Entry 9, NARA.

22. Bateman-House and Fairchild, "Medical Examination of Immigrants at Ellis Island."

23. File: 52516/11-A, RG 85, Entry 9, NARA.

24. Frank Sargent to Secretary of Commerce and Labor, January 13, 1905, File: 51444, RG 85, Entry 9, NARA.

25. Oscar Straus to Acting Secretary of State Alvey Adee [?], April 2, 1908, and Supervising Inspector Burkoning [?] to Commissioner-General of Immigration, March 28, 1908, File: 51800, RG 85, Entry 9, NARA.

26. Sarah Galtieri in *Between Arab and White* has made an important contribution to the history of Syrian immigrants in the United States by analyzing the complex racial identities of early Syrian/Lebanese migrants and the legal history of decisions concerning their racial classification in the United States. Samuel Barbari to Robert Watchhorn, October 28, 1906, and March 29, 1907, File: 51423/2-A, RG 85, Entry 9, NARA.

27. S. A. Seraphic to Commissioner-General of Immigration, January 8, 1907, File: 514231, RG 85, Entry 9, NARA.

28. Ibid.

29. T. F. Schumacher [?], Inspector in Charge, El Paso, Texas, to Commissioner-General of Immigration, December 10, 1905; Hunter Course, Inspector in Charge, Laredo, Texas, to Commissioner-General of Immigration, July 7, 1905; Nagib Abdou, to Hunter Course, May 20, 1905, File: 51522/17, RG 85, Entry 9, NARA.

30. Draft of Fiscal Year 1906 Annual Report, October 20, 1906, File: 514444, RG 85, Entry 9, NARA.

31. New York State Senate Bill, Albany, February 16, 1914, File: 52730/3-C, RG 85, Entry 9, NARA.

32. Byron Uhl to Commissioner-General, October 30, 1913, File: 529030, RG 85, Entry 9, NARA.

33. Memo to Commissioner-General of Immigration, January 13, 1914, File: 52903/60A, RG 85, Entry 9, NARA.

34. Albert Warren Ferris to William A. Williams, July 23, 1909, File: 52730/75, RG 85, Entry 9, NARA.

35. Homer Folks to Charles Nagel, August 27, 1912, File: 51564/3-C, RG 85, Entry 9, NARA.

36. Deposed Statement by Katharine Tucker, August 12, 1912, File: 51564/3-C, RG 85, Entry 9, NARA.

37. Byron Uhl to Commissioner-General of Immigration, September 10, 1912, File: 51564/3-C, RG 85, Entry 9, NARA.

38. Russian Imperial Consul General to George B. Campbell, M.D., August 14, 1912, RG 85, Entry 9, NARA.

39. Sadie American, Council of Jewish Women, to Benjamin S. Cable, Assistant Sec-

retary, Department of Commerce and Labor, October 3, 1912, File: 515643-C, RG 85, Entry 9, NARA.

40. Ibid.

41. Kaplan and Kaplan to Commissioner-General of Immigration, December 5, 1912, and Benjamin Cable to Sadie American, Council of Jewish Women, December 5, 1912, File: 41564/3-F, RG 85, Entry 9, NARA.

42. John Garrett to Secretary of State, September 25, 1909; William Williams to Commissioner-General of Immigration, December 13, 1909, File: 515643, RG 85, Entry 9, NARA.

43. Memo, April 8, 1912, File: 52423/46A, RG 85, Entry 9, NARA.

44. For background on the climate giving rise to immigration restriction and the popularity of eugenics in the United States in the Progressive Era, see Higham, *Strangers in the Land*. Recent works that discuss the relationship between the two include Guterl, *The Color of Race in America*; Jacobson, *Whiteness of a Different Color*; King, *Making Americans*; E. Lee, "Enforcing the Borders"; Ngai, "The Architecture of Race in American Immigration Law"; R. Smith, *Civic Ideals*; Gerstle, *American Crucible*.

45. The category was not mentioned in the 1903 annual immigration report. United States, "Annual Report on Immigration" (1904). Robert DeCourcy Ward to William A. Williams, January 17, 1905, December 21, 1910, and July 9, 1910, Box 2, William A. Williams Papers, New York Public Library. Williams resigned his political appointment in January 15, 1905, but was reappointed to the position in 1909. Williams received congratulatory letters from Prescott F. Hall on July 14, 1909, Madison Grant on July 16, 1909, and Joseph Lee of the Immigration Restriction League on July 28, 1909, William A. Williams Papers. Cannato, *American Passage*, published after my research and writing was complete, discusses Williams's controversial administration, as well as health- and poverty-related inspections by Ellis Island officials.

46. *Boston Evening Transcript*, April 12, 1905.

47. This section of the chapter was originally presented as "Immigrant Advocates, Ethnic Bias, and Public Health in Progressive Era U.S. Immigration Policy," at the American Historical Association Annual Meeting in January 2003. The "poor physique" controversy in also discussed briefly by Kraut, *Silent Travelers*, and in more detail in Baynton, "Defectives in the Land." See also comments by Amy Fairchild, David Gerber, Alan Kraut, and Catherine Kudlick in that same issue. I am arguing that "poor physique" was a diagnosis that was not accepted among physicians but was a designation that was inscribed into immigration policy by nonmedically trained eugenics who wished to limit the number of Jews and Southern and Eastern Europeans who were admitted into the United States before the National Origins Act was enacted.

48. Robert DeCourcy Ward to Lawrence Murray, Assistant Secretary, Department of Commerce and Labor, April 12, 1905, File: 51490/19, RG 85, Entry 9, NARA.

49. Ward to Frank P. Sargent, Commissioner-General of Immigration, January 11, 1905; Ward to Lawrence Murray, April 12, 1905; Murray to Ward, April 15, 1905; Ward to Murray, April 19, 1905; Sargent to Ward, April 25, 1905 (in response to Ward's letter to Murray on April 19), File: 51490/19, RG 85, Entry 9, NARA.

50. J. W. [Joseph Williams] Schereschewsky to Commissioner of Immigration, Balti-

more, March 28, 1905, File: 51490/19, RG 85, Entry 9, NARA. Schereschewsky worked on a variety of public health issues and later became a recognized authority on early cancer research.

51. Dr. George Stoner, Public Health and Marine-Hospital Service to Commissioner of Immigration, March 30, 1906, File: 51490/19, RG 85, Entry 9, NARA.

52. Letter to Walter Wyman, M.D., Surgeon-General, Public Health and Marine Hospital Service, Treasury Department, December 22, 1906, File: 51490/19, RG 85, Entry 9, NARA.

53. Straus to Leslie Shaw, February 4, 1907, File: 51490/19, RG 85, Entry 9, NARA.

54. Memo, "Some of the Cases in Which the Hebrew Sheltering and Immigrant Aid Society Has Filed Appeals," April 2, 1913, File: 536201/84, RG 85, Entry 9, NARA. I am grateful to Ellen Pearlstein of Arlington, Virginia, and her grandfather, Samuel Gordon of Worcester, Massachusetts, for their help in determining whether some names listed in the memo are female or male.

55. Moloney, *American Catholic Lay Groups*, chap. 3.

56. Kohler, "Immigration and the Jews of America," *American Hebrew*, February 3, 1911, 407, in File: 53173/12, RG 85, Entry 9, NARA.

57. Both quotes in Kohler, "Immigration and the Jews of America," *American Hebrew*, January 27, 1911, 375, in File: 53173/12, RG 85, Entry 9, NARA.

58. Kohler, "Immigration and the Jews of America," *American Hebrew*, February 3, 1911, 408, in File: 53173/12, RG 85, Entry 9, NARA.

59. Ibid., 409.

60. Interestingly, while the census does not include religious affiliation in its surveys, my previous research using the 1910 census taken in Waterbury, Connecticut, suggests that at least some census takers categorized Jews from Russia or Poles distinctly from non-Jews from those countries. Tellingly, they did not note the religion of those who were not Jewish.

61. Fishberg, *The Jews*.

62. Ripley, "Races in the United States." This fear of immigrant longevity was the flip side of a related concept of "race suicide," popularized by Theodore Roosevelt and others. Many elites in the early twentieth century expressed their concern that higher birth rates among immigrant women, coupled with decreased birth rates among native-born women, was leading to race suicide. See, for example, King and Ruggles, "American Immigration, Fertility, and Race Suicide."

63. Memo, by Commissioner William A. Williams, April 2, 1913, File: 536201/84, RG 85, Entry 9, NARA.

64. "Information in Relation to Certain Features of the Immigration Law, with Particular Reference to the Inspection Work Conducted on the Registry or Inspection Floor, Ellis Island," Folder 13, Box 48, Foreign Language Information Service, Immigration History Research Center.

65. Transcript of address by Assistant Commissioner of Immigration, H. R. Landis, April 26, 1924, Conference on Immigration Policy, Folder 14, Box 48, Foreign Language Information Service, Immigration History Research Center.

66. Memo to the Acting Secretary from F. H. Larned, July 22, 1909; Memo to the Acting Secretary from Daniel O'Keefe [undated, circa March 1913], File: 52533/21; John

McMullen, Medical Officer in Command, to Commissioner of Immigration at Ellis Island, July 6, 1906, File: 50627/16, RG 85, Entry 9, NARA.

67. ARA to Edward Corsi, May 18, 1932. The copy of this letter has no signature but indicates the sender's initials. It appears to be from someone in the Washington office of the Bureau of Immigration. File: 52729/9, RG 85, Entry 9, NARA.

68. D'Agostino, "Craniums, Criminals."

69. Frederick Ciampi to Arthur D. Healey, July 14, 1934; APA to Edward Corsi, May 1932, File: 52729/9, RG 85, Entry 9, NARA.

70. Hans Sulzer to Frank L. Polk, January 17, 1920, File: 52729/9, RG 85, Entry 9, NARA.

71. David Montgomery has discussed the ambiguous role of factory foremen in his book, *Workers' Control in America*, as has Hugh Aitken in *Scientific Management in Action*.

Chapter 5

1. Said, *Orientalism*.

2. Ibid., 42.

3. Ibid., 75.

4. *Los Angeles Times*, June 22, 1901.

5. Jacobson, *Barbarian Virtues*.

6. U.S. Consul at Basel, Switzerland, to John Davis, May 9, 1883, File: 715, Box 4, Entry 7, RG 85, NARA.

7. W. Robertson to Charles Folger, June 6, 1883, and John Davis to Charles Folger, May 22, 1883, File: 715, Box 4, RG 85, Entry 7, NARA.

8. Said, *Orientalism*, 62.

9. S. Gordon, "The Liberty of Self-Degradation," quotations, 835 and 829. See also Burgett, "On the Mormon Question."

10. "List of Debarred Aliens," August 12, 1910, File: 52737/499. Eight of the forty-three Muslim individuals (all males) on this list were deported to Turkey on charges of polygamy. The remainder was deported on LPC grounds. The Turkish ambassador (representing the Imperial Ottoman Embassy) issued a formal complaint about deportations of Muslim immigrants and questioned whether Turkish immigrants were being treated unfairly by immigration officials. J. B. Densmore to [William Jennings Bryan], Secretary of State, May 9, 1914, File: 52737/499. Both files in RG 85, Entry 9, NARA.

11. Burgett, "On the Mormon Question."

12. For more on this issue, see Flake, *The Politics of American Religious Identity*.

13. United States House of Representatives, Report No. 848, 56th Cong., 1st sess., 1900; Theodore Roosevelt, "State of the Union Address," 59th Cong., 2nd sess., 1906.

14. Finkel, *Osman's Dream*.

15. "The United States and the Moslems," *Progrès de Salonique*, February 22, 1910, File: 52737/499, RG 85, Entry 9, NARA.

16. Ibid.

17. George Horton to the Secretary of Commerce and Labor, January 3, 1913, File: 52737/499, RG 85, Entry 9, NARA.

18. Huntington (Carlson?, Assistant Secretary of State) to Nagel, April 21, 1910, File: 52737/499, RG 85, Entry 9. NARA.

19. "Examination of alien applicants for the purpose of determining whether a polygamist or a person who believes in the practice of polygamy," May 5 and June 16, 1913, File: 52737/499, RG 85, Entry 9, NARA.

20. Charles Nagel to the Secretary of State, January 9, 1913, File: 52737/499, RG 85, Entry 9, NARA.

21. Memorandum for the Acting Secretary, Appeal of Ismal Mustafa, May 3, 1913, File: 53595/110, RG 85, Entry 9, NARA.

22. Rehearing Testimony of Ismail Mustafa, U.S. Immigration Station, Boston, May 14, 1913, File: 53595/110, RG 85, Entry 9, NARA.

23. Caminetti to Commissioner of Immigration, Ellis Island, May 19, 1913, File: 53595/110, RG 85, Entry 9, NARA.

24. Youssouf Zia to William Jennings Bryan, February 4, 1914, File: 52737/499, RG 85, Entry 9, NARA.

25. Secretary [Charles Nagel?] to William Jennings Bryan, April 14, 1910, RG 85, Entry 9, NARA.

26. Jensen, *Passage from India*, 246–47, 254–55.

27. Ibid., 256–57.

28. Commissioner [in San Francisco] to Commissioner-General of Immigration, July 30, 1910, RG 85, Entry 9, NARA.

29. Ibid.

30. U.S. District Court Western District of Washington Northern Division, No. 2532, filed September 1913, Herbert W. Meyers for Petitioners, C. F. Riddall and E. B. Brockway, Respondents, File: 536250-E, RG 85, Entry 9, NARA. The cases referenced were *Ekin v. United States*, 142 U.S. 650; *Yamataya v. Fisher*, 189 U.S. 86; *United States v. Ju Toy*, 198 U.S. 253; *Lee Moon Sing v. United States*, 158 U.S. 538; and *Chin Yow v. United States*, 208 U.S. 8.

31. File: 55685/886, RG 85, NARA.

32. Yogananda, *Autobiography of a Yogi*. For more on the early interest in Asian religions among Americans, see Tweed and Prothero, *Asian Religions in America*.

33. Yogananda, *Autobiography of a Yogi*, 350.

34. Tweed and Prothero, *Asian Religions*, 14–15.

35. Jensen, *Passage from India*, 15. The census figure included people born in India to English parents stationed in the colonial government.

36. Board of Special Inquiry Transcript of Swami Giri Yogananda case, October 26, 1936, File: 55685/886, RG 85, Entry 9, NARA.

37. "Immigration and Naturalization Legislation," appendix 1.5–1.6, *Statistical Yearbook, 1986*, http://www.ins.gov/graphics/aboutms/statistics/stateyrbook96/appendix.pdf.

38. Board of Special Inquiry Transcript of Swami Giri Yogananda case, October 26, 1936; financial issues discussed on pp. 12–14.

39. Adele Calhoun to U.S. Immigration Service, April 30, 1935, File: 55685/886, RG 85, Entry 9, NARA.

40. V. W. Tomlinson to Commissioner, July 8, 1925, File: 55685/886, RG 85, Entry 9, NARA.

41. Chan, *Asian Americans*, 60–61.

42. One such example is analyzed in Jew, "'Chinese Demons.'"

43. Hilda Concorde Brodeur Allen to the secretary of the Sri Ramakrishna Mission, January 21, 1933, File: 55685/886, RG 85, Entry 9, NARA.

44. Ibid.

45. Yogananda, *Autobiography of a Yogi*, 352, 418. Memo, "In connection with Swami Yogananda's request . . . ," [undated and unsigned but stamped "Received October 26, 1936, Warrant Division"], File: 55685/886, RG 85, Entry 9, NARA.

46. V. W. Tomlinson to Commissioner, July 8, 1925, File: 55685/886, RG 85, NARA.

47. Bureau of Special Inquiry Transcript of Swami Giri Yogananda case, October 26, 1936. All questions from p. 10. The questions and answers are in consecutive order, but there are others that are not excerpted.

48. Dinitia Smith, "The Death and Delirious Life of Doris Duke," *New York Magazine*, December 6, 1993, 44.

49. Ashcraft, *The Dawn of the New Cycle*, 17–19.

50. Ibid., 53.

51. Ibid., 24–25; *Los Angeles Times*, March 29, 1901, and June 22, 1901.

52. Ashcraft, *The Dawn of the New Cycle*.

53. "Otis Chandler: Publisher Established *Los Angeles Times* as Respected Voice," *Washington Post*, February 28, 2006.

54. *Los Angeles Times*, January 13, 1903.

55. See, for example, *Los Angeles Times*, December 30, 1902 (article mentions separation from parents). On food, see December 25, 1902; on Muslin dress, March 31, 1901 (the article refers to outfits as "nightgowns").

56. *Los Angeles Times*, December 30, 1902.

57. *Los Angeles Times*, September 17, 1910.

58. *Los Angeles Times*, August 9, 1901.

59. On Van Pelt, see John William Leonard, ed., *Woman's Who's Who of America: A Biographical Dictionary of Contemporary Women of the United States and Canada, 1914–1915* (New York: American Commonwealth, 1914), 831; "Thirty-seventh Annual Announcement of the Woman's Medical College of Philadelphia, North College Ave. and Twenty-First Street, Philadelphia Session of 1886–87," http://archives.drexelmed.edu/womanmd, accessed May 16, 2006, in "Women Physicians," Drexel University College of Medicine Archives and Special Collections."

60. *Los Angeles Times*, November 2, 1902.

61. *Los Angeles Times*, March 31, 1901.

62. ["Cuban Children Case,"] Proceedings of the U.S. Board of Special Inquiry of Ellis Island, November 1, 5, and 7, 1902, File: 51841/57, RG 85, Entry 9, NARA.

63. *Los Angeles Times*, November 14, 1902.

64. "Cuban Children Case," 15–16.

65. Ibid.

66. Ibid.

67. L. Gordon, *The Great Arizona Orphan Abduction.*

68. Edward Parker, Testimony at the Board of Special Inquiry Hearing, 75–77, File: 51841/57, RG 85, Entry 9, NARA.

69. "Cuban Children Case."

70. *Los Angeles Times*, November 14, 1902.

71. *Los Angeles Times*, November 18, 19, 22, and 23, and December 5 and 7, 1902. Morals quotation on December 7, 1902. Egyptian gate remark in November 23, 1902, issue.

72. *Los Angeles Times*, April 3, 1906.

73. *Los Angeles Times*, November 2, 1902.

Chapter 6

1. The classic work on this period is Preston, *Aliens and Dissenters.*

2. H. Cohen, "The (Un)Favorable Judgment of History."

3. *New York World Telegram*, March 23, 1933; Louis Post, *Deportations Delirium* (Chicago: Charles H. Kerr, 1923), 166–67.

4. See Zolberg, *A Nation by Design.*

5. Bisbee Deportation Collection, University of Arizona Library.

6. *Bisbee Daily Review*, June 27, 1917, Bisbee Deportation Collection.

7. Ibid.

8. *Bisbee Daily Review*, July 7, 1917.

9. *Los Angeles Times*, July 13 and 15, 1917; "Cochise County Clerk's Office: Bisbee Deportation Documents," Bisbee Deportation Collection.

10. Recent scholarship on the Bisbee Deportations includes Capozzola, "The Only Badge Needed Is Your Patriotic Fervor," and Benton-Cohen, "Docile Children and Dangerous Revolutionaries"; Department of Labor, "Report on the Bisbee Deportations Made by the President's Mediation Commission to the President of the United States," November 6, 1917, Bisbee Deportation Collection.

11. Report, Bisbee Deportation Collection.

12. Byrkrit, *Forging the Copper Collar*; Benton-Cohen, *Borderline Americans*, chap. 7.

13. Department of Labor, "Sixth Annual Report of the Secretary of Labor for the Fiscal Year Ended June 30, 1918," Washington, D.C., 1918, Bisbee Deportation Collection.

14. There are many biographies of Hoover. Among them are Charles, *J. Edgar Hoover and the Anti-interventionists*; Hack, *Puppetmaster*; Theoharis, *J. Edgar Hoover, Sex, and Crime.* Theoharis's short biography is essentially a refutation of claims that Hoover was gay. Whether he was or not, however, he was clearly obsessed with race, sexuality, and power.

15. Falk, Zborny, and Hall, eds., Emma Goldman Papers, microfilm edition, Reel 63, Notes, xv.

16. Ibid., notes. On Garvey, see Grant, *Negro with a Hat*, 153.

17. "I.W.W. Deportation Cases: Hearings before a Subcommittee of the Committee on Immigration and Naturalization," 66th Cong., April 27 to 30, 1920 (Washington, D.C.: Government Printing Office, 1920), Bisbee Deportation Collection.

18. Ibid., 18.

19. Manager, American Press Bureau, to Robert Scott, December 24, 1919, Immigration and Refugee Services of America Records, Immigration History Research Center, University of Minnesota.

20. Chafee, *Freedom of Speech*, 250.

21. Ibid., 252.

22. Ibid., 253–55.

23. Ibid., 260, 265.

24. *New York World Telegram*, March 23, 1933.

25. Falk, Zborny, and Hall, eds., Emma Goldman Papers, microfilm, Reel 1, Introductory Essays, 49–51.

26. Ibid.

27. Ibid., Reel 58.

28. Ibid.

29. Ibid., Reel 57, "Introduction to Reels 57–60," vi–viii, and "U.S. v. Goldman and Berkman, July 2, 1917," Transcript, 14.

30. Ibid., Reel 57, July 2, 1917, Transcript, 19–22, 36–39, 100, and 121–22.

31. Ibid., "Introduction to Reels 57–60," microfilm edition, viii.

32. Ibid., Reel 63, Warrant Issued by John Abercrombie, September 5, 1919.

33. Ibid., Alice Stone Blackwell to Albert Caminetti, September 17, 1919.

34. Ibid., Statement by Alexander Berkman in re Deportation, September 18, 1919.

35. Ibid., Introduction to Reel 63, xxvi–xxv.

36. Ibid., Harry Weinberger to Albert Caminetti, August 15, 1919.

37. Ibid.

38. *Attorney General A. Mitchell Palmer on Charges Made against the Department of Justice* and *Investigation of Administration of Louis F. Post in the Matter of Deportation of Aliens*, Hearings before House Committee on Rules, 66th Cong., 2nd sess., Parts 1 and 2 (1920), cited in Chafee, *Free Speech in the United States*, 207–8. On history of Deer Island, see Tanis, "Education in John Eliot's Indian Utopias, 1646–1675"; *Boston Globe*, May 18, 2008; and http://www.bostonislands.org/isle_deer.html, accessed October 27, 2009.

39. *New York Times*, November 10, 1919.

40. Shubert, "The Palmer Raids in Connecticut." On labor and manufacturing in the Connecticut Valley, see Montgomery, *The Fall of the House of Labor*.

41. *Hartford Courant*, November 20, 1919.

42. *Hartford Courant*, November 1919, various issues.

43. File: 54859/525, RG 85, Entry 9, NARA.

44. J. Edgar Hoover to Anthony Caminetti, March 16, 1920, File: 54859/525, RG 85, Entry 9, NARA.

45. Memorandum for the Assistant Secretary, "In Re: Worth or Wirth. . . . December 26, 1919," File: 54859/525, RG 85, Entry 9, NARA.

46. Ibid.

47. Ibid.

48. Ibid.

49. Ibid.

50. U.S. Department of Labor, Immigration Service, "Report of Hearing," 4, no date, Chicago File: 2050/204"; File: 54811/528, RG 85, Entry 9, NARA.

51. See the references in n. 50 above.

52. File: 54811/528, RG 85, Entry 9, NARA.

53. Ginger, *Carol Weiss King*, 27, 33–34; Rogers, "Judge George W. Anderson and Civil Rights."

54. Rogers, "Judge George W. Anderson and Civil Rights," 13–16, and 20–23.

55. "Warrant–Deportation of Alien, March 23, 1920," File: 54810/209, RG 85, Entry 9, NARA.

56. "Opinion of the Court, 11 January 1922," *Skeffington v. Katzeff, ex. Rel William T. Colyer*," File: 54810/209, RG 85, Entry 9, NARA.

57. Ibid.

58. "Rehearing, February 4, 1920," [Amy Colyer], File: 54810/209, RG 85, Entry 9, NARA.

59. Ibid.

60. Ibid.

61. *Attorney General A. Mitchell Palmer on Charges Made against the Department of Justice* and *Investigation of Administration of Louis F. Post in the Matter of Deportation of Aliens*, Hearings before House Committee on Rules, 66th Cong., 2nd sess., Parts 1 and 2 (1920), 326; "Rehearing, February 4, 1920," [Amy Colyer], File: 54810/209, RG 85, Entry 9.

62. "Rehearing, February 4, 1920," [Amy Colyer], File: 54810/209, RG 85, Entry 9.

63. *Hartford Courant*, November 17, 1919.

64. Kanstroom, *Deportation Nation*, 75.

65. Rolinson, *Grassroots Garveyism*.

66. *Hartford Courant*, November 16, 1919.

67. *Time Magazine*, December 12, 1927.

68. Spiro, *Defending the Master Race*, 258–64.

69. See, for example, Rolinson, *Grassroots Garveyism*; U. Taylor, *The Veiled Garvey*; Harold, *The Rise and Fall of the Garvey Movement*.

70. Cronon, *Black Moses*.

71. H. Hill, *The Marcus Garvey Papers*, vols. 10:397–98. On Ireland, 1:501.

72. H. Hill, *Marcus Garvey Papers*, 1:xxx.

73. Ibid., 1:305.

74. Ibid., 1:305–7.

75. Ibid., 1:327.

76. Cronon, *Black Moses*, 141–42.

77. "Philosophy and Opinions of Marcus Garvey," edited by Amy Jacques Garvey, vol. 2 (December 1925), written by Marcus Garvey in the Atlanta Federal Penitentiary, http://www.international.ucla.edu/africa/mgpp/lifesamp.asp, accessed June 17, 2008.

78. Harold, *The Rise and Fall of the Garvey Movement*, 117.

79. Anonymous letter, August 11, 1919, enclosed with a note from Robert P. Stewart to William Wilson, Secretary of Labor, in Hill, *Marcus Garvey Papers*, 1:484.

80. Davies, *Left of Karl Marx*. On Ashwood Garvey, 2.

81. Ibid., xxiii.

82. *Chicago Defender*, February 25, 1939.

83. *Chicago Defender*, 134–36.

84. Claudia Jones, "Dear Comrade Foster: The Following is the Autobiographical (Personal, Political, Medical) History that I Promised . . . Comradely, Claudia Jones (December 6, 1955)."

85. Cherny, "The Making of a Labor Radical."

86. Ginger, *Carol Weiss King*, 21.

87. "In re Harry Bridges," *Yale Law School Journal* 52, no. 1 (December 1942): 108–29; Ginger, *Carol Weiss King*, 259 and 264.

88. Ginger, *Carol Weiss King*, 301–2, 329.

89. Kutler, *The American Inquisition*.

90. Klehr and Haynes in "The Comintern's Open Secrets," 34–35.

Chapter 7

My sincere appreciation goes to Hiroshi Motomura, Daniel Kanstroom, and Philippa Strum for sharing their legal expertise and for reviewing this chapter.

1. Congressional representation is apportioned by U.S. population, not by U.S. citizenship, a fact that was widely argued by abolitionists in nineteenth-century political debates on slavery. In 1995, a federal appeals court held in the *American-Arab Comm. v. Thornburgh* case that "the same First Amendment protections apply to citizens and non-citizens alike." Half a decade earlier, federal legislation removed the provisions for deportation on ideological grounds that had been used to deport political radicals earlier in the century, while adding provisions to deport aliens based on terrorist activity. Motomura, *Americans in Waiting*, 107.

2. On *Padilla v. Kentucky* decision, see www.supremecourt.gov/opinions/09pdf/08-651.pdf, accessed July 30, 2011.

3. Maurice A. Roberts, "Background and Development of the Board of Immigration Appeals," unpublished Paper, 1977. Maurice A. Roberts Papers, Immigration History Research Center, University of Minnesota; Kanstroom, *Deportation Nation*, 178.

4. Motomura, "The Curious Evolution of Immigration Law."

5. Ibid.; *Washington Post*, April 12, 2009.

6. Kanstroom, *Deportation Nation*, 63–95; quotation, 65.

7. Ibid.

8. Weisselberg, "The Exclusion and Detention of Aliens"; G. Chin, "Chae Chan Ping and Fong Yue Ting"; Motomura, *Americans in Waiting*, 24–36.

9. See the references in n. 8 above.

10. *Wong Wing v. U.S.*, 163 U.S. 228 (1896).

11. Moloney, *American Catholic Lay Groups*; Connolly, *The Triumph of Ethnic Progressivism*; Rodgers, *Atlantic Crossings*.

12. For biographical data on Oppenheimer, see "The Judges in Maryland," June 29, 1960, and "Judge Oppenheimer Is Appointed to Court of Appeals," Maryland State Archives, Baltimore, Md.

13. United States, Wickersham Commission, Reports, 87.

14. Ibid., 97.

15. Ibid.
16. Ibid., 3.
17. Ibid., 3–4.
18. Ibid., 75–76.
19. Ibid., 4, 23, 26–27.
20. Ibid., 4.
21. Ibid., 17–18.
22. Ibid., 21.
23. Ibid., 51–52.
24. Ibid., 21.
25. Ibid., 28–30.
26. Ibid., 30–31.
27. Ibid., 32–33.
28. Ibid., 31, 85.
29. Ibid., 100.
30. Ibid., 8–12.
31. Kane, "The Challenge of the Wickersham."
32. *Time Magazine*, July 13, 1931.
33. United States, Wickersham Commission, Reports, 4. Van Vleck, Administrative Control.
34. Alexander, *Rights of Aliens*, 79–80.
35. Ibid., 34.
36. Ibid., 87.
37. Obituary, *New York Times*, October 27, 1981.
38. Carey, *Deportation*, 9, 54, 58.
39. Hoffman, "Stimulus to Repatriation."
40. Irwin, *Strange Passage*.
41. Ibid., 225.
42. Ibid., 279–80.
43. Ibid.
44. Ibid., 282.
45. Ellis Island Committee, Report of the Ellis Island Committee, New York, 1934.
46. Offen, "Dealing with 'Defectives.'"
47. Ellis Island Committee, Report, 132–33.
48. Ibid., 141–42.
49. Ibid., 80.
50. Ibid., 47.
51. Ibid., 81.
52. Weisselberg, "The Exclusion and Detention of Aliens," 955–60.
53. Ibid., 960–63.
54. Ibid.
55. Waters, Ueda, and Marrow, *The New Americans*.
56. Zolberg, *A Nation by Design*; McGirr, *Suburban Warriors*.
57. Abraham, Hamilton, et al., *Immigration and America*.

58. Ibid.; Miller, "Citizenship and Severity." On the *Wing* case, see Richbourg, "Liberty and Security," 3.

59. *New York Times*, June 7, 2003.

60. Neuman, "The Assault on Habeas Corpus in Immigration Law"; Gonzalez's remarks in *San Francisco Chronicle*, January 24, 2007.

61. *New York Times*, October 12, 2007, and January 27, 2007; King and Massoglia, "Banishment as Social Control"; García, "Local Challenges to Labor Organizing in Mexican Immigrant Enclaves."

62. *Washington Post*, April 12, 2009; "9050 Liberty," PBS, aired January 12, 2011.

63. *Washington Post*, October 2, 2007 (Prince William County), and October, 2007.

64. *Washington Post*, November 27, 2007.

65. Ibid. On Arizona decision, see *New York Times*, May 27, 2011.

66. *New York Times*, July 27, 2007.

67. *New York Times*, June 26, 2007; Kerwin and Yi-Ying Lin, "Immigrant Detention"; *Washington Post*, June 14, 2009; *New York Times*, May 27, 2011.

68. *New York Times*, June 26, 2007, and August 17, 2009. Asylum seekers are discussed in Amnesty International, "The United States of America, Lost in the Labyrinth," 5.

69. U.S. Department of Homeland Security, United States Citizenship and Immigration Service, Annual Report, Enforcement Procedures (2007), http://www.dhs.gov/xlibrary/assets/statistics/publications/enforcement_ar_07.pdf, accessed November 5, 2008.

70. For overviews on twentieth-century U.S. civil rights activism, see Sullivan, *Days of Hope*; Ransby, *Ella Baker*; Payne, *I've Got the Light of Freedom*; Vargas, *Labor Rights Are Civil Rights*; Rosen, *The World Split Open*; Cruikshank, *The Gay and Lesbian Liberation Movement*; Marcus, *Making History*. I do not subscribe to post-racial, post-feminist perspectives, or an interpretation that emphasizes inevitable progress over time. Much remains unequal, and hate crimes and discrimination persist. But, while tangible gains have been made for African Americans, women and gay, lesbian, and transgendered peoples in the U.S. since 1955, as measured by public attitudes, legal rights, and economic gains, this is less true for immigrants. Moreover, attitudes toward immigrants have become increasingly hostile since 2001.

71. Motomura, *Americans in Waiting*, 191–94.

72. Aleinikoff, *Semblances of Sovereignty*, especially chap. 7.

73. *New York Times*, June 30, 2004.

74. Cole, *Enemy Aliens*.

75. *Zadvydas v. Davis* 533 U.S. 678 (99–7791) (2001).

76. Ishay, *The History of Human Rights*, 267–73.

77. Grey, *Ghost Plane*.

78. *Washington Post*, July 29, 2003.

79. Congressional Research Service, Report, "*Boumediene v. Bush*: Guantanamo Detainees' Right to Habeas Corpus," September 8, 2008, http://fas.org/sgp/crs/natsec/RL34536.pdf, accessed February 22, 2010.

80. *Washington Post*, December 5, 2007; *New York Times*, December 5, 2007.

81. *New York Times*, December 5, 2007.

82. Article 2 of the United Nation's Universal Declaration of Rights states: "Everyone is entitled to all the rights and freedoms set forth in this Declaration, without distinction of any kind, such as race, colour, sex, language, religion, political or other opinion, national or social origin, property, birth or other status. *Furthermore, no distinction shall be made on the basis of the political, jurisdictional or international status of the country or territory to which a person belongs, whether it be independent, trust, non-self-governing or under any other limitation of sovereignty*" (emphasis added). http://www.un.org/en/documents/udhr, accessed June 8, 2009. See also Ishay, *The History of Human Rights*, 267–73.

83. *Washington Post*, October 6, 2009; *New York Times*, February 12, 2010; Syracuse University, Transactional Records Access Clearinghouse, Report, http://trac.syr.edu/immigration/reports/224/, accessed November 5, 2008.

Conclusion

1. Pew Hispanic Center, Report, "The Hispanic Vote in the 2008 Election"; Wong, *Democracy's Promise*.

2. On the European Union, see Tilly, Welfens, and Heise, *Fifty Years of EU Economic Dynamics*.

3. Joppke, *Immigration and the Nation-State*, 100–101; Hansen, *Citizenship and Immigration*.

4. Joppke, *Immigration and the Nation-State*, 114–19; Hansen, *Citizenship and Immigration*, 19–20, 29; Moch, *Europeans on the Move*, 176.

5. Joppke, *Immigration and the Nation-State*, 114–19; Hansen, *Citizenship and Immigration*, 19–20, 29.

6. On Spain, Bledsoe, Houle, and Sow, "High Fertility Gambians in Low Fertility Spain"; on Italy, *Morning Edition*, NPR, January 13, 2009; on France, Catherine Raissiguier, "Blood Matters: Sarkozy's Immigration Policies and Their Gendered Impact."

7. Joppke, *Immigration and the Nation-State*, 62–63; Mandel, *Cosmopolitan Anxieties*.

8. See *New York Times*, February 25, 2008, and www.citizensinformation.ie/categories, accessed March 6, 2010.

9. United Kingdom, Home Office, Report, "Control of Immigration." On Spain, see *New Statesman*, May 7, 2009.

10. See, for example, Lesser, *Welcoming the Undesirables*; Skidmore, *Black into White*; Guy, *Sex and Danger in Buenos Aires*; Masterson and Funada-Classen, *The Japanese in Latin America*.

11. Cornelius, Martin, and Hollifield, *Controlling Immigration*, 3–4, 28–33.

12. On the globalization perspective, see, for example, Sassen, *Territory, Authority, Rights*; Soysal, *Limits of Citizenship*; Benhabib, *The Rights of Others*, 29–31 and 50–52.

13. Benhabib, *The Rights of Others*, 20–21; Carens, "The Case for Amnesty." Thanks to Rebecca Kingston and Matthew Gibney for guiding me toward the literature in this debate.

BIBLIOGRAPHY

Manuscript Collections

ARCHIVES

Minneapolis, Minn.
  Immigration History Research Center, University of Minnesota
    Immigration and Refugee Services of America Records
    Maurice A. Roberts Papers
New York, N.Y.
  New York Public Library
    William A. Williams Papers
  YIVO Institute for Jewish Research
    Hebrew Immigration Assistance Service Records
Notre Dame, Ind.
  University of Notre Dame
    Thomas F. Mahony Papers
Washington, D.C.
  American Catholic History Research Center and University Archives, Catholic University of America
    United States Conference of Catholic Bishops Records
    Immigration Bureau/Department, National Catholic Welfare Council (NCWC)
  National Archives and Records Administration
    Immigration and Naturalization Records

DIGITAL AND MICROFILM COLLECTIONS

Berkeley, Calif.
  University of California
    Emma Goldman Papers, microfilm, Cambridge: Chadwyck-Healy, 1991.
Philadelphia, Pa.
  Drexel University
    "Women Physicians," College of Medicine Archives and Special Collections, http://archives.drexelmed.edu/womanmd
Tucson, Ariz.
  University of Arizona Library
    Bisbee Deportation Collection, http://www.library.arizona.edu/exhibits

Newspapers and Periodicals

Atlantic Monthly (Boston)
Boston Globe
Chicago Defender
Congressional Record
El Paso Daily Times
Evening Transcript (Boston)
Excelsior
Hartford Courant
La Opinion (Los Angeles)
Los Angeles Times

McClure's (New York)
New Statesman
New Yorker
New York Magazine
New York Times
New York University Law Review
New York World Telegram
San Francisco Chronicle
Time
Washington Post
Yale Law Review

Government Reports and Publications

Ellis Island Committee. Report of the Ellis Island Committee. New York, 1934.

Roosevelt, Theodore. "State of the Union Address." 59th Cong., 2nd sess., 1906.

United Kingdom. Home Office. Report. "Control of Immigration: Quarterly Statistical Summary." October–December 2008 (2nd edition). http://www.homeoffice.gov.uk/rds/pdfs09/immiq408.pdf, accessed March 1, 2010.

United States. "Annual Report of the Commissioner-General of Immigration." 1892–1940. [Departments of Treasury, Commerce, Labor and Commerce, and Labor].

United States. Wickersham Commission. *Reports*. Washington, D.C.: Government Printing Office, 1931. [Including the Oppenhcimer Report].

U.S. Department of Health and Human Services. "HHS Joins the INS and State Department in Clarifying 'Public Charge' Guidance." Press Release. May 26, 1999. http://archive.hhs.gov/news/press/1999pres/990526.html, accessed December 9, 2002.

U.S. Department of Homeland Security. Enforce Alien Removal Module (EARM). February 2009. Enforcement Case Tracking System (ENFORCE). December 2008.

U.S. Department of Homeland Security. *Yearbook of Immigration Statistics: 2008*. Washington, D.C.: U.S. Department of Homeland Security, Office of Immigration Statistics, 2009. http://www.dhs.gov/xlibrary/assets/statistics/yearbook/2008/ois_yb_2008.pdf, accessed January 3, 2010.

———, Bureau of Immigration and Customs Enforcement. "Endgame: Office of Detention and Removal Strategic Plan, 2003–2012 Detention and Removal Strategy for a Secure Homeland." August 15, 2003. www.fas.org/irp/agency/dhs/endgame.pdf, accessed January 5, 2010.

U.S. House of Representatives. Report. "Europe as an Emigrant-Exporting Continent and the United States as an Immigrant-Receiving Nation": Hearings before the Committee on Immigration and Naturalization, 68th Cong., 1st sess., March 8, 1924. Statement of Dr. Harry H. Laughlin, 1231–1437. Washington, D.C.: Government Printing Office, 1924.

U.S. House of Representatives. Report No. 848. 56th Cong., 1st sess., 1900.

U.S. House of Representatives. "To Provide for Removal at Government Expense of Certain Financially Distressed Aliens who Apply for Permission to Return to Their Native Country." 74th Cong., 1st sess., Report 120 (1935).

United States, Wickersham Commission. *Reports*. Washington, D.C.: Government Printing Office, 1931. [Including the Oppenheimer Report].

Published Primary Sources

Addams, Jane. *A New Conscience and an Ancient Evil.* New York: Macmillan, 1912.

Alexander, Norman. *Rights of Aliens under the Federal Constitution.* Montpelier, Vt.: Capitol City Press, 1931.

Chafee, Zechariah. *Freedom of Speech.* New York: Harcourt, Brace, and Howe, 1920.

Fishberg, Maurice. *The Jews: A Study of Race and Environment.* New York: Walter Scott Publishing, 1911.

Hill, Hamilton Andrews. *An Inquiry into the Relations of Immigration to Pauperism.* Boston: Mudge and Son, 1876.

Hill, Robert A. *The Marcus Garvey and Universal Negro Improvement Association Papers.* Vols. 1–10. Berkeley: University of California Press, 2006.

Irwin, Theodore. *Strange Passage.* New York: Harrison Smith and Robert Haas, 1935.

Jones, Claudia. "Dear Comrade Foster: The Following is the Autobiographical (Personal, Political, Medical) History that I Promised . . . Comradely, Claudia Jones (December 6, 1955)," with an introduction and bibliography by Peter Meyer Filardo. *American Communist History* 4, no. 1 (2005): 85–93.

Kane, Francis Fisher. "The Challenge of the Wickersham Deportations Report." *Journal of Criminal Law and Criminology* 23, no. 4 (1932): 575–613.

Post, Louis. *Deportations Delirium.* Chicago: Charles H. Kerr, 1923.

Ripley, William Z. "Races in the United States." *Atlantic Monthly* 102, no. 6 (December 1908): 745–59.

Turner, George Kibbe. "Daughters of the Poor: A Plain Story of the Development of New York City as Leading Center of the White Slave Trade of the World, under Tammany Hall." *McClure's* 34 (November 1909): 45–61.

Yogananda, Paramahansa. *The Autobiography of a Yogi.* 1946. Reprint, Nevada City, Calif.: Crystal Clarity Publishers, 1995.

Broadcast: Television and Radio

"Annapolis, Maryland, Immigration Raid." News Story. WAMU Radio. Aired July 14, 2008. Lagan Sebert, reporter.

Morning Edition. NPR. Aired January 13, 2009.

"9050 Liberty." PBS. Aired January 12, 2011.

Secondary Sources

BOOKS AND ARTICLES

Abraham, Spenser, Lee H. Hamilton, et al. *Immigration and America: A New Chapter (Report of the Independent Task Force on Immigration and America's Future).* Washington, D.C.: Migration Policy Institute, 2006.

Aguila, Jaime. "Mexican/U.S. Immigration Policy Prior to the Great Depression." *Diplomatic History* 31, no. 2 (April 2007): 207–25.

Aitken, Hugh. *Scientific Management in Action: Taylorism at Watertown Arsenal, 1908–1915.* Princeton: Princeton University Press, 1985.

Aleinikoff, T. Alexander. *Semblances of Sovereignty: The Constitution, the State and Citizenship.* Cambridge, Mass.: Harvard University Press, 2002.

Anbinder, Tyler. *Nativism and Slavery: The Northern Know Nothings and the Politics of the 1850s*. New York: Oxford University Press, 2004.

Archdeacon, Thomas. *Becoming American*. New York: Free Press, 1983.

Arnesen, Eric. "Scholarly Controversy: Whiteness and the Historians' Imagination." In special issue of *International Labor and Working-Class History* 60 (2001): 3–32.

Ashcraft, W. Michael. *The Dawn of the New Cycle: Point Loma Theosophists and American Culture*. Knoxville: University of Tennessee Press, 2002.

Balderrama, Francisco, and Raymond Rodriguez. *Decade of Betrayal: Mexican Repatriation in the 1930s*. Albuquerque: University of New Mexico Press, 1995.

Bay, Mia. *To Tell the Truth Freely: The Life of Ida B. Wells*. New York: Hill and Wang, 2009.

Baynton, Douglas C. "Defectives in the Land: Disability and American Immigration Policy, 1882–1924" (and scholars' responses to it). *Journal of American Ethnic History* 24, no. 3 (Summer 2005): 31–44.

Beer, Janet, and Katherin Joslin. "Diseases of the Body Politic: White Slavery in Jane Addams' 'A New Conscience and an Ancient Evil' and Selected Stories by Charlotte Perkins Gilman." *Journal of American Studies* 33 (1999): 1–18.

Benhabib, Seyla. *The Rights of Others: Aliens, Residents, and Citizens*. Cambridge: Cambridge University Press, 2004.

Benton-Cohen, Katherine. *Borderline Americans*. Cambridge, Mass.: Harvard University Press, 2009.

———. "Docile Children and Dangerous Revolutionaries: The Racial Hierarchy of Manliness and the Bisbee Deportation of 1917." *Frontiers* 24, nos. 2 and 3 (2003): 30–50.

Bergoffen, Debra, Paula Ruth Gilbert, Tamara Harvey, and Connie L. McNeeley, eds. *Confronting Global Gender Justice: Women's Lives, Human Rights*. London: Routledge, 2010.

Bledsoe, Caroline, Rene Houle, and Papa Sow. "High Fertility Gambians in Low Fertility Spain: The Dynamics of Child Accumulation across Transnational Space." *Demographic Research* 16 (May 2007): 375–412.

Bodnar, John. *The Transplanted: A History of Immigrants in Urban America*. Bloomington: Indiana University Press, 1985.

Bredbenner, Candice. *A Nationality of Her Own: Women, Marriage and the Law of Citizenship*. Berkeley: University of California Press, 1998.

Burgett, Bruce. "On the Mormon Question: Race, Sex, and Polygamy in the 1850's and 1890's." *American Quarterly* 57, no. 1 (2005): 75–102.

Byrkrit, James W. *Forging the Copper Collar: Arizona's Labor-Management War of 1901–1921*. Tucson: University of Arizona Press, 1982.

Canaday, Margot. *The Straight State: Sexuality and Citizenship in Twentieth-Century America*. Princeton: Princeton University Press, 2009.

Cannato, Vincent J. *American Passage: The History of Ellis Island*. New York: Harper, 2009.

Capozzola, Christopher. "The Only Badge Needed Is Your Patriotic Fervor: Vigilance, Coercion, and the Law in World War I America." *Journal of American History* 88, no. 4 (March 2002): 1354–82.

Carens, Joseph. "The Case for Amnesty: Time Erodes the State's Right to Deport." *Boston Review*, May–June 2009. http://bostonreview.net/BR34.3/ndf_immigration.php, accessed January 15, 2010.
Carey, Jane Perry Clark. *Deportation of Aliens from the United States to Europe*. 1931. Reprint, New York: Arno Press, 1969.
Carpenter, Niles. "The New Immigration Policy and the Labor Market." *Quarterly Journal of Economics* 45, no. 4 (August 1931): 720–23.
Chan, Sucheng. *Asian Americans: An Interpretative History*. Boston: Twayne, 1991.
———, ed. *Entry Denied: Exclusion and the Chinese Community in America*. Philadelphia: Temple University Press, 1994.
Chang, Kornel. "Circulating Race and Empire: Transnational Labor Activism and the Politics of Anti-Asian Agitation in the Anglo-American Pacific World, 1880–1910." *Journal of American History* 96, no. 3 (December 2009): 678–701.
Charles, Douglas W. *J. Edgar Hoover and the Anti-interventionists: FBI Political Surveillance and the Rise of the Domestic Security State, 1939–1945*. Columbus: Ohio State University Press, 2007.
Cherny, Robert. "The Making of a Labor Radical: Harry Bridges, 1901–1934." *Pacific Historical Review* (1995): 363–80.
Chin, Gabriel J. "Chae Chan Ping and Fong Yue Ting: The Origins of Plenary Power." In *Immigration Law Stories*, edited by David Martin and Peter Schuck, 7–30. New York: Foundation Press, 2005.
Chin, Rita. *The Guest Worker Question in Postwar Germany*. Cambridge: Cambridge University Press, 2008.
Cohen, Harlan Grant. "The (Un)Favorable Judgment of History: Deportation Hearings, the Palmer Raids, and the Meaning of History." *New York University Law Review* 78, no. 4 (October 2003): 1431.
Cohen, Stanley. *Folk Devils and Moral Panics*. 3rd ed. London: Routledge, 2002.
Cole, David. *Enemy Aliens: Double Standards and Constitutional Freedoms in the War on Terrorism*. New York: New Press, 2003.
Compomanes, Oscar V. "Images of Filipino Racialization in the Anthropological Laboratories of the American Empire: The Case of Daniel Folkmar." *PMLA* 123 (2008): 1692–99.
Connolly, James J. *The Triumph of Ethnic Progressivism: Urban Political Culture in Boston, 1900–1925*. Cambridge, Mass.: Harvard University Press, 1999.
Coon, Carlton S. *The Living Races of Man*. New York: Knopf, 1965.
Cornelius, Wayne, Philip L. Martin, and James F. Hollifield. *Controlling Immigration: A Global Perspective*. Stanford: Stanford University Press, 1994.
Cott, Nancy. *Public Vows: A History of Marriage and the Nation*. Cambridge, Mass.: Harvard University Press, 2000.
Crenshaw, Kimberlé. "Demarginalizing the Intersection of Race and Sex: A Black Feminist Critique of Antidiscrimination Doctrine, Feminist Theory, and Antiracist Politics." *University of Chicago Legal Forum* (1989): 139–67.
———. "Mapping the Margins: Intersectionality, Identity Politics, and Violence against Women of Color." *Stanford Law Review* 43, no. 6 (1991): 1241–99.
Cronon, E. David. *Black Moses: The Story of Marcus Garvey and the United Negro*

Improvement Association. 1955. Reprint, Madison: University of Wisconsin Press, 1969.

Cruikshank, Margaret. *The Gay and Lesbian Liberation Movement*. New York: Routledge, 1992.

D'Agostino, Peter. "Craniums, Criminals and the 'Cursed Race': Italian Anthropology in U.S. Racial Thought." *Comparative Studies of Society and History* 44 (April 2002): 319–43.

Daniels, Roger. *Guarding the Golden Door: American Immigration Policy and Immigrants since 1882*. New York: Hill and Wang, 2004.

———. "No Lamps Were Lit for Them: Angel Island and the Historiography of Asian American Immigration." *Journal of American Ethnic History* 17, no. 1 (Fall 1997): 3–19.

Davies, Carole Boyce. *Left of Karl Marx: The Political Life of Black Communist Claudia Jones*. Durham, N.C.: Duke University Press, 2007.

Davis, Allen F. *Spearheads for Reform: The Social Settlements and the Progressive Movement, 1890–1914*. New York: Oxford University Press, 1967.

Delaney, Enda. *Demography, State and Society: Irish Migration to Britain, 1921–1971*. Montreal: McGill-Queens, 2000.

Diffee, Christopher. "Sex and the City: The White Slavery Scare and Social Governance in the Progressive Era." *American Quarterly* 57, no. 2 (2005): 411–37.

Diner, Hasia. *Erin's Daughters in America: Irish Immigrant Women in the Nineteenth Century*. Baltimore: Johns Hopkins University Press, 1983.

———. "The World of Whiteness." *Historically Speaking*, September–October 2007, 20–22.

Divine, Robert. *American Immigration Policy, 1924–1952*. New Haven: Yale University Press, 1957.

Dorr, Gregory. *Segregation's Science: Eugenics and Society in Virginia*. Charlottesville: University of Virginia Press, 2008.

Dowbiggin, Ian. *Keeping America Sane: Psychiatry and Eugenics in the United States and Canada, 1880–1940*. Ithaca: Cornell University Press, 1997.

Fairchild, Amy. *Science at the Borders: Immigrant Medical Inspection and the Shaping of the Modern Industrial Labor Force*. Baltimore: Johns Hopkins University Press, 2003.

Finkel, Caroline. *Osman's Dream: The Story of the Ottoman Empire, 1300–1923*. New York: Basic Books, 2005.

Flake, Kathleen. *The Politics of American Religious Identity: The Seating of Senator Reed Smoot*. Chapel Hill: University of North Carolina Press, 2004.

Foner, Eric. *Free Soil, Free Labor, and Free Men: The Ideology of the Republican Party before the Civil War*. New York: Oxford University Press, 1970.

———. *Reconstruction: America's Unfinished Revolution, 1863–1877*. New York: Harper Collins, 1988.

Foucault, Michel. *The History of Sexuality*. New York: Pantheon, 1978.

Fox, Cybelle. *Three Worlds of Relief: Race, Immigration, and the American Welfare State from the Progressive Era to the New Deal*. Princeton: Princeton University Press, 2012.

Gabaccia, Donna. *From the Other Side: Women, Gender and Immigrant Life in the U.S., 1820–1920*. Bloomington: Indiana University Press, 1994.

———. "Women of the Mass Migrations: From Minority to Majority, 1820–1930." In *European Migrants: Global and Local Perspectives*, edited by Dirk Hoerder and Leslie Moch, 90–111. Boston: Northeastern University Press, 1996.

Gabaccia, Donna, and Franca Iacovetta, eds. *Women, Gender, and Transnational Lives: Italian Workers of the World*. Toronto: University of Toronto Press, 2002.

Galtieri, Sarah. *Between Arab and White: Race and Ethnicity in the Early Syrian Diaspora*. Berkeley: University of California Press, 2009.

Gardner, Martha. *Qualities of a Citizen: Women, Immigration, and Citizenship, 1870–1965*. Princeton: Princeton University Press, 2005.

Gerstle, Gary. *American Crucible: Race and Nation in the Twentieth Century*. Princeton: Princeton University Press, 2001.

Gilman, Sander. *Disease and Representation: Images of Illness from Madness to AIDS*. Ithaca: Cornell University Press, 1990.

Ginger, Ann Fagan. *Carol Weiss King: Human Rights Lawyer, 1895–1952*. Boulder: University of Colorado Press, 1993.

Glenn, Susan. *Daughters of the Shtetl: Life and Labor in the Immigrant Generation*. Ithaca: Cornell University Press, 1991.

Goldberg, David J. *Discontented America: The United States in the 1920s*. Baltimore: Johns Hopkins University Press, 1999.

Gomez, Laura. *Manifest Destinies: The Making of the Mexican American Race*. New York: New York University Press, 2008.

González, Gilberto G. *Mexican Consuls and Labor Organizing: Imperial Politics in the American Southwest*. Austin: University of Texas Press, 1999.

González, Manuel G. *Mexicanos: A History of Mexicans in the United States*. Bloomington: Indiana University Press, 1999.

Gordon, Linda. *The Great Arizona Orphan Abduction*. Cambridge, Mass.: Harvard University Press, 2001.

———. *Pitied but Not Entitled: Single Mothers and the History of Welfare, 1890–1935*. New York: Free Press, 1994.

———. "Putting Children First: Women, Maternalism, and Welfare in the Early Twentieth Century." In *U.S. History as Women's History*, edited by Linda K. Kerber, Alice Kessler, and Kathryn Kish Sklar, 63–86. Chapel Hill: University of North Carolina Press, 1995.

Gordon, Sarah Barringer. "The Liberty of Self-Degradation: Polygamy, Woman Suffrage, and Consent." *Journal of American History* 83, no. 3 (December 1996): 815–47.

Gould, Steven J. *The Mismeasure of Man*. New York: W. W. Norton, 1996.

Grant, Colin. *Negro with a Hat: The Rise and Fall of Marcus Garvey*. Oxford: Oxford University Press, 2008.

Grey, Stephen. *Ghost Plane: The True Story of the CIA Rendition and Torture Program*. New York: St. Martins, 2007.

Guglielmo, Thomas A. "Fighting for Caucasian Rights: Mexicans, Mexican

Americans, and the Transnational Struggle for Civil Rights in World War II Texas." *Journal of American History* 92, no. 4 (March 2006): 1212–37.

Guterl, Matthew. *The Color of Race in America, 1900–1940*. Cambridge, Mass.: Harvard University Press, 2000.

Guy, Donna. *Sex and Danger in Buenos Aires: Prostitution, Family, and Nation in Argentina* Omaha: University of Nebraska Press, 1991.

Gyory, Andrew. *Closing the Gate: Race, Politics, and the Chinese Exclusion Act*. Chapel Hill: University of North Carolina Press, 1998.

Hack, Richard. *Puppetmaster: The Secret Life of J. Edgar Hoover*. Beverly Hills: New Millennium Press, 2004.

Haney-López, Ian. *White by Law: The Legal Construction of Race*. 2nd ed. New York: New York University Press, 2006.

Handlin, Oscar. *The Uprooted*. Boston: Little, Brown, 1951.

Hansen, Randall A. *Citizenship and Immigration in Post-War Britain: The Institutional Origins of a Multicultural Nation*. Oxford: Oxford University Press, 2000.

Harold, Claudrena N. *The Rise and Fall of the Garvey Movement in the Urban South, 1918–1942*. New York: Routledge, 2007.

Hartog, Hendrik. *Man and Wife in America*. Cambridge, Mass.: Harvard University Press, 2000.

Hernández, Kelly Lytle. *Migra!: A History of the U.S. Border Patrol*. Berkeley: University of California Press, 2010.

Higham, John. *Strangers in the Land: Patterns of American Nativism, 1860–1925*. New Brunswick, N.J.: Rutgers University Press, 1955.

Hirata, Lucie Cheng. "Free, Indentured, Enslaved: Chinese Prostitutes in Nineteenth-Century America." *Signs* 5 (1979): 23–29.

Hoffman, Abraham. "Stimulus to Repatriation: The 1931 Federal Deportation Drive and Los Angeles Mexican Community." *Pacific Historical Review* 42, no. 2 (May 1973): 205–19.

Hsu, Madeline. *Dreaming of Gold, Dreaming of Home: Transnationalism and Migration between the United States and South China, 1882–1943*. Palo Alto: Stanford University Press, 2000.

Hughes, Jonathan, and Louis P. Cain. *American Economic History*. 7th ed. Reading, Mass.: Addison-Wesley, 2006.

Igra, Anna R. "Likely to Become a Public Charge: Deserted Women and the Family Law of the Poor in New York City, 1910–1936." *Journal of Women's History* 11, no. 4 (Winter 2000): 59–81.

Iocovetta, Francesca, and Wendy Mitchinson. *On the Case: Explorations in Social History*. Toronto: University of Toronto Press, 1998.

Ishay, Micheline. *The History of Human Rights: From Ancient Times to the Globalization Era*. Berkeley: University of California Press, 2004.

Jacobson, Matthew F. *Barbarian Virtues: The United States Encounters Foreign Peoples at Home and Abroad, 1876–1917*. New York: Hill and Wang, 2000.

———. *Whiteness of a Different Color: European Immigrants and the Alchemy of Race*. Cambridge, Mass.: Harvard University Press, 1998.

Jensen, Joan M. *Passage from India: Asian Indian Immigrants in North America*. New Haven: Yale University Press, 1988.
Jew, Victor. "'Chinese Demons': The Violent Articulation of Chinese Otherness and Interracial Sexuality in the U.S. Midwest, 1885–1889." *Journal of Social History* 37, no. 2 (2003): 389–410.
Johnson, Hugh. *The Voyage of the Kogmagata Maru: The Sikh Challenge to the Canadian Colour Bar*. Oxford: Oxford University Press 1979.
Joppke, Christian. *Immigration and the Nation-State*. Oxford: Oxford University Press, 1999.
Jordan, Winthrop. *White over Black: American Attitudes toward the Negro, 1550–1812*. Chapel Hill: University of North Carolina Press, 1968.
Kanstroom, Daniel. *Deportation Nation: Outsiders in American History*. Cambridge, Mass.: Harvard University Press, 2007.
Keire, Mara L. "The Vice Trust: A Reinterpretation of the White Slavery Scare in the United States, 1907–1917." *Journal of Social History* 35, no. 1 (2001): 5–41.
Kevles, Daniel. *Genetics and the Uses of Human Heredity*. Cambridge, Mass.: Harvard University Press, 1995.
King, Desmond. *Making Americans: Immigration, Race, and the Origins of the Diverse Democracy*. Cambridge, Mass.: Harvard University Press, 2000.
King, Desmond, and R. Hansen. "Eugenic Ideas, Political Interests and Policy Variance: Immigration and Sterilization Policy in Britain and the US." *World Politics* 53 (2001): 237–63.
King, Miriam, and Steven Ruggles. "American Immigration, Fertility, and Race Suicide at the Turn of the Century." *Journal of Interdisciplinary History* 20, no. 3 (1990): 347–69.
Klehr, Harvey, and John Haynes. "The Comintern's Open Secrets." *American Spectator* 25, no. 12(December 1992): 34–35.
Kraut, Alan M. *Silent Travelers: Germs, Genes, and the "Immigrant Menace."* New York: Basic Books, 1994.
Kutler, Stanley. *The American Inquisition: Justice and Injustice in the Cold War*. New York: Hill and Wang, 1982.
Leavitt, Judith Walzer. *Typhoid Mary: Captive to the Public Health*. Boston: Beacon Press, 1997.
Lee, Erika. *At America's Gates: Chinese Immigration during the Exclusion Era, 1882–1943*. Chapel Hill: University of North Carolina Press, 2003.
———. "Enforcing the Borders: Chinese Exclusion Along the U.S. Borders with Canada and Mexico, 1882–1924." *Journal of American History* 89, no. 1 (June 2002): 54–86.
———. "The Yellow Peril and Asian Exclusion in the Americas." *Pacific Historical Review* 76, no. 4 (2007): 537–62.
Lee, Erika, and Judy Yung. *Angel Island: Immigrant Gateway to America*. New York: Oxford University Press, 2010.
Lee, J. J. *Ireland, 1912–1985*. Cambridge: Cambridge University Press, 1989.
Lesser, Jeffrey. *Welcoming the Undesirables: Brazil and the Jewish Question*. Berkeley: University of California Press, 1995.

Lombroso, Cesare, and Guglielmo Ferraro. *Criminal Woman, the Prostitute and the Normal Woman.* 1893. Translated, with a new introduction, by Nicole Hahn Rafter and Mary Gibson. Durham: Duke University Press, 2004.

Luibhéad, Eithne. *Entry Denied: Controlling Sexuality at the Border.* Minneapolis: University of Minnesota Press, 2002.

Mandel, Ruth. *Cosmopolitan Anxieties: Turkish Challenges to Citizenship and Belonging in Germany.* Durham, N.C.: Duke University Press, 2008.

Masterson, Daniel M., and Sayaka Funada-Classen. *The Japanese in Latin America: The Asian American Experience.* Urbana: University of Illinois Press, 2004.

McCall, Leslie. "The Complexity of Intersectionality." *Signs* 30, no. 3 (Spring 2005): 1771–1800.

McGirr, Lisa. *Suburban Warriors: The Origins of the New American Right.* Princeton: Princeton University Press, 2001.

McKeown, Adam. *Chinese Migrant Networks and Cultural Change: Peru, Chicago, Hawaii, 1900–1930.* Chicago: University of Chicago Press, 2001.

———. *Melancholy Order: Asian Immigration and the Globalization of Borders.* New York: Columbia University Press, 2008.

Marcus, Eric. *Making History: The Struggle for Gay and Lesbian Equal Rights, 1945–1990: An Oral History.* New York: Harper Collins 1992.

Markel, Howard. "When Germs Travel." *American Scholar* 68, no. 2 (Summer 1999): 61–69.

Miller, Teresa A. "Citizenship and Severity: Recent Immigration Reforms and the New Penology." *Georgetown Immigration Law Journal* 10 (Summer 2003): 611–66.

Mink, Gwendolyn. *The Wages of Motherhood: Inequality in the Welfare State, 1917–1942.* Ithaca: Cornell University Press, 1995.

———. *Welfare's End.* Ithaca: Cornell University Press, 1998.

Moch, Leslie Page. *Europeans on the Move: Migration in Western Europe since 1650.* Bloomington: Indiana University Press, 1992.

Molina, Natalia. *Fit to Be Citizens? Public Health and Race in Los Angeles, 1879–1939.* Berkeley: University of California Press, 2006.

Moloney, Deirdre M. *American Catholic Lay Groups and Transatlantic Social Reform in the Progressive Era.* Chapel Hill: University of North Carolina Press, 2002.

———. "Women, Sexual Morality, and Economic Dependency in Early U.S. Deportation Policy." *Journal of Women's History* 18, no. 2 (Summer 2006): 95–122.

Montgomery, David. *The Fall of the House of Labor: The Workplace, the State, and American Labor Activism, 1865–1925.* Cambridge: Cambridge University Press, 1987.

———. *Workers' Control in America: Studies in the History of Work, Technology and Labor Struggles.* Cambridge: Cambridge University Press, 1980.

Motomura, Hiroshi. *Americans in Waiting: The Lost History of Immigration and Citizenship in the United States.* New York: Oxford University Press, 2006.

———. "The Curious Evolution of Immigration Law: Procedural Surrogates for Substantive Constitutional Rights." *Columbia Law Review* 92, no. 7 (November 1992): 1625–1704.

Neuman, Gerald. "The Assault on Habeas Corpus in Immigration Law." American

Bar Association, *Human Rights Magazine*, Winter 2001. http://www.americanbar.org/publications/human_rights_magazine_home/irr_hr_winter01_neuman.html, accessed April 14, 2011.

Ngai, Mae. "The Architecture of Race in American Immigration Law: A Reexamination of the Immigration Act of 1924." *Journal of American History* 86, no. 1 (June 1999): 67–92.

———. *Impossible Subjects: Illegal Aliens and the Making of a Modern America*. Princeton: Princeton University Press, 2004.

Offen, M. Lewis. "Dealing with 'Defectives': Foster Kennedy and William Lennox on Eugenics." *Neurology* 61, no. 5 (2003): 668–73.

Orloff, Leslye. "Women Immigrants and Domestic Violence." In *Women Immigrants in the United States*, edited by Philippa Strum and Danielle Tarantolo, 49–58. Washington, D.C.: Woodrow Wilson Center for Scholars Press, 2002.

Parenas, Nancy, and Don Fowler. *Anthropology Goes to the Fair: The 1904 Louisiana Purchase Exposition*. Lincoln: University of Nebraska Press, 2009.

Payne, Charles. *I've Got the Light of Freedom: The Organizing Tradition and the Mississippi Freedom Struggle*. Berkeley: University of California Press, 1995.

Peck, Gunther. *Reinventing Free Labor: Padrones and Immigrant Workers in the North American West*. Cambridge: Cambridge University Press, 2000.

———. "White Slavery and Whiteness: A Transnational View of the Sources of Working-Class Radicalism and Racism." *Labor: Studies in Working-Class History of the Americas* 1, no. 2 (2004): 41–63.

Peffer, George. *If They Don't Bring Their Women Here: Chinese Female Immigration before Exclusion*. Urbana: University of Illinois Press, 1999.

Peglar-Gordon, Anna. *In Sight of America: Photography and the Development of U.S. Immigration Policy*. Berkeley: University of California Press, 2009.

Peiss, Kathy. *Cheap Amusements: Working Women in Turn-of-the-Century New York*. Philadelphia: Temple University Press, 1987.

Posadas, Barbara. *The Filipino Americans*. Westport, Conn.: Greenwood Press, 1999.

Preston, William. *Aliens and Dissenters: Federal Suppression of Radicals, 1903–1933*. New York: Harper and Row, 1963.

Ransby, Barbara. *Ella Baker and the Black Freedom Movement: A Radical Democratic Vision*. Chapel Hill: University of North Carolina Press, 2005.

Richbourg, John S. "Liberty and Security: The Yin and Yang of Immigration Law." *University of Memphis Law Review* 33 (Spring 2003): 475–507.

Rockman, Seth. *Welfare Reform in the Early Republic: A Brief History with Documents*. New York: Bedford Books, 2003.

Rodgers, Daniel T. *Atlantic Crossings: Social Politics in a Progressive Age*. Cambridge, Mass.: Belknap Press, 1998.

Rodriguez, Clara E. *Changing Race: Latinos, the Census and the History of Ethnicity in the United States*. New York: New York University Press, 2000.

Roediger, David. *The Wages of Whiteness: Race and the Making of the American Working Class*. London: Verso, 1991.

Rogers, Alan. "Judge George W. Anderson and Civil Rights in the 1920's." *Historian* 54, no. 2 (Winter 1992): 289–304.

Rolinson, Mary G. *Grassroots Garveyism: The Universal Negro Improvement Association in the Rural South, 1920–1927*. Chapel Hill: University of North Carolina Press, 2007.

Rosen, Ruth. *The Lost Sisterhood: Prostitution in America*. Baltimore: Johns Hopkins University Press, 1982.

———. *The World Split Open: How the Modern Women's Movement Changed America*. Rev. ed. New York: Penguin, 2006.

Rosenberg, Clifford. *Policing Paris: The Origins of Modern Immigration Control between the Wars*. Ithaca: Cornell University Press, 2006.

Ruiz, Vicki. *Cannery Women, Cannery Lives: Mexican Women, Unionization, and the California Food Processing Industry, 1930–1950*. Albuquerque: University of New Mexico Press, 1987.

Rygiel, Philippe. *Destins immigrés: Cher, 1920–1980, Trajectoires d'immigrés d'Europe*. Besançon: Annales littéraires de l'Université de Franche Comté, 2001.

Said, Edward. *Orientalism*. 1978. Reprint, New York: Vintage Books, 2003.

Salyer, Lucy. *Laws Harsh as Tigers: Chinese Immigrants and the Shaping of Modern Immigration Law*. Chapel Hill: University of North Carolina Press, 1995.

Sánchez, George. *Becoming Mexican American: Ethnicity, Culture, and Identity in Chicano Los Angeles, 1900–1945*. New York: Oxford University Press, 1993.

Sassen, Saskia. *Territory, Authority, Rights: From Medieval to Global Assemblages*. Princeton: Princeton University Press, 2006.

Schrover, Marlou. "Family in Dutch Migration Policy, 1945–2005." *History of the Family* 14 (2009): 191–202.

Shah, Nayan. *Contagious Divides: Epidemics and Race in San Francisco's Chinatown*. Berkeley: University of California Press, 2001.

Shenton, James P. "Ethnicity and Immigration." In *The New American History*, edited by Eric Foner, 251–79. Philadelphia: Temple University Press, 1990.

Shubert, Bruce. "The Palmer Raids in Connecticut, 1919–1920." *Connecticut Review* 5, no. 1 (1971): 53–69.

Skidmore, Thomas. *Black into White: Race and Nationality in Brazilian Thought*. New York: Oxford University Press, 1974.

Skocpol, Theda, Peter B. Evans, and Dietrich Rueschemeyer, eds. *Bringing the State Back In*. Cambridge: Cambridge University Press, 1985.

Smith, Marion L. *A Historical Guide to the U.S. Government*. Edited by George T. Kurian. New York: Oxford University Press, 1998.

Smith, Rogers. *Civic Ideals: Conflicting Visions of Citizenship in U.S. History*. New Haven: Yale University Press, 1997.

Soysal, Yasemin. *Limits of Citizenship: Migrants and Postnational Membership in Europe*. Chicago: University of Chicago Press, 1995.

Spiro, Jonathan D. *Defending the Master Race: Conservation, Eugenics, and the Legacy of Madison Grant*. Burlington: University of Vermont Press, 2009.

Stern, Alexandra M. *Eugenic Nation: Faults and Frontiers of Better Breeding in Modern America*. Berkeley: University of California Press, 2005.

Sullivan, Patricia. *Days of Hope: Race and Democracy in the New Deal Era*. Chapel Hill: University of North Carolina Press, 1996.

———. *Lift Every Voice: The NAACP and the Making of the Modern Civil Rights Movement*. New York: New Press, 2009.

Takai, Yukari. "Navigating Transpacific Passages: Steamship Companies, State Regulators, and Transshipment of Japanese in the Early-Twentieth-Century Pacific Northwest." *Journal of American Ethnic History* 30, no. 3 (Spring 2011): 7–34.

Tanis, Norman E. "Education in John Eliot's Indian Utopias, 1646–1675." *History of Education Quarterly* 10, no. 3 (Autumn 1970): 308–23.

Tavan, Gwenda. *The Long Slow Death of White Australia*. Melbourne: Scribe, 2005.

Taylor, Jeffery, Isabel Vitek, Virginia Enriquez, and Jeffrey Smedley. "A Continuing Focus of Hansen's Disease in Texas." *American Journal of Medical Hygiene* 60, no. 3 (1999): 449–52.

Taylor, Ula Yvette. *The Veiled Garvey: The Life and Times of Amy Jacques Garvey*. Chapel Hill: University of North Carolina Press, 2002.

Theoharis, Athan. *J. Edgar Hoover, Sex, and Crime: An Historical Antidote*. Chicago: Ivan Dee, 1995.

Tilly, Richard, Paul J. J. Welfens, and Michael Heise, eds. *Fifty Years of EU Economic Dynamics: Integration, Financial Markets, and Innovations*. Berlin: Springer, 2007.

Tweed, Thomas, and Stephan Prothero. *Asian Religions in America: A Documentary History*. New York: Oxford University Press, 1999.

Van Vleck, William. *The Administrative Control of Aliens; a Study in Administrative Law and Procedure*. New York: Commonwealth Fund, 1932.

Vargas, Zaragosa. *Labor Rights Are Civil Rights: Mexican American Workers in Twentieth-Century America*. Princeton: Princeton University Press, 2007.

Vecoli, Rudolph. "Contadini in Chicago: A Critique of the Uprooted." *Journal of American History* 51, no. 3 (1964): 404–17.

Walkowitz, Judith. *Prostitution and Victorian Society: Women, Class, and the State*. Cambridge: Cambridge University Press, 1982.

Waters, Mary C., Reed Ueda, and Helen B. Marrow, eds. *The New Americans: A Guide to Immigration since 1965*. Cambridge, Mass.: Harvard University Press, 2007.

Weaver, Vesla. "Frontlash: Race and the Development of Punitive Crime Policy." *Studies in American Political Development* 21 (Fall 2007): 230–65.

Weisselberg, Charles D. "The Exclusion and Detention of Aliens: Lessons from the Lives of Ellen Knauff and Ignatz Mezei." *University of Pennsylvania Law Review* 143 (1995): 933–1034.

Wong, Janelle. *Democracy's Promise: Immigrants and American Civic Institutions*. Ann Arbor: University of Michigan Press, 2006.

Yans-McLaughlin, Virginia. *Family and Community: Italian Immigrants in Buffalo, 1880–1930*. Urbana: University of Illinois Press, 1978.

Yung, Judy. *Unbound Feet: A Social History of Chinese Women in San Francisco*. Berkeley: University of California Press, 1995.

Zolberg, Aristide. *A Nation by Design: Immigration Policy in the Fashioning of America*. Cambridge, Mass.: Harvard University Press, 2006.

UNPUBLISHED AND DIGITIZED REPORTS, PAPERS, AND DISSERTATIONS

Amnesty International. "Report on Women of Juarez and Chihuahua." 2006. http://www.amnestyusa.org/violence-against-women/justice-for-the-women-of-juarez-and-chihuahua/page.do?id=1108394, accessed February 22, 2009.

———. "The United States of America, Lost in the Labyrinth: Detention of Asylum Seekers." Report. New York, 1999.

Anderson, Christopher G. "Restricting Rights, Losing Control: Immigrants, Refugees, Asylum Seekers, and the Regulation of Canada's Border, 1867–1988." Ph.D. diss., McGill University, 2006.

Bateman-House, Alison, and Amy Fairchild. "Medical Examination of Immigrants at Ellis Island." April 2008. http://virtualmentor.ama-assn.org/2008/04/mhst1-0804.html, accessed May 3, 2009.

Century Foundation. "Immigration Reform." Report. 2000.

Evans, Patricia Russell. "'Likely to Become a Public Charge': Immigration in the Backwaters of Administrative Law, 1882–1933." Ph.D. diss., George Washington University, 1987.

García, Victor. "Local Challenges to Labor Organizing in Mexican Immigrant Enclaves: Kaolin Mushroom Workers Union in Southeastern Pennsylvania." 2007 Conference paper, University of Nebraska. Omaha, Nebraska. www.unomaha.edu/ollas/pdf/Papers%20cumbre07/garcia,%20victor%20Final%20paper.pdf, accessed February 23, 2010.

Haskins, Ron, Mark Greenberg, and Shawn Fremstad. "Federal Policy for Immigrant Children: Room for Common Ground?" Report. Brookings Foundation. Summer 2004. http://www.brookings.edu/articles/2004/summer_demographics_haskins.aspx, accessed December 22, 2010.

Kerwin, Donald, and Serena Yi-Ying Lin. "Immigrant Detention: Can ICE Meet Its Legal Imperatives and Case Management Responsibilities?" Report. Washington, D.C.: Migration Policy Institute, 2009. www.migrationpolicy.org/pubs/2009.php.

King, Ryan, and Michael Massoglia. "Banishment as Social Control: Politics, Labor Markets, and Criminal Deportations in United States History." Paper presented at the annual meeting of the American Sociological Association, New York City, August 11, 2007. http://www.allacademic.com/meta/p181604_index.html, accessed January 24, 2010.

Leal, David, with Jacqueline Hagan and Nestor Rodriguez. "Deporting Social Capital: The Removal of Salvadoran Migrants from the United States." Paper presented at the conference "Deportation and the Development of Citizenship," sponsored by the Department of International Development, Refugee Studies Centre, and Centre on Migration, Policy, and Society, Oxford University, December 11–12, 2009.

Loza, Mireya. "The Bracero Project: Collective Memory, Cultural Memory and Public History." Paper presented at the annual conference of the Organization of American Historians, Washington D.C., April 21, 2006.

Merchant, Emily, Brian Gratton, and Myron P. Gutmann. "Race and Deportation: Mexicans in the 1930 and 1940 Censuses." Paper presented at the Social Science History Association, Miami. 2008.

National Immigration Law Center. "New INS Guidance on Public Charge." May 27, 1999. http://www.nilc.org/immspbs/bu/ebupdate995.htm, http://www.neighborhoodlaw.org/Files/1999NILCQA.pdf, accessed December 9, 2002.

Pew Hispanic Center. Report. "The Hispanic Vote in the 2008 Election." December 7, 2007. http://pewhispanic.org/reports/report.php?ReportID=98, accessed May 15, 2008.

Raissiguier, Catherine. "Blood Matters: Sarkozy's Immigration Policies and Their Gendered Impact." Conference paper, Social Science History Conference (SSHA), Long Beach, Calif., November 2009.

Roberts, Maurice A. "Background and Development of the Board of Immigration Appeals." Unpublished Paper. 1977. Maurice A. Roberts Papers. Immigration History Research Center, University of Minnesota.

INDEX

MIX
Paper from
responsible sources
FSC® C013483
FSC
www.fsc.org